Research Methods
for Counselors

Wiley Series in Counseling and Human Development
Leo Goldman, Editor

Community Counseling: A Human Services Approach
Judith A. Lewis and Michael D. Lewis

Research Methods for Counselors:
Practical Approaches in Field Settings
Leo Goldman, Editor

RESEARCH METHODS FOR COUNSELORS:

PRACTICAL APPROACHES IN FIELD SETTINGS

LEO GOLDMAN, EDITOR

Graduate School and University Center
City University of New York

JOHN WILEY AND SONS
New York   Santa Barbara   Chichester   Brisbane   Toronto

Library of Congress Cataloging in Publication Data

Main entry under title:

Research methods for counselors.

(Wiley series in counseling and human development)
Includes bibliographies and indexes.
1. Personnel service in education.   2.   Educational
reports.   I.   Goldman, Leo, 1920-
LB1027.5.R466   371.4'072   77-10950
ISBN 0-471-02339-6

Printed in the United States of America

10 9 8 7 6 5 4 3 2 1

PREFACE

We prepared this book primarily for use in courses in which counselors in training (and students in other human services professions) are introduced to research methods. Our position is that counselors prepared at the master's level, and even at the undergraduate level, should have a consumer's understanding of the more technical types of research methods and actual skill in using the less technical types of research methods. With this kind of preparation, professional practitioners in the helping fields will be in a position both to keep up with the more technical published research and to do practical studies of their own in their schools, colleges, agencies, and other settings.

We also address the book to practicing counselors (and to practitioners in other human services fields) in the belief that they will find the methods described here and the suggested applications in various settings to be valuable tools in their daily work.

For helping practitioners, research ideally will become part of the job—not an esoteric activity reserved for the "pure" or highly technical researcher but rather the systematic use of what are essentially simple and logical ways to answer everyday questions. Obtaining these answers should enable us to be more helpful and to demonstrate to our organizations and communities that we are offering a responsible and effective service.

For students planning theses and dissertations, and for specialists in research, we hope that these methods will be attractive as alternates or supplements to the traditional quantitative approaches heretofore seen as the only acceptable "scientific" methods of study.

As editor of the volume, I invited chapter authors each of whom is an expert in a type of research or work setting. I chose not to impose a uniform outline on them. Instead, each was given a general topic and goals for the chapter and was then encouraged to design a structure and approach best suited to that chapter's topic and that author's own style. I believe the result is a more interesting variety of chapters than would otherwise have resulted. In addition to diversity of styles, these approaches also resulted in a number of bonuses when authors included treatments of specific topics I had not thought of when planning the book.

If we are successful in our goals for this book, there will be far more valuable and useful research produced both by people who are essentially practitioners and those who are essentially researchers. If that happens, research will truly become an underpinning for practice, and the researcher and practitioner will see themselves and each other as collaborators in a common enterprise.

LEO GOLDMAN

CONTRIBUTORS

WAYNE P. ANDERSON is Professor of Psychology and Counseling Psychologist in the Counseling Services at the University of Missouri —Columbia.

JANE L. ANTON is Assistant Professor of Education in the Graduate Institute of Education of Washington University, St. Louis, Missouri.

ROGER F. AUBREY is Coordinator of Human Development Counseling Program and Associate Professor in the Departments of Psychology and Education at George Peabody College for Teachers, Nashville, Tennessee.

RICHARD M. BALABAN is Coordinator of Children and Youth Service for the Community Mental Health Center in Bloomington, Indiana.

DONALD N. BERSOFF is Assistant Professor of Law at the University of Maryland and Professor of Psychology at Johns Hopkins University. He holds doctoral degrees in both school psychology and law.

HARMAN D. BURCK is Professor of Education in the College of Education of Florida State University—Tallahassee.

KEVIN R. CONTER is a graduate student in the College of Human Development of Pennsylvania State University—University Park.

STEVEN J. DANISH is Associate Professor of Human Development in the College of Human Development of Pennsylvania State University —University Park.

URSULA DELWORTH is Professor of Counselor Education and Director of the University Counseling Service at the University of Iowa—Iowa City.

LEO GOLDMAN is Professor of Education in the Graduate School and University Center of the City University of New York.

LENORE W. HARMON is Professor of Educational Psychology in the School of Education of the University of Wisconsin—Milwaukee.

ALLEN E. IVEY is Professor of Education in the School of Education of the University of Massachusetts—Amherst.

DWIGHT R. KAUPPI is Assistant Professor in the Rehabilitation Counselor Training Program of the State University of New York at Buffalo.

FRANCIS W. MC KENZIE is Coordinator of Pupil Personnel Services for the Public Schools of Brookline, Massachusetts and Adjunct Professor in the Department of Counselor Education at Boston University.

ENA VAZQUEZ NUTTALL is Assistant Professor of Education in the School of Education of the University of Massachusetts—Amherst and Senior Research Associate in the Laboratory for Statistical and Policy Research at Boston College.

MARSHALL P. SANBORN is Professor of Education in the School of Education of the University of Wisconsin—Madison.

CONTENTS

Research Methods
for Counselors

INTRODUCTION

CHAPTER 1
Introduction and Point of View

Leo Goldman

This book grew out of conflict and ambivalence. On the one hand, each author has been involved in research in the counseling field in different roles—as active researcher, instructor of graduate courses, supervisor of research workers, and advisor on theses and dissertations. Each, therefore, has been in some way identified with "research" as a major function, and all have utilized research findings in their counseling work. On the other hand, all the authors in this book, to varying extents, agree with the position that much or most of the research published in the counseling field has made little contribution to practice in the field.

Each author has made a personal resolution of this internal conflict; the individual chapters state and in fact to some extent represent those resolutions. My own view grew mainly out of my roles as a teacher of counselors and an editor of a journal. In the first role I have tried for some twenty-five years to teach counselors-in-training at least to understand the importance of using published research in their work. Toward this end I tried to help them to understand enough about statistics and the methods and principles of research so that they could read the literature of the field intelligently. In addition I tried to persuade some of them—especially those who went on for advanced graduate study or had a special flair for research—that they should also be producers of research. I recognized that for most students of counseling this was very difficult and very uninteresting subject matter, but I persuaded myself, and tried to persuade them, that it was important and useful.

Increasingly I came to doubt the value of that instruction and to doubt that it really was all that important. Yet my professional-professorial conscience continued to tell me that it would be a disservice to the field if we let people become counselors who did not have at least a good consumer's knowledge of research methods and an appreciation of the specific contributions that research has made as a foundation for professional practice. Further, the conscience said that some counselors—certainly those with doctorates—should be doing their own research and submitting it for publication, as their contributions to theory and knowledge in the field.

From 1969 to 1975 I was editor of the *Personnel and Guidance Journal*. I resolved from the beginning that we would publish only those articles that had something to say to counseling practitioners, that we were a reader's, not a writer's journal. We found almost no research manuscripts during those years that satisfied that criterion; quite a few research reports were received, especially in the earlier years, but almost every one of them either was so technical that it could not be truly understood except by very research-sophisticated people, or was so limited in its implications that it really had nothing to offer the practicing counselor. But it remained a conflict situation for most of us involved with producing the journal, a conflict that was aroused whenever we received critical comments from readers —often highly respected people in the field—indicting us for weakening the profession by failing to give research a major place in the all-Association journal of the American Personnel and Guidance Association. Over the years, I wrote several editorials trying to explain and justify our position, and yet somehow I felt a sense of incomplete resolution of the conflict.

Finally, for me at least, the pieces began to fall in place in 1975 as a result of several experiences that occurred within a period of a year or so. During that year I taught a course in research methods to an unusually able class of full-time master's students in counseling. I used one of the traditional textbooks in educational research and, in addition, had the class read each week one or two research articles drawn from the current literature of the field. In the following semester each of the students was required to plan and carry through a research project. In applying the textbook's standards to the articles they read, they found most of the studies either quite flawed in design or execution or simply lacking in meaningful implications; of course, they resolved that their studies would be better.

In the same semester in which I taught the course, I participated in a symposium at the 1975 APGA Convention on major populations whose needs we, as a field, were not meeting—women, the poor, minority groups, and the incarcerated. My assignment was to answer the question: what contributions have been made by research toward meeting those needs? This was the first time I had taken a long look at this question, and when I did, I had to conclude that the existing body of research had almost nothing to say to the topic of the symposium and, in fact, had little to say regarding *most* of the concerns of counselors and their clients.

It was at that point that I came to the realization that the problem was not "research" as a general idea but rather the *kinds* of research that have predominated in our field. I became convinced that the kinds of research methods and the kinds of research studies that prevail in the field are largely inappropriate or inadequate for most of the kinds of knowledge and insight counselors require in their daily work. Ironically, I now had a difficult time persuading my students to use for their individual projects some of the kinds of research that I now felt *were* the more desirable kinds; they had learned the other methods all too well!

This book arose from the experiences of that year and is an effort to present to counselors in all specialties and all settings the kinds of research that *they* can do and that would be a real contribution to their own professional work. This book does not replace the traditional research textbooks, but rather takes the position that most of the methods described in those books are appropriate more for the advanced researcher—the professional researcher, the doctorally trained researcher, the researcher who is concerned more with contributing to the science of counseling, and to theory building and theory testing, than to the immediate improvement of practice. Therefore, with the exception of Chapter 2, we present here only those methods that we believe are feasible and useful for people who are primarily practitioners and who are in the midst of or have completed a master's degree program in the field. Chapter 2 does deal with the traditional research methods, but from the *consumer's* point of view. We do not expect practioners to use those methods, but they need to have some awareness of them, so that they can at least be critical consumers.

Some of the authors who have collaborated in this work, myself included, would go even further and would take the position that the less rigorous, less technical, more informal methods of research described in this book would, in many instances, serve the field better than the traditional methods, even for the kinds of basic or scientific study done by doctoral candidates, graduate school professors, and professional researchers. The remainder of this chapter explains my own position on this matter (also described in two articles, published in 1976 and 1977), which is essentially that the traditional models of research used in our field have overemphasized precision and quantification and the artificial conditions of the laboratory. The kinds of problems we are concerned with in counseling will be far better served by research methods that study people in their real contemporary worlds and that study them with methods much more qualitative in nature. Not all the chapter authors agree with my belief that these methods would also be more useful for much of the "scientific" research in the field, but all agree that these methods are more appropriate for the kinds of research that are, or should be, done by practicing counselors.

WHY RESEARCH
IN COUNSELING?

Research in the counseling field serves several purposes, or at least it is believed to. In a broad sense, as Harmon explains in the next chapter, research is one of the three legs supporting the counseling field, the other two being theory and practice. Ideally, there is constant interaction among the three. The theorist tries to formulate what is at any one time the most comprehensive and most advanced explanation of the phenomena we deal with—people's thoughts, feelings, and needs, and the activities that comprise the counselor's work. The theorist builds upon the experiences of counselors and the accumulated research and, in effect, provides a blueprint for future research by offering new formulations to test. Meanwhile, the researcher is also looking toward practice as a source of problems to study and as the activity to influence. The practitioner's role in all this is twofold. First, it is to let the theorist and researcher know what problems are being faced, what lessons are being learned, what insights are being obtained, and what methods seem to be producing what results in practice. Second, the counselor looks to published research for answers, insights, and suggestions that should feed into daily applied activities. At least ideally, that is what should happen; in fact, there is little interaction between practitioners and the other two and much of the research is not dealing meaningfully or helpfully with the current major concerns of practitioners (Berdie, 1973). It follows that counselors do not find much of the published research to be of value to them, and in fact do not bother to read much current research.

In this book we are concerned mostly with applied research that seeks to answer practical questions. This is the research that helps evaluate one's programs and practices, the research that helps understand better the people and settings one is dealing with. *It is research for action.* It is research that should, among other things, help persuade the people who employ counselors that we know what we are doing and are doing something valuable. This kind of research is done all too seldom, for reasons discussed later in this chapter and elsewhere in the book. For now, it is necessary to state one important reason, namely, that counselors have not learned how to do these more practical kinds of research and have instead been offered, as a model for their own research activities, the much more technical, highly quantitative methods of the "scientific" researcher. In fact, counselors, even those who completed doctoral programs, have been discouraged from doing research because the models they have been offered are so forbidding and of so little practical value.

THE FAILURE OF
RESEARCH MODELS
OF THE PAST

A number of writers have been reaching similar conclusions in recent years. Rausch (1974) has stated the conclusion about professional psychology in general:

> So far as one can see, again with the possibility of behavior modification methods, research has not influenced practice. (p. 678)

> The practitioner, whether as producer or consumer, rejects the traditional model of statistical research because it is of no value to him. (p. 679)

> We have all been sold a parochial definition of science, and those of us who are teachers continue to foist it on students. They buy once—they have to get their degrees—but they are rarely return customers. Traditional research procedures serve only an academic clientele. (p. 679)

Rausch was referring to professional psychology. Sprinthall (1975) now refers to counseling in educational settings:

> What have been the scientific breakthroughs, the great leaps forward? We have heard something about learning nonsense syllables (it's easier to remember the first one and the last one), and something about not learning two foreign languages simultaneously because of negative transfer and, in reading, something about teaching letters first. But the effectiveness of teaching has yet to be established. The effectiveness of counseling and psychotherapy remains problematic. After 60 years, where are the guidelines, where is the wall of knowledge, the scientific basis for practice? We are only told, "You see, we are still in the basic research stage;" or, "In another 15 to 20 years we'll have some valid evidence." (pp. 310–311)

These statements are strong medicine, but their essential validity is confirmed time after time in reviews of the research literature on any single topic in the counseling field. After careful detailed examination of study after study, and after trying to tease out generalizations, the typical review-of-research article concludes that little or nothing can be stated with confidence and that further research is needed in order to clear up the ambiguities of all the preceding research. The problem is that the further research that is contemplated is of the same types that have failed in the past, and the failure in fact results in part from the use of those inappropriate methods of research.

The Failure of the Laboratory

So many contemporary thinkers are saying, directly or by implication, that the venerated laboratory experiment has been highly overrated as a way to gain understanding of human behavior as it exists in real life. The traditional valuation of the laboratory was inherited from the physical sciences, along with the associated values of precision, mathematical formulation, objectivity, and isolation from contamination by any but the treatments or interventions that we are interested in studying.

A number of observers of the research scene have been concluding that the laboratory has become so "pure" that it has little or nothing to say about how people function in real life. Gadlin and Ingle (1975) question the "external" validity of the laboratory experiment; it may be *internally* valid in the sense that, because of all the careful controls, one does indeed know what happened during the experiment and perhaps what caused it to happen, but the experiment lacks *external* validity in that we have placed the person in such artificial conditions that we have no way to judge whether that person would behave in that same manner outside of the sterile laboratory. Proshansky (1976) in describing his development as an environmental psychologist concludes:

> First, we not only have put aside the laboratory physical-science model for our research, but we have abandoned without regret the conception of simple cause-and-effect relationships in understanding how the built environment and human behavior and experience are related. We worry far less about experimental controls in doing our research and far more about what, when, and how to describe ongoing events, an approach that is possible because we are not looking for the usual independent-dependent variable relationships. We are looking in contrast for patterns of relationships between the observed and described properties of physical settings and described reactions of people in these settings. (p. 309)

Proshansky is saying, in effect, that the relationships among people-factors and environment-factors are so complex in reality that it is no loss to give up the laboratory, whose main virtue is that it isolates one factor from the other. In this case, the virtue is not a virtue at all but a distortion of reality.

Sometimes, laboratory studies even use simulated counseling methods, because the "clients" are not real clients who have sought help but draftees or volunteers, often college students, who are asked to participate as subjects in a study. In such cases, neither the clients nor the counseling methods are genuine, which decreases even further any possible application of the results to real people and real counseling.

It has often been stated that the laboratory study is the ultimate in scientific method, and that the less precise and less controlled methods of field observation are merely preludes to really scientific study. In fact, one may wonder whether, in counseling and other human behavioral fields, the opposite is the case. The laboratory may permit exploration of variables and may suggest things about people and methods, but only real-life studies can provide the bases for conclusions and generalizations about people and about helping activities.

The Failure of Purity and Rigor

Other writers have emphasized the fact that all research knowledge acquisition occurs in a cultural framework and within a set of values and beliefs about truth and goodness and, indeed, about the role of science in society. Therefore, it is self-deluding to think that it is possible to study any psychological phenomenon in a pure or culture–free sense (Buss, 1975).

Cronbach (1975), viewing scientific psychology as a whole, makes the point that it has tried too much for eternal truth and enduring theoretical structures and concludes:

> Too narrow an identification with science, however, has fixed our eyes upon an inappropriate goal. The goal of our work, I have argued here, is not to amass generalizations atop which a theoretical tower can someday be erected. . . . The special task of the social scientist in each generation is to pin down the contemporary facts. Beyond that, he shares with the humanistic scholar and the artist in the effort to gain insight into contemporary relationships, and to realign the culture's view of man with present realities. To know man as he is is no mean aspiration. (p. 126)

Similar ideas have been expressed at more applied levels. In assessing Project TALENT, a large-scale research program that, among other things, followed groups of students into their further education and work, McKenzie (1973) expressed the opinion that it was of little value to continue along those lines. His reasoning was that more recent populations have grown up in such different times that any truths discovered about the career development of a sample from one period in time do not necessarily have validity for a sample that has grown up during another era. In a cogent statement he says:

> . . . any creditable study of the future can no longer rely heavily on sophisticated statistical treatment of rather sterile categorical responses to questionnaires unaccompanied by more probing survey and analytical procedures. (p. 106)

He goes on to recommend that future studies reflect the influence on people's career development of such factors as the high unemployment rate of one era, the drug-stimulated culture of another, the 12-year involvement in Vietnam, the sex revolution, women's liberation, and other broad societal changes. How far this is from the simple administration of questionnaires and standardized tests as a mode of research!

It has been traditional also to value the most rigorous types of research design—for example, careful arrangements for subjects not to know what the purposes of the study are, lest they be contaminated. Argyris (1968), in a careful and detailed analysis, incorporates some of the experiences of psychologists in industry on research design. His position is essentially that an overly rigorous experimenter can have undesirable effects on research subjects, much as an overly rigorous supervisor can have undesirable effects on workers. Among the effects in both instances are dependency, overt and covert withdrawal, aggression, and eventual banding together—against the researcher in the one case and the supervisor in the other—in order to protect their own interests. Under such conditions, the researcher cannot be certain that the subjects are responding or behaving genuinely, and the results of the research may therefore be seriously distorted.

Before leaving the topic of rigor, we should heed Levine's (1974) caution that rigor does not necessarily inhere *only* to laboratory and quantitative kinds of research. We will later in this chapter examine some of his ideas, the essence of which is that the intelligent human mind is as effective a research tool as the pseudoprecise instruments customary in "rigorous" research.

We may well conclude this section with a cogent statement by Rausch (1974):

> I would suggest that we scuttle a narrow, parochial, outdated definition of research— one that would eliminate major contributors ranging from Darwin to Freud to Piaget— in favor of definitions appropriate to natural and social sciences and the humanities. (p. 679)

NEW DIRECTIONS
FOR RESEARCH

This book is directed mainly to counseling practitioners, and all the authors who have contributed to it are in agreement that practitioners should be doing research of a less traditional nature. The principles now to be proposed, and the methods and practices described throughout the book, are intended mainly for that audience. But most of the chapter authors, and certainly most of the writers cited and quoted in this chapter, are also in agreement that the traditional methods of research have not been especially productive even for the pure or basic researcher, and that *both* basic and applied research would benefit from a change to methods that place less emphasis on precision, objectiveness, quantitative methods, and the isolation of the laboratory. The following pages are addressed to both kinds of researcher.

Study Current Problems

Research in counseling is so much more useful and alive when it deals with current problems and current situations. Too much research—in psychology as a whole as well as in counseling—has sought to establish basic laws of human function for all time. As Cronbach (1975) was earlier quoted as saying, it is enough of a challenge to understand how people function during any one period. One way to do that is to begin our quest for research topics in the more advanced centers of professional activity—in those schools, colleges, and agencies whose counselors are in the vanguard of professional functioning and are trying out new ideas and new methods. In this book, we have done just that; we have, for the most part, focused on the newer conceptualizations of counselor role in these various settings. If we all do that, we will be less likely in the future to repeat the situation that Berdie (1973) bemoaned as a journal editor:

> During the past several years, the Journal of Counseling Psychology has received few or no papers that have described or evaluated counseling programs for alcoholics. No papers have described a systematic theory of the development and structure of measured vocational interests. Few papers have described or evaluated team or multiple counseling treatment. Counseling of runaways has been given no attention. (p. 393)

The experience of the *Journal of Counseling Psychology* is probably typical of most research journals, and it is not therefore surprising to hear practitioners say that they do not bother reading those journals.

To correct a situation, one should have some idea of its causes. Here we can only speculate. It may be that most published research is done by people who themselves are not practitioners in the newer modes. One can speculate that the people who are in the forefront of new modes of practice are often found in service departments and institutions where research and publication are not as highly valued as they are in academic departments of colleges and universities. One can speculate that the kinds of people who initiate and implement new ideas in practice tend not to be inclined to write but more often to thrive in the action scene. One can speculate that, for the most part, it is easier and more comfortable to do research in traditional, relatively unchanging settings and on traditional and relatively unchanging topics. Among all these speculations there probably are some grains of truth.

Later in this chapter, we consider the question of how to spur more research activity in the action scenes. For now, we only suggest that those who do research, and journals that publish research, should place much higher value on studies of the current scene, even if that means some sacrifice in precision and rigor, and certainly if it means more discomfort because of the not-fully-crystallized and constantly changing nature of the leading edges of our field. Certainly, journal editors and manuscript reviewers should apply to each proposed article the criterion: how much does this add to our knowledge of what is happening in the counseling world today?

Study in the Field

Previous sections have assessed the inadequacies of the laboratory and the controlled experiment as means of understanding how people function and react in real life. "Unobtrusive" or "nonreactive" research (Webb, Campbell, Schwartz, and Sechrest, 1966) certainly raises many problems of ethics and research design and technique. These are the methods that observe what is happening rather than ask people questions or perform experiments. Social psychologists have used such methods quite a bit to learn, for example, how people behave in crowds, without letting them become aware that they are being watched. To observe and study people as they function in classrooms, in families, on the job, and in counseling activities—to do this unobtrusively and to see how people act rather than how they react to questions or interventions—calls for the utmost in care and tact. Indeed, the results of such study often do not give one the feeling of comfort that everything has been neatly controlled or accounted for. The conditions of field study are often messier than those of the laboratory, not necessarily more difficult, but messier. Our conclusion, however, in weighing the advantages and disadvantages of the two approaches, is that the rougher field conditions will offer more insights and will permit much greater generalization of the findings to the real world in which our counselees and consultees live, learn, work, play, and receive help from counselors.

One of the most important values of field-based research is that it provides an unusually rich opportunity to engage in a continuing process of relating theory, research, and practice. Sprinthall (1975) describes it in the following manner:

Natural-setting research implies a constant interplay between investigation and analysis of significant questions. The action/reflection sequence (try out, examine, then try out again) should replace the classical hypothesis-testing basis for research. The feedback cycle will provide the means to analyze and correct any error before the next step. (pp. 314–315)

The chapters in Part 3 spell out many specific approaches that may be used in field-based research—studies of individuals responding to environmental changes, participant–observer studies, longitudinal studies, and evaluations of programs and projects. Then, in Part 4, the authors suggest many kinds of field studies for specific settings—school, college, rehabilitation, vocational and employment agency, and community counseling. Readers, whether practitioner–researchers or specialists in research, will find in both sections a wealth of useful ideas for field-based studies. Practicing counselors would do well to take advantage of these rich opportunities. Specialists in research are advised to seek active collaboration with practitioners in field settings so that together they can foster the kinds of interaction that have thus far been more of an ideal than a reality.

Study Individuals Rather than Groups

Traditionally, research in counseling deals with *numbers* of people and their *central tendencies* (means, medians, and modes) and their *variation* (standard deviations and ranges). Most published studies describe the *average* or *typical* ability level of students in a school or college, or of workers in an occupation, or of some other group. Many studies report the *correlation* for a group of people between two measures, say of interest on the one hand and satisfaction in some field on the other, and ask the question, in general, do the people who have more interest in an area tend to be happier in it? Some studies describe the use of a counseling technique with a number of people and report how many respond positively to it, or how the people who respond more positively tend to rank on other measures. Chapter 2 explains these kinds of studies, and Chapter 11, in particular, gives many examples drawn from the vocational counseling literature.

In all of these kinds of studies, and many others, the results are almost never about *individuals* but about *types of people*, or groups of people, or people who have something in common. True enough, if one's interest is in *selecting* students or employees, such studies can provide usable information and can often spell out how many poor choices can be avoided and how many dollars saved by reducing turnover if certain selection devices or methods are used. If enough people are involved, even a test or an interview or other selection technique that correlates quite low with success in college or on a job may increase the efficiency of selection by avoiding the admission or hiring of people who would probably have failed. Every such mistake avoided is that many dollars saved in training, supervision, counseling, and the paper work to hire and fire, not to speak of the personal discomfort of those involved. Any selection procedure, of course, also inevitably makes mistakes—either by selecting people who later turn out to be failures, or by rejecting people who would have been successful. But we are thinking now *only* of the interest of the school or company doing the selecting. From the selector's point of view, the saving of money and time may justify the procedure; relatively simple studies provide the data for that judgment.

However, the usefulness of most of these studies for *individuals* has been greatly overstated. Correlation coefficients in the .40's, .50's, or even .60's that are regarded as "moderate" or "good" for *group* predictions are, for the most part, of little or no value if we are trying to make statements about individuals (Goldman, 1973). Even with a correlation of .60, say between a college aptitude test and grades in one specific college, which is about as high as one ever finds, the statement as to the probable grade average that any one student with a given test score is likely to attain has to be given within such a wide range as to be ridiculous. (As an illustration, with a correlation of .60, a student who receives a score at the 84th percentile on the aptitude test would have two chances in three of standing somewhere between the 42nd and 92nd percentiles in college grade average. If we wanted to extend the band so that it included the nine in ten chances of probability, the range would be so wide as to become truly ludicrous.) Most correlations for success or satisfaction on specific occupations or jobs are well below .60, so the usefulness for any one individual, though it may be "statistically significant," is for practical purposes close to nil.

Rarely are studies designed in such a way as to permit one to conclude how any one person, with his or her makeup of abilities, interests, and temperamental characteristics, is likely to function in a school, college, job, or indeed in a counseling experience. To take an example that has been much studied over many years, "underachievement" has been found typically to be correlated moderately with each of a number of different factors, such as too much socializing, not enough academic interest, excessive anxiety, poor study habits, and others. Journals continue to publish studies that show such simple correlations, with some variation from study to study depending on what population was sampled and what aspects of the students are studied. Multiple correlations are only slightly better. Though they show the combined predictive power of two or more tests, school grades, and other factors, they still tell only how people with those total scores did in school or on the job, not about the achievement of individuals and why those individuals achieved as they did. Almost never does anyone study *constellations* of factors as they operate within individuals. How one longs sometimes for a few case studies to give life to the phenomenon being examined and to give one a basis for understanding better the occurrence of underachievement in any one student.

To *understand individuals*, and to be able to apply those understandings in helping efforts with individuals, it is necessary to *study individuals*. Several research designs for that purpose are described in Parts 3 and 4. They include systematic observation of what happens to individuals as rewards or other interventions are applied; case studies; and long-term follow-up of individuals. These methods not only have the advantage of permitting applications to specific individuals, but they also involve a minimum of statistical work and therefore bring the research methods within the reach of working master's level counselors. (For me, the absence of esoteric and complex statistical methods has an additional virtue: sometimes researchers become so absorbed in the statistics and the search for "significance" through statistical tests that they lose sight of the data themselves and their actual meaning and value. To put it another way, high-powered statistics sometimes camouflage low-powered data.)

The systematic and even quantified study of individuals as they respond to environmental changes has been highly refined in recent years and has become quite widely used, especially with behavioral methods of intervention. (See Chapter 4 for details). More neglected and much in need of revival as a respectable form of research is the case study or case history. No doubt precautions must be taken to avoid bias in selection, presentation, and interpretation of case study material; with such precautions, the case study has much to offer. As Rausch (1974) points out, such clinical studies need not be restricted to individuals but can focus on families, groups, institutions, plays, novels, or films. Rausch describes them as case histories that focus systematically on psychological themes or theories. They certainly deserve a major place among the research models used in the counseling field.

Study the Whole Individual

It probably is typical for research in almost any field to begin by studying large-scale segments or phenomena and then to break the discipline into smaller and smaller segments—a move from macroscopic to microscopic levels of examination. This kind of development has probably been fruitful in the physical sciences, but it may well have been counter-productive in the social sciences and the humanities. The common saw that "doctoral students learn more and more about less and less until they know a great deal about almost nothing" is a reflection of the belief on the part of some that this kind of development is not entirely in the interest of humanity and may sometimes make people less effective rather than more.

The rationale, of course, is that as a field grows in complexity, one person can know only smaller and smaller portions of it and that it is necessary to isolate smaller and smaller segments in research. The problem in applying this principle to human behavior is that the *interaction* among thoughts, feelings, perceptions, values, and experiences is so vital that one sometimes finds microscopic studies of any one of these to be of little meaning. Buss (1975), Proshansky (1976), and McKenzie (1973) were previously cited on the point that, when studying any one reaction or attitude of a person, it is important that the reaction or attitude be studied only in the light of the pertinent things about the person's (and the researcher's) total being and environment at that time.

Aside from the fact that microscopic-size studies often are trivial in meaning, they defy interpretation. To know that counselees reacted in such-and-such a manner to counselor questions or reflections has little meaning if we do not know how those counselees perceived the counselor and the situation at that moment, and what else of pertinence was happening in their lives at that time. Indeed, if it was a pseudo-counseling situation, as so often is the case in published research, or a simulation through videotape or other medium, one can only wonder how the "counselees" viewed what was happening and whether their reactions bore any resemblance to what they were doing in real life. [See the earlier reference to Argyris's (1968) analysis of the unintended consequences of rigor in research.]

Certainly it is not possible for every study to include every pertinent aspect of each subject's life. However, it is important that most studies at least try to find out what the subjects' perceptions were of what was happening during the study and to ask them to assess the generalizability of their behavior during the study. This raises the question of the subject's role in the entire research enterprise; that calls for some discussion as a separate topic.

Involve the "Subject" as Collaborator

Many have objected to the word "subject" because it is so dehumanizing and because it suggests such a passive, manipulated person. In fact, as Argyris (1968) points out, this status may backfire on the researcher; people who are being questioned or manipulated for purposes they do not under-stand may defend themselves by withholding or distorting their responses. One of his suggestions is in fact to inform the participants, insofar as possi-ble, as to the purposes of the study and to develop in them some feeling that they are active participants in a search rather than passive reactors to an ambiguous searcher. Gadlin and Ingle (1975) suggest that we borrow a leaf from anthropology and regard our "subjects" as "informants" rather than as uninformed objects.

One of the presumed advantages of this recasting of the place of the subject in counseling research would be a mitigation of the ethical concern that one must always bear in mind—the concern that the subjects are doing things they would rather not do if they were fully aware of what is happen-ing, or are revealing things they would not consciously reveal, or actually suffer some undue effects from the study. True, informing the person of everything about the study could contaminate the results, and certainly one is justified in withholding some things, at least until after the subject's par-ticipation has been completed.

On the whole, though, one would probably be well advised in most cases to err in the direction of sharing too much rather than too little. In addition to the reasons already stated, there are two more. One is that the researcher may unwittingly be influencing the results of the study by giving cues or misreading observations (Rosenthal, 1966). Another reason is the tendency that we all carry to some extent—the belief that because one's research is in the interest of increased knowledge or improved professional practice it is all right to manipulate and even deceive people somewhat; after all, the experimenter knows that it is all for a worthy cause. However, the American Psychological Association (1973) found it necessary to de-velop a separate set of ethical principles for research, for the very reason that no person, even the most competent and conscientious, can be trusted to do the ethical thing at all times and to protect fully the privacy and rights of the individual being studied.

In many ways, what is proposed here is that the counselor as researcher enter into a kind of contractual relationship with research subjects, much as the counselor as helper enters into a kind of contractual relationship rather than just "doing things" to people. True, we stand to lose some freedom of professional movement in both instances, but in the total scene there will probably be more honesty all around and therefore a net increase in the value of the research, just as most counselors these days believe that their helping activities are more valuable when counselees collaborate with full awareness of what is happening and full commitment to the process.

Make Place for the Subjective and Qualitative

As we have seen over and over, the counseling field, like all of psychology and probably the social sciences as a whole, has become increasingly concerned (I would say "obsessed") with precision, quantification, and microscopic-level examination of people and of the counseling process. The time has come for a return to respectability of the less formal, more subjective, even looser methods that seem to be acceptable in the early days of a discipline, the days when creativity and imagination are valued. The intelligent mind and perceptive eyes and ears of the researcher should again have a position not only of acceptability but of prominence. As Levine (1974) states:

> It is my feeling that disciplined human judgment can do at least as effective a job in many tasks as a reliance on pseudoprecise instruments and imperfect designs. . . . the basic research instrument is the human intelligence trying to make sense out of what it observes. . . . (p. 674)

Levine goes on to spell out a legal kind of model, where one person acts as an adversary and someone else as a witness, to monitor any bias or error that may result from such subjective processes. This model is discussed in Chapter 7.

In an editorial written during his term of office as president of the American Psychological Association, Donald Campbell (1976), who had been a leading writer for years on rigorous, quantitative methods of research, considered the inadequate state of research in psychotherapy and concluded that:

> We need to reactivate earlier and less pretentious models, which in their day produced valuable research. Much of this research will be "qualitative" in nature. Such qualitative study is an essential underpinning of quantitative science. (p. 2)

Campbell made specific suggestions. One is that each psychotherapist (for which we can read "counselor") offer a free visit one year after termination, during which there would be an updating of the patient's ("client's") life situation and an attempt together to evaluate the effects of the treatment. Campbell also suggests reviving the practice of systematic note-taking and record-keeping after each session, to be accompanied by the patient's own record and view of what was happening.

Another example of a more subjective and qualitative method is the use of the *interview* as contrasted with the questionnaire as research tools.

For most purposes, I would rather have 25 or 50 well-done interviews than 1000 questionnaires. There is a greater likelihood of approaching 100 percent response from the people whom one asks to participate in an interview study than those to whom one sends a questionnaire. Even more important, there usually is no way of knowing why the nonrespondents to a questionnaire (who typically comprise 20 percent to 50 percent of a sample) did not respond. Further, the data from a questionnaire have the serious disadvantage of not indicating how any given respondent perceived the questionnaire as a whole or any specific item on it. As a result, no matter how fastidiously the questionnaire was constructed and tried out, responses to it remain essentially ambiguous and equivocal in their interpretation. Of course, this has not stopped researchers from reporting questionnaire data as if they were facts or at least precise measures, and diligently calculating means and standard deviations to two or more decimal points, thus giving them an air of the precision they do not have. (To claim that in a large enough sample individual differences in perception and interpretation of items will balance each other out is hardly reasonable. Ambiguity multiplied by any number remains ambiguity.)

The interview, by contrast, when well done, permits follow-up questions to clarify a response and allows much greater depth than a questionnaire. One must, of course, take measures to minimize the risks of inaccurate recording and misinterpretation of responses. With the advent of the cassette recorder, it is easy enough to record every interview so that at least a sample of them can be checked by an independent judge for accuracy of recording and interpretation. In those cases where people refuse permission or are reluctant to record, at least each interviewer can be carefully trained and a sample of practice interviews checked for accuracy.

We are in a field that deals with nonprecise phenomena, with intangible qualities, and with constantly changing people and situations. It is therefore highly appropriate that our major research methods include the subjective and the qualitative and the relatively unfettered approaches. To capture the reality of a human life or an encounter is more an artistic than a scientific accomplishment—at least if we define science as it is usually defined in the physical sciences. Ours is not an exact science or an exact practice. It is therefore illusory to expect that our research will be exact.

This is not to suggest that no cautions are needed and that one may use any subjective approaches in any way one wishes without impedence. All research methods require a careful statement of the specific purposes and the expected outcomes of the study. Whether interviews or questionnaires are used, questions must be phrased carefully to avoid ambiguity or confusion. Even more critical, measures must be included in the study to detect and reduce to a minimum the possibilities of bias in the interpretation of responses. Fortunately, there are well-established methods for avoiding these and other flaws in a study—preliminary tryouts of questionnaires and inventories, independent interpretation of a sample of responses to check the researcher's own interpretations, careful training of interviewers, and others. More sophisticated methods may be warranted in some studies; Levine's (1974) legal model, already mentioned in this chapter, is one example.

And of course each research method has its limits. For instance, if appropriate sampling and statistical methods have not been used, then one cannot generalize beyond the people studied. However, for the vast majority of studies that practitioners can and should do for their own information and for the improvement of their work, sampling and statistical inference may be of little or no concern. This point is emphasized over and over in this book, but especially in Chapter 6 where the distinction is made between applied evaluation and theoretical research.

By using appropriate checks and not overstating the conclusions of their studies, researchers may use these more subjective and qualitative methods for a large portion of the problems that concern us as practitioners and scientists.

Planning for Research Implementation

Too often research has stopped with the writing of a report or an article, as if with the expectation that it would now be read and used by many people. The more usual experience is that few, except other researchers, ever read research reports. To some extent, this is because so few research reports have any immediate application in practice.

But it is unrealistic to expect that almost any research reports, even those that do have immediate implications for practice, will be read and used. For one thing, counselors are inundated with journals and books and special reports. Even with the aid of systematic methods, such as those described in Appendix B, for locating published and unpublished studies —the ERIC system, abstracts of various kinds, locater services, and so on—it is still an overwhelming scene that confronts the conscientious counselor who would like to keep up with research.

The first task then is to bring to counselors' attention the facts and ideas that have been uncovered in one's study. The second task is to get them to consider the meaning and implications of these facts and ideas. And the third task is to get them to do something with what they have learned, assuming that the findings do imply change of some kind. As Glaser (1973) says, "Ideas *alone* will not generate and sustain change" (p. 437).

The situation is similar in some ways to counseling; the counselor now is in the position of the client who needs information, who needs help in interpreting and weighing and accepting the information and in deciding then what to do about it, by way of action.

If research is to influence practice, something akin to a counseling process is needed. The information must be seen or heard, and it must be understood and its legitimate implications accepted. The usual technical research report is pretty forbidding to start with and often includes little or nothing by way of implications for practitioners. (The journals themselves are not entirely to blame; journal editors quite generally find that they must push authors pretty hard, and repeatedly, to get them to stick out their necks into the realm of counseling practice and discuss specific implications and applications of their research findings.)

We must therefore seek new styles and modes for reporting research findings. For some people, the printed word or a paper read at a conference are excellent means of communication, but these days most people have become accustomed to more interesting and engaging methods such as films, television, slide-and-cassette, and the hands-on and interactive features of workshop experiences. A full program of such dynamic dissemination should be a part of each research plan; to be certain that this will happen, it is wise to include a plan for meaningful dissemination as part of the total research project before beginning the study itself (Glaser, 1973).

As Glaser cautions us, even a well-rounded meaningful program for dissemination is not enough. There needs to be a continuing interaction with the potential users of the research, to help them to deal with the many internal and external barriers to change, and to give them continuing support and help in the process of decision and change. Here we can bring to bear what we have learned from the experience of counseling, consultation, and organizational development. In each of these areas, there is a considerable body of wisdom about the ways in which change occurs. Institutions are resistant enough to change under the best conditions; many counselors work in institutions where the conditions for change are much less than the best, so the task is a formidable one indeed.

Perhaps we need a new kind of intermediary between research and practice, a linking agent (Glaser, 1973) who will help bring together in continuing ways the producers and the consumers of research. Someone who will play this role is almost certainly needed in connection with published research that is to be used in many different settings. But a linking agent may be needed even when the research is in-house, even when it was done by counselors on the staff of the organization. The understandings and skills needed by such a person probably are very close to those needed to do consultation and even counseling itself.

Many ideas regarding the dissemination of research findings are found in later chapters. In particular, Chapter 3 examines in considerable detail all aspects of communicating research to its consumers, and Chapter 10 describes some exemplary programs in the rehabilitation field.

HELPING COUNSELORS DO RESEARCH

Most people who select careers as counselors tend to be uncomfortable with courses that involve statistics, such as measurement and research methods. Further, counselors tend to be people-oriented and action-oriented and by temperament usually find the activities that go into research work not especially congenial. All of this constitutes a very real barrier between counselors and research activities.

Another barrier arises from the kinds of research models that have been presented to counselors in their courses, textbooks, and journals. Studies that are regarded as good quality, in addition to being few and far between, tend to involve rather forbidding techniques and procedures. Certainly for many practice-oriented people the experience of doing a good dissertation under rigorous professorial supervision is enough to discourage them from ever trying it again, especially on their own.

Finally, counselors tend to work in busy service arms of schools, colleges, and agencies where there is little time, money, or assistance for research activities. Conscientious counselors may actually find discouragement of their efforts to do research, even if they request no time, money, or assistance. Research is not high in the hierarchy of values in most of these settings (though again it must be said that the failure of most research in the past to make any discernible contribution to practice is a very real factor).

In effect, this book is an attempt to at least whittle away at the first two barriers. The kinds of studies we emphasize call for a minimum of statistical competence, in many instances none at all. We stress qualitative research and practical studies that should be within the reach of most practitioners. For the most part, we focus on local studies that may or may not be of interest to other institutions. In many cases they would not be suitable for publication because they have only local significance. This should in no way be viewed as a downgrading of such studies; in fact, local studies probably have far more to offer counselors than "national" studies, both in terms of the useful information they provide to the counselors, and in terms of supplying evidence of the value of the counseling program.

So, we are inviting readers to join us in an exploration of truly task-oriented, meaningful studies where research means a *search* for understanding and good ideas. We are not concerned with the publish-or-perish motivation to do research. Not that we expect to see much change in that tradition which, unfortunately, has produced so many journals full of trivial, unimaginative, and largely useless research reports (though some journals have recently broadened their conception of appropriate articles) but that is not where we are or, we hope, our readers. Instead, we believe that the vast gap between practitioners and researchers can be closed, at least partly, if practitioners become researchers and if researchers offer practitioners the kinds of research that will have real meaning on the firing line.

REFERENCES

American Psychological Association. *Ethical principles in the conduct of research with human participants.* Washington, D.C.: Author, 1973.

Argyris, C. Some unintended consequences of rigorous research. *Psychological Bulletin,* 1968, *70,* 185–197.

Berdie, R.F. Editorial. *Journal of Counseling Psychology,* 1973, *5,* 393–394.

Buss, A.R. The emerging field of the sociology of psychological knowledge. *American Psychologist,* 1975, *30,* 988–1002.

Campbell, D.T. Research in psychotherapy. *APA Monitor,* 1976, *7* (1), 2.

Cronbach, L.J. Beyond the two disciplines of scientific psychology. *American Psychologist,* 1975, *30,* 116–127.

Gadlin, H., and Ingle, G. Through the one-way mirror: The limits of experimental self-reflection. *American Psychologist,* 1975, *30,* 1003–1009.

Glaser, E.M. Knowledge transfer and institutional change. *Professional Psychology,* 1973, *4,* 434–444.

Goldman, L. Test information in counseling: A critical view. In *Proceedings of the 1973 Invitational Conference on Testing Problems.* Princeton, N.J.: Educational Testing Service, 1973.

Goldman, L. A revolution in counseling research. *Journal of Counseling Psychology,* 1976, *23,* 543–552.

Goldman, L. Toward more meaningful research. *Personnel and Guidance Journal,* 1977, *55,* 363–368.

Levine, M. Scientific method and the adversary model: Some preliminary thoughts. *American Psychologist,* 1974, *29,* 661–677.

McKenzie, F.W. Implications for further research. *Vocational Guidance Quarterly,* 1973, *22,* 104–108.

Proshansky, H.M. Environmental psychology and the real world. *American Psychologist,* 1976, *31,* 303–310.

Rausch, H.L. Research, practice, and accountability. *American Psychologist,* 1974, *29,* 678–681.

Rosenthal, R. *Experimenter effects in behavioral research.* New York: Appleton-Century-Crofts, 1966.

Sprinthall, N.A. Fantasy and reality in research: How to move beyond the unproductive paradox. *Counselor Education and Supervision,* 1975, *14,* 310–322.

Webb, E.J., Campbell, D.T., Schwartz, R.D., and Sechrest, L. *Unobtrusive measures: Nonreactive research in the social sciences.* Chicago: Rand McNally, 1966.

THE COUNSELOR AS CONSUMER OF RESEARCH

CHAPTER 2
The Counselor as Consumer of Research

Lenore W. Harmon

Most counselors working in educational settings and social agencies are busy people. The more innovative and successful they are at their work the busier they are. They are concerned with helping as many people as possible and there are always more people to help (Schofield, 1964; Greenberg, 1965). Busy as they are, counselors would want to keep up with research in the field if they thought this would make them better helpers, but most have felt that research is not as helpful in their work as they would like it to be. Many research results are indeed too narrow or too equivocal to tell the practitioner much about how to improve counseling practice. However, I believe that the practicing counselor should be a consumer as well as a producer of research. The first portion of this chapter is devoted to a discussion of that position. Later portions of the chapter investigate how the counselor can become a consumer of research, and the remainder of the book indicates some practical ways and areas in which practicing counselors can become producers of research.

WHY READ RESEARCH?

That some research has not fulfilled the needs of practicing counselors is a poor reason for giving up on research in general. Such reasoning is analogous to the thought processes of the man who decided to stop using ammunition in his gun because he never hit anything. Obviously, there were other more effective adjustments he could have made. The magnitude of his folly is directly proportional to the importance of his shots. That is, if he was shooting at his food supply, his error is much more serious than if he was shooting beer cans off a fence. Counseling is much more important than shooting beer cans off a fence. Thus, it is important that we not neglect a potentially useful tool—research—just because it has not yet been very useful.

Counselors should be consumers of research for several reasons: (1) there are potential effects on their own professional development and effectiveness with clients; (2) their own research will be influenced by their knowledge or lack of knowledge regarding previous research; (3) only the counselor can really take responsibility for the quality of service offered to clients. Each of these reasons, as well as the relationships among theory, practice, and research, is discussed further.

Reading Research Contributes to Professional Development

As in all fields, ideas in psychology have increased exponentially in recent years. The practicing counselor must be aware of new developments but at the same time be critical and selective in applying them. Many of the "theories" that have been proposed for application to counseling are little more than collections of ideas with meager evidence to support either the relationships claimed in the theory or the effectiveness of the theory as applied to counseling. There is a period in the development of new theories and techniques when this situation is natural—however, it should be temporary. Client-centered theory and therapy provide a good example of how a theory developed and was subjected to empirical test. Rogers (1959) tells of his early search for ways to test his ideas; subsequent major research projects resulted from his determination to do so (Rogers and Dymond, 1954; Rogers, Gendlin, Kiesler, and Truax, 1967). Applications of learning theory to counseling have also been demonstrated through research (e.g., Lazovik and Lang, 1960; Krasner and Ullmann, 1965; Mann and Rosenthal, 1969; Spiegler, Cooley, Marshall, Prince, Puckett, and Skenazy, 1976). However, many so-called "theories" have existed for too long as untested ideas, to the extent that they approach the status of fads. Without an awareness of current research the practicing counselor is a prey to faddism in psychology. There is evidence, for instance, that Perls (1969) was concerned that gestalt therapy was being accepted at the level of a fad by practitioners who made little attempt to understand its theoretical basis. Reading research can help practicing counselors to identify well-researched new theories and techniques that may be applied to their own practice.

Although the title of this chapter implies that the counselor consumes research, this is not strictly so. To "consume" is "to destroy or expend by use" (Stein, 1967). Actually, the counselor does not destroy or expend research by using it, but the service offered, counseling, *is* destroyed or expended by use. No counseling hour or minute can be relived. To the extent that time spent with a client is less effective than it could be, the efforts of the counselor and client are wasted. Knowledge of research can help the counselor be more effective in the limited time available for each client. Counselors who spend some of their time trying to find ways to make their services more effective—by reading research and by attending conferences and workshops—are more likely to be effective.

AN EXAMPLE.   I was taught as a practicum student that clients who disclose too much in early interviews often defect from counseling. This information was presented as the clinical insight of a practicing psychologist. As I gained experience as a practitioner, I observed the same thing. My approach to the problem was to attempt to control the amount of client disclosures in early interviews although I felt uncomfortable about doing it because of a competing belief that clients needed to disclose their problems as freely as possible for maximum growth. The work of Heilbrun (1973) suggested a solution to my dilemma. He was interested in female defectors from therapy and had previously hypothesized that dependent females drop out of therapy as a response to frustration with the nondirective behavior of male therapists. The new hypothesis he explored in his 1973 work was that females disposed to leave therapy early have a history of difficulty in self-disclosure especially with men. His results showed just the opposite. Females who were disposed to leave therapy early had a history of greater self-disclosure and greater self-disclosure to the men than women not disposed to leave therapy. He concluded that women who have disclosed more to males and fathers in particular would be especially frustrated by nondirective male counselors. He did acknowledge that these defectors from therapy might not be frustrated but instead gratified that someone had listened, and he suggested further research along that line. His research was extremely specific, and its major findings were about female clients and male counselors, but I did find it very useful. I generalized from these findings to male and female clients and to male and female therapists. I changed my counseling emphasis from one of preventing extreme self-disclosure in early interviews to one of providing more structure about what might happen next in counseling during early interviews where a great deal of self-disclosure took place. I did this more by summarizing and highlighting options for my client than by controlling the course of therapy completely.

It could be argued that I have generalized too much from Heilbrun's findings and that the issues involved have not been resolved, and I would agree. However, my current practice is based on better data than my previous practice was, and I am aware that more data are likely to be forthcoming from Heilbrun and his associates.

I could check out my application of Heilbrun's findings if I worked in a large counseling center devoted to research. This could be done by administering the Adjective Check List, which he used, to each client before counseling began and scoring it on the Readiness for Counseling Scale to determine the client's propensity to terminate counseling prematurely. Clients would be randomly assigned to male and female counselors who had been trained to offer two different conditions in the initial interview. One condition would be an extremely nondirective approach and the other would be a more structured and directive approach. If women with low readiness for counseling left nondirective counseling with male counselors more often than women with high readiness for counseling, Heilbrun's idea that women are frustrated by nondirective counseling from male counselors would be supported. If women with low readiness for counseling left nondirective counseling with either male or female counselors more often than they left more structured and directive counseling with either male or female counselors, my application of Heilbrun's work would be supported. That is, the defection from counseling would be more highly related to the counseling conditions offered than to the sex of the counselor. Using male clients as well as women would afford an opportunity to contrast the effects of the treatments across sexes. I could also follow up those who dropped out of counseling to determine their frustration level in order to explore Heilbrun's suggestion that the perceptions of defectors from therapy should be explored.

My findings would have implications for further research, and for whether or not certain types of clients continue in therapy and resolve problems that concern them.

Reading Research Stimulates Better Research

The underlying thesis of this book is that practicing counselors can and should do research that takes place in the field settings they work in. Ways of doing this are described in subsequent chapters. Such research can be improved by a knowledge of more theoretically and experimentally based studies. The more a researcher knows and understands about previous research in an area, the better study the researcher can plan.

AN EXAMPLE: HOLLAND'S THEORY.   A real and important example is the development of John Holland's theory of careers. In his 1973 explication of this theory he attributes its first formulation (Holland, 1959, 1966) in part to his experience as a vocational counselor and as a reader of the vocational literature (p. 5). He proposed that there are six types of people: realistic, investigative, artistic, social, enterprising, and conventional. A series of empirical studies showed that when individuals were assigned to these categories or types using a variety of means (vocational choice, major field, scores on inventories), there were demonstrable differences among the groups in how they described themselves and in their educational behavior (Holland, 1962, 1963, 1963–1964, 1964, 1968; Holland and Nichols, 1964). Holland developed an instrument—the Vocational Preference Inventory (Holland, 1958)—for assigning individuals to types and subtypes. At the same time, other studies showed that environments could be categorized using the same typology (Astin and Holland, 1961; Astin, 1963). Holland, Viernstein, Kuo, Karweit, and Blum (1972) showed later that a classification system derived from Dictionary of Occupational Titles job descriptions (McCormick, Jeanneret and Mecham, 1969; Jeanneret and McCormick, 1969) could be related to Holland's system of classification. In addition, Holland, Whitney, Cole and Richards (1969) demonstrated that the classifications within the system had specific relationships among themselves. For instance, people who are basically artistic types are more likely to have investigative or social subtypes than a conventional subtype. The result of this body of research is that the current theory asserts a relationship between the personalities of individuals and occupational environments in which they work, as well as a relationship between the types of individuals and their vocational behavior, such as employment stability and such attitudes as job satisfaction. Research has expanded and changed the theory, as a comparison of the 1966 and the 1973 formulations will show. Holland counted over 100 studies stimulated by his theory in 1973 and there are many more by now. Because the theory is becoming more precise, with well-defined concepts and clearly derived predictions, it will probably continue to change and grow as a result of this research.

Because the theory relates individuals and jobs (environments) using the same category system, it is extremely useful for vocational counselors. Holland (1973) suggests several ways of assessing the personality types of individuals and provides a listing of occupations according to that typology in The Occupations Finder (Holland, 1970). Obviously, this gain for the practitioner and for clients is based on growing and changing theory so they cannot afford to assume its stability. However, practice has been improved. Thus, practice and reading research led Holland to develop a theory that was changed and expanded by research and that ultimately influenced practice. This illustrates precisely the relationships suggested by Figure 2.1.

If knowledge moves in only one direction across the arrows in Figure 2.1, or if one component is removed from the figure, the whole system suffers. If, for instance, Practice is removed from the system, then Theory and Research have no impact on the world of behavior and vice versa. Theory and Research are rendered sterile intellectual exercises and Practice is devoid of any rationale.

The Counselor's Responsibility

The counselor is a kind of intermediary who works between the pure science of psychology and the needs of human beings. The quality of the counseling service provided is an ethical concern, yet the practicing counselor is not usually found pondering over the latest research in counseling the way that a surgeon, for instance, ponders over the latest research into surgical techniques. When a counselor neglects the latest knowledge in the field, such neglect is a tacit affirmation that the counselor believes counseling is strictly an individualistic art form rather than a science-based professional practice that can be taught. This is a legitimate position but not one that should be taken by practitioners who are at the same time arguing that counseling should be limited to those with certain types and amounts of education. I prefer to view counseling as a skill that can be learned by a wide variety of people (Egan, 1975).

Only the counselor can take responsibility for the quality of service provided. The nature of the counseling service, the way counseling is evaluated by employers, and the position of the client make it nearly impossible for anyone else to take that responsibility.

Since the product offered to the public is intangible, and the criteria used to determine its effectiveness are usually quite subjective, it is easy to assume that the job has been done well because the client "feels better" or terminates. Because there is no right way to deal with any particular client—only a way that works in a particular client–counselor relationship—counselors are very much "on their own" regarding treatment of clients. To assume they can get no help from reading and thinking about their work negates the idea that counseling skills can be taught and improved by knowledge.

Counseling agencies have been at a loss to evaluate counseling for the same reasons—because it is so intangible and because there are various means to the same ends. Most often the criterion applied has more to do with quantity than quality. Thus, hours of client contact or number of closed cases may serve as indicators in some agencies but these criteria have only a tangential relationship to quality or effectiveness. Even the client is not in a very good position to evaluate counseling. If a positive result is obtained and clients are pleased about the results of counseling, they rarely question whether more effective and efficient methods might have been used. If on the other hand, clients are dissatisfied, it is difficult to pinpoint the source of their complaints without referring to personal issues. Most clients are unwilling to do this.

Only individual counselors are in positions to improve their skills and understandings by a thoughtful attention to current research literature. Employees, clients, even bodies that give certificates and licenses on the basis of past education and performance cannot insure that counselors do everything in their power to provide the best possible service.

Likewise, only practicing counselors can direct pure scientists to important problems for research. Thus, we arrive at the conclusion that counselors must know about research to improve their practice, so that they can engage in the research process themselves, and so that they can influence the research being done.

BACKGROUND NEEDED FOR READING COUNSELING RESEARCH

In order to read counseling research effectively it is important for the reader to understand how theories are developed and tested. Understanding of the more technical research elements such as measurement, statistics, and research design is useless unless there is an understanding of how they relate to theory development.

Theory Building

Theories are sets of definitions and statements specifying the relationships between the defined concepts. They help us to understand the world around us, to predict what will happen next, and ultimately to control those happenings. For instance, if it has been demonstrated that a certain set of conditions and behaviors are likely to produce addictive personalities, then we can intervene in the experiences of an identified group who live under the specified conditions and exhibit the specified behaviors to help prevent the development of addictions. The counselor may be the intervenor but the theory helps indicate when and how to intervene.

Note that while a theory usually starts out as a belief held by a person or group, this belief must ultimately be tested and confirmed. If we believe that a certain set of conditions and behaviors contribute to the development of addictive personalities, the relationship must be demonstrated unequivocally. This demonstration is called research. Usually the idea that a relationship exists is based on observation in the same way that Newton noticed that objects fall toward the earth and that Freud noticed that sexual repression occurred in his neurotic patients.

This type of reasoning is called "inductive" and it is characterized by starting with specific observations and making general statements based on them. However, there is always the danger that what is observed in specific cases is not, in fact, general; that, for example, more objects fall away from the earth than toward it or that neuroses are not all rooted in the displacement of sexual energies. For this reason, it is important that theories stated in general terms be logically consistent (that is, not violate the rules of formal logic) and that the implications of the theory be tested. Even if the scope of the theory is quite narrow, it is important that we ask how the general theory can now be tested in specific cases. This involves "deductive" reasoning from the general case to the specific case. The testing involved here usually occurs under much more rigorous and controlled conditions than the observations involved in inductive reasoning, although deductive reasoning is surely a type of observation.

For an empirical test it is necessary that the concepts of the theory be defined precisely and that the hypothesized relationships between them be stated explicitly. Once this is done, a test is conducted under controlled conditions that minimize the chances for the outcomes to be attributed to any factors other than those hypothesized in the theory as being causal or related to the outcomes. Actually, such tests are never as comprehensive or general as the theory itself, so a successful empirical test can only be said to contribute to the confirmation of a theory, not to "prove" it.

The most difficult problems in setting up research studies designed to test theories include defining and putting constructs into operation ("operationalizing" them), stating the hypothesized relationships in ways that are testable, and controlling all the extraneous variables. Control of variables is especially difficult when the theory in question is a theory of human behavior because we have moral inhibitions and ethical prohibitions against intervening in certain ways in the lives of other human beings for such abstract purposes as increasing knowledge and conducting research.

Operationalizing Theoretical Constructs

Dictionary definitions of words and ideas are made up of other words. In ordinary conversations these definitions serve quite well, although problems in communication can often be traced to a lack of precision in how different individuals define abstract concepts such as "love," "trust," and "beauty." For psychological research purposes, it is necessary to define the concepts being studied in such a way so that we know precisely when a certain trait or behavior is present and often in what quantities it is exhibited. This is called operational definition. For example, Auerswald (1974) did a study of the effects of restatement and interpretation in the counseling interview. She wisely noted that it was important to specify in behavior terms what a "good" effect or positive change in the client is. She chose to use client expression of affect in the interview as her criterion of a "good" change in client behavior. But a very precise method was used to measure affect. Counseling interviews were taped and then typed. A specific procedure was used for breaking each typescript into smaller units of analysis and for determining whether or not each unit contained a self-reference affect statement. The resulting proportion of affect responses served as an operational definition of client expression of affect and ultimately of client change. It is important that every concept involved in a research hypothesis have just such a specific operational definition. Obviously, if Auerswald had simply said she was interested in the relationship of restatement and interpretation to client change without specifying exactly what kind of client change and how it was measured, her results would be quite useless to a practitioner trying to explore the relative effects of the two techniques by reading research reports. On the other hand, to argue that all that is meant by the positive effect of counseling is an increase in the proportion of affect responses made by the client is ridiculous. This is a good illustration of how operational definitions always narrow the concepts they define at the same time as they sharpen our understanding of those concepts. It also illustrates why research can only help to confirm a theory, not to prove it.

Other concepts have been operationalized by standardized tests, questionnaires, and physiological measures. For instance, the early intelligence tests of Binet as adapted in this country by Terman (1916) helped to operationalize the concept of human intelligence. Woodworth (Symonds, 1931) developed a questionnaire called the Personal Data Sheet to detect neuroticism in soldiers. It served as a prototype for many more modern personality inventories that are used to operationally define personality characteristics. As to physiological measures, Droppleman and McNair

(1971) have introduced a finger sweat print as a method of operationally defining anxiety.

Measurement—Means to Operational Definition

Basically, an operational definition includes a statement of how the concept defined can be measured. It is at the level of operational definition where the whole science of measurement becomes important to counselors who want to read and understand research. And, of course, measurement principles are also important to counselors who use tests in their work with individuals. There are a number of books that cover both aspects of this topic admirably and at length so that only a limited discussion of the problems of reliability and validity is offered here. Textbooks by Anastasi (1976), Brown (1976), Cronbach (1970), Horst (1966), and Tyler (1971) provide good introductions to psychological measurement in the context of standardized testing. Levine and Elzey (1970) and Miller (1972) cover the same topic in programmed format. Guilford (1954), Gulliksen (1950), and Magnusson (1966) treat measurement from a more theoretical viewpoint. Goldman (1971) covers the applications of measurement in counseling.

RELIABILITY.   It is important to note here that unless the procedure by which a concept is measured is reliable, that measurement is useless. If my scale weighs the same object at 5 pounds today and 10 pounds tomorrow, it is quite useless in determining how much an object really weighs—it is unreliable. Although the above books discuss various types of reliability, the ones most important for good operational definition are stability over time and stability over raters. If I use a standardized test or questionnaire as an operational definition of a trait or attitude, I want to know that if nothing changes in the individual I will get approximately the same score if I test the individual tomorrow or next month or next year. The reason the test must measure with reliability over time is that I want to be able to attribute changes in the scores of individuals or groups of individuals to the effects of some intervention —such as counseling—rather than to instability in my measurement.

As a journal editor, I find that researchers often conduct research using elaborate designs in which they control for error from every source except from their measuring instruments—the inventories, questionnaires, and scales they use to determine to what group an individual belongs or whether an individual has changed. Error in the measuring instrument is synonymous with unreliability. It can occur as a result of ambiguous items, subjective scoring procedures, or poor testing conditions. Yet it is so unusual for researchers to provide reliability estimates for the various unpublished questionnaires and surveys they use that one of my consulting editors recently wrote me a note extolling the virtues of an author who *had* provided reliability information in the manuscript I sent him for review.

Stability over time is most often expressed as a correlation coefficient between scores on two administrations of the same test. These coefficients can range between -1.0 and $+1.0$ but in reliability estimates they are most likely to range between 0 and $+1.0$. A correlation of 1.0 would indicate perfect reliability, which is never found in psychological instruments. It is not unreasonable, however, to expect correlations in the .80 to .95 range. The higher the correlation coefficient, the more reliably and stably the instrument measures.

When raters assess behavior as they did in Auerswald's study, their reliability can be expressed as a correlation coefficient between the ratings of two raters or as a percentage of agreement between them. It is important, if the ratings are to be used to express change, that any changes found can be attributed to the treatment or intervention—in Auerswald's study it was restatement and interpretation—rather than to error and instability of judgment in the raters.

Whenever a concept is operationally defined, as it must be in research, a statement about the reliability of the measuring process inherent in that operational definition should be given.

VALIDITY.   There should be some evidence that the measuring process measures what it is supposed to measure. This is called validity. Validity is discussed in detail in the textbooks mentioned earlier but the kind of validity most essential in research is construct validity (Cronbach and Meehl, 1955; APA, 1974).

Construct validity is inferred from evidence that scores on the test are related to appropriate behavior and attributes, or scores on other measures for which such evidence is available. Often the appropriate relationships must be predicted from the particular theory the measuring instrument is designed to help operationalize, and considerable research must be done on the instrument before it can be used to advance research on the theory. For instance, the Career Maturity Inventory (Crites, 1973) was designed to measure career maturity as hypothesized by theorists who propose a developmental model of individual careers (Ginzberg, Ginsburg, Axelrad and Herma, 1951; Super, 1953, 1957). One of the pieces of evidence for the construct validity of this instrument is that scores increase with grade, as Crites (1965) hypothesized that they should in a developmental inventory.

Various paper and pencil measures of intelligence that are more easily administered and scored than individual measures of intelligence demonstrate construct validity by indicating their relationship to individual measures of intelligence. In these cases it is possible to represent the amount of relationship between scores on the instrument in question and behavior or other test scores by computing a correlation coefficient between the two sets of measures. Thus, validity can also be expressed as a coefficient ranging from -1.0 to $+1.0$. Occasionally a negative correlation, which indicates an inverse relationship between the variables correlated, gives important evidence bearing on the construct validity of the measures (Campbell, 1960). Validity coefficients are not usually as high as reliability coefficients; $\pm.40$ to .60 represents a reasonable range for validity coefficients. The books cited above give more detailed information on how to determine the adequacy of validity coefficients and they also discuss other noncorrelational ways of expressing reliability and validity.

Any measuring procedure used to operationally define a concept for research purposes must have both reliability and validity.

Testing Hypotheses

Every research study is undertaken because there is a question. This is sometimes difficult to see because researchers do not always state the underlying question explicitly. Nor do they always state the research hypothesis, a statement about what relationship they expect to observe or what kind of change they expect to bring about. It is important for a researcher to consider how results contrary to the hypothesis of the study might be explained—before the study is begun. Too many studies have been completed in a burst of enthusiasm, only to have the researchers find that the results neither give a clear answer to the underlying question nor contribute to a much greater understanding of anything. A manuscript of this type is usually returned to a journal editor from a reviewer with the comment: "I cannot understand why this study was done."

Unfortunately, there is usually nothing the author can do *post hoc* to salvage the study when the problem is that the research was started without a clear understanding of what the researcher wanted to do. Sometimes the specific problem is with the operational definitions of the important concepts; either the important concepts were not operationally defined at all, or a measure with poor reliability or validity was used. Sometimes the specific problem is that the study was designed in such a way so that the important variables could not be isolated.

Some questions and hypotheses cannot be answered or tested because, although we know what it would take to confirm a specific hypothesis, we cannot do that thing and therefore cannot test the hypothesis. Carnap (1953) made this distinction between confirmability and testability. For instance, the hypothesis "A three stage rocket launched from earth can land on the moon" was confirmable but not testable until a solid fuel was developed that could be used to power such a rocket over the distance.

In another case, we might hypothesize that children raised in Skinner cribs (Skinner, 1945) will exhibit less social behavior than children not raised in Skinner cribs. To test this hypothesis we would need to start with a sample of babies, all from the same population, and randomly assign them to one treatment or the other, specifying exactly how the outcomes would be measured. This hypothesis is confirmable because we do know how to test it, but it is probably untestable because it is extremely unlikely that we can find a sample of babies available for random distribution to either a Skinner crib environment or a nonSkinner one. Because parents feel quite strongly about the early environment of their babies, it is not likely that many would agree to participate in such a study. Those babies whose parents are willing or who have no parents to object would probably live in situations that differ substantially from those of most children in our society, so the general hypothesis when applied to all babies would not be tested.

Research Design

Good research design insures that a testable hypothesis, with its concepts well operationalized (another way of saying this is that its variables are well measured), actually is tested. In testing any specific hypothesis, the researcher has dozens of decisions to make. The way these decisions are made dictates whether the hypothesis is adequately tested. Some of the decisions include answers to these questions: Who will be studied? How will they be assigned to treatment groups? When will measurements be taken? What variables, in addition to those included in the major hypothesized relationships, will be included in the design so that their effects can be studied? Although this section only describes briefly some basic principles of research design, there are many books covering the subject at length (Campbell and Stanley, 1963; Myers, 1966; Borg and Gall, 1971; Kerlinger, 1973). Johnson and Solso (1971) present a very effective case study approach to understanding experimental design.

SELECTING PEOPLE.   The people or units chosen for study should be representative of some larger group to whom the findings will be generalized; this is much easier to understand than to implement, however. It is difficult to secure the cooperation of representative groups of children, parents, workers, nonworkers, believers, atheists, clients, and nonclients. Therefore, the people chosen for study are often those whom the researcher can control to some extent. The most popular group used in counseling research is students in institutions where researchers work. A report by Holcomb and Anderson (1977) shows that few studies on students in technical or community colleges, workers, handicapped persons, or elderly people are conducted in the area of vocational guidance despite the obvious need for research using these populations. The group studied certainly influences the usefulness of research findings.

ASSIGNING PEOPLE.   Some kinds of research designs do not really assign people to different groups at all. Whenever the researchers cannot assign people to groups, a great deal of control is lost and the resulting designs give less definitive information. This is the case whenever a researcher studies only one group or two or more different but already existing groups. In studies on only one group, the researcher usually wants to say that an experience that the group has had (e.g., incarceration) or will have as a result of the research (e.g., a new type of counseling technique) has some specific effect. Unfortunately, if that effect *is* demonstrated, it is impossible to conclude that it is the result of the particular experience. It may have occurred as a result of some other experience or growth in the people, or changes in their society. In the absence of a comparison group that did not have the experience, it is impossible to attribute the demonstrated effect to any cause.

If two different groups are used—one which has had or will have a specific experience and one which has not had the experience—any difference between them cannot necessarily be attributed to the experience. It may be the result of initial differences between the groups. For example, an early attempt to assess the impact of counseling by Williamson and Bordin (1940) was open to criticism (Campbell, 1965) because it did not control for the fact that the counseled group, who were judged to be better adjusted and to have more appropriate career plans one year later, were different from the control group in that the former *sought* counseling. Thus, it was impossible to conclude on the basis of the data (which did show some differences between the groups) whether the superior progress of the counseled group was related to the experience of being counseled or to being the kind of person who seeks counseling. Actually, Campbell (1965) did attempt to demonstrate that the observed effects were due to counseling by studying a subgroup of the control group who sought counseling later.

In all of these cases of single group or different group designs, many extraneous sources may influence the results and there is no way to control for them. On the other hand, whenever the researcher starts with one group of people and assigns them randomly to two or more groups or matches them and then assigns them randomly to two or more groups, the researcher can be much more definitive about the causes of whatever effects are observed. If the people come from essentially the same population and are assigned randomly, then one can conclude that any effects observed are not a result of the groups being different, of the growth of the people, or the effect of the society in which they live. Applying this principle, Volsky, Magoon, Norman, and Hoyt (1965) also studied the effects of counseling, but they randomly assigned students who sought counseling to an experimental group who received counseling and a control group who did not receive counseling during the period of the study. This procedure assured that any differences found could not be attributed to changes that would occur for most students with the passage of time or to differences between the groups initially.

TIMING OF MEASURES.   The timing of the measurements is also important. If one measures the status of the people in the study only at the end of the study, it is difficult to conclude that anything in the research caused the final scores although it may appear to be reasonable to do so if there are differences between an experimental and control group at the end. Another approach is to measure both the experimental and control groups before and after the experimental group receives whatever special experience or treatment is of interest. However, it is possible, in this case, to argue that the measurement changes the people in some way. For instance, if the incoming clients in a study are given a questionnaire on their attitudes toward the family before counseling and then are randomly assigned to counselors some of whom are trained as family therapists and others as vocational counselors, it is possible that they may be alerted to the importance of family topics by the prior measurement. This readiness to talk about family topics would probably meet with differential acceptance by the two types of counselors. If the attitudes of the group counseled by family therapists change more than those of the other group, it is difficult to know what effect the pre-counseling questionnaire had in creating the change.

A pretest-posttest design with two groups cannot answer this question. However, a design with people randomly assigned to four groups—two experimental groups and two control groups, where one experimental and control set are both pretested and posttested and one experimental and control set are only posttested—can help control for the effects of the measurement itself. Although this design proposed by Solomon (1949) has been called ideal, it is difficult to implement because it requires more subjects and introduces considerable complexity to the practical arrangements for the study.

Another example of how the timing of measurements is used in research design is in time series studies. In these, one group of people is measured repeatedly to determine whether important changes have occurred over time. Between two of these measures an experimental treatment is introduced. If a greater change is observed during this period, it is attributed to the treatment. For instance, if a sample of students receive grade reports every six weeks, it is possible to observe whether the fluctuation in grades is greater from beginning to end of a six-week period when counseling groups designed to increase motivation to do well and to give assistance in developing good study habits is offered than from beginning to end of other six-week periods. This method controls for the effect of the measurement itself, and for the effects of maturation in the individuals, assuming this maturation is a relatively smooth process, but the effects of external events are not ruled out by this design. If the PTA simultaneously held a meeting on the merits of paying students to get good grades and 75 percent of the parents in school decided to adopt this practice, it would be impossible to determine whether any increase in grades should be attributed to the group program or the parents' promise to pay.

VARIABLES.   Even if the researcher is interested in the effect of a treatment (the independent variable) on the outcome (the dependent variable), other potentially important influencing factors or variables must often be taken into account.

Although the researcher may be interested in the effect of a certain counseling technique or a specific behavior, it may also be important to know if the technique is differentially effective for clients of different ages, sexes, ability levels, or socioeconomic levels. If the technique works best for females at a certain age, it is important that the study be planned to allow for testing that possibility. Thus, planning a study requires an ability to choose which independent variables may be fruitfully incorporated in the research design. This ability may be intuitive but it is more likely to be enhanced by a wide knowledge of previous research.

The independent variables included in a research design may be obvious status variables such as sex or they may be measures of constructs like "anxiety" whose presence and level are inferred from scores on an inventory. These measures must have adequate reliability and validity if the purpose of the study is to be fulfilled.

The way the independent variables are incorporated in the research design is as important as choosing and measuring them. A factorial design that allows for contrasting the effects of each independent variable singly and in all possible combinations with other independent variables is best but it is not always possible to use such a design because some combinations of the independent variables do not occur independently in the population studied. For instance, if a researcher determined that both sex and race were important independent variables in a study of the effects of group counseling, the effects of sex and race could not be studied in a factorial design if only black females and white males were available for participation in the study. A more definitive study could be designed if participants representing all four possible combinations of these variables were available.

A knowledge of experimental design is necessary for doing research and a knowledge of why good design is important is necessary for reading research critically. Overall, the researcher must make decisions about people, assignments to groups, timing, and important variables in designing good research. The researcher must also determine a method of statistical analysis to be used in analyzing the data once they are collected.

Statistical Analysis

Basically, statistical analysis helps us to answer the question: "Are these findings important or could they have occurred by chance?"

As a graduate student, I once collected data for a study and then looked for a statistical test that would answer that question, using the data I had collected. To my chagrin, I found that there was no such test. Surely there are times when it is appropriate to present data without benefit of statistical analysis. For instance, statistical significance seems superfluous when the data show large differences that are of obvious practical importance. However, because one never knows what the data will show until after they are collected, it is imperative that choosing a means of statistical analysis be incorporated into the planning of a research study and *not* left until after the data are collected.

There are hundreds of statistical tests designed to answer this question of statistical significance under various conditions and many books to explain them, e.g., McNemar, 1969; Blalock, 1972; Ferguson, 1966; Guilford and Fruchter, 1973; Mendenhall and Ott, 1972; Minium, 1970; Siegel, 1956; and Winer, 1971). Tanur (1972) discusses the study of statistics from a case study approach and Terrace and Parker (1971) offer a set of programmed units for the study of statistics.

For our purposes it is most important to understand that research findings usually involve a comparison, whether with a theoretical expectation or a comparison group. For instance, Hanson and Rayman (1976) compared how well two types of interest inventory scales classified college-bound men and women into vocational preference groups. They concluded that both types of scales had a hit rate that was far better than what would have resulted from random assignment. The hit rate for random assignment in this case was derived theoretically, a technique sometimes used in studies. The authors reasoned that if the people were randomly assigned to five categories, each assignment had one chance in five of being correctly assigned, and that over the whole group only 20 percent would be correctly classified. Both of the types of scales in question classified nearly 40 percent of the people correctly, so the authors concluded that both types were quite effective.

Unless statistical tests are applied, observed differences may appear to be large and meaningful when, in fact, they are not. The number of people studied, the distribution of their scores (which operationally define some concept) are all factors entering into the determination of whether the findings are "statistically significant." This term is used to indicate that there is a low probability that a given finding could be attributable to chance factors. An acceptable level of probability is specified. Levels most often specified are .01 and .05, meaning that there are one and five chances in one hundred that these results could be obtained by chance in situations where, indeed, there is no real difference.

With a basic understanding that the concepts utilized in research must be operationally defined, and that they are often defined by psychological measuring techniques, that the hypothesis must in fact be testable, that good research design insures a clear test of the hypothesis, and that statistical methods allow us to understand the importance of the findings, we can now examine various types of research.

These basic understandings should be supplemented by more detailed reference material. Every counselor's library should contain at least one textbook in each of the following areas: measurement, research design and statistics (listed previously), as well as a good general work on research (Arnoult, 1976; Asher, 1976; Helmstadter, 1970; Hopkins, 1976; Runkel and McGrath, 1972). Hardyck and Petrinovich (1973) and Millman and Gowin (1974) are particularly helpful general books for those who wish to learn to read research because they utilize the case study approach.

TYPES OF RESEARCH

Basically, theory, research, and practice interact as indicated in figure 2–1. Some types of research begin at the practical real world level and influence theory. Other types of research begin at the theoretical level and ultimately influence practice. The first type of research is essentially descriptive or survey research designed to answer the question "What have we here?" in an inductive fashion. Descriptive research helps to understand a given situation. The second type of research is designed to aid us in spelling out relationships between the elements of a theory. It is designed to answer questions like "If we did this, what would happen?" This is a deductive approach to research.

Among the types of research discussed in this section, the descriptive, correlational, causal comparative, and historical are basically inductive, while the experimental type of research is deductive.

Descriptive Research

Descriptive research helps us to describe the current situation. We often do descriptive research when we want to find out whether a hunch we have is borne out by the data. For instance, in 1968 Strong wrote an article in which he drew on social psychology to make some hypotheses about the nature of successful counseling. One of his ideas was that counselors who are perceived as expert by their clients will be more effective in influencing their clients. To find out how clients actually did perceive expertness in counselors, Schmidt and Strong (1970) taped interviews between six counselors at different levels of expertise as indicated by education and experience and one person playing the role of client. They asked students (who were not real clients) to listen to the tapes and rate the counselors in terms of expertness and give the reasons for their ratings. They found that the students did not rate the counselors in accord with their expertness as defined by the authors. However, the variables identified by the students were used to define expert and inexpert roles in a subsequent study of expertness and influence in counseling (Strong and Schmidt, 1970). This study helped expand our understanding of how people perceive expertness in counselors; as it turned out, the results were contrary to the authors' hunches. It is a good example of why it is necessary to do descriptive research.

FIELD AND LABORATORY SETTINGS.   Descriptive research can take place either in the field or in laboratory. Field research is conducted in real, ongoing life situations. For instance, anthropological research where the researcher actually observes the ongoing process of a society is field research. So is the more technologically sophisticated research in which an observer uses a one-way vision screen to observe and describe the behavior of subjects in natural settings. This allows the observer to work without influencing the situation being observed, whereas when the observer is perceived by the subjects it is likely that their behavior will be changed in some way. Brandt (1972) discusses research in natural settings at length and Webb, Campbell, Schwartz, and Sechrest (1966) examine how the researcher can actually measure important variables in natural settings.

Laboratory research is not done in a natural setting. Instead, the subjects are brought into some new situation for purposes of participating in the research. There are particular problems involved with descriptive research of this kind. Subjects must agree to participate and often they are only analogous to the group the researchers are really interested in. In the Schmidt and Strong study (1970) described above, the authors were interested in how clients would perceive the expertness of counselors. The counselors they used were real but the research subjects were male students in introductory psychology classes. Obviously, the authors wanted to generalize from these subjects to all counseling clients. However, whether counseling clients and introductory psychology students react similarly to counselors has not been demonstrated. Schmidt and Strong might have attempted to engage clients currently in counseling or past clients, or even clients being held on a waiting list to participate in their research. Even if they had, it is doubtful that all the clients requested to participate would have done so. Whenever participation rates vary substantially from 100 percent, the unanswerable question of how the nonparticipants vary from the participants can be asked. Research done in laboratory settings must always confront the issues of generalizability and participation rates.

Descriptive research in which subjects are asked to complete tests and questionnaires either in a laboratory setting or in a mailed format are most like laboratory studies in that the participants are asked to do something that they would not naturally do in the course of their daily lives. The same problems of generalizability and participation rates apply.

CORRELATIONAL RESEARCH.   This descriptive research technique is basically used to explore how psychological traits or behaviors are related.

In correlational studies, some measures of the variables of interest are employed and later correlated. A study by Westbrook (1976) illustrates this approach and is also a good example of how correlational studies can be used to explore the accuracy of theories. Westbrook studied the relationship between Career Choice Competencies and Career Choice Attitudes as measured by various scales of the Career Maturity Inventory, the Career Development Inventory, and the Cognitive Vocational Maturity Test. Each of the ten scales on the three instruments was classified as either a measure of career choice attitude or competency. Crites (1965, 1974) had previously predicted that *within* each area the correlation among measures would be in the .50's and .60's, while *between* the two areas correlations among measures would be only in the .30's and .40's. Westbrook explored the accuracy of Crites' predictions by administering all three inventories to ninth graders and intercorrelating their scores on all 10 of the scales. This resulted in 43 correlation coefficients that were arranged within the two areas showing the level of relationship between each pair of scales and within and between types of measures.

The correlations supported some of the specific hypotheses Westbrook derived from Crites' theory but not all of them. Table 2–1, which is reprinted from Westbrook's article, illustrates a correlational table that includes means and standard deviations for all the variables as well as the correlations between them. The correlations between competency measures were all above .50, but none of the correlations between attitude measures were above .50. Correlations between measures of attitude and measures of competency ranged from .04 to .64. These findings from a correlational study are helpful in illustrating one additional point. It is difficult to know in a study where some of the hypotheses were not upheld whether the fault is with the theory from which the hypotheses were derived or from the measures used.

Another analysis that Westbrook employed in an attempt to understand the relationships among the ten variables was factor analysis. Factor analysis is a statistical means of asking how many factors or dimensions may be used to explain a set of correlation coefficients such as those derived by Westbrook, and how much of the variability in the obtained scores can be explained by those factors. In his study, Westbrook found two factors roughly corresponding to the attitudinal and competency dimensions, as Crites' theory suggested. However, one of the attitude measures (The Career Maturity Inventory Attitude Scale, Number 1 on Table 2–1) was more highly related to the competency measures than to the other attitudinal measures. Another way of saying this is: "One attitude measure loaded highly on a factor that contained other competency measures." Factor loadings can themselves be defined as correlation coefficients between each measure and a factor representing a kind of summation or average of several variables that are related. Correlational techniques and factor analysis are discussed in much more detail in many of the statistical textbooks cited earlier.

It is important to remember that correlational studies show association or relationship but do not show causation. As a result of a correlational study we can say what traits or behaviors occur together in a given population but we cannot conclude that one caused the other.

When correlation coefficients are high, it is possible to predict the scores on one variable (called the criterion variable) from a knowledge of

TABLE 2-1
MEANS, STANDARD DEVIATIONS, AND INTERCORRELATIONS OF CAREER MATURITY VARIABLES [a,b] CLASSIFIED AS CAREER CHOICE ATTITUDES AND CAREER CHOICE COMPETENCIES OF NINTH-GRADE PUPILS

Career Maturity Variables	Mean	SD	1	2	3	4	5	6	7	8	9	10
Career Choice Attitudes												
1. Career Maturity Inventory Attitude Scale	34.58	4.95		18	12	50	54	64	55	59	60	64
2. Career Development Inventory Planning Orientation	96.47	18.80			48	09	17	13	04	17	17	17
3. Career Development Inventory Resources for Exploration	237.50	45.08				14	04	18	10	09	12	20
Career Choice Competencies												
4. Career Development Inventory Information and Decision-Making	14.76	4.52					56	57	56	61	51	51
5. Cognitive Vocational Maturity Test Fields of Work	13.96	4.48						62	73	72	64	64
6. Cognitive Vocational Maturity Test Job selection	8.24	3.10							65	68	64	64
7. Cognitive Vocational Maturity Test Work conditions	15.44	4.17								76	65	60
8. Cognitive Vocational Maturity Test Education required	13.31	4.20									61	64
9. Cognitive Vocational Maturity Test Attributes required	13.30	5.32										84
10. Cognitive Vocational Maturity Test Duties	14.24	6.85										

[a] Decimals have been omitted from correlations.
[b] $N = 90$.

*B. W. Westbrook, "Interrelationship of career choice attitudes of ninth-grade pupils: Testing hypotheses derived from Crites' model of career maturity. *Journal of Vocational Behavior*, 1976, 8, 1–12. Reprinted by permission of the publisher, Academic Press, Inc.

scores on another variable (the predictor variable) with some degree of accuracy. This process is called regression. It is also possible to correlate more than one variable at a time with a criterion variable to see how each contributes to the strength of the relationship or to find the best combination of measures to be used in predicting the criterion variable. This is called multiple regression.

For example, when it became possible after World War I to test students with paper and pencil measures of academic ability, counselors were interested in two questions that could be answered by correlational research. First, are academic ability and grades in school related? Second, can grades in school be predicted from measures of academic ability? The answers, of course, were that academic ability and performance or grades are related but that the obtained correlations (usually about .60) do not account for all of the variability in the sets of scores. To determine what percentage of the variability in a set of scores is explained by the relationship between two variables, the correlation between them is squared. Thus, if the correlation between an ability measure and grades is .60, then 36 percent of the variance in grades can be attributed to ability and 64 percent must be accounted for by other factors. Nevertheless, scores on ability tests can be used to make broad predictions about grade attainment in specific academic situations.

For instance, one can make up the kind of expectancy table shown in table 2–2 that shows the relationship between ability and grades based on actual experience in a specific college. In this fictitious example, 2000 students entered as freshmen. The distribution of their scores on the entrance exam, a measure of college aptitude, is described in the first two columns. For each subgroup, the row reflects their experience. For instance, of the 150 students who scored between 91 and 100 on the entrance exam, 20 percent obtained a grade point average (GPA) of less than 2.00 for the first year; 45 percent obtained GPA's between 2.01 and 2.99; and 35 percent obtained GPA's of 3.00 or above. It is clear from Table 2–2 that the correlation between scores and grades is not perfect. Some other factors besides ability must be influencing GPA. Yet, the table provides a prospective student at Fictitious University with a probability statement about that student's performance. If the student scores between 51 and 60, there are 65 chances in 100 that the student will earn a GPA above 2.00 based on the experience of other students with scores in the same range who enrolled at that university.

This information is useful for the counselor who is helping a client make educational plans—but it is predictive only. It will not help answer

TABLE 2-2
EXPECTANCY TABLE FOR FRESHMEN GRADES
Fictitious University
(N = 2000 freshmen)

Scores on the Fictitious University Entrance Examination	N	CHANCES IN 100 OF		
		Obtaining a GPA of 2.00 or below	Obtaining a GPA between 2.01 and 2.99	Obtaining a GPA of 3.00 or above
91–100	150	20	45	35
81–90	225	20	50	30
71–80	250	25	50	25
61–70	300	30	50	20
51–60	400	35	55	10
41–50	300	40	55	5
31–40	150	45	55	0
21–30	125	50	50	0
11–20	75	60	40	0
01–10	25	75	25	0

such questions as, "What type of remedial work will help a low scorer on the academic achievement test exceed the grade point average predicted?" That question can be answered only by an experimental study.

Correlational studies may be conducted in field or laboratory settings. The variables correlated can range from observation of behavior to measures of psychological traits or attitudes.

The use of correlation rests on an assumption that we are looking for a linear relationship. For instance, if 100 percent of the freshmen who score above 80 in Table 2–2 received a GPA of 3.00 or more and 100 percent of the freshmen who scored below 20 also received a GPA of 3.00 or more, traditional correlational analysis would probably tell us there is no relationship between the college aptitude test and GPA. Actually, there would be a relationship but not a linear one where scores on both variables increase together or where scores on one variable go up while scores on the other variable go down.

Correlational studies must use reliable and valid measures of the variables of interest. If the grade point average in a given school is distorted because all athletes are given A's on the basis of their participation in athletics, then it will be difficult to find a relationship between academic ability and GPA even though one may exist for most students. On the other hand, if the measure of academic ability used is unreliable or unstable over time, any relationship between academic ability and performance may be here today and gone tomorrow.

The people whose characteristics are measured in correlation studies deserve particular attention because they must be representative of the population the researcher is interested in if the results are to be useful. If a correlation is found between two variables in a population of college sophomores (who are often available for studies of this type), can the relationship found be generalized to all adults? There are obvious differences in age, scholastic ability, and socioeconomic status that cannot be ignored.

Not only must the people measured represent the population of interest, but there must be enough of them to insure that the resulting correlations are quite stable. Correlations based on fewer than 25 or 30 cases do not usually meet this criterion.

Because the measurements for correlational studies are usually made at one time, they usually do not help us to understand temporal influences. For instance, a researcher might find a high relationship between purchasing gifts and purchasing fir trees if the study was conducted in the month of December and no relationship at all between the two if the study was conducted in June.

Correlational studies are extremely valuable in showing what measures vary together. They tell us nothing about the absolute levels of the variables studied, temporal relationships, or causation. When the intent is to describe relationships, correlational studies are appropriate.

CAUSAL COMPARATIVE RESEARCH.   One way to attempt an understanding of causation is to study two groups that differ in some way and to search their history for differing factors that may explain the differences. Strictly speaking, this is still descriptive research, which is not really capable of determining causation. However, it is useful in describing differences that may be incorporated into subsequent experimental studies.

A study by DiMarco and Whitsitt (1975) is a good example. No hypotheses were stated but the study illustrates the problems implicit in this type of research and how the authors recognize the equivocal nature of their results. DiMarco and Whitsitt studied two groups of female supervisors, one employed by business and one employed by government. They measured the organizational structures in the two settings and the life-style orientations and interpersonal needs of the women and found certain differences between the groups. Because all the measures were taken in the present there is really no temporal difference that can be hypothesized to cause the difference. In fact, the authors point out that their results suggest two possible interpretations: (1) organizations hire people like those who already work in the organization, or (2) organizations change people after they are hired. It is extremely difficult to design a causal comparative study that does not present this type of problem.

Those causal comparative studies that do find the variables in the past that differentiate between the groups in a way suggestive of specific causation do not always lend themselves to further experimental study. A study I did (Harmon, 1972) is illustrative. In comparing women persisters and nonpersisters in three college curricula, one of the most significant differences between the two groups was that the persisters were more likely to be first-born. That is clearly a temporal difference that suggests causation. However, no experimental method for testing the relationship is available because of social prohibitions against controlling conception and childrearing practices.

Causal–comparative studies can be heuristic but the researcher must first determine that temporal differences implying causation are really being studied and that those differences once identified are amenable to more rigorous examination.

All of these descriptive studies basically reflect what exists now. They are useful in that they suggest directions for future research and also define problems.

Experimental Research

This type of research always begins with a population of subjects that can be randomly assigned to two or more treatment groups. Experimental research is most often conducted in a laboratory setting although field experiments can occasionally be carried out. For instance, in educational settings it is sometimes possible to randomly assign classrooms as a unit for one treatment or another—the experimenter wants to be able to say that the only difference between the groups was the treatment they received. Thus, any change after the treatment can be attributed to the treatment itself, not to extraneous variables. A good experimental research design does allow us to make statements about causation. For instance, if a sample of individuals who are deficient in certain skills are randomly assigned to two treatments designed to alleviate that deficiency, and one group makes better progress than the other, we can assume that the treatment caused the progress and that if the groups were reversed, the group now receiving the effective treatment would be the one to make progress. Random assignment assures that every subject has as much chance of being assigned to one treatment group as to another. Consequently, the characteristics of the subjects assigned to each treatment group should be pretty typical of the sample as a whole.

The independent variables in an experimental design are those controlled by the experimenter. They include the various treatments to be applied but they also include variables thought relevant to the research question such as age, sex, socioeconomic status, or score on a psychological test. If the experimenter controls each of the variables so that its effects can be known, less is left to chance and more can be explained.

The dependent variable in experimental research is the measure or measures that the experimenter expects to vary in relationship to the independent variables. It is clear that this measure must be highly reliable and valid or the whole experiment will be worthless. For instance, suppose an experimenter hypothesized that under certain conditions specific organisms produced electricity that could be collected and used to light an electric bulb in a special apparatus. The experimenter might spend a great deal of time and effort building the apparatus and creating and varying the conditions, but if the light bulb used to measure the production of electricity had a broken filament that would never light, or would light only when the broken filament ends happened to fall into physical contact, the results would be worse than useless. Because of an unreliable measure of the dependent variable, erratic results that appear to come from a well-controlled study can be worse than no results at all because they are so confusing.

Experimental studies are most often analyzed by using statistical techniques called analysis of variance. They allow for the control of a number of variables and for the study of the effects of each independent variable *as well as* for interactions between independent variables. Thus, an experimenter might find that one specific treatment worked best for one age group but that another treatment worked best for another age group.

Experimental studies in counseling are quite difficult to design. The major reason is that populations of interest are not easy to engage in research. Many of the studies on counseling process have been conducted as analogue studies requiring the assumption that the available population, often college students, are analogous to clients. Assigning real clients to specific and sometimes short-term treatment processes is difficult because counselors believe that the proper treatment of clients requires a counselor to be a diagnostician and prescriber who is free to use the whole range of treatment modalities unhampered by concerns of research design. For example, the study reported by Rogers and Dymond (1954) suggests that some clients who should have been placed in the control group and not treated immediately were not put into that group because of their immediate need for treatment. That decision is consistent with the humanistic goals of counseling but not with the goal of producing well-controlled experimental research.

Increasingly, researchers have turned to the use of videotape and analogue designs to study the counseling process. (For example, review any recent issue of the *Journal of Counseling Psychology*.) Although this allows for tight experimental control, too often the study is so far removed from the actual counseling process that it is not clear whether the results generalize to the counseling process. When counseling outcomes are studied, real clients are more likely to be used but the process is not often well described so the value for practice or future research is limited.

Thus, while experimental designs allow us to learn more than any other type of research, they are also the most difficult kinds of research studies to implement. In the counseling field they are extremely challenging but not impossible. The study by Stulman and Dawis (1976) reprinted later in this chapter is a good example of the application of experimental techniques to a counseling related problem.

Historical Research

Historical research differs considerably from the other types of research discussed here. It is rarely conducted in counseling, probably because counseling has a relatively short history. Historical research is an attempt to understand some specific aspects of the past. It is a potentially useful method in a field like counseling, where the subject studied—clients and their behavior—is very similar to the person doing the study. It is possible that any research on human behavior is biased by the human beings doing the research in ways that will be apparent only after a number of years have passed. A historical study in counseling should allow us to understand a period of time, its events, and its people, and how they interacted to produce what we think of as the counseling literature. Behind each theory proposed, each piece of research printed, there is a social, cultural, economic, and political era and there is a person who is unique in his or her needs and interests. Understanding more about how our counseling heritage was produced by these forces might help us to understand more about the forces that impinge on us as counselors and researchers.

I learned some new and startling things about how researchers work from reading *The Double Helix,* James Watson's account of how the structure of the DNA molecule was discovered (1968) and the *Oppenheimer Case* (Stern, 1969), which chronicles some of the events surrounding the development of the first atomic weapons. These books helped me to see how the researcher's values and cultural milieu influence the research process and ultimately to understand how my values interact with my work.

Historical studies in counseling might explore such questions as "What is the relationship between warfare and trait and factor theories in counseling (1914–1974)?" or "How do the early histories of Albert Ellis, Fritz Perls, and Carl Rogers differ?"

It is obviously difficult to apply scientific methodology to historical questions. This type of research is open to criticism on the basis of lack of experimental control. Whole books have been written about historical methodology (e.g., Barzun and Graff, 1957; Nevins, 1962). The major point to be made here is that the historical study of counseling has the potential to teach us something about what we are doing today.

READING RESEARCH
IN COUNSELING

The first thing you need to know about reading research in counseling is where to find it. The *Journal of Counseling Psychology* is one of the most research oriented journals in the counseling area as well as the most general in terms of content. For a reader who is just beginning to explore the counseling literature, it is a good place to start. Other journals that publish some counseling research, usually in specific areas, include *Counselor Education and Supervision, Elementary School Guidance and Counseling,* the *Journal of Educational Research,* the *Journal of Employment Counseling,* the *Journal of Vocational Behavior, Measurement and Evaluation in Guidance,* the *Rehabilitation Counseling Bulletin,* and the *Vocational Guidance Quarterly.*

Figure 2-2 suggests a method for reading and evaluating research. It serves as a framework for the following paragraphs, which discuss the several stages shown in the figure.

1. Most research articles are preceded by an abstract. You should be able to tell from reading the abstract whether an article is of interest to you. If not, go on to read another (it is hoped, more engaging) abstract. Nobody reads all the research articles in counseling.

2. From the introduction the purpose of the study should be clear to you. It should have some theoretical or practical import or the author is collecting data just for the fun of it. In experimental studies, formal hypotheses should be given in addition to a general statement of purpose.

3. Either in the introductory section or in the methods section, you should be told how each of the important terms and concepts in the study will be operationally defined. These definitions should be presented early and used consistently throughout the manuscript.

4. If either step 2 or 3 above has been violated, discontinue reading unless the topic is of such great interest to you that you are willing to put forth great effort to gain a hazy understanding. Such studies should not be published, but they are.

5. Read the methods section to determine whether:
    (a) the reliability and validity of the measures used have been established and are satisfactory.
    (b) the subjects are appropriate to the study and whether the results will generalize to an appropriate counseling situation. Is there a large enough number of subjects to draw any conclusions?
    (c) the design that was used tests the hypothesis or explores the question posed. A common fault at this level is to design a study in such a way that it does not answer the questions posed.
    (d) the statistical analysis is appropriate to the problem. It is not uncommon to find researchers computing a number of simple tests that make it difficult to interpret the probability of the results, where one complex test would be more appropriate and informative.
    (e) the overall logic of the method is sound. This means that you don't have a nagging feeling that the hypotheses have not been tested, the sample is too small, or the statistical analysis is inappropriate. Any one of these questions should cause you to do some checking in the books mentioned throughout this chapter or with experts to test out your hunches.

6. If you have questions at all, they will probably lead you to question the results and discussion. If you do, you will already be thinking about how you or someone else might design and conduct the study better. Act on these ideas and design your own study or write to the author, who can benefit from your ideas.

7. Even if you have no problems with the methods and accept the results, you may find that you have ideas about application of the

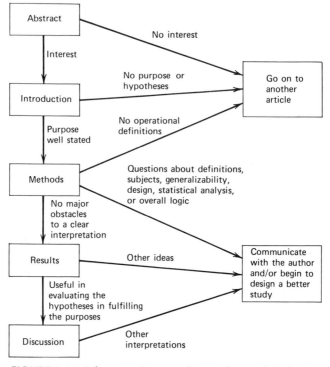

FIGURE 2.2   Schematic Diagram for Reading and Evaluating Research.

findings in your setting that differ from those of the author. Or you may have ideas for extending the research the author did not have. Communicate with the author about them. That's what caused the interaction in Figure 2–1.

Many studies that do not meet all the criteria implied in the steps suggested above are published. In my own career as a journal editor I have accepted some. Very few studies are perfect and if journal editors waited until they came along, not much would be published. On one hand, that might be considered a good thing. On the other, it is sometimes useful to publish an imperfect study. I occasionally make the judgment that one particular well-designed, nearly perfect study is less valuable than an imperfect one because the nearly perfect one tells us nothing new, while the imperfect one introduces fresh new ideas that will generate considerable new thinking and research. In such cases I usually ask the authors to acknowledge and discuss the limitations of their work.

The reader of research should be aware that imperfect research is published and be prepared to read critically. The general editorial review process that most research goes through before it appears in journals is usually designed to insure merit but not perfection.

AN EXAMPLE. A study by Stulman and Dawis is reprinted here because it represents a good, well-written, and creative experimental study. However, parallel to it is an example of how it could have been written less well and what a journal editor might say about the "parody." The original article appears in roman type, the parody in bold face type, and a running critique of the parody alongside it in italics.

Experimental Validation of Two MIQ Scales*

David A. Stulman and René V. Dawis
University of Minnesota

Two Minnesota Importance Questionnaire (MIQ) scales, Creativity and Independence, were validated by experiment. Subjects were exposed to four task conditions representing joint combinations of high or low levels of Creativity and Independence. As a behavioral criterion of preference, subjects were then required to work for 12 sessions, each session under any (of the four) task conditions of their choice. The behavioral results were consistent with the subjects' MIQ score levels on the two scales, thereby validating the scales.

Experimental Validation of Two Scales: A Parody for Pedagogical Purposes

Comments by a Prototypic Reviewer Regarding "A Parody . . . "

Lenore W. Harmon
University of Wisconsin – Milwaukee

ABSTRACT

Two inventory scales were investigated by an experimental procedure that exposed subjects to four conditions and then required them to choose among them. Significant results were obtained.

What inventory?
What scales?
What conditions?

Why was this done?
Not enough information to help the reader decide whether to read further.

Over the years psychologists have been exhorted to "reconcile" the "two disciplines of scientific psychology" (Bindra & Scheier, 1954; Coffield, 1970; Cronbach, 1957; Dashiell, 1939; Owens, 1968). Simply put, the "experimentalists" have been urged to consider individual differences in their experiments and theories, while the "correlationists" have been admonished to utilize theory and experiment

*(From D. A. Stulman and R. V. Dawis, Experimental validation of two MIQ scales. *Journal of Vocational Behavior*, 1976, 9, 161–67. Reprinted by permission of the publisher, Academic Press, Inc.)

in the investigation of their "applied" problems. The present study is an attempt at utilizing experiment in what is ordinarily a correlational problem: the validation of a psychometric instrument.

Inventories are usually validated by correlating scores with some criteria. The purpose of this study was to use an experimental design to accomplish that purpose.

The author seems to imply that correlational validations lack something. Why? What?

The Minnesota Importance Questionnaire (MIQ; Gay, Weiss, Hendel, Dawis, & Lofquist, 1971) is a 20-scale, paired-comparison self-report instrument designed to measure vocationally relevant needs, i.e., preferences for reinforcers. Utilizing scaling methods developed under the assumptions of Thurstone's classic Case V of the Law of Comparative Judgment (Guilford, 1954), MIQ scale values are calculated to reflect the relative importance of 20 work or vocational reinforcers to the respondent. The scale values are anchored to a "zero point" (separating the important from the "not important" reinforcers), thereby enabling comparison across individuals. An idea of the MIQ's content domain can be gleaned from the following scale titles: (a) Ability Utilization, (b) Achievement, (c) Activity, (d) Advancement, (e) Authority, (f) Company Policies and Practices, (g) Compensation, (h) Co-workers, (i) Creativity, (j) Independence, (k) Moral Values, (l) Recognition, (m) Responsibility, (n) Security, (o) Social Service, (p) Social Status, (q) Supervision-Human Relations, (r) Supervision-Technical, (s) Variety, and (t) Working Conditions.

As in the case of many other psychometric instruments, the validity of the MIQ has been based on evidence from correlational and "natural variation" (i.e., non-manipulated) studies, such as studies of group differences and concurrent prediction (Gay et al., 1971, pp. 46-55). It occurred to the authors that scales measuring preferences might be amenable to validation in a laboratory setting, with experimental conditions being manipulated as in conventional experimentation. It might be possible, for example, to expose subjects to varying conditions under which a task might be performed and then to determine which of the conditions was most preferred. Such "experimental" preference could then be used to validate the preference scores generated by the MIQ.

Two MIQ scales appeared to be most promising for such experimentation: Creativity ("I could try out some of my own ideas") and Independence ("I could work alone on the job"). The Creativity statement suggests two contrasting conditions: one, permissive, and the other, prescriptive. The Independence statement suggests the two contrasting conditions of working alone and working with others. Since the two scales correlate very little ($r = .26$), it would be possible to cross the two sets of conditions, yielding four conditions: permissive and working alone; permissive and working with others; prescriptive and working alone; and prescriptive and working with others.

After exposing subjects to the four conditions (in random sequence), a criterion of *behavioral* preference could be determined by requiring each subject to work for a given number of sessions but allowing the subject to choose, for each session, under which of the four conditions he/she would work.

The inventory chosen for study was the Minnesota Importance Questionnaire (MIQ) which measures needs (Gay, Weiss, Hendel, Dawis, and Lofquist, 1971). Within the MIQ, two scales, Creativity and Independence, were selected. They are not highly correlated so it was possible to cross the two sets of conditions to create four sets of conditions.

Not enough information is given about the MIQ–Does it have any established reliability or validity? What is it designed to measure? How were these scales developed?

How much are they correlated? I would rather know the correlation than the author's evaluation of it.

METHOD

Subjects.   Subjects were 68 college students, 40 females and 28 males, enrolled in an introductory psychology course at a state university in the fall of 1973. The 68 subjects were chosen from an original group of 284 volunteers because they could be classified on the basis of their MIQ scores (adjusted scale values) into one of four categories: High Creativity-High Independence, High Creativity-Low Independence, Low Creativity-High Independence, and Low Creativity-Low Independence. High and Low levels represented approximately the upper and lower thirds, respectively, of the original group's distributions of Independence and Creativity scale scores. Minimum scores of High levels were 1.3 for Creativity and .1 for Independence. Maximum scores for Low levels were .8 for Creativity and −.6 for Independence.

METHOD

Subjects.   From 284 volunteers, 68 subjects were chosen because they could be classified on the basis of their MIQ scores into one of the four groups needed for study. Some of the remaining volunteers were used as members of the Low Independence groups.

Not enough information is given about the subjects and how they were selected. It would be hard to replicate this study or to generalize from it.

The four groups needed have not been clearly explained. Thus, the status of the remaining volunteers is still unclear.

Procedure.   The work task each subject had to perform was the assembly of a set of Tinker Toy elements. A model to be replicated was prescribed for the Low Creativity condition. No model was prescribed for the High Creativity condition; the subject could design his/her own Tinker Toy figure. Working alone was the High Independence condition; working with two other persons of the same sex as the subject's was the Low Independence condition. (The "two others" for the Low Independence condition were drawn from the remainder of the original group of 284.)

Each subject had to work for 7 min under each of the four task conditions: (a) High Creativity-High Independence (working alone without a model); (b) High Creativity-Low Independence (working in a group without a model); (c) Low Creativity-High Independence (working alone with a prescribed model to replicate); and (d) Low Creativity-Low Independence (working in a group with a model to replicate). The sequence of conditions was randomized for each subject. After being exposed to all four conditions, the subject was required to work for 12 4-min sessions, with 1-min rest periods in-between. For each 4-min session, the subject chose the condition under which he/she preferred to work. Thus, the number of sessions spent on each task condition was a direct behavioral measure of preference for the task condition.

Procedure.   Each   subject   was given a work task—assembling elements of a set of toys. In the Low Creativity condition a model was given but in the High Creativity condition the subject could assemble the elements in any way he/she desired.
Each subject first worked under each task condition for a specified period of time. Then the subject was required to work for 12 sessions but he/she could choose which one of the four conditions he/she preferred for each task served as a measure of preference for each task condition.

Was the form the elements "should" take implied by the elements? Were they parts of a train for instance? Or Lincoln Logs? If so, the presence of a model is not as important as spatial and mechanical ability in the case of the train, and prior experience in the case of Lincoln Logs.

Do we have two or four task conditions here? How long were these sessions? Could fatigue have been a factor? Or sequencing?

RESULTS

Table 1 shows the means and standard deviations for the number of sessions spent by the various groups in each of the four task conditions. The subjects are grouped by sex and MIQ score pattern (i.e., those scoring "high" on both Creativity and Independence, "high" on one and "low" on the other, or "low" on both scales). Regardless of group, the highest means (i.e., the longest amount of time spent) are generally observed for the High Creativity-High Independence condition, while the lowest means generally obtained for the Low Creativity-Low Independence condition. Considering each task condition separately, the highest mean is observed for the group with the appropriate MIQ score pattern, with one exception. The only exception is that under the High Creativity-Low Independence task condition for males, the High Creativity-High Independence group had the highest mean.

RESULTS

Table 1 shows the time spent in each condition by each group. It is clear that the appropriate groups scored high on the appropriate task.

I read Table 1 to show that within groups the highest scores were for the appropriate condition except in the High Creativity-Low Independence Group. However, most groups like high creativity a lot. Which brings us back to the question of where these subjects came from.

A multivariate analysis of variance was conducted on the data, using the computer program UMST 570 of the University Computer Center at the same state university. (UMST 570 is capable of handling unequal cell frequencies. An unweighted means analysis was used because the sums of squares in such an analysis would be conceptually more meaningful. If a weighted means analysis were used, some of the main effect contributions would be removed when interaction effects are re-

TABLE 1
MEAN AND STANDARD DEVIATION FOR NUMBER OF SESSIONS SPENT ON EACH OF FOUR TASK CONDITIONS, BY SEX AND MIQ GROUP

Group	(N)	Task condition[a]							
		HC-HI		HC-LI		LC-HI		LC-LI	
		(M)	(SD)	(M)	(SD)	(M)	(SD)	(M)	(SD)
Female									
High Creativity-High Independence	11	6.18[b]	2.32	3.36	2.84	2.00	2.15	0.46	0.69
High Creativity-Low Independence	10	4.10	2.23	5.30	3.09	1.60	1.17	1.00	1.49
Low Creativity-High Independence	10	6.00	3.13	2.10	2.69	2.20	2.74	1.70	1.16
Low Creativity-Low Independence	9	5.33	1.87	3.33	1.80	1.56	1.33	1.78	1.56
Male									
High Creativity-High Independence	8	5.88	3.18	4.50	3.51	0.75	0.89	0.88	0.64
High Creativity-Low Independence	6	5.50	1.64	3.50	1.76	1.00	1.27	2.00	2.10
Low Creativity-High Independence	8	5.75	3.28	2.00	2.07	3.13	2.59	1.13	1.55
Low Creativity-Low Independence	6	3.33	3.39	4.67	2.58	1.00	1.27	3.00	1.27

Note: maximum score = 12.
[a] H = High; L = Low; C = Creativity; I = Independence.
[b] Means are underscored for the task condition corresponding to the group MIQ pattern.

moved, thereby confusing the interpretation of main effects.) The vector of dependent variables in this case consisted of three variates, number of sessions spent, respectively, in the High Creativity-High Independence, High Creativity-Low Independence, and Low Creativity-High Independence task conditions. (Number of sessions spent in the Low Creativity-Low Independence condition was completely determined by the number of sessions spent in the other three task conditions and therefore was not free to vary.) The independent variables in this analysis were MIQ Creativity and Independence levels and sex. The results of the multivariate analysis of variance are summarized in Table 2.

TABLE 2

MULTIVARIATE ANALYSIS OF VARIANCE FOR NUMBER OF SESSIONS SPENT IN EACH OF FOUR TASK CONDITIONS

Effect	F ratio (3,58)	p value
Creativity	2.74	.05
Independence	4.25	.01
Creativity × Independence	0.78	.51
Sex	1.07	.37
Creativity × Sex	1.25	.30
Independence × Sex	1.33	.27
Creativity × Independence × Sex	1.37	.26

As Table 2 shows, only the effects due to MIQ Creativity and Independence scores were statistically significant. Sex was not a significant source of variation, nor were the various interactions significant sources of variation.

Table 2 shows that only the effects due to creativity and independence were significant in a multivariate analysis.   *Why and how was this analysis done?*

Subsequently, univariate analyses of variance were conducted separately for each task condition to determine the significance of differences between High and Low Creativity groups (combined across Independence groups) and between High and Low Independence groups (combined across Creativity groups) in the number of sessions spent in each task condition. (It should be noted that these F tests are not independent and therefore the p values are probably underestimates. However, the results are suggestive of tendencies.) Table 3 shows the summary statistics for these analyses.

Table 3 shows that the High Creativity group spent more time (number of sessions) than the Low Creativity group in the High Creativity task conditions, while the Low Creativity group spent relatively more time in the Low Creativity task condition. However, the High Creativity-High Independence task condition appeared to be behaviorally preferred about equally by both High and Low Creativity groups, and the Low Creativity-High Independence was unattractive almost equally to both groups. The High Creativity group behaviorally preferred the High Creativity-Low Independence condition significantly more than the Low Creativity group, which in turn preferred the Low Creativity-Low Independence condition significantly more than the High Creativity group.

An analogous but more pronounced pattern of results is observed for the High and Low Independence groups, with the findings being significant for three of the four task conditions. As Table 3 shows, the High Independence group behaviorally preferred the High Independence task condition relatively more than did the Low Independence group, while the latter preferred the Low Independence task condition relatively more than did the High Independence group.

TABLE 3

MEAN AND STANDARD DEVIATION OF NUMBER OF SESSIONS SPENT IN EACH
OF FOUR TASK CONDITIONS, BY MIQ GROUP

Task condition	MIQ Creativity Group				F ratio (1,64)	p value
	High Creativity		Low Creativity			
	M	SD	M	SD		
High Creativity-High Independence	5.34a	2.48	5.21	2.95	0.003	.84
High Creativity-Low Independence	4.23	2.93	2.96	2.42	3.92	.05
Low Creativity-High Independence	1.42	1.54	1.97	2.20	1.46	.23
Low Creativity-Low Independence	1.00	1.32	1.86	1.47	6.66	.01
	MIQ Independence Group					
	High Independence		Low Independence			
	M	SD	M	SD		
High Creativity-High Independence	5.97a	2.83	4.58	2.35	4.60	.04
High Creativity-Low Independence	2.95	2.88	4.25	2.48	4.06	.05
Low Creativity-High Independence	2.04	2.29	1.35	1.23	2.30	.13
Low Creativity-Low Independence	1.04	1.12	1.82	1.68	5.62	.02

Note: Maximum score = 12.
a Means are underscored for the task conditions corresponding to the MIQ score-level group.

Table 3 shows that significant differences between the High and Low Creativity Groups and the Creativity Groups and the High and Low Independence Groups resulted from univariate F tests.

I couldn't tell what was done here without looking at Table 3. The problem is that the groups contrasted are not clearly delineated.

CONCLUSION

The experiment described above has shown that preferences for two reinforcers, Creativity and Independence, as expressed in a paired-comparison, self-report questionnaire, are consistent with preferences presumably for the same reinforcers expressed through behavioral choice. The experimental results provide support for the validity of the Creativity and Independence scales of the MIQ as measures of preferences for the corresponding reinforcers, i.e., as measures of vocational needs. The study is, of course, not without its limitations. Only two of the 20 MIQ scales were validated; only two levels were used for each factor (scale); only college students served as experimental subjects. Different results might have been obtained with more (or other) scales, more levels, or a different population. Furthermore, in the present study, while *within* a given task condition the most time is spent by the appropriate group in the appropriate task condition, *across* task conditions, the behavioral preference is decidedly for the High Creativity-High Independence condition (a finding which might be related to the use of college students as subjects). Nonetheless, the study does show that experimentation can be utilized and is useful in what has long been a private preserve of correlational methodology, the validation of a psychometric instrument.

CONCLUSION

This study showed that subjects chose tasks consistent with their scores on two MIQ scales, Creativity and Independence, thus validating these scales. It seems reasonable to expect that other MIQ scales could also be validated in a similar fashion. Although college students were used as subjects here (with an attendant preponderance of preferences for creativity and independence) it seems safe to assume that even more pronounced trends would be evident with a more general population.

The author generalizes far too freely from the data.

The relationship of the sample and a high level of preference for creativity and independence should have been discussed earlier, not just hinted at here.

Overall, this may be a good study but this report of it does not deal with some of the major pieces of information needed to determine whether it is or not.

This study was part of the doctoral dissertation of the first author conducted under the supervision of the second author. The study was supported in part by grants from the Department of Psychology and the University Computer Center, University of Minnesota. Special acknowledgment is due Dr. Kinley Larntz for his assistance in the statistical analysis. The first author is now a psychologist with the U.S. Army at Fort Hood. Requests for reprints should be sent to René V. Dawis, Department of Psychology, University of Minnesota, Minneapolis, MN 55455.

REFERENCES

Bindra, D., & Scheier, I. H. The relation between psychometric and experimental research in psychology. *American Psychologist,* 1954, 9, 69–71.

Coffield, K. E. Research methodology: A possible reconciliation. *American Psychologist,* 1970, 25, 511–516.

Cronbach, L. J. The two disciplines of scientific psychology. *American Psychologist,* 1957, 12, 671–684.

Dashiell, J. F. Some rapprochements in contemporary psychology. *Psychological Bulletin,* 1939, 36, 1–24.

Gay, E. G., Weiss, D. J., Hendel, D. D., Dawis, R. V., & Lofquist, L. H. Manual for the Minnesota Importance Questionnaire. *Minnesota Studies in Vocational Rehabilitation,* 1971, No. XXVIII.

Guilford, J. P. *Psychometric methods.* New York: McGraw Hill, 1954.

Owens, W. A. Toward one discipline of scientific psychology. *American Psychologist,* 1968, 23, 782–785.

If you can follow the seven steps outlined in this section and apply them to the article illustrated above, many of the apparent contradictions from research studies will become clearer. You will see how differing results can be obtained by sampling from different populations and using different operational definitions even though the researchers claim to be studying the same question. Of course, you will need to educate yourself in measurement, statistics, and research design to a certain extent. However, you will not be likely to throw out research results because they are inconclusive or too restricted. You will understand why they are inconclusive or not very general as well as which soundly derived results you can begin to apply to your counseling practice. You will begin to believe that questions about counseling are answerable if the researcher is careful and persistent enough.

However it *is* difficult to understand human behavior; Lincoln Barnett (1948) wrote:

> Man's inescapable impasse is that he himself is part of the world he seeks to explore; his body and proud mind are mosaics of the same elemental particles that compose the dark drifting dust clouds of interstellar space; he is, in the final analysis, merely an ephemeral confirmation of the primordial space-time field. Standing midway between macrocosm and microcosm, he finds barriers on every side. . . .

Since he wrote that, we have made monumental leaps in our understanding of both interstellar and intracranial space, yet it is still true. It will probably always be true. Yet we will continue to increase our knowledge of the world and our control over it through research. These efforts will be enhanced by active communication between practitioner, researcher, and theoretician.

REFERENCES

American Psychological Association. *Standards for educational and psychological tests* (2nd edition). Washington, D.C.: Author, 1974.

Anastasi, A. Psychological testing (4th edition). New York: Macmillan, 1976.

Arnoult, M. D. *Fundamentals of scientific method in psychology* (2nd edition). Dubuque, Iowa: W.C. Brown, 1976.

Asher, J. W. *Educational research and evaluation methods.* Boston: Little Brown and Company, 1976.

Astin, A. W. Further validation of the environmental assessment technique. *Journal of Educational Psychology,* 1963, *54,* 217–226.

Astin, A. W., and Holland, J. L. The environmental assessment technique: A way to measure college environments. *Journal of Educational Psychology,* 1961, *52,* 308–316.

Auerswald, M. C. Differential reinforcing power of restatement and interpretation on client production of affect. *Journal of Counseling Psychology,* 1974, *21,* 9–14.

Barnett, L. *The universe and Dr. Einstein.* New York: Harper and Brothers, 1948.

Barzun, J., and Graff, H. F. *The modern researchers.* New York: Harcourt Brace Jovanovich, 1957.

Blalock, H. M., Jr. *Social statistics* (2nd edition). New York: McGraw-Hill, 1972.

Borg, W. R., and Gall, M. D. *Educational research: An introduction* (2nd edition). New York: David McKay, 1971.

71

Brandt, R. M. *Studying behavior in natural settings.* New York: Holt, Rinehart, and Winston, 1972.

Brown, F. G. *Principles of educational and psychological testing* (2nd edition). New York: Holt, Rinehart and Winston, 1976.

Campbell, D. P. *The results of counseling: Twenty-five years later.* Philadelphia: W. B. Saunders, 1965.

Campbell, D. T. Recommendations for APA test standards regarding construct, trait, and discriminant validity. *American Psychologist,* 1960, *15,* 546–553.

Campbell, D. T., and Stanley, J. C. *Experimental and quasi-experimental designs for research.* Chicago: Rand McNally and Company, 1963.

Carnap, R. Testability and meaning. In *Readings in the philosophy of science.* Feigl,H. and Brodbeck, M. (Eds.). New York: Appleton-Century-Crofts, 1953. (Reprinted from *Philosophy of Science,* 1937, *3* and 1937, *4).*

Crites, J. O. *Measurement of vocational maturity in adolescence: I. Attitude test of the Vocational Development Inventory. Psychological Monographs,* 1965, 79 (2, Whole No. 595).

Crites, J. O. *Career Maturity Inventory.* Monterey, Calif.: CTB/McGraw-Hill, 1973.

Crites, J. O. *The Career Maturity Inventory.* In D. E. Super (Ed.), *Measuring vocational maturity for counseling and evaluation.* Washington, D.C.: National Vocational Guidance Association, 1974, 23–39.

Cronbach, L. J. *Essentials of psychological testing* (3rd edition). New York: Harper & Row, 1970.

Cronbach, L. J., and Meehl, P. E. Construct validity in psychological tests. *Psychological Bulletin,* 1955, *52,* 281–302.

DiMarco, N., and Whitsitt, S. E. A comparison of female supervisors in business and government. *Journal of Vocational Behavior,* 1975, *6,* 185–196.

Droppleman, L. F., and McNair, D. M. An experimental analogy of public speaking. *Journal of Consulting and Clinical Psychology*, 1971, *36*, 91–96.

Egan, G. *The skilled helper: A model for systematic helping and interpersonal relating*. Monterey, Calif.: Brooks/Cole, 1975.

Ferguson, G. A. *Statistical analysis in psychology and education* (2nd edition). New York: McGraw-Hill, 1966.

Ginzberg, E., Ginsburg, S. W., Axelrad, S., and Herma, J. L. *Occupational choice*. New York: Columbia University Press, 1951.

Goldman, L. *Using tests in counseling* (2nd edition). New York: Appleton-Century-Crofts, 1971.

Greenberg, J. *The Monday voices*. New York: Avon Books, 1965.

Guilford, J. P. *Psychometric methods* (2nd edition). New York: McGraw-Hill, 1954.

Guilford, J. P., and Fruchter, B. *Fundamental statistics in psychology and education* (5th edition). New York: McGraw-Hill, 1973.

Gulliksen, H. *Theory of mental tests*. New York: Wiley, 1950.

Hanson, G. R., and Rayman, J. Validity of sex-balanced interest inventory items. *Journal of Vocational Behavior*, 1976, *9*, 279–292

Hardyck, C., and Petrinovich, L. F. *Understanding research in the social sciences*. Philadelphia: W.B. Saunders, 1973.

Harmon, L. W. Variables related to women's persistence in educational plans. *Journal of Vocational Behavior*, 1972, *2*, 143–153.

Heilbrun, A. B., Jr. History of self-disclosure in females and early defection from psychotherapy. *Journal of Counseling Psychology*, 1973, *20*, 250–257.

Helmstadter, G. C. *Research concepts in human behavior: Education, psychology, sociology*. New York: Appleton-Century-Crofts, 1970.

Holcomb, W. R., and Anderson, W. P. Vocational guidance research: A five year overview. *Journal of Vocational Behavior*, 1977, *10*, 341–346.

Holland, J. L. A personality inventory employing occupational titles. *Journal of Applied Psychology*, 1958, *42*, 336–342.

Holland, J. L. A theory of vocational choice. *Journal of Counseling Psychology*, 1959, *6*, 35–45.

Holland, J. L. Some explorations of a theory of vocational choice: I. One and two year longitudinal studies. *Psychological Monographs*, 1962, *76* (26, Whole No. 545).

Holland, J. L. Explorations of a theory of vocational choice and achievement: II. A four year prediction study. *Psychological Reports*, 1963, *12*, 537–594.

Holland, J. L. Explorations of a theory of vocational choice: IV. Vocational preferences and their relation to occupational images, daydreams, and personality. *Vocational Guidance Quarterly*, published in four parts in Summer, Autumn, and Winter issues, 1963–64: 1963, *11*, 232–239; 1963, *12*, 17–21 and 21–24; 1963–64, *12*, 93–97.

Holland, J. L. Explorations of a theory of vocational choice: V. A one year prediction study. Moravia, New York: Chronicle Guidance Professional Service, 1964.

Holland, J. L. *The psychology of vocational choice: A theory of personality types and model environments.* Waltham, Mass.: Blaisdell, 1966.

Holland, J. L. Explorations of a theory of vocational choice: VI. A longitudinal study using a sample of typical college students. *Journal of Applied Psychology*, 1968, *52*, 1–37.

Holland, J. L. *The Self-Directed Search.* Palo Alto, Calif.: Consulting Psychologists Press, 1970.

Holland, J. L. *Making vocational choices: A theory of careers.* Englewood Cliffs, N. J.: Prentice-Hall, 1973.

Holland, J. L., and Nichols, R. C. Explorations of a theory of vocational choice: III. A longitudinal study of changes in major field of study. *Personnel and Guidance Journal,* 1964, *43,* 235–242.

Holland, J. L., Viernstein, M. C., Kuo, H., Karweit, N. L., and Blum, Z. D. A psychological classification of occupations. *Journal Supplement Abstract Service,* 1972, *2,* 84.

Holland, J. L., Whitney, D. R., Cole, N. S., and Richards, J. M., Jr. An empirical occupational classification derived from a theory of personality and intended for practice and research. ACT Research Report No. 29. Iowa City: The American College Testing Program, 1969.

Hopkins, C. D. *Educational research: A structure for inquiry.* Columbus, Ohio: Charles E. Merrill, 1976.

Horst, P. *Psychological measurement and prediction.* Belmont, Calif.: Wadsworth Publishing Co., 1966.

Jeanneret, P. R., and McCormick, E. J. The job dimensions of "worker-oriented" job variables and their attitude profiles as based on data from the Position Analysis Questionnaire. Office of Naval Research Contract N–1100 (28), Report No. 2. Lafayette, Ind.: Occupational Research Center, Purdue University, 1969.

Johnson, H. H., and Solso, R. L. *An introduction to experimental design in psychology: A case approach.* New York: Harper & Row, 1971.

Kerlinger, F. N. *Foundations of behavioral research* (2nd edition). New York: Holt, Rinehart and Winston, 1973.

Krasner, L., and Ullmann, L. *Research in behavior modification.* New York: Holt, Rinehart, and Winston, 1965.

Lazovik, A. D., and Lang, P. J. A laboratory demonstration of systematic desensitization psychotherapy. *Journal of Psychological Studies,* 1960, *11,* 238–247.

Levine, S., and Elzey, F. F. *A programmed introduction to educational and psychological measurement.* Belmont, Calif.: Brooks/Cole, 1970.

Magnusson, D. *Test theory*. (translated by H. Mabon.) Reading, Mass.: Addison-Wesley, 1966.

Mann, J., and Rosenthal, T. Vicarious and direct counter conditioning of test anxiety through individual and group desensitization. *Behavior Research and Therapy*, 1969, 7, 359–367.

McCormick, E. J., Jeanneret, P. R., and Mecham, R. C. The development and background of the Position Analysis Questionnaire. Office of Naval Research Contract N–1100 (28), Report No. 5. Lafayette, Ind.: Occupational Research Center, Purdue University, 1969.

McNemar, Q. *Psychological statistics* (4th edition). New York: Wiley, 1969.

Mendenhall, W., and Ott, L. *Understanding statistics*. Belmont, Calif.: Duxbury Press, 1972.

Miller, D. M. *Interpreting test scores*. New York: Wiley, 1972.

Millman, J., and Gowin, D. B. *Appraising educational research: A case study approach*. Englewood Cliffs, N. J.: Prentice-Hall, 1974.

Minium, E. W. *Statistical reasoning in psychology and education*. New York: Wiley, 1970.

Myers, J. L. *Fundamentals of experimental design*. Boston: Allyn & Bacon, 1966.

Nevins, A. *The gateway to history*. New York: Anchor Books, Doubleday & Co., 1962.

Perls, F. S. *Gestalt therapy verbatim*. Lafayette, Calif.: Real People Press, 1969.

Rogers, C. R. A theory of therapy, personality and interpersonal relationships as developed in the client-centered framework. In S. Koch (Ed.), *Psychology: A study of a science*. Volume III. New York: McGraw-Hill, 1959.

Rogers, C. R., and Dymond, R. F. *Psychotherapy & personality change*. Chicago: University of Chicago Press, 1954.

Rogers, C. R., Gendlin, E. T., Kiesler, D., and Truax, C. B. *The therapeutic relationship and its impact: A study of psychotherapy with schizophrenics.* Madison, Wis.: University of Wisconsin Press, 1967.

Runkel, P. J., and McGrath, J. E. *Research on human behavior: A systematic guide to method.* New York: Holt, Rinehart & Winston, 1972.

Schmidt, L. D., and Strong, S. R. "Expert" and "inexpert" counselors. *Journal of Counseling Psychology,* 1970, *17,* 115–118.

Schofield, William. *Psychotherapy: the purchase of friendship.* Englewood Cliffs, N. J.: Prentice-Hall, 1964.

Siegel, S. *Nonparametric statistics for the behavioral sciences.* New York: McGraw-Hill, 1956.

Skinner, B. F. Baby in a box. *Ladies Home Journal,* October, 1945.

Solomon, R. L. An extension of control group design. *Psychological Bulletin,* 1949, *46,* 137–150.

Spiegler, M. D., Cooley, E. J., Marshall, G. J., Prince, H. T., II, Puckett, S. P., and Skenazy, J. A. A self-control versus a counterconditioning paradigm for systematic desensitization: An experimental comparison. *Journal of Counseling Psychology,* 1976, *23,* 83–86.

Stein, J. (Ed.) *The Random House dictionary of the English language.* New York: Random House, 1967.

Stern, P. M. *The Oppenheimer case: Security on trial.* New York: Harper & Row, 1969.

Strong, S. R. Counseling: An interpersonal influence process. *Journal of Counseling Psychology,* 1968, *15,* 215–224.

Strong, S. R., and Schmidt, L. D. Expertness and influence in counseling. *Journal of Counseling Psychology,* 1970, *17,* 81–87.

Stulman, D. A., and Dawis, R. V. Experimental validation of two MIQ scales. *Journal of Vocational Behavior,* 1976, *9,* 161–167.

Super, D. E. A theory of vocational development. *American Psychologist,* 1953, *8,* 185–190.

Super, D. E. *Psychology of careers.* New York: Harper & Row, 1957.

Symonds, P. M. *Diagnosing personality and conduct.* New York: Appleton-Century-Crofts, 1931.

Tanur, J. M. (Ed.). *Statistics: A guide to the unknown.* San Francisco: Holden-Day, 1972.

Terman, L. M. *The measurement of intelligence.* Boston: Houghton Mifflin, 1916.

Terrace, H., and Parker, S. (Eds.). *Psychological statistics,* (Units 1–15). San Rafael, Calif.: Individual Learning Systems, 1971.

Tyler, L. E. *Tests and Measurements* (2nd edition). Englewood Cliffs, N. J.: Prentice-Hall, 1971.

Volsky, T., Jr., Magoon, T. M., Norman, W. T., and Hoyt, D. P. *The outcomes of counseling and psychotherapy.* Minneapolis: University of Minnesota Press, 1965.

Watson, J. D. *The double helix.* New York: Atheneum, 1968.

Webb, E. J., Campbell, D. T., Schwartz, R. O., and Sechrest, L. *Unobtrusive measures: Nonreactive research in the social sciences.* Chicago: Rand McNally & Company, 1966.

Westbrook, B. W. Interrelationship of career choice competences and career choice attitudes of ninth-grade pupils: Testing hypotheses derived from Crites' model of career maturity. *Journal of Vocational Behavior,* 1976, *8,* 1–12.

Williamson, E. G., and Bordin, E. S. Evaluating counseling by means of a control group experiment. *School and Society,* 1940, *52,* 434–440.

Winer, B. J. *Statistical principles in experimental design* (2nd edition). New York: McGraw-Hill, 1971.

THE COUNSELOR AS RESEARCHER

CHAPTER 3
Research for Action: The Tradition and Its Implementation

Ena Vazquez Nuttall and Allen E. Ivey

How do you justify your services? Couldn't the money be spent somewhere else more effectively? Did the life-planning workshop really make a difference? How effective are your counseling and guidance programs, *really*? Are your activities and programs responsive to the demonstrated needs and wants of the people you serve? Do we as professional helpers really "make a difference"? Counselors need to prove their worth and improve their wares.

How can counselors meet all these challenges? They are often ill-equipped to provide systematic assessments of their services and programs. Perhaps equally troublesome is the fact that counselors are often unacquainted with the basic research in their field. They desperately need more information and new skills in order to begin to carefully construct answers to the many difficult questions that lie ahead.

This chapter demonstrates how counselors can involve themselves more fully in the assessment of needs and services and communicate better with the publics they serve. Specifically, this chapter seeks to:

1. Present the tradition of *action research*, both as background for all the applied research methods described in the chapters of Section 3, and as a point of view eminently well suited to the practical research needs of counselors.

2. Explain in detail how research for action can be implemented so that practitioners can initiate and complete their own projects.

3. Discuss the process of diffusion and implementation of research findings in order to help counselors make effective use of the

research findings produced by others and to set up their own research projects so that the results can be put into practice and made known to others.

THE TRADITION
OF ACTION RESEARCH

Kurt Lewin stated it succinctly: "No research without action, no action without research." Action research provides a systematic framework in which the practicing counselor, therapist, or other professional in the helping field can solve problems and determine the effectiveness of his or her work. Action research provides a model for the evaluation of the effectiveness of an individual, a single program, or a totality of guidance services.

The tradition of action research dates back to the late 1930s and the arrival of a social psychologist named Kurt Lewin in this country. Lewin, having been seriously affected by Nazism, the Depression, and World War II, wanted to know why people and groups behaved as they did and what could be done to change their behavior. He was a scientist concerned not only about the direct benefits to be derived from social action, but also that interventions in social systems be done in ways that would at the same time contribute to the accumulation of knowledge. During his brilliant career Lewin inspired and helped set up many different institutions such as the Center for Research in Group Dynamics at MIT, the Commission on Community Interrelations, and the National Training Laboratories (Marrow, 1969). Most of these projects combined action with research. In a document of the Commission on Community Interrelations (Marrow, 1969) three distinguishing characteristics of action research were outlined. First, "it would be conducted jointly with people who wanted practical answers; second, it would be carried out under community rather than laboratory conditions; and third, measurement of attitudes and behavior would be made both before and after each action step to discover which methods succeeded and which failed." (p. 7)

Stated in its most elementary form, action research may be described as *the introduction of a planned change and the observation of its results* (Cherns, 1969). Action research involves: (1) the explicit statement of the experimental intervention (this may be a specific counseling intervention or it may be as general as a total counseling services program); (2) the explicit statement of the goals of the intervention; and (3) the determination of whether or not those goals were achieved. Action research can evaluate on a simple level individual, group, or program interventions and determine whether or not stated goals were achieved. However, complex experimental designs are also possible within the broad-based conceptual frame that is action research.

In contrast to basic research, action research builds diffusion of findings and their implementation directly into the research design. Research that does not lead directly to future action is considered irrelevant. In short, action research is always for a purpose: to check whether or not a helper intervention has benefited a client, to examine whether or not a specific new program made a difference in the lives of participants, to evaluate the effectiveness of an organized set of helping services. Then, having determined the effectiveness of the intervention or program, the helper is prepared to take additional steps as a result of feedback from the evaluation.

As Kurt Lewin stated, action research appeals to mission-oriented practitioners:

> If we speak of research, we mean "action research," that is, action on a realistic level, action that is always followed by self-critical objective reconnaissance and evaluation of results. Since we like to learn rapidly, we will never be afraid to face our shortcomings. We aim at "no action without research; no research without action." (quoted in Marrow, 1969, p. 193)

Four Varieties of Action Research

Among the Lewinian group Chein, Cook, and Harding (1948) concentrated on spelling out different types of action research and the problems inherent in each. They outlined four varieties of action research: diagnostic, participant, empirical, and experimental. The following pages contain a discussion of each of these four types of action research, an outline of the steps involved in performing each type, and brief examples illustrating how to accomplish each step. After that, we present an extended illustration of the application of the four steps in a counselor training method.

The *diagnostic research* paradigm represents perhaps the most typical and simple problem-solving strategy of the helper faced with problems and crises on the job. Diagnostic action research consists of: (1) the emergence of a problem, (2) a diagnosis of its causes, (3) formulation of all the possible avenues of remediation, and (4) recommendations for a possible solution.

An example of the diagnostic action research approach in a counseling setting is the frequent problem that emerges during the summer months with teenagers roaming the streets, creating problems to the community.

1. This usually becomes known officially after several teenagers are arrested by the police. Let us suppose that you are a counselor working in a community mental health center and the mayor of the town asks for your

help in the solution of this problem. Now the problem has emerged and you are in charge of finding a solution.

2. Your next step is to obtain a clear idea of what the causes of the problem are. In order to do this you should identify and talk to all the important actors taking part in the drama. Talking to the teenagers arrested and other teenagers in the community to find out what they think is causing the problem will add clarity to the scenario. Interviewing police officers, parents, school personnel, business owners, recreation personnel, and other community members about their perceptions of the causes and possible remedies to the problem would further enlighten the picture.

3. After obtaining an accurate assessment of the situation from the interviews with all the relevant actors, the counselor formulates a series of possible solutions to the problem. In this case it may be that the difficulties experienced by the teenagers were due to lack of meaningful activities appropriate to their age. The counselor then brainstorms all the possible solutions, among them: making available more summer jobs for teenagers, providing more educational opportunities, creating more leisure time activities, hiring a streetworker to help the teenagers, approaching the churches to offer programs for teenagers, and contacting the parents of the teenagers involved to see if they can offer their own solutions.

4. After studying the different possible solutions, the counselor makes a final set of recommendations. If the recommendations are accepted and followed by the appropriate agencies, the diagnostic action research project can be considered a success. However, if the recommendations are not followed, the project is judged a failure because this model conceives of the process as a whole unit involving diagnosis, research, and attempts at remediation.

Another example of the use of the diagnostic action research approach is the hypothetical case of a director of a college counseling service who is asked to analyze the problem of and possible solutions to the large number of transfers from and high vacancy rates of the tallest dormitory on campus, a forty story high-rise building. (1) The problem thus is the lack of popularity of this particular dormitory. (2) The second step is to investigate the reasons why the students do not like to live in that dormitory. To accomplish this goal, the director interviews the administrative staff of the dormitory, the students living in it, those who transferred out, and many other relevant parties. (3) After this information is gathered and there is a clear idea about what is causing the problem, the director formulates a series of possible solutions. Among the solutions could be to fire or transfer the administrative staff of the dormitory, to change the system of roommate allocation, to replace the food services director, increase the services and facilities available in the building, or change the use of the building. (4) From this set of recommendations the director chooses those that seem more feasible and appropriate to the specific circumstances.

Another variety of action research is *participant action research*. This approach seeks to remedy some of the pitfalls of the first approach, namely, that recommendations are not always implemented and that the failure to implement them is mostly due to lack of involvement of the relevant publics from the very beginning of the project. The most distinctive characteristic of this type of action research is the involvement of the people who will later participate in whatever action is recommended.

The steps to follow in the participant action research model are as follows: (1) observing the emergence of a problem, (2) involving all important parties relevant to the causes and remediation of the problem, (3) brainstorming all the possible causes of the difficulty with participating members, (4) defining the problem and determining whether further data are needed before intervening, (5) designing an interview or questionnaire to obtain further data, (6) training community participants to administer the instrument, (7) analyzing the data, (8) making final recommendations, and (9) involving the participants and others in carrying out the recommendations.

An example of this approach takes place in a community being plagued by excessive vandalism of its schools and businesses. The school committee and the chamber of commerce ask the director of the mental health center to help the town find a solution to the problem.

1. The problem is: What are the causes of this increase in vandalism and what possible solutions are there?

2. The director of the mental health center immediately contacts all those who have some involvement with the problem either because they know some of the causes or because they are likely participants in the solution of the problem. Among those invited are principals of the schools, owners of the businesses affected, members of the schools' PTA's, police department staff, members of the school guidance and counseling services, officers of youth organizations, organizers of church youth programs, members of adolescent self-help groups, staffs of adolescent mental health services groups, and many others.

3. Once the group is contacted, a brainstorming session concerning all the possible causes of the problem, the possible remedies, and the availability of resources is organized and conducted.

4. The group may decide after deliberations that the problem is not totally clear and that it needs more information. It decides to survey all the

school principals and business owners to ask them about the extent of vandalism, hours and days at which it occurs, possible culprits, and possible solutions.

5. An interview is then designed to obtain the relevant information and community people are trained to conduct the interview.

6. Once the data are obtained, they are analyzed using the simplest statistics. The data are then prepared for presentation using simple tables and easy-to-follow graphic materials.

7. The new information is then presented to the group of participants in order to determine possible solutions to the problem in light of the new data gathered.

8. The group narrows down the recommendations to those that are more feasible and cost effective.

9. By virtue of their involvement with the project from the beginning, the participants that have positions in agencies that are to implement the recommendations will now take over and help to initiate and perform the appropriate action.

Empirical action research involves using a certain type of intervention and keeping accurate records of what is done and what happens. It is analogous to the clinical wisdom developed by a physician who keeps track of illnesses, the remedies prescribed, and the results obtained from the different interventions. The specific steps involved are: (1) performing the intervention, (2) keeping a record of the activities the helper engages in and the clients' reactions to these activities, (3) assessing the effects of the activities on the clients, and making changes in the interventions according to the results.

Examples of this type of action research occur very frequently in the work of counselors. For instance, a counselor running assertiveness training groups who wants to use the empirical action research model begins by (1) deciding to perform a particular type of intervention, in this case a group of about 15 women that meets once a week for sixteen weeks. (2) Next, the counselor keeps an accurate record of everything she does during each of the sessions of the sixteen week intervention. Furthermore, the counselor records the clients' reactions to and evaluations of the different aspects of the intervention. For example, do the women react more positively to role playing than to small group discussions? (3) Throughout the intervention period and especially at the end, the helper tries to find out what kinds of changes have occurred in the lives of the women. Has their behavior in situations requiring assertiveness changed? Are their attitudes toward being assertive more positive? (4) Using the results obtained from evaluating the effects of the intervention, the counselor may decide not to repeat the treatment, to change certain parts of it, or, if the results of the analyses have been positive, to repeat the treatment in the same fashion.

The fourth kind of action research is *experimental action research.* Experimental action research is the brand of action research that comes closest to what is generally regarded as the ideal research paradigm —experimental control group design. However, the experiment is carried out in the field, not in the laboratory. Another difference is that the object of experimental action research is to solve practical problems, while in the classical experimental design the experiment does not necessarily need to have practical relevance.

Experimental action research might be used when the counselor wants to find out the relative effectiveness of two or more methods of intervention or action. This type of action research requires taking pre and post measures of the variables that are supposed to change with the intervention. Usually the design also includes the use of a comparison or control group.

Sometimes experimental action research will be used when the counselor is examining the effectiveness of a single intervention. Here the design would use pre and post measures of the relevant variables and may use several measures over time to examine the effects of the intervention at several periods of time. The research questions would be: Does the intervention accomplish the goals it was supposed to accomplish? Is this type of intervention useful?

Among the four types of action research, the experimental type has the most to offer for the advancement of knowledge. If the experimental action research has been well executed, the study can give more definite answers to the theoretical questions.

This type of design involves the following steps: (1) the decision to determine the relative effectiveness of an intervention, (2) explicit statement of the hypothesis to be investigated, (3) a research design that tests the hypothesis, (4) selection of appropriate measures, (5) obtainment of pre and post measures, (6) analysis of the data, (7) a decision about which of two or more interventions is better or whether a particular intervention is effective, and then changing the practice accordingly.

To better understand the steps of the experimental action research paradigm, let us suppose that you are a counselor in a mental health setting and that you have been given the job of training a group of paraprofessionals to work as counselors. (1) You would like to find out which of two different training methods will do the job most effectively. Which of two training methods will create the best counselors? (2) You decide to use two very different training styles: one a systematic step-by-step approach and the other an intuitive, creative, spontaneous approach. Based on careful analysis of pertinent theories, you hypothesize that the systematic approach will produce more effective counselors than the intuitive spontaneous one. (3) Your research plan is to train two groups of paraprofessionals, each with a different method. Measures of counseling competence will be taken before and after the training. People are assigned to the two training groups by random or other acceptable methods to avoid any sampling bias. (4) The question of finding a measure of counseling competence that is reliable, valid, and well-researched is a difficult one. Choose one that best fits your project. (5) Administer the measures of counseling competence before and after the training to both groups. (6) Analyze the data. (7) If the data reveal that those persons trained with the systematic step-by-step approach are better counselors than those trained through the more informal approach, you will have reliable information on which to make decisions about paraprofessional training in the future.

Summary of the Four Varieties of Action Research

The four varieties of action research—diagnostic, participant, empirical, and experimental—represent a continuum ranging from somewhat crude, local, nongeneralizable research to more sophisticated, representative research generalizable to other populations. Experimental action research represents the highest degree of research sophistication and diagnostic the lowest.

Diagnostic and participant action research are very similar to each other. The main difference between the two is that the participant action research model includes in the planning and conduct of the study those people who will be involved in the application of the study's findings. Participant action research is an improvement over diagnostic because of the built-in diffusion measures. However, participant action research encounters more difficulties in its implementation because the researcher has to deal directly with the community, which is composed for the most part of people who are not sophisticated in the conduct or use of research. The participant action researcher has to be adept not only in research but also in human relations, and must be very careful about how to phrase questions, train interviewers, and explain the results of the investigation.

Empirical and experimental action research are also related to each other. Experimental action research is an improvement over the empirical action research variety. The empirical action research paradigm does not adhere to the canons of science as much as its experimental counterpart. The empirical action research model deals with the same types of problems but with simpler and cruder methods. There are no attempts at using control groups, administering pre and post measures, or using valid and reliable instruments. The empirical action research approach is really a sophisticated common sense approach to the problems of day-to-day practice. Experimental action research attempts to satisfy as many of the classical experimental design features as it can in the real world.

All these four types differ from the classic experimental model in that they are oriented toward obtaining results relevant to practice and are conducted in the real world instead of in the artificial conditions of the laboratory.

Microcounseling: Action Research in Action

Microcounseling (Ivey, 1971) is a videobased counselor training program that systematically studies the helping process. The original work for microcounseling was completed in 1966 and first published in 1968 (Ivey, Normington, Miller, Morrill, and Haase). Microcounseling has since become one of the more widely used counselor and paraprofessional training methods in the United States and Canada. It began with an action research problem: *How can one define the specific dimensions of the helping process and how can these dimensions be most effectively taught?* Out of this highly action-oriented question has arisen an array of highly clinical, action-research, and experimental studies. The purpose of this section is to examine microcounseling as a specific example of action research conducted by a team over a period of several years.

MICROCOUNSELING DEFINED.   First, it is necessary to define precisely what microcounseling is and the goals of this orientation to helper training. Microcounseling is a scaled-down sample of counseling in which the counselor, therapist, or lay trainee talks with volunteer clients during brief five minute sessions that are videorecorded. Rather than teach helping "all-at-once" as done in traditional training programs, microcounseling focuses on specific single skills. Thus, through a highly systematized form, trainees quickly learn important aspects of the total helping process.

The most vital fact about microcounseling, however, is the recent discovery that the skills of helping need not be restricted to professional and paraprofessional helpers—they can be taught systematically to the general lay public. Parents (Bizer, 1972), junior high school students (Aldrige, 1971), and elementary school children (Goshko, 1973) have all demonstrated their ability to learn and profit from the microcounseling framework and its adaptations. Extensions have also been made into systematic work with psychiatric patients (Donk, 1972; Ivey, 1971, 1973) that suggest a teaching approach for behavior change is a valuable therapeutic alternative.

The standard paradigm for microcounseling training consists of the following steps (Ivey, 1974, p. 6).

1.   Videotaping of a five minute segment of therapy or counseling, or, if it is a couple or a family, five minutes of interaction around a selected topic.

2.   Training. First a written manual describing the single skill being taught is presented to the trainee(s). Next, video models of an "expert" therapist or "good" communication illustrating the skill are shown, thus giving trainees a gauge against which to examine the quality of their own behavior. Trainees then view their own videotapes and compare their performance on the skill in question with the written manual and video model. Seeing oneself as others see you has a particular impact. Finally, a trainer-supervisor provides didactic instruction and emotional support for the trainees.

3.   Videotaping of a second five to ten minute session.

4.   Examination of the last session and/or recycling of the entire procedure as in step 2, depending on the acquired skill levels of the trainee.

The time period for the training is approximately one hour and a recycling to step 2 adds another 30 to 45 minutes. The procedures of microcounseling involve cue discrimination, modeling procedures, and operant reinforcement by the trainer of newly learned behavior (typically, the trainer ignores ineffective behavior and rewards positive behavior change).

THE FIRST STAGE—DIAGNOSTIC ACTION RESEARCH.   The first issue encountered by the research team attempting to define the single skills of the helping process was to diagnose that very helping process. What is it that can be recognized as effective helping? What are behaviors that can be clearly identified and measured?

Diagnosing the helping interview involved reading books on helping sessions by a variety of authors and inviting in a panel of experts to give their views. Although these efforts were helpful, it was finally found that direct videotaping of the helping session itself and diagnosing specific component portions of the interview was basic.

The first set of specific behaviors diagnosed was termed "attending behavior" and included dimensions of eye contact, body language, and verbal following behavior. Through direct observation and diagnosis of videotapes it was found that ineffective helpers tended to break eye contact frequently, have distracting body communication, and topic jump frequently.

Subsequent to this identification process, three action research studies were designed to test the effectiveness and reality of the diagnosed constructs (Ivey, Normington, Miller, Morrill, and Haase, 1968). The first study involved a simple pretest posttest comparison of beginning helpers-in-training. Thirty-eight trainees were divided into an experimental and a control group. Videotapes with specific behavioral ratings of eye contact, body language, and topic jumps were made before training and compared with videotapes made after microcounseling training in the specific skills. The target of this study was to demonstrate that the constructs diagnosed could be identified and measured and that training could improve behavior of beginning helpers. Results on this first study were positive. Specifically, the action goals were attained.

Two subsequent studies in this same series examined the counseling skills of reflection of feeling and summarization of feeling, two helping constructs considered important in active listening. The design used in these studies employed a simple pretest—training—posttest design and no control groups were used. The focus in these studies was to demonstrate that the goal of changed behavior in the interview was achieved. Each study used small groups (N's of 11 and 10 respectively) because action research is often done with small groups who seek to change specific behaviors or action. Once again, the action goals of changed helper behavior were achieved in a short time.

These first studies have been followed by an array of diagnostic research into the nature of the helping interview. Skills of questioning , paraphrasing, minimal encouragements, directions, self-disclosure, interpretation, and others have been diagnosed and assessed in the microcounseling paradigm (cf. Moreland, Ivey, and Phillips, 1973; Sherrard, 1973; Authier and Gustafson, 1975; Chadbourne, 1975; and a complete review of the microcounseling literature in Kasdorf, in press).

The significance of the diagnostic phase of microcounseling research on the practicing counselor may be described as follows:

1.   Any counselor who wishes to diagnose his or her own behavior, the behavior of paraprofessional helpers, or the effectiveness of training in helping now has a systematic format for diagnosing the present status of helper functioning and behavior.

2.   This system may be used by beginning helpers to rate changes in their own personal behavior or the behavior of others as a result of helper training programs. In effect, diagnostic efforts by the microcounseling group now make it possible to integrate past research into present training practices (an important dimension when one considers diffusion of results).

Let us assume that a counselor wishes to engage in a helper training program. The results of the diagnostic phase of microcounseling are available and may be used to assess the beginning functioning of helpers. This assessment may in turn be used to design training programs to increase helper functioning. Finally, the measures of diagnosis may be used to present competency-based data demonstrating that the program of paraprofessional training is effective. Specifically, easily assembled and measured data are available to show that a program achieved its goals (cf. Ivey and Gluckstern 1974 a and b; 1976 a and b).

THE SECOND STAGE—PARTICIPANT ACTION RESEARCH. The diagnostic research described above is helpful in that the interview is described more completely, but such action research does not speak to the needs of individuals who may wish to develop their own conceptual frames and devices for helping others. Gluckstern (1972, 1973) provides an interesting illustration of how microcounseling can be integrated into the needs of a participant group.

A suburban community was faced with severe drug problems and decided to build a program to combat this issue. (It may be noted that the diagnostic phase is built in already; the community has identified a problem—drug abuse.) Community members were involved in deciding what to do about the problem. Parents, schools, and social agencies met to devise a solution. The first seven of the nine steps of participant action research in this project may be considered: (1) the emergence of the drug problem; (2) important parties were involved to define and develop ideas for the problem; (3) many areas of difficulty were brainstormed (but not all, more on this issue later); (4) and, (5) data were obtained and a decision for action was made. There was no formal questionnaire or instrument developed to increase community ownership and participation (steps 6 and 7).

It was decided to institute a program for community training of paraprofessionals in drug abuse counseling. A training program combining information on drug abuse, group counseling, microcounseling, and community intervention was developed. Pre and posttesting on drug information, interpersonal relationships, helping skills, and community intervention knowledge was conducted. Evaluation research revealed in each case that program objectives were achieved. The relatively brief training program produced knowledgeable, skilled individuals who had ability to counsel effectively on problems of drug abuse.

Two levels of helping effectiveness were considered in this participant action research study. The first was the effectiveness of the training program. As noted, immediate testing following training and six-month follow-up revealed significant improvement in helping skills that was retained over time. The second question is the effectiveness of the total program in the community. Six-month and one-year data indicated that the program was off to a good start and was effective in that numbers of people were seen and provided helping services.

However, in the second year of this project, professional groups began to question the project aims. A large number of individuals were being seen by nonprofessionals, thus threatening the image of more highly paid agency workers. The end result of this questioning was pressure on the community advisory board and the eventual discontinuation of a heretofore successful action project that had been shown by demonstration and research to be effective.

Why the failure? One needs simply to return to the nine-step model of participant action research. The community *appeared* to be involved, but really adequate planning and involvement had not been completed. Athough time-consuming, it seems increasingly apparent that effective programs must include highly careful planning in the beginning stages or even the best attempts at action will fail. In this case the action research clearly demonstrated the effectiveness of the program, but effectiveness in terms of outcome and helping services does not mean that all interested parties will regard the program as effective.

The implications of this research example for the practicing counselor seem to be that action research models to be effective must still touch all bases. Effectiveness of a program is insufficient unless strong community support is built in at the beginning and efforts are made continuously during the program to maintain solid interpersonal and professional relationships. Action research that does not take into account all important variables and plan to meet them may ultimately be ineffective. It is here that action research most clearly departs from traditional research efforts. Clearly, the development of an effective program is important, and traditional research efforts are most often satisfied at this level, but unless all community issues are considered, the action taken may be wasted effort.

THE THIRD PHASE—EMPIRICAL ACTION RESEARCH.   A major question a counselor often asks is "are my interventions making a difference in the life of my client?" The microcounseling model is only recently being used to determine the effect of action research interventions on the client population.

Perhaps the first illustration of this effort comes in Ivey's application of microcounseling (1973) to work with psychiatric patients. The specific intervention was teaching life skills to the patient. Authier, Gustafson, Guerney, and Kasdorf (1975), Carkhuff (1969), and others have suggested that direct teaching of coping skills to clients may be more appropriate than therapy, counseling, or interviewing that are, in actuality, indirect efforts at helping people change their lives. Ivey's intervention consisted of videotaping a patient in interpersonal interaction. The videotape was then reviewed and patients determined what they themselves wished to change or learn; a wide array of verbal and nonverbal behaviors was selected. Patients were then taught in microcounseling-like training sessions skills such as attending behavior, use of questions, appropriate nonverbal communication, and so on. The immediate laboratory outcome was change in behavior as observed by both therapist and patient. Behavioral contracts were developed with each individual to encourage generalization of learned behavior to ward and home settings. One important possibility for this type of action-evaluation research is whether or not a single individual reaches his or her goals.

Let us look at this study from the four aspects of empirical action research. First, the intervention as described was performed. Second, a record of baseline behavior for the patient was developed by the therapist and patient. Third, the behavioral contracts were examined constantly to ensure that learned behavior had generalized to the home or to the ward. Fourth, as appropriate, changes were made in treatment plans when the intervention was less successful.

This model originated with psychiatric patients, but has been applied to elementary school children by Goshko (1973) and adapted to parent training programs by Bizer (1972). In each case, the individual identifies the behavior, demonstrates it in role-played, audiotaped, or videotaped practice sessions, and then contracts to practice that specific behavior in daily life situations.

Similarly, this model of action research in microcounseling can be studied in paraprofessional or peer counseling programs by examining the reactions of clients to those trained in helping skills. Hearn (1976), Chadbourne (1975), and Gluckstern (1972), for example, found that client verbal statements changed markedly after the training periods. Specifically, clients were more able to talk about themselves rather than about external irrelevant topics and expressed more affect in the interview. What is needed at this point is further data that requires a more detailed examination of the *actions* clients take as a result of helping.

It may be seen that empirical action research is concerned with determining whether or not a programmatic intervention *makes a difference*. The simple asking of that question reveals weaknesses of programs and areas of needed evaluation. Microcounseling, for example, has strong evidence that significant changes are produced in individuals trained. The data, however, are more limited at the point where specific effects on client life style are considered. This same issue may also be considered a problem in all types of counseling interventions. The specificity of the goal-oriented microcounseling format forces the helper to look more precisely at what he or she is doing and provides alternatives for investigating the usefulness of one's activities.

What are the implications of these examples for the practicing counselor? They seem to suggest that, first, specific interventions if clearly defined can produce specific and measureable outcomes, and second, that it is not enough to show that an intervention has produced a short-term change. What are the long-term outcomes of the intervention on clients? The microcounseling interventions with single patients, parents, and children illustrate one way that the busy professional helper can indeed demonstrate that he or she is making a difference in the lives of others. It is possible to demonstrate empirically that counselors are effective, but we too often fail to examine ourselves, what we do, and its specific effects on those with whom we work.

PHASE FOUR—EXPERIMENTAL ACTION RESEARCH. Relatively few practicing counselors can be expected to find time to engage in action research that involves carefully constructed experimental designs. Nonetheless, it is sometimes necessary to compare the effectiveness of alternative strategies to achieve the same goal. We often stay in a similar tired rut of professional practice only because we know the route. Experimental action research can provide data that will help us move out of this rut and test our present programs against alternatives.

Toukmanian and Rennie (1975) provide one good example of experimental action research. They wished to compare the effectiveness of a microcounseling training program in helping skills with that of the human resource development (HRD) model of Carkhuff (1969). Twelve students were trained with microcounseling and twelve with HRD. Pretraining and posttraining tapes were rated for the types of skills identified earlier in this section and for the more subjective construct of empathy. It was found that both groups improved on skills and that the microcounseling group improved more on empathy dimensions.

The above is as simple an experimental model as one can find where two efforts toward the same goals may be compared. Two groups are divided into matched pairs and then external evaluation is conducted to see which treatment is most effective. Other examples of this type of research in microcounseling include Moreland, Ivey and Phillips (1973), Dunn (1975), and Hearn (1976).

The seven-step model of experimental action research in this type of comparative study was outlined earlier in this chapter. The first three steps involve defining what methods one wishes to compare, making the hypotheses clear, and suggesting the methods to make the research design explicit. The issue of finding specific measures of counseling competence is more complex. In the study cited, measures used by microcounseling (behavioral skills counts) and by HRD (subjective empathy ratings) were both employed. The advantage of this approach is that measures are closely yoked to training methods. This advantage turns into a sometimes harrowing disadvantage in that training and research have become closely related and the danger of "teaching toward the test" becomes apparent. The yoking of outcome measures to treatment or training designs may be highly desirable, but other important aspects of measuring the effectiveness of the program may be missed. Thus, it is suggested that *both* yoked and nonyoked measurements be employed.

The remainder of the model (administration of test, analysis of data, and decision making based on the results) should be readily apparent. *What is not immediately apparent, however, is that some of the important aspects of diagnostic action research, participant action research, and empirical action research are lost when the "more sophisticated" control group designs are used.* In effect, the more carefully you control your study, the greater danger of losing relevance to the clientele being served.

INTEGRATING FOUR TYPES OF ACTION RESEARCH IN A LARGE-SCALE PROJECT.   Microcounseling research has, of necessity, been developed in a piecemeal fashion. Although extensive diagnostic, participant, empirical, and experimental research on effectiveness exists, it has not been possible because of funds, time, and the developing state of the art to determine the full effectiveness of the program. This obvious criticism of microcounseling research can also be stated as a basic criticism of virtually all research. Few, if any, research programs or projects in helping or counseling have been able to fill all the gaps of full evaluation of the effectiveness of a program.

One application of microcounseling currently conducted by a pharmaceutical company illustrates the ideal of research that includes all dimensions of action research mentioned here. The problem is a "simple" outcome study on the subject of how can one improve specifications for a product when to do so is clearly in the patient's best interest? The ultimate

criterion is clear. Let us consider how this company applied the microcounseling model to an action research problem.

The first stage involved careful *diagnosis* of the discussion with physicians about a product. Through examination of videotapes and audiotapes
of those discussions, it was discovered that company representatives tended
to only talk about their product and not inquire into the specific needs of the
busy physician. Skills of questioning, paraphrasing, and summarization
were often missing from the discussion. The representative tended primarily
to give information and worked to influence the physician to prescribe a
specific product when indicated.

Out of the diagnostic work, a concept of the interview was developed
and tested. It involved breaking down the interview into phases and gave
special attention to training in attending skills so that individual physician
informational needs could be determined. Once that determination was
made, appropriate alternatives would then be suggested. Preliminary testing
was made to determine whether the skills were indeed teachable, and pilot
sales training programs were developed. Meanwhile, *participants* who were
to be affected by the training program were interviewed and included actively in all stages of the action research model. The training program was
reviewed and commented on. Appropriate executives and other individuals
were consulted for their opinions and suggestions.

The *empirical* phase of the research included two prime dimensions.
The first is an extension of the diagnostic phase. Company representatives
were taught the skills and an effort was made to determine their views of the
program and their ability to acquire the newly defined version of the interview. On the basis of all the above data, the program was revised and a
major field test in one state was implemented. Two types of criteria for this
test could be identified. The first is the simple pre-post examination of
whether or not personnel could demonstrate the specific interviewing skills
taught in the program. This is a yoked measure that ties in specifically with
the training program. The unyoked and crucial measure was defined as
increase in sales. Pre-post comparisons revealed that sales had increased.
However, the lack of a control group limits the conclusions one can make
about the program's effectiveness. It could be simply that the attention given
to the company's personnel made the difference or that a new type of illness
or new drug was responsible. The empirical phase of this research does not
tell us whether or not the program "made the difference." It is possible that
some unknown factor might be causal. It is important also to remember that
this phase included continual involvement and participation of all relevant
parties and decision makers.

Therefore, *experimental research* is currently under way nationally in which two groups of pharmaceutical representatives have been taught the new training program and a control group has not. This should provide an effective test of the value of the program. The central criterion of the effectiveness of this program, of course, is the unyoked volume of dollar sales. In sales, skills may be "nice," but unless they make a difference in the life of the company, they are irrelevant.

This model of action research encompasses all phases. Microcounseling research, still in its infancy after 10 years of work, here comes closest to full bloom in an industrial setting. What this says about the values and integrated efforts of the educational establishment is, of course, most interesting. Constructing such a large-scale research project would be impossible for the highly diffuse and individually oriented helping professions. Nonetheless, it seems apparent that we can use this large study as a model for the examination of microcounseling research in its totality, and this model can then be used by the practicing counselor in her or his own work setting. Consider the following when you wish to introduce an innovation and include as many phases of action research as you can.

1.   Diagnose the system carefully. Know what you want to have happen and the specific steps that might make it likely to happen.

2.   Involve participants actively in your work. They are the ones who will live with your research and will determine whether your time was wasted or not.

3.   Test your work to see its effect on clients. This may be as far as you get. But an innovation or intervention that does not include some form of systematic empirical evaluation is akin to witchcraft. One must produce some data indicating that one is making a difference in the lives of clients.

4.   Where possible, develop experimental action research that involves testing of your treatment *and* testing of more general unyoked issues related to your treatment.

Finally, let us face the fact that most of those who read these words do not consider themselves researchers. Perhaps it is time for all of us to rethink our role as practitioners and researchers. Practitioners who cannot evaluate what they are doing may not be doing anything. Researchers who can develop carefully controlled experimental design may not be doing anything either. Action research provides a bridge between research and practice. Action without research and research without action are all too often meaningless.

IMPLEMENTING RESEARCH FOR ACTION

In this section we delineate the stages involved in applied research studies, which should be applicable at least in a general way to all the types of research described in Parts 3 and 4 of this book.

Selecting an Issue or Problem

Select for research and action an issue or problem that relates to your day-to-day professional activities or to major decisions that must be made. The issue can also be brought to your attention by a concerned citizen of the community, colleagues, clients, or any other source. Are career information services more effective when given in small groups or in large groups? Why are the mental health services given by your clinic used more by middle class clients than lower class and minority clients? Is it better to train paraprofessionals with a systematic method or is it better to be spontaneous and informal? Is a program designed to make underachieving students do better academically actually doing its job?

Defining the Problem and Involving the Relevant People

After a problem is selected for study, the counselor convenes a group of people that includes all those judged important to the understanding and remediation of the issue. For example, clients, employers, supervisors, teachers, parents, and others may be part of this group. The group is called together to brainstorm all the relevant factors involved in the problem, define its boundaries, its causes, and, most important, possible avenues of action. This group can meet several times, adding more people if desirable for the purpose of clarifying all the relevant aspects. Getting a clear idea of what the problem is and involving those who will probably participate in the action are the most important elements in this step.

An example of this step is the case of a counselor working in a prison setting faced with the reluctance of black inmates in contrast to white to take advantage of a program offering the opportunity to obtain a college degree while in prison. The staff running the program is puzzled and unhappy about this situation. One action research approach to this problem is first to organize a meeting of all the relevant actors including black and white inmates, the director of the prison, the staff running the program, and any others.

In this group the issue of black inmates' participation in all aspects of prison life is examined to determine whether this reluctance is a general or a specific response. If the problem is a general one, then actors taking parts in the larger scenario should be invited to join the group. Once the nature of the problem is clarified and ways of obtaining more information are outlined, the group concentrates on developing ways of solving the problem. It is important that those who will have to implement the solution be involved in this group from the very beginning.

Examining the Available Literature and Data Sources

Once the problem has been clarified, plan to conduct or order a literature search before designing your study. It is quite easy nowadays to do literature searches using the ERIC or PASAR computerized systems. (See Appendix B for further information about these and other retrieval systems.) In particular, look for the types of instruments and measures other people have used. It may well turn out that your problem has been solved by a study conducted by someone else, or that their method is just what you need to replicate in your case. Do not, however, spend too much time in researching the literature. It is easy to get bogged down in reading and not deal with your problem.

If at all possible, use existing data sources such as the United States or town census, State Department of Education data, student records, already collected test data, or other such sources. Do not plan to collect new data if you can possibly find out what you want to know from existing data sources. The reference librarians of public or university libraries can be of major help in locating data sources. If, for example, you are in a school setting and the principal is concerned about the increasing number of students dropping out of school and you want to determine whether this is a true problem or merely an impression of the principal, you should consult national data for dropouts published by the National Center for Educational Statistics and local data collected by the secretaries and unit chairpersons of your school.

Another example of making use of available data sources would be a helper working in a community mental health center who is given the charge of determining the needs of the elderly population. The first step should be to consult the Census Reports and determine how many elderly are located in the region by inspecting the county census and the town resident lists.

Determining the Research Strategy

Once the problem has been defined, a research strategy that leads to studying the right issues should be followed. The basic questions you should ask are: "Are we researching the questions properly? Will the questions that we are researching bring us the answers that we need for action? Why are we researching these questions?" Often counselors with the best of intentions engage in research studies that do not yield the answers they need.

One common example of this situation is a high school counselor who wants to find out the effectiveness of a vocational orientation program. In order to assess whether the program is effective, the counselor usually sends questionnaires to the seniors who have graduated asking them about their whereabouts after they left school. The counselor then compiles the data and produces a series of percentages of how many students went to college, are working, are in the armed forces, or have gotten married.

Some counselors assume that if many students from their schools are opting for college they have been doing a good job. The truth is that the proportion of students going to college is probably more a function of the social class background of the students than of the quality of the counseling at the school they attend. Also, a very tight job market will increase the number of people going to college regardless of whether they receive a good college orientation or not. If counselors want to assess the effectiveness of their career orientation program, they should follow a different research strategy. One should at least obtain measures, before and after the career orientation program, of the amount of career information the students possess, and the clarity of their vocational choices. Ideally, a group of students who are not receiving the intervention or who are served with a totally different approach could serve as a control group and would also be tested pre and post intervention. Following this research strategy the counselor will be able to answer the basic question: What are the effects of the vocational orientation services?

Selecting the Appropriate Measures

Once the problem has been clearly defined and a research strategy designed to deal with it, appropriate measures must be found or constructed for the major variables. If at all possible, use an existing test or scale or inventory rather than creating your own. It is very difficult and actually quite a technical problem to create a good measuring instrument. Also, results obtained with a home-made instrument will be hard to compare with those of other studies. If you use an instrument or measure that has a history, you can compare your results with those of others using the same device. Also, someone else will likely have done the hard work of establishing evidence of reliability and validity. In selecting an instrument, look for those that (1) measure what you are interested in, (2) have reasonable reliability indices, (3) have been used in projects similar to your own, (4) seem to have some conceptual relevance to a larger body of theory, and (5) are not offensive to the general public. Some books where you can find measures already developed and available for use are presented in Appendix A.

Delineating the Relevant Populations

Determining whom to focus on is an important aspect of all research. The population to be used will of course depend on the nature of the problem. In cases such as those typical of diagnostic and participant action research, many community groups would have to be interviewed or sent questionnaires. In experimental and empirical action research, groups receiving the intervention will be the target of the research.

Finding a Comparison Group

If you are trying to determine the effectiveness of one method of intervention, try to find a comparison group that is either receiving another treatment or no treatment at all. It is possible to use the experimental group as its own control by comparing pre and postmeasures, but the use of a separate comparison group treated the same as the experimental group—except for the method of intervention that is being studied—permits firmer conclusions.

Trying to Use Pre and Post Measures

In designing a study, try to use pre measures as well as post measures on your groups. If you cannot arrange for a control or comparison group, at least obtain pre and post data on the group you are servicing. If the nature of your problem does not allow this, then you must settle for post measures alone, but it will then be very difficult to reach any conclusion as to whether any changes occurred.

Using Simple Statistics

Remember that a major component of action research is feeding back the findings to people who do not know statistics. Plan to use bar graphs, means, and percentages to present your results. Use the relatively simple t-tests or chi-square to test for statistical significance of any differences that were found. *Plan* your research so that you can use simple statistics.

Meeting Your Deadlines

Many action research projects are oriented toward assisting decision making. Decisions must usually be made by a given date. Information arriving after that date is useless in helping to make that decision. Keep in mind the deadlines and design and conduct your research so that the results will be available when needed, and in a form the decision makers can understand.

Feeding Back the Results to Relevant Others

The people most concerned with the problem you are researching should be participating in the study. All people involved and those for whom the action research is relevant should be informed about the findings of your research. You should plan to spend as much time informing people about the results as you spend in actually conducting the study. In that way the results are more likely to achieve change led by those who are in a position to translate them into action.

Modifying Your Practice

If the results of your research indicate that one method or combination of methods is more effective than other interventions, then modify your practice accordingly. If none of your interventions prove effective, start again the process just described since you now have another action research problem.

THE DIFFUSION AND IMPLEMENTATION OF RESEARCH FINDINGS

One of the most frustrating and unfortunate situations in the field of counseling is the small influence research findings have in the practice of the profession. Many counselors are not aware of major research findings; many just do not read their journals. Garvey and Griffith (1965) report that about one-half of the research reports in journals are read or skimmed by only one percent or less of a random sampling of psychologists. The most striking feature of the process of dissemination of research findings in psychology is the small amount of information that is easily available to the professional and scientific community (Garvey and Griffith, 1965). The public dissemination of research findings occurs late, takes only a few forms, and in its final presentation has a very small audience. Actually, the national professional conventions such as those of the American Psychological Association, American Personnel and Guidance Association, National Association of Student Personnel Administration, and others occupy key positions in the dissemination process, because they give the earliest and most democratic access to research findings.

Dissemination in any field is the dynamic process between the system of dissemination and the behavior of the professional within the system. The greatest contributor to the dynamics of the system is the individual professional; it is the *individual counselor* who determines the effectiveness of the dissemination process. The counselor is involved in the diffusion and implementation of findings in two ways: as a producer of research and as a receiver of the research findings of others. The counselor who is producing research findings wants to make the results known to others and to see them effectively implemented. The counselor accomplishes this role by reading papers at conventions, publishing articles and books, and offering workshops, courses, and training sessions. The counselor as receiver of the research products of others wants to know where the specific information needed is and how to put it into practice. In order for counselors to fulfill this role, they must solicit information, attend meetings and workshops, take courses, and read journals and books.

Each of these two roles is very important to the advancement of the profession of counseling and to the professional development of the individual counselor. For these tasks to be accomplished, the counselor has to be seriously committed to their realization and be willing to interact actively with other professionals and the counseling establishment. In order to prepare the counselor to fulfill these roles effectively, we will discuss the following topics:

Characteristics of present dissemination-implementation models

Factors important in the dissemination and implementation process.

Dissemination Models

The natural cycle of research is: first to be generated, then disseminated and diffused, and finally implemented or utilized. In this section we concentrate on the way research is disseminated, that is, moved from the originating researcher to other researchers or possible users.

Research dissemination literature is extensive and contains many models of the dissemination/utilization process (Davis and Salasin, 1975; Shaskin, Morris, and Horst, 1973). One of the most complete categorizations of all the available diffusion/implementation models is that of Havelock (1975). He classifies available diffusion models into three types: the research and development perspective, the problem-solver perspective, and the social interaction perspective.

The *research and development perspective* begins with a scientist-developer perceiving the need of the consumer for a particular innovation or product. The developer identifies a problem, gathers data, invents or designs a package, tests and evaluates the product, promotes, informs, demonstrates, trains, and helps the consumers use it. The consumers in turn become aware of the innovation, idea, or package; show interest, evaluate it, try it, install it, adopt it, and finally institutionalize it. In this model the focus is on the activity phases of the developer as he or she designs a potential solution. In the field of counseling this approach is best exemplified by the aptitude, interest, and intelligence test materials developed by researchers, such as the Differential Aptitude Tests, the Strong-Campbell Interest Inventory, the Minnesota Multiphasic Personality Inventory, and many others. The researchers produce these materials because they believe that practitioners need them to fulfill their function.

In contrast to the research and development perspective that focuses on the originator of the innovation, the *problem-solver model* centers its attention on the receiver. The consumer initiates or senses a need and sets out to find possible ways of fulfilling it, usually by establishing a relationship with an outside expert or resource person. The way in which the problem is solved depends on the resources available in the particular field and the knowledge the individual or group has of the availability of those resources. The distinctive quality of this approach is the active role played by the consumer. The receiver searches for the solutions, establishes goals and priorities, weighs and evaluates possible solutions, selects the best possible alternatives, and plans for implementation.

An example of this model in a counseling setting is the situation in which one needs more information about a certain area such as parent counseling in schools. The counselor begins to search out ways of addressing these needs; this might include a literature search through the ERIC or PASAR system to learn about the work of others who are counseling in schools with parents, locate a summary of relevant studies on this topic in the *Journal of Counseling Psychology*, or find out from colleagues or through reading professional publications who can give special training in the parent counseling area. The counselor is the sole initiator of the actions in this model.

The third model, *the social interaction perspective,* like the research and development model, centers its attention on the producer of the innovation. The producer determines the receiver's needs and sends along a package or product for the receiver to accept or reject. The social interaction networks that make possible the diffusion and implementation of the new idea are the focus of attention of this approach. Proponents of this model believe that the key to the adoption of an innovation is the social interaction that takes place among members of the adopting group. Most of the work in this area has been done by rural sociologists interested in the adoption of agricultural innovations; they have been especially interested in the process individuals go through in adopting innovations. An example of this approach would be studies focused on the social networks used by counselors in obtaining information about a certain idea and to whom they passed on this information. The results of the research would enable those people interested in disseminating information through that system to know who are the important gatekeepers and what are the most important contacts in the transmission of the information.

The best known model of the innovation adoption process has been postulated by Rogers (1962). He proposes a five-stage process composed of awareness, interest, evaluation, trial, and adoption. The first stage, awareness, consists of exposing the individual to a new idea; it is hoped that this exposure will create a need for that idea. The individual is not actively seeking a new idea but a government agency, a private company, or colleagues are trying to stimulate the counselor's interest in one. The interest stage is characterized by active seeking of information about the innovation. At the evaluation stage the individuals mentally try out the innovation in their setting.

The trial stage is the one in which the prospective user actually tries out the innovation on a small scale. Adoption is the final stage in which the results of the trials are evaluated and the decision is made to continue using the innovation or to reject it. In agricultural science this model has been operationalized thorough the extension agent. In counseling there have not been change agents of this nature, except for some work in the rehabilitation area that is described in Chapter 10. The field of education has tried a similar role and labelled it the education extension agent. Because of its importance and direct applicability to the field of counseling the education extension agent is discussed below.

Three states participated in the *education extension agent* program, conducted mainly in rural and small town areas (Siebert, 1974). Seven extension agents were employed full time to meet with clients and help them diagnose their needs. When the client had a clear idea of what she or he wanted the agent transmitted this information to a retrieval staff who performed either computer or manual searches of ERIC, CIJE, and other standard educational resources. The information obtained, which might be in microfiche or hard copy and might include abstracts, bibliographies, or other contents, was then delivered to the client. The extension agents helped the clients interpret, use, and adapt the information.

The program was successful both in its diffusion and knowledge utilization functions. A much larger percentage of requests was generated from areas using this program than from other areas. In the actual use of the information obtained, half of the respondents reported that it had given them new resources for helping other staff members and more than a quarter said that it had helped solve administrative problems. Another fifth of the users claimed that it had assisted them in developing instructional packages.

These results are very promising especially when one considers that this was the first time such a system was tried and people were not used to this type of service. Siebert points out that among the factors responsible for the program's success were that the expertise resided in the use of the research resources and was independent of the agent; the extension agent was not presented to the clients as a change agent or problem solver but as a simple conveyor of information; and the clients were given the freedom to define their needs and choose their solutions. This client-controlled approach, suitable for independent-minded professionals who like to follow their own styles, is very appropriate for the field of counseling.

Factors for Effective Dissemination and Implementation

The factors conducive to the successful dissemination and implementation of research findings can be organized in three realms: the characteristics of the particular innovation or finding, the characteristics of potential consumers of the new ideas, and the manner and extent of the diffusion and utilization effort.

CHARACTERISTICS OF THE INNOVATION.   Glaser (1973) postulates seven attributes that he considers important elements in the eventual acceptance of a new idea or behavior pattern: credibility, observability, relevance, relative advantage, ease in understanding and installation, compatibility, and trialibility, divisibility, or reversibility.

The first of the attributes characterizing an innovation is *credibility*. A credible innovation or research finding is one that is espoused by a reputable source or is based on sound evidence. An example of a credible innovation in the field of counseling is behavior modification, which is being increasingly adopted by counselors for use in their practice. Among the reasons are the extensive research literature documenting the effectiveness of behavior modification techniques, the practicality and generalizability of the theories underlying this modality, and the stature and reputation of Skinner and other behavioral theorists.

Observability of an innovation concerns its concreteness and tangibility—that is, how much can the practitioner actually observe the method in use? Using behavior modification as an example, the opportunity for the practitioner to see behavior modification techniques being employed with a client and to try using them under supervision would enhance the probability of the counselor accepting the method and trying it in practice.

Relevance pertains to the degree that an innovation fulfills an urgent need. Innovations that touch on those areas of concern to a counselor (such as therapeutic counseling) are more likely to be given serious consideration than those that deal with less central areas. Again using behavior modification techniques as an example, it is easy to see that because of its demonstrated effectiveness in doing a task that counselors consider of utmost priority, behavior modification has been accepted by more counselors than many other new modalities in this field.

Relative advantage means that an innovation, in order to be adopted, has to prove its superiority over other competing methods currently in practice. For counselors to change their ways of behaving they have to be certain that the new approach is worth all the trouble of learning a new method. Thus, a counselor who was operating with satisfaction under a Rogerian model would have to be convinced of the superiority of another method before deciding to change to another approach.

Ease in understanding and installation is another quality important to the successful acceptance of an innovation. Ideas or products that are hard to install or to understand are less likely to be adopted. For example, counseling methods utilizing video feedback techniques are less likely to be accepted and tried than techniques that only require talking between two people or a group of people.

The *compatibility* of an innovation refers to the congruence it has with the values, ways of functioning, and facilities of the counseling setting and the counselor. Returning to the behavior modification example, incompatibility is one of the greatest barriers in the acceptance of this innovation. Many counselors' values are in conflict with the conscious manipulation and control used by social learning based therapies. Counselors who perceive behavior modification in this way often reject its use because it clashes with their basic values.

Trialibility, divisibility, or reversibility pertains to the flexibility allowed to the system or person to try out the innovation. The more flexibility an innovation possesses, the greater its chance of being implemented. Thus, if an innovation can be tried out one step or part at a time, the system has an easier time of accepting it. Most innovations are never really adopted, rather, they are "adapted" to the needs of the receiving organization. The more flexible an innovation is, the greater its likelihood of being accepted and incorporated into the system.

The enterprising counselor who has produced a new technique or idea should study the factors discussed previously and try to consider them in planning the diffusion and implementation of the idea. If after careful examination the counselor discovers that the innovation will have difficulty in some of these areas, efforts should be made to eliminate or lessen the effect.

THE CHARACTERISTICS OF THE POTENTIAL CONSUMERS OF THE NEW IDEAS.   Effective use of research findings includes at least these three characteristics of the consumer organization or institution: the leadership and organizational climate; characteristics of the staff; and the financial resources. Each of these is now discussed.

Leadership and Organizational Climate.

Among the most important factors in the eventual adoption of an innovation are the type of leadership and the organizational climate present in the setting in which the change is being introduced. As stated by Glaser (1973, p. 436), "A leadership style that sets a role model of willingness to entertain challenge of one's own operation, a style that encourages a nondefensive, self-renewing organizational climate" is a very important component in the acceptance of new ideas. In whatever setting a counselor works, the style of leadership of the administrators and the climate of the institution will determine to a great extent the amount of change that is allowed from the outside or encouraged from the inside. The following quote from the Rand Corporation Change Agent Study (Berman and McLaughlin, 1975) illustrates this point further:

> In particular, the local organizational climate and the motivations of the project participants had major effects on perceived success and on change in teacher behavior. More specifically, high morale of teachers at a school, the active support of principals who appear to be the "gatekeepers" of change, the general support of the superintendent and district officials, and the teachers' willingness to expend extra effort on the project all increased the chances of teacher change

and perceived success. The attitudes of administrators in effect tell the staff how seriously they should take the project's objectives. Unless the project seems to represent a district and school priority, teachers may not put in the extra effort and emotional investment necessary for successful implementation. Thus, when these elements were not in evidence, projects were likely to break down or be implemented symbolically without significant change. (p. 20)

The support given by administrators to the efforts of their staff to seek new ways of performing their jobs and to keep abreast of developments in the field is extremely important. Administrators who do not value and reward staff information-seeking and implementation of new ideas will have outdated, poorly informed, and demoralized staff members. The behavior of the administrators in this connection will be modeled by the staff; when the leaders show interest in keeping abreast and are open to new ideas and experience, the staff finds it easy to do the same. However, if the administrator does not think that research has anything to offer to practitioners and that new ideas are not worth pursuing, the front-line professionals will have a difficult time trying to further their growth.

The support of the administration is of crucial importance when a practitioner learns about a new idea and wants to try to implement it in his or her own practice. Encouragement, alternative suggestions, and accomplishment of the administrative tasks that will make possible implementation of the innovation are vital. I vividly remember one director of guidance services who, after I presented him with my ideas for a new program, responded: "Go home and think about the possible dangers that this idea could bring and then call me back." A year later the innovation was adopted by some high school teachers with whom I had discussed the idea. The town newspapers carried several laudatory articles on the project and the town annual report selected a picture of the project in operation as its front cover. Another administrator, not concerned about the dangers but about the benefits that this project could bring to the children, students, and parents of the town, had helped make it a reality and was proud of being the moving force behind its implementation.

Indifference to an innovation is often as prejudicial to its enactment as a negative reaction. Administrators and staff members who react negatively to new ideas and those who do not get involved constitute a kiss of death for change (Berman and McLaughlin, 1975).

Staff Characteristics

The quality of the staff of the potential user of the innovation is another very important factor in the adoption and successful implementation of a new idea. The staff has to be competent and able to carry out the new procedures properly. Not only must the administration be interested, but the staff that is going to be directly involved in using the ideas or new patterns must also be concerned and eager to participate. Thus, even if a new way of delivering after-care services is approved by the higher level administration of the outpatient unit of a mental hospital, it will not be successfully implemented unless the front-line personnel trying out the new method feel positively toward it.

In addition to the level of competence, the staff's degree of professional motivation and commitment is another very important factor in the utilization of research findings. Counselors who perceive themselves in process of continuous growth, learning, and changing are the ones eager and willing to use and implement new ideas. Counselors with low interest in their professional competence, those who feel they have reached the peak of professional excellence, those who feel threatened by the creative work of others or who are rigid or afraid of learning new things will usually not be interested in learning about and using the new developments in their field.

Counselors and administrators who define their role to include time to read journals and books, review the literature on a certain topic, attend meetings, and other similar activities tend to be more innovative. A few hours a week spent reading the most important journals in the field of counseling will save ten or more hours a week trying to re-invent the wheel by designing tests that others have already constructed or programs that others have already tried and evaluated. Even if a counselor does not attend national meetings, a weekly reading of the most important counseling journals will help keep one in contact with new developments.

The practitioner who is to understand research articles needs a certain *basic knowledge of research methods* such as elementary statistics, reading of graphs and tables, research design, and sampling procedures. Of extreme importance is the necessity for the practitioner to evaluate research findings. Counselors should be able to answer such questions as: Does this study demonstrate that the new method of doing counseling is effective? Is the sample on which this test was normed representative of the population whom I serve? (Chapter 2 discusses this topic in greater detail.)

The practitioner has to know how to *translate research findings into practical applications.* Many authors fail to point out the practical uses of their work or do not discuss fully the considerations that should be taken into account when their findings are implemented. Research courses for counselors should give training in translating research findings into practice. Many excellent research findings lie dormant waiting for an imaginative practitioner to put the ideas into use.

Financial Resources of the Organization.

The financial resources needed to put new ideas into practice and to keep abreast of research findings are a very important component of the utilization and dissemination system. Without appropriate funding to buy supplies or to hire the new personnel needed, an organization cannot introduce new patterns of behavior. Money to provide a well-stocked, up-to-date professional library or access to one is another necessity. Counselors need to read books, journals, and magazines, do literature searches, and perform other educational tasks in order to get acquainted with new innovations in the field. Money to attend professional meetings both locally and nationally is another serious need.

THE MANNER AND EXTENT OF IMPLEMENTATION EFFORTS.   The way in which a new idea or behavior pattern is diffused and implemented is a very critical factor in its eventual acceptance and adoption. In the action research models described previously, dissemination and implementation efforts are built in from the initial stages. Researchers work hand in hand with communities, social agencies, schools, and other practicing organizations from the very beginning. Because most models of research and evaluation fail to involve the front-line practitioner from the start, they have great difficulty having any effect on the practical operation of the programs they evaluate. Thus, among the first things researchers interested in implementing their findings must do is to involve in the project as many of the possible users of the results as they can.

However, not all research projects can follow this principle. In some instances participants cannot be included and in others when an innovation is being disseminated on a larger scale a different model has to be used. Many have found that *personal contact* between the possible adopter and the innovator is the most effective route (Glaser and Wrenn, 1971; Fairweather, 1971, among others). Workshops, information packages, conferences, and other means of dissemination are not sufficient. As Glaser (1973) states: "The most effective single means that can be used to increase information utilization is personal interaction, and the strategic contact is the well informed colleague (gatekeeper)" (p. 438).

When personal contact between the researcher and the possible user is not possible, a valuable approach is the linking agent. This person helps to connect the counselor in need with the available resources. The education extension agent experiment (Siebert, 1974) described earlier is a good example of this approach. (See Kauppi's description of the utilization specialist program in the rehabilitation area in Chapter 10.) Other important factors in the successful adaptation of an innovation are adaptive planning, staff training keyed to the local setting, and local materials development (Berman and McLaughlin, 1975).

To facilitate the transmission of their findings to the practitioner, researchers should ask in their grant proposals for dissemination and implementation funds that will enable them to offer free workshops, training sessions, and continuous support to counselors while they need it. Funds can also be used to pay for a linking agent that will bring together the practitioner and the research findings.

CONCLUSION

The purpose of this chapter is to make clear to counselors that there is an imperative need to do research and to make use of the research findings of others. The action research tradition was presented because it fits so well with the practical orientation of the front-line counselor. This chapter has offered a basic set of principles and practices that should serve well for all the practical research that counselors can engage in and use in their work. As such, the chapter provides a foundation for the remaining chapters in Part 3, each describing in detail one type of research approach.

Most of the studies that counselors can do on the job are aimed at action of some kind—either to confirm the merits of current practices or to suggest changes. The traditions of action research are still highly valid as the counselor plans a study, conducts it with maximum involvement and collaboration of all concerned, and then applies the results to the problem at hand. The reader may find it helpful to return to this chapter frequently while examining the many research methods and research settings that comprise most of the remainder of this book.

REFERENCES

Aldrige, E. *The microtraining paradigm in the instruction of junior high school students in attending behavior.* Unpublished doctoral dissertation, University of Massachusetts–Amherst, 1971.

Authier, J. and Gustafson, K. Applications of supervised and non-supervised microcounseling paradigms in the training of paraprofessionals. *Journal of Counseling Psychology,* 1975, *22*, 74–78.

Authier, J., Gustafson, K., Guerney, B., and Kasdorf, J. The psychological practitioner as teacher: A theoretical-historical and practical review. *The Counseling Psychologist,* 1975, *5* (2), 31–50.

Berman, P., and McLaughlin, M. W. *Federal programs supporting educational change, Volume IV: The findings in review.* Santa Monica, Calif. Rand Corporation, 1975.

Bizer, L. *Parent program in behavioral skills.* Unpublished manual, Amherst, Massachusetts, Regional Public Schools, 1972.

Carkhuff, R. *Helping and human relations. Vol I & II.* New York: Holt, Rinehart, and Winston, 1969.

Chadbourne, J. *The efficacy of the Ivey Taxonomy of group leader behavior for use with classroom teachers.* Unpublished doctoral dissertation, University of Massachusetts–Amherst, 1975.

Chein, S., Cook, S. W., and Harding, J. The field of action research. *American Psychologist,* 1948, *3*, 33–44.

Cherns, A. Social research and its diffusion. *Human Relations,* 1969, *22*, 209–218.

Davis, H. R., and Salasin, S. E. The utilization of evaluation. In E. L. Struening and M. Guttentag, *Handbook of evaluation research.* Beverly Hills, Calif.: Sage Publications, 1975.

Donk, L. Attending behavior in mental patients. *Dissertation Abstracts International,* 1972, *33* (2), order No. 72–22, 569.

Dunn, J. *Comparative effects of three counselor training techniques on reflection of feeling.* Paper presented at the meeting of the Canadian Psychological Association, Quebec City, June 18, 1975.

Fairweather, G. W. *Methods of changing mental hospital programs* (Progress report to NIMH, Grant No. R12-17888). East Lansing: Michigan State University, 1971.

Garvey, W., and Griffith, B. Scientific communication: The dissemination system in psychology and a theoretical framework for planning innovations. *American Psychologist,* 1965, *20,* 157–164.

Glaser, E. M. Knowledge transfer and institutional change. *Professional Psychology,* 1973, *4,* 434–444.

Glaser, E. M., and Wrenn, C. G. *Putting research, experimental, and demonstration findings to use.* Washington, D.C.: Office of Manpower Policy, Evaluation and Research, U.S. Department of Labor, 1971.

Gluckstern, N. *Parents as lay counselors: The development of a systematic parent program for drug counseling.* Unpublished doctoral dissertation, University of Massachusetts–Amherst, 1972.

Gluckstern, N. Training parents as drug counselors in the community. *Personnel and Guidance Journal,* 1973, *51,* 676–680.

Goshko, R. Self-determined behavior change. *Personnel and Guidance Journal,* 1973, *51,* 629–632.

Havelock, R. G. Research on the utilization of knowledge. In M. Kochen, (ed.) *Information for action: From knowledge to wisdom.* New York: Academic Press, 1975.

Hearn, M. *Three modes of training counselors: A comparative study.* Unpublished doctoral dissertaion, University of Ontario, London, 1976.

Ivey, A. The clinician as a teacher of interpersonal skills: Let's give away what we've got. The Clinical Psychologist, 1974, 27, 6–9.

Ivey, A. Media therapy: Educational change planning for psychiatric patients. Journal of Counseling Psychology, 1973, 20, 338–343.

Ivey, A. Microcounseling: Innovations in interviewing training. Springfield, Ill. Charles C. Thomas, 1971.

Ivey, A., Normington, C., Miller, C., Morrill, W., and Haase, R. Microcounseling and attending behavior: An approach to pre-practicum counselor training. Journal of Counseling Psychology, 1968, 15, Part II (Monograph Separate), 1–12.

Ivey, A., and Gluckstern, N. Basic attending skills: Leader and participant manuals. North Amherst, Mass.: Microtraining, 1974a, 1974b.

Ivey, A., and Gluckstern, N. Basic influencing skills: Leader and participant manuals. North Amherst, Mass.: Microtraining, 1976a, 1976b.

Kasdorf, J. Research implications of microtraining. In A. Ivey and J. Authier (eds.), Microcounseling: Innovations in interviewing, counseling, and psychotherapy training. Springfield, Ill.: Charles C. Thomas, in press.

Marrow, A. J. The practical theorist: The life and work of Kurt Lewin. New York: Basic Books, Inc., 1969.

Marrow, A. J. Risks and uncertainties in action research. Journal of Social Issues, 1964, 3, 5–20.

Moreland, J., Ivey, A., and Phillips, J. An evaluation of microcounseling as an interviewer training tool. Journal of Clinical and Consulting Psychology, 1973, 41, 294–300.

Rogers, E. Diffusion of innovation. New York: Free Press, 1962.

Shaskin, M., Morris, W. C., and Horst, L. A comparison of social and organizational change models: Information flow and data use processes. Psychological Review, 1973, 80, 510–526.

Sherrard, P. Predicting group leader/member interaction: The efficacy of the

Ivey Taxonomy. Unpublished doctoral dissertation, University of Massachusetts–Amherst, 1973.

Siebert, S. D. Trends in diffusion research: Knowledge utilization. *Viewpoints*, 1974, *50*, 61–81.

Toukmanian, S., and Rennie, D. Microcounseling vs. human relations training: Relative effectiveness with undergraduate trainees. *Journal of Counseling Psychology*, 1975, *22*, 345–352.

CHAPTER 4
Studying Individual Change

Jane L. Anton

As counselors, our primary concern is the growth and change of individuals. Regardless of setting or theoretical orientation, we are all faced with two important questions: Are the clients I am currently working with changing in desired ways? And, how can I be more effective with future clients? To answer the first question, we usually rely on "clinical judgment," "intuition," or clients' answers to such questions as "Are things getting any better?" Unfortunately, all of these methods produce unreliable answers. In order to answer the second question, we ought to be aided by research in counseling. However, most counseling research fails to meet the simple test of relevance suggested by Krumboltz (1967, p. 191): "What will counselors do differently if the results of this research come out in one way rather than another?" Consequently, alternative methods for integrating research and practice in counseling must be used.

This chapter presents an introduction to and description of methods for the systematic study of a single individual. These methods have two major advantages. First, they allow us to take a more "intimate" look at the process of individual growth and change and examine effects of counseling on specific individuals that have been obscured by traditional counseling research methodology. Second, these methods are particularly appropriate for the practitioner/researcher in counseling. Although the traditional distinction between counseling research and counseling practice still exists, this separation of research and practice can be reduced. Valid and well-designed research can and should be carried out by counselors in practice.

As in learning how to be an effective counselor, there is no substitute for experience, experimentation, and practice in learning how to be an effective researcher. This chapter presents the rationale and the basic principles of observation, design, and analysis for single subject research in sufficient detail so that you will begin to apply these methods and techniques. Only by trying, failing, and trying again will you begin to experience the joy and satisfaction of improving your own effectiveness and contributing to the understanding of others.

WHATEVER HAPPENED TO
THE INDIVIDUAL?

The systematic study of an individual is certainly not new to the fields of counseling or psychology. Some of the most significant breakthroughs in clinical work have been a result of work with individuals (Dukes, 1965; Lazarus and Davison, 1971). Allport (1937) and Lewin (1935) stressed the importance of the systematic study of the individual. Allport championed the "idiographic" method while Lewin argued that understanding and explaining individual performance required an examination of the "here and now" of contemporary events (Thoresen, 1972). The work of B. F. Skinner (1945, 1953) is based totally on the systematic observation of individual animals in highly controlled environments.

But this is an age of science, and counseling researchers, like other social scientists, want to be "scientific." We know that individual performance changes from situation to situation, and from person to person. In order for the results of a specific study to be generalized to other persons and situations, we must somehow account for this individual variation. Following the lead of psychology, the physical science model, with its emphasis on the "average" and resultant statistical procedures, has been adopted as the basis for counseling research. This model not only fails to consider *individual* performance as lawful and systematic, but treats the individual as a random event or unexplained variance. Consequently, in our quest to be scientific, we have all too often substituted "statistical control" for disciplined inquiry.

Much of counseling research is devoted to correlations between one descriptive measure and another, such as the correlation between a personality inventory and an academic achievement test. Although various statistical procedures allow us to determine the extent to which two or more variables correlate, the conclusions from such studies cannot legitimately be interpreted as describing causal relationships, although there is a great temptation to do so. In addition, such designs provide absolutely no information to the counselor concerned with the factors that influence a particular student's academic achievement.

Recognizing the limitation of correlational research, many counseling researchers have argued for more experimental research in counseling (Whiteley, 1967). Unfortunately, "experimental" research in counseling has become synonymous with comparative group designs (Campbell and Stanley, 1966). The typical counseling experiment involves at least two groups: an experimental group, which experiences the counseling treatment, and a control group, which does not. In such an experiment, the usual question asked is whether the average performance of one group differed significantly from that of the other group(s). In such an experiment, the subject's performance is seldom observed during treatment. Usually, an estimate of the group's pretreatment performance, as assessed by some pretest, is compared with the group's posttest.

In such a design, statistically significant differences in the *average* performance of the two groups does not demonstrate that the difference was effective for *all* subjects (Chassan, 1967). The reliance on the average performance of a group obscures the effects of a treatment on individuals. Although the average performance of a group may improve, specific individuals may in fact "get worse," or a few subjects may change dramatically while most subjects remain unchanged. And yet, in the view of most counseling researchers, the comparative group design represents the only "proper" research method.

The emphasis on statistical analysis has not only mathematically erased the individual in counseling research, but has furthered the separation between researcher and practitioner. Most counselors were traumatized rather than inspired by their usually brief introduction to counseling research in graduate school, and have neither the time nor facilities to perform elaborate group designs.

Scientific inquiry requires the use of standardized procedures to permit testing in the public arena, yet no single scientific method is valid without consideration for the phenomenon under investigation. A science is only as good as its methodology and any rigid orthodoxy in psychological experimentation can only lead to a reduction in the usefulness of such experiments. Consequently, counseling research must utilize a variety of methods including the systematic study of a single subject.

We do need alternative methods for the description and experimental study of individual behavior, but it is a mistake to assume that the absence of elaborate statistics and group designs will make counseling research "easier." We must return to the difficult and often painstaking process of *thinking*. Instead of turning to a textbook for a design or analysis procedure, the counselor/researcher is required to observe, describe, think, rethink, create, analyze, and continually invent new procedures that match the specific problem to be studied.

Although a "single subject" in counseling research usually refers to an individual person, the "subject" can also be a larger unit such as a school, family, classroom, or community. In fact, while these methods are seldom applied in counseling or psychological research, their use in other social sciences such as anthropology, economics, political science, and sociology has been extensive.

QUALITATIVE METHODS FOCUSING ON AN INDIVIDUAL

The primary focus of this chapter is to examine experimental methods for the study of a single subject, but there are also a variety of useful *descriptive* methods (Lofland, 1971; Franklin and Osborne, 1971). The case study is most often used to describe individuals. Although case reports from practicing counselors lack the degree of control and objectivity to provide information on *why* something is happening, a careful description of *what* is happening can play several important roles in the scientific study of the individual. Specifically, case studies have been used in the following ways.

1. Case studies can provide valuable information on specific types of individual behavior that occur too infrequently to be studied repeatedly. For example, the relatively rare phenomenon of multiple personality was reported by Thigpen and Cleckley (1954). The now classic case of Eve White, Eve Black, and Jane is one of the few detailed accounts of this phenomenon and, consequently, the primary source of information about it.

2. The description of a single case can provide disconfirmation of allegedly universal beliefs. For example, Freud's belief that his female patients' reports of sexual assaults by their fathers or uncles were accurate descriptions of events was changed when he learned that one of his patients could not have been present at the time of the incident. As a result of this single case he realized that some of these assaults were fantasies and began to rethink the "meaning" of his patients' recollections (Davison and Neale, 1974).

3. Perhaps the most important role of a case study is to generate "hunches" about the nature and causes of individual behavior. Because the case study is often exploratory it is possible to examine new and perhaps important hypotheses that would not be uncovered in controlled investigation. This use of the case

study requires that the counselor collect extensive data about the subject. If we want to study an individual child's disruptive behavior, for example, it would be wise to examine not only the frequency, timing, and conditions of the behavior but also numerous other factors about the child whether or not they appear to be related to the problem—family situation, health, academic achievement, self-concept, physical and social development, and so on (Miller and Warner, 1975).

Although the case study can be used to answer questions about what is happening now, different kinds of methods are required to answer such questions as "Is my client changing? If so, is that change related to something I did? If so, what was it?" This leads us to the quantitative methods.

QUANTITATIVE METHODS—
INTENSIVE EXPERIMENTAL DESIGNS

A variety of labels have been applied to methods that permit a systematic and quantified observation of changes in an individual—"intensive designs," "multiple baseline methods," "same subject research," "N-1," "interrupted time series," "empirical case studies"—but here these methods will all be referred to as intensive experimental designs. These methods all share the underlying assumption that human beings change continuously and that one must observe change as a process rather than as a single movement from pretreatment (before the counseling intervention) to posttreatment (after the intervention). That is to say, a single observation before treatment compared to a single observation after treatment can lead to an erroneous conclusion about treatment effects. A single observation, whether it is a test score, a count of specific behaviors, or the client's self report, may tell us what is happening at a given moment but does not give us any information about the *direction* in which the client is changing. Again we are faced with the problem of individual variation, and a single point estimate may be misleading. For example, suppose a colleague of yours reported the following evaluation of the effects of group counseling in working with an extremely shy fifth grade girl.

She almost never talked or played with other kids before or after school or during recess. So on the Wednesday before the group began, I had the playground monitor count the number of times she was interacting with another child. The monitor recorded three interactions during recess. After the counseling group, I had the monitor count again and this time Mary interacted nine times with other kids. So I knew the group was effective for her.

Most of us would be persuaded by such information that the counseling group indeed had produced a change. But Figure 4-1 shows what the counselor would have seen if the playground monitor had been observing Mary each day. As we can see, the frequency of social interactions is already increasing before counseling. Thus, counseling cannot be said to have brought about this upward trend despite the fact that the comparison of two points (day 2 compared to day 12) shows a "significant" change.

Not only might we mistakenly conclude that counseling had produced a change when it had not, we might also mistakenly conclude that counseling was not effective when in fact it was. In the case represented in Figure 4-2, we can see that simply comparing the observations on day 3 (before treatment) and day 11 (after treatment) would lead us to conclude that counseling had no effect. Obviously, counseling had a dramatic effect in changing the trend or direction of change.

The preceding examples highlight the fundamental principle underlying intensive experimental research methods.

Principle 1: *An empirical study of a single subject requires that the counselor/researcher make a series of observations over some period of time in order to determine both the degree and direction of change.*

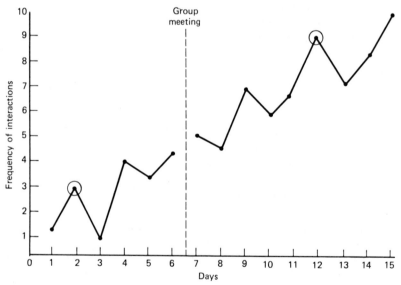

FIGURE 4.1   Client Change Not Necessarily Due to Group Counseling.

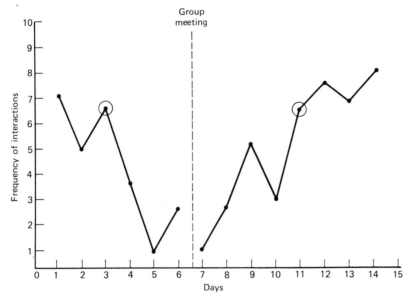

FIGURE 4.2   Client Change Probably Due to Group Counseling.

A set of such observations is referred to as a time series and relies on a second major assumption—that the observations in a time series reflect a continuous process of change. For example, if we observed a client on Monday, Wednesday, and Friday, we know that the process of change is occurring on Tuesday and Thursday even though we have not observed it. Consequently, we must estimate the "real" process of change, since we have only observed part of it. This assumption leads us to a general principle for using time series to study an individual.

Principle 2: *In order to estimate the continuous process of change, observations in a time series should be as continuous and frequent as possible.*

What to Observe

Most applications of intensive experimental research have come from psychologists utilizing a behavioral approach. Because the behavioral counselor is likely to define a client's problem in terms that can be observed with some frequency over time (Krumboltz and Thoresen, 1969), this type of research can be more readily applied. The application of this research method does not require the counselor to utilize a behavioral approach to counseling, but it does require that the counselor be able to express objectives and relevant variables in observable terms (to "operationalize" them) in order to monitor them over a period of time.

Traditional counseling research has relied heavily on standardized tests and other forms of psychometric assessment. These methods are inappropriate for our purposes for four reasons. First, these methods attempt to assess *unobservable* qualities or characteristics such as dependency, anxiety, or self-concept. Second, they are designed to assess individual performance only as relative to group performance. For example, an individual score on the D (Depression) subscale of the MMPI does not assess the individual's actual feelings of depression, but describes the individual's responses to the test items in terms of "group norms." Consequently, if we are interested in changes within a *group*, these measurement techniques are appropriate. However, they tell us little about an individual.

Third, this type of instrument cannot be administered repeatedly to the same individual unless alternate forms are used. Since most psychological tests have only one or two forms, they cannot be used to assess the same client repeatedly over time. Fourth, and most important, this type of assessment frequently assumes that individuals possess certain personality "traits" that are stable across situations. For example, the assumption is that an aggressive child is aggressive on the playground, in the classroom, at home, at church, and at a baseball game. However, most human behavior is not so consistent (Mischel, 1973). An individual may be relaxed and talkative around close friends and yet tense and quiet at a staff meeting. The attempt to assess stable personality traits has obscured the *interaction* between the individual's behavior and environmental characteristics.

A major obstacle in conducting intensive experimental research is frequently the counselor's attitude toward observation and measurement. One often hears counselors say something like, "All right, you can count the number of times the kid gets out of his seat without asking permission, but you can't count something really important like his self-concept." It is true that we cannot make an actual assessment of such constructs as self-concept, independence, and mental health, but we can assess related observable variables and use them as an index of progress. This procedure is similar to a physician's monitoring such variables as a patient's blood pressure, heart rate, respiration, and temperature as an index of the construct of the patient's "health." Unfortunately, the relevant observable indexes of "psychological health," "personal growth," or "healthy development" have not been established. Consequently, the couselor/researcher must carefully examine and define constructs and invent appropriate assessment indexes.

Let's take, for example, the construct "self-concept" that is usually considered both important and unmeasurable. Imagine you are seeing a client who has a very low opinion of herself and her abilities, despite ample evidence to the contrary. You decide that a goal of counseling should be to raise her self-concept. How will you monitor her progress toward that goal?

One solution to this type of problem is presented by John Gottman and Sandra Leiblum (1974). In working with a child who thought of himself as a "loser," Gottman and Leiblum reasoned that the child's self-concept would be reflected in his predictions of how well he would do in certain specific situations. A child with a "positive self-concept" would expect to do well, while a child with a "negative self-concept" would expect to do poorly. The procedure for this child involved periodically listing situations the child was to encounter and asking him how well he would do. Figure 4-3 shows seven situations that came up in the child's ratings.

Date:	Expect to do:	(1) Bad	(2) Average	(3) Good
1. Behave with the babysitter on Friday night		x		
2. Do well on math test on Wednesday			x	
3. Win at cards with my sister		x		
4. Win at hockey game			x	
5. Finish homework this weekend		x		
6. Not fight with sisters		x		
7. Not sass back mom		x		
		x		
TOTAL		5	4	= 9

FIGURE 4.3   Rating Form for Child's Expectations. (From *How To Do Psychotherapy and How To Evaluate It* by John M. Gottman and Sandra R. Leiblum. Copyright © 1974 by Holt, Rinehart and Winston, Inc. Reprinted by permission of Holt, Rinehart and Winston.)

His "self-concept score" was the percent of the maximum number of points. During the course of ten sessions a graph of his self-concept scores was plotted (Figure 4-4). In addition, the scores were analyzed separately for areas of self-concept involving parents, schools, siblings, and peers. This type of data analysis not only allows the counselor to monitor the overall effectiveness of counseling, but provides ongoing information that can be used in the process of counseling.

Another approach to operationalizing the construct of self-concept is presented by Hannam, Thoresen, and Hubbard (1974) in an attempt to increase the self-esteem of teachers. They operationalize the construct as follows:

> A positive self-concept was defined as a high frequency of positive (reinforcing) self-evaluations combined with a low frequency of negative (punishing) self-evaluations; a negative self-concept was viewed as the converse, that is, as many negative evaluations and few positive ones. (p. 146)

After an initial interview where self-thoughts were defined and a list of common self-thoughts was generated, each teacher was asked to self observe positive and negative thoughts about self during a specified hour each day. The teacher recorded each self-observation on one of two wrist counters. An example of a positive self-thought was "I am patient with children." A negative self-thought may have been "I'm wasting my time here, I should be doing something more important." Figure 4-5 shows how this index of self-concept was used to monitor changes in three teachers over time. During the baseline phase, the teachers were asked to observe and record both positive and negative self-thoughts. In the next phase, teachers learned to subvocalize the word stop and imagine a stop sign immediately following the occurrence of a negative thought. Teacher number 3 did not participate

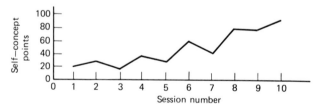

FIGURE 4.4 Index of "Self-Concept" Plotted Over Ten Counseling Sessions. (From *How To Do Psychotherapy and How To Evaluate It* By John M. Gottman and Sandra R. Leiblum. Copyright © 1974 by Holt, Rinehart and Winston, Inc. Reprinted by permission of Holt, Rinehart and Winston.)

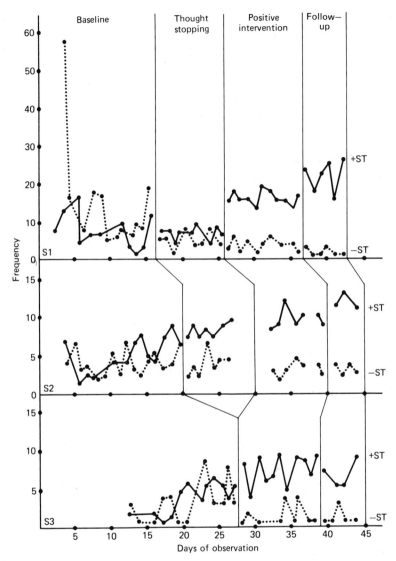

FIGURE 4.5 Positive Self-Thoughts (+ST) and Negative Self-Thoughts (−ST) as an Index of Self-Concept. (From *Self-Control: Power to the Person* by M. J. Mahoney and C. E. Thoresen. Copyright © 1974 by Wadsworth Publishing Co., Inc. Reprinted by permission of the publisher, Brooks/Cole Publishing Co., Monterey, Calif.)

in this procedure but continued the baseline phase. The third phase, for all three teachers, was designed to increase positive thoughts by placing "cues" (e.g., a blue decal on the clock) in order to prompt the teacher to think a positive thought while engaging in routine actions.

Although the preceding examples use very different methods to operationalize the construct "self-concept," they illustrate two important points. First, "unmeasureable" constructs can be operationalized to provide useful data to monitor change over time. To be useful, the selection of what is observed is tailored to the individual client or problem under investigation. This does not mean that the counselor/researcher must "re-invent the wheel" every time, but learns and revises observation strategies based on experiences with different clients. Second, there is no "right answer" or perfect solution to the question of what to observe. Not only are there an infinite number of solutions, but deciding what to observe is a continuous process rather than a single decision. Unfortunately, this part of the process is often left out of research reports, and it appears that the investigator came up with the solution with practically no effort. This is usually not the case and especially so for the counselor just beginning to observe or have clients self observe specific actions. This process is sometimes difficult but there is a growing number of resources and models to which the counselor can turn. A variety of systems have been developed for observing teacher behavior and classroom interactions (Medley and Mitzel, 1963; Flanders, 1970). Examples of operationally defining constructs related to individual counseling can be found in Risley and Wolf (1972), Dustin and George (1973), Rimm and Masters (1975), and Krumboltz and Thoresen (1976). Thoresen and Mahoney (1974) have described various methods of self-observation that make "private events" available for investigation. In addition, Liberman (1970, 1972) and Krumboltz and Potter (1973) suggest ways of operationalizing such concepts as cohesiveness, trust, empathy, and intimacy, which are frequently considered important in group counseling. It is then possible to study the group as a "single subject" and monitor the development of "cohesiveness" over time.

Technical Considerations

There are several important criteria that influence how well or how poorly we are able to make appropriate conclusions from the results of an experimental design, whether it is a comparative group design or a correlational study or an intensive experimental design. Since these concepts are discussed in detail elsewhere, the discussion here is brief and limited to their application to intensive experimental designs.

VALIDITY.   How do you determine if you measured or observed what you actually intended to? Although this is frequently a significant problem in psychometric assessment, it is less so in intensive experimental research because we are more likely to be observing the actual actions or characteristics of an individual and not inferring them from a test score. The problems of validity within an intensive experimental design are faced when you begin to answer the question "what to observe" as discussed above.

RELIABILITY.   How accurate are the measurements or observations? Often the answer to this question appears to be simple when it is not. Many factors can affect the accuracy of such "simple" actions as seeing and counting. In general, the counselor/researcher can increase the accuracy of observation by careful and detailed attention to the following four factors.

1.   *What is being observed.* There is no substitute for a detailed, well-defined description of the target behavior. It is the only way the observer knows what to count and what not to count. For example, if we are interested in a child's disruptive behavior, we could simply ask the teacher to count the number of times the child is disruptive in class. However, we would have no way of knowing if "disruptive" had the same meaning for the teacher as it did for us. By defining disruptive as any occasion when a child's behavior requires direct attention from the teacher that is not related to the ongoing classroom activities, we have increased the likelihood that the teacher will make more accurate observations. We could increase the reliability still further by describing the specific act that would be considered disruptive, for example, yelling, swearing, pounding on desk, dropping books, or slamming the door.

2.   *Where and when the behavior is observed.* We can further increase the accuracy of observations by specifying the conditions for those observations. If we ask the teacher in the preceding example to observe the child in the classroom, during reading, for 45 minutes a day, we are likely to get more reliable observations than if the teacher observed "only when I thought about it."

3.   *How the observations are counted.* The procedures for counting and recording observations should be specified and should make the act of recording as easy as possible. For example, instead of

having a teacher record every instance of disruptive behavior, which might be difficult to do while carrying out the normal activities of teaching, we could ask the teacher to take a moment at the end of each hour and simply check whether or not the disruptive behavior had occurred. This "time sampling" procedure would increase the consistency of the teacher's observations.

4.   *Who the observer is.* Numerous characteristics of the individual doing the observation as well as that person's interaction with the conditions under which the observations are made influence the reliability of the observations. The usual procedure for checking the observer's reliability is to have two or more individuals observe the same things under the same conditions at the same time, and then compute their "agreement." Often as counselors we are interested in thoughts, feelings, and images that take place within an individual and cannot be observed by someone else. In such cases, we must have the client observe him/herself. There are several distinct advantages to self-observation, and the factors affecting one's ability to accurately monitor one's own behavior are only beginning to be explored (Kazdin, 1974; Thoresen and Mahoney, 1974).

UTILITY.   The final and often ignored characteristic of measurement is the ratio between the cost of obtaining the information and the benefit derived from the information. For example, if I were interested in increasing a client's personal responsibility during counseling sessions, I could tape record each session and do a content analysis to find out how many "responsibility taking" statements the client made. Such a procedure might produce very reliable and valid data but it is not practical for the practicing counselor without a large research budget. Fortunately, there are several inexpensive and often useful data sources. Since the cheapest kind of data is data already collected, the counselor/researcher should not overlook records that are routinely kept by schools, agencies, or institutions.

Designing an Intensive Experimental Study

The most important factor in determining how to design a particular study is the answer to the question "What do I want to know?" That may sound simplistic, but only by answering that question carefully can the counselor/researcher determine what factors are important in the design of a study. No textbook can tell you how to design the study you want to do. The process of experimental design is not one of following rules generated by some authority, but rather the diligent application of logic and common sense (Anton, in press).

The major purpose of an "experimental" research design is to explore cause and effect relationships but it is essential to keep one fundamental principle in mind when designing and interpreting such studies. We can never design an experiment or set of experiments that *prove* a causal relationship exists. For any experimental finding there are always alternative explanations. The value of any single type of design is relative to the number and types of alternative explanations it eliminates. For example, if a counselor used assertive training procedures with several married couples with equal success in improving their relationship, we have some evidence that those procedures may be related to improving marital relationships. However, it is just as likely that the improvement was "caused" by some characteristics of the particular counselor involved and not related to the procedures per se. The only way to rule out one or the other of these rival hypotheses would be an experiment using the same procedures and different counselors.

No experimental design is "good" or "bad" in any absolute sense. The merits of any particular design can be evaluated only in terms of the questions under investigation. The following section provides a description of basic designs used in intensive experimental research.

ANNOTATED TIME SERIES.   The most elementary level of investigating causal relationships is to examine the fluctuations in a series of observations and begin to pinpoint variables that covary with these fluctuations. For example, in working with a 45-year-old depressed woman, I was interested in examining those factors that covaried with shifts in her depressed mood. She kept daily records of her mood by completing the Depression Adjective Check List (DACL) (Lubin, 1965) and kept a daily diary of "significant events." Figure 4-6 presents the series of DACL scores that has been annotated with references to specific significant events that occurred on the same days.

An examination of this chart revealed that unpleasant events such as those on days 5, 16, and 23 are followed by three or four days of acute depression; whereas pleasant events, such as those on days 13 and 21, seemed to have an immediate but temporary effect on alleviating the client's mood. Further, the type of unpleasant experience that increased the depression was a conflict with another person. As a result of discussing the chart,

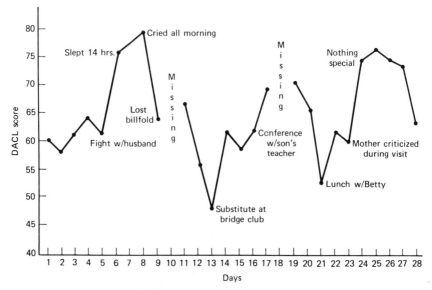

FIGURE 4.6 Annotated Time Series of Depression Adjective Checklist Standard Scores and Significant Events.

we set the following objectives that seemed likely to reduce the client's depression: to learn skills to manage interpersonal conflict, to decrease the time spent "worrying" about conflicts with others, and to increase the number of pleasant activities in which the client engaged.

Although Figure 4–6 presents what seem to be obvious relationships between significant events and changes in mood, it was only after careful examination and some "detective" work that the specific events presented were isolated. By looking carefully at events both preceding and following a shift in the time series, the counselor can begin to generate hypotheses. Frequently, the most "significant" events are not the most obvious, and considerable persistence and creativity may be required. An example of how such apparently unrelated events can be of importance is illustrated by Edwards and Cronbach's (1952) discussion of Fisher's (1921) analysis of wheat yields.

> [Fisher] found that after he controlled variety, and fertilizer, there was considerable variation from year to year. This variation had a slow up and down cycle over a 70 year period. Now Fisher set himself on the trail of the residual variation. First he studied records from other sections to see if they had the trend; they did not. He considered and ruled out rainfall as an explanation. Then he started

reading the records of the plots and found weeds as a possible factor. He considered the nature of each species of weed and found that the response of specific weed varieties to rainfall and cultivation accounted for much of the cycle. But the large trends were not explained until he showed that the upsurge of weeds after 1875 coincided with a School Attendance Act which removed cheap labor from the fields, and that another cycle coincided with the retirement of a superintendent who made weed removal his personal concern. (p. 64)

Another method of searching for concomitant variation is to examine two sets of observations at once and look for parallel fluctuations. This method is illustrated in Figure 4-7, which represents a set of self-observations made by a graduate student in counseling as part of a self-change project.

The student was concerned about his inability to fall asleep shortly after going to bed and the frequent experiences of anxiety that "came on for no reason at all." At first, the student considered these separate and independent problems; however, after plotting both sets of observations on the same charts, he discovered a remarkable correspondence between the number of "anxiety attacks" experienced each day and the length of time it took him to fall asleep.

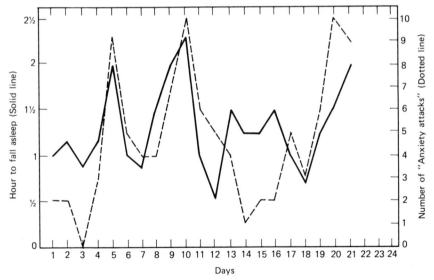

FIGURE 4.7 Concomitant Variation Between "Anxiety Attacks" and Time to Fall Asleep.

The annotated time series design is most often useful as an exploratory or first order examination of causal relationships; it is also useful in program evaluation to monitor changes over time in order to confirm or disconfirm the effects of specific events. For example, teachers in a program for potential high school dropouts assumed they had made major breakthroughs as a result of a long, emotional, intimate talk with a student. Such talks occurred with three different students. A time series analysis, however, questioned the conclusion that these talks produced beneficial effects. The analysis showed that following the talk each of the students significantly avoided the teacher, did not improve in academic performance, and significantly increased classroom disruptive behavior (Gottman, 1971).

INTERRUPTED TIME SERIES OR AB DESIGNS.   The basic problem of experimental design is how to rule out alternative explanations for specific effects. Because no single experimental design, whether comparative group or intensive, can rule out all alternatives except one, experimentation should be viewed as a process rather than a specific "experiment." Several basic design options for intensive experimental research are described in the following section. Each of these design options involves somehow "interrupting" a time series of observations. The following notation is used to designate different phases or periods of the time series:

A   Baseline phase (before treatment)

B   First treatment use

C   Second treatment phase

D   Third treatment phase

A'   Return to baseline phase (after treatment)

The AB Design.

The simplest of the intensive designs is the AB design where a series of baseline observations (A) are compared to a series of treatment observations (B). The A phase serves as the "control" phase—that is, we can use this phase to estimate what would happen without treatment. Consequently, this design allows us to rule out the possibility that the observed changes are a result of pretreatment trends as illustrated in Figure 4-1. A major weakness of this design is that it fails to control for the effects of history, that is, other events occurring at the same time as treatment that could account for the change. For example, widespread media coverage of a construction worker falling from the 23rd floor of a building would present problems if it occurred simultaneously with the onset of a treatment for acrophobia for one's client.

In addition, the results of a single AB study cannot be generalized to other individuals with confidence. However, this leads us to an important distinction between intensive experimental research and the use of comparative group designs. In most group designs the ability to generalize findings with "statistical significance" from the specific subjects in the study to a larger population is based on assigning several subjects at random to treatment groups. Generalization within an intensive experimental method is based on the systematic replication of results rather than statistical significance per se. If the counselor can demonstrate comparable results with the same client each time a technique is used (intraindividual replication) or with other clients (interindividual replication), then confidence is increased that the counseling procedure is effective. In this way, the question of generalization can gradually be answered—that is, whether the counseling technique works with different clients, different counselors, and different problems.

The major advantage of the AB design is that it is compatible with the "real life" work of the counselor. The goal of counseling is to produce desired changes even if the counselor cannot be certain as to what produced the changes. This design does document the fact of change without pinpointing the process producing the change.

The ABAB Design.

This is the most commonly used intensive experimental design and is frequently referred to as the reversal design (Risley and Wolf, 1972; Sidman, 1960; Kazdin, 1973). The primary purpose of this design is to demonstrate a functional relationship between a phenomenon under observation and the treatment procedures, thus increasing confidence that it is the treatment itself that is producing the observed changes. If the counselor can demonstrate that the observed change occurs only when the treatment is "on" (B) and that the phenomenon under investigation "returns to baseline" when the treatment is "off" (A and A'), then a functional relationship has been established. Although it is still possible that extraneous factors may have produced the observed changes, the counselor makes such explanations less plausible by showing that the changes covary with the presence or absence of the specific treatment.

An example of the ABAB design is presented in Figure 4-8. In this study

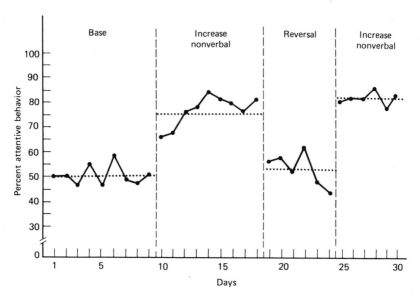

FIGURE 4.8 ABAB Design Investigating the Effects of Teacher Nonverbal Approval. (From Kazdin and Klock, 1973.)

(Kazdin and Klock, 1973) the effect of teacher praise on the attending behavior of retarded children in a special education classroom was examined. After the baseline observations were made, the teacher was instructed to increase her use of nonverbal approval to the students by smiling, physically patting them on the back, and nodding approvingly for paying attention to her. During this phase, the students' attentive behavior increased. The teacher was then instructed to discontinue the use of nonverbal approval and the students' behavior "returned to baseline." The treatment procedures were then reinstated and again the students' behavior increased.

The ABAB design is the most powerful design for demonstrating causal relationships, especially if replicated with different subjects and different situations, yet there are several factors that limit its utility. First, it may be impossible to remove or reverse the effects of treatment. For example, learning a new skill, such as how to respond empathically, cannot be "turned off" since the person has acquired a new response. A variety of responses once learned cannot be unlearned (Bandura, 1969). Second, while a particular behavior may be "reversible," the treatment procedures may have changed the subject and/or others in the environment. Once a teacher learns that the use of "I-messages" decreases disruptive behavior in class, she or he may be unlikely to terminate the use of such statements even if consciously intending to. Third, the removal of treatment procedures may be highly undesirable or unethical. For example, if a treatment is successful in eliminating the self-injurious behavior of a child, the risks associated with withdrawing that treatment are not justified in order to establish experimental control over the behavior. Fourth, it is usually the task of the counselor to establish relatively permanent changes in behavior rather than transitory or highly "reversible" ones. Consequently, the maintenance of behavior change is more important than the establishment of causal relationships.

MULTIPLE TIME SERIES DESIGNS.   As mentioned previously, a major weakness of a single time series design is its failure to control for the effects of concurrent events. One method of controlling for these events is the use of two or more subjects, or multiple time series design (Gottman, McFall, and Barnett, 1969). One of the subjects is randomly assigned to the treatment while the other serves as a control subject. Once the treatment effect has been established, the treatment can then be applied to the control subject. A study by Hall, et al. (1970) illustrates this design (see Figure 4-9).

Three tenth grade students who had been earning D or F grades on class quizzes were selected. Baseline data was collected on each student. The treatment, which consisted of required tutoring contingent upon D or F grades, was applied on the tenth day to Dave. Five days later, after observing the increase in Dave's grades, the treatment was applied to Roy. Now Roy's grades increased after the beginning of his tutoring. Finally, five days later, the procedures were applied to Debbie, and the same effect was demonstrated. Because the increase in grade was observed for each student only after that student's tutoring began, we can be more confident that the treatment, rather than some other simultaneous event, produced the change. This "time-lagged" design has several advantages. First, such a design meets all the criteria for the internal validity of an experiment (Campbell and Stanley, 1966). Second, it avoids any ethical problems associated with permanently withholding treatment from a subject. Third, it provides the opportunity for immediate replication of results.

MULTIPLE BASELINE DESIGNS.   Another major design option involves multiple observations on the same individual. The two major types of multiple baseline designs are: (1) across situations, where the same behavior is observed in different situations; (2) across behaviors, where two or more different behaviors are observed in the same situation.

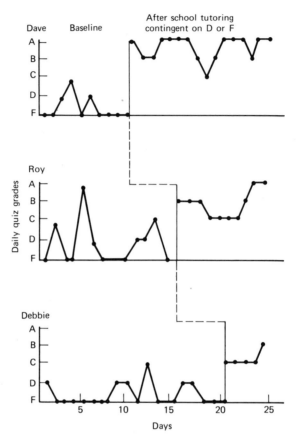

FIGURE 4.9 Time Lagged Multiple Time Series Design. (From R. V. Hall, C. Cristler, S. Cranston, and B. Tucker, Teachers and parents as researchers using multiple baseline designs. *Journal of Applied Behavior Analysis,* 1970, *3,* 247–55. Reprinted by permission of the *Journal of Applied Behavior Analysis,* Department of Human Development, University of Kansas, Lawrence.)

Across Situations.

Figure 4-10 is an example of a multiple baseline design across situations. In this study (Schmidt, 1974) a fourth grade boy's aggressive responses (e.g., biting, kicking, spitting) were observed during both Reading and Math classes. The treatment intervention consisted of having the teacher respond to the aggressive behavior with an "I message" (e.g., "I'm scared to death that you will hurt someone seriously when you kick.") The treatment was

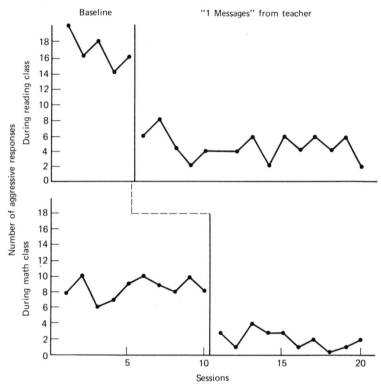

FIGURE 4.10 Multiple Baselines of Frequency of Aggressive Response During Reading and Math Class. (From J. A. Schmidt, Research techniques for counselors: The multiple baseline. *Personnel and Guidance Journal,* 1974, 53, 200–6. Copyright 1974 American Personnel and Guidance Association. Reprinted with permission.)

first introduced during Reading class, following the fifth session, and resulted in a reduction in the number of aggressive responses. However, the child's aggressive behavior in Math class did not change as a result of the intervention in Reading class. Only when the treatment was applied during Math class, beginning after the tenth session, did the number of aggressive responses reduce.

The major advantage of this type of design is that it allows us to examine the relationship between the individual's behavior and the stimulus or environment. There is increasing evidence that an individual's responses are less a function of "personality traits" such as aggressiveness, but rather a result of interaction with certain stimulus conditions such as time, place, type of activity, or behavior of another person (Mischel, 1973). The situations in this type of design are not necessarily two specific places, but rather two sets of stimulus conditions that share some important characteristic. For example, in studying the effects of assertive training you could observe assertive behavior in response to men and women, strangers and friends, supervisors and those supervised, and so on. By repeatedly examining different situational or stimulus properties, the most relevant variables affecting the phenomenon should emerge.

Across Behaviors.

This design involves repeated observations on two or more behaviors followed by the application of treatment procedures to one behavior at a time. It has often been used to evaluate the effects of reinforcement contingencies (Schwarz and Hawkins, 1970; Risley and Hart, 1968; Hall, et al., 1970). In such studies two or more target behaviors are selected that are assumed to be independent of each other. For example, a female college student wanted to increase her frequency of social interaction and to decrease the amount of time she "procrastinated" during study periods. Both of these behaviors were monitored continuously. The treatment intervention consisted of a "self-contract" (Thoresen and Mahoney, 1974) where the client established her own goals (e.g., to initiate a conversation with another person at least three times a day) and then reinforced herself (e.g., buying a new plant) if she attained the goal. After the self-contracting was established as effective in increasing the frequency of social interactions, the client then applied the same procedures in order to decrease the amount of time spent procrastinating. This type of multiple baseline design is very useful for demonstrating the effects of contingency arrangements when the behaviors are assumed to be functionally independent and it is also useful in examining the components of complex social skills. Hersen and Bellack (1976) used the multiple baseline design to examine the components of assertive behavior with a chronic schizophrenic. Figure 4-11 presents observations of four specific behaviors viewed as components of assertiveness for the particular subject involved. The same treatment, consisting of giving the client instructions and feedback on a target behavior during videotape "probe" sessions, was sequentially applied to each of the four behaviors. First, the client was given feedback on and instruction for increasing the amount of eye contact while talking; then for increasing the duration of speaking, then for increasing the number of requests made, and finally, for decreasing compliances. Throughout the study, the client's overall assertiveness was assessed as well as the frequency of each target behavior (Figure 4-11). This design demonstrates that the treatment procedures were effective in changing each of the target behaviors and additionally illustrates the cumulative effect of each change on the client's overall assertiveness.

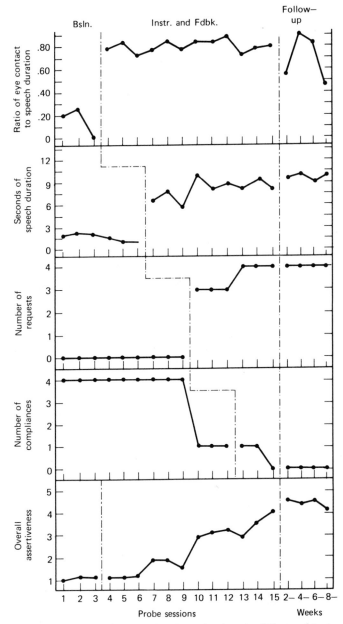

FIGURE 4.11 Multiple Baseline Design Investigating the Effects of Instruction and Feedback on Assertive Behaviors. (From M. Hersen and A. A. Bellack, A multiple baseline analysis of social skills training in chronic shizophrenics. *Journal of Applied Behavior Analysis*, 1976, 9, 239–45. Reprinted by permission of the Journal of Applied Behavior Analysis, Department of Human Development, University of Kansas, Lawrence.)

COMBINATION DESIGNS.   The preceding section has presented some of the basic design options in intensive experimental research. However, there are infinite possibilities for combining and adding to any specific design. Again, the design you use or create depends on what questions you are asking and what kinds of alternative explanations you wish to investigate. For example, you may begin by evaluating the effects of a specific treatment with an AB design. You may also be interested in the effects of an additional treatment, C. This raises the additional question of "Does it make any difference which treatment comes first?" In addition, you might want to control for concurrent events by using control subjects. In any case, the possibilities are limitless.

Analysis of Results

Careful and detailed analysis is critical when analyzing the results of an intervention using an intensive design: first, because a time series can change in a variety of ways as a result of an intervention, and second, because changes in a time series may be only in the "eye of the beholder."

A time series of observations has two important dimensions, either of which may change as a result of an interaction—a certain level of magnitude and a trend or slope in the direction in which it is moving. Figure 4-12 illustrates different types of changes that can occur as a result of an intervention.

In determining the level and slope of a time series, it is most tempting to say, "Well, I can tell how things are going just by looking at it." Sometimes you can, but frequently you may be deceived. Consider the following case. A counselor was working with a client who wanted to decrease the number of nonassertive responses he made at work. The counselor had the client observe and record the number of nonassertive statements he made each day. After 10 days, the counselor wanted to determine if the client was improving just by observing his behavior. The client's observations were recorded on a chart (Figure 4-13) to assess changes in the trend over time. Most people estimate that the trend is going downward and, consequently, that the client is changing as desired. However, if you cover up points 2 and 7 (the highest and lowest points), the trend looks flat. Extremely high or low points tend to mislead us visually when we examine a chart.

Several procedures exist for analyzing the trend in time series data, but the simplest and most useful for the counselor/researcher is the Split-Middle method (White, 1972). If you follow the simple steps presented below you will be able to plot the slope for a set of data points (Thoresen and Anton, 1973).

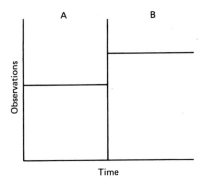

1. Change in level only

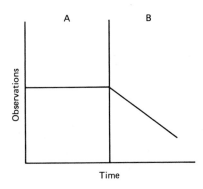

2. Change in slope only

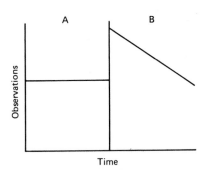

3. Change in both level and slope

FIGURE 4.12 Changes in a Time Series as a Result of an Intervention.

143

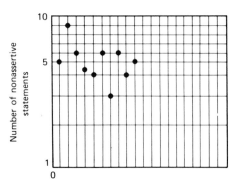

FIGURE 4.13 How Is the Client Changing?

1.   Your data should be plotted on a semi-log chart where the vertical axis is in a logarithmic scale and the horizontal is represented in equal intervals (e.g., days). This type of chart "transforms" your data and tends to reduce the variability in it from day to day. The objective is to represent the data by a straight line, primarily because a straight line can be readily understood and used.

2.   Draw a line on the chart so that you have divided the data points in half (see the broken line in Figure 4-14a). If you have an odd number of points, your line will run through the middle point.

3.   Draw a line through the middle point in each half (solid heavy vertical lines in Figure 4-14a). If you have an even number of points, this line will fall between two points.

4.   Draw a line through the middle rate, that is, the point with an equal number of points above and below it (heavy horizontal lines in Figure 4-14b). Frequently, there will be more than one point on the middle rate line. Simply draw the lines through all the points at the middle rate.

5.   Draw a line through the intersections of the middle point and the middle rate lines in each half (diagonal line in Figure 4-14c). This is called the slope or line of progress.

6.   Check to see if the line "splits the data in half" (i.e., are there an equal number of points above and below the line?). In this case

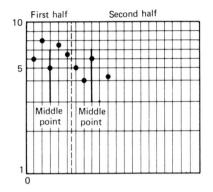

FIGURE 4.14a Finding the Middle Point.

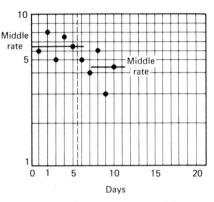

FIGURE 4.14b Finding the Middle Rate.

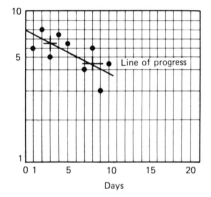

FIGURE 4.14c Drawing the Line of Progress.

there are five points above the line, four points below, and one on the line. If the line does not "split" the points, move it up or down so that there are equal numbers of points on each side. When moving the line, be sure to keep it parallel to the original line.

*Semi–log charts are available from Behavior Research Company, Box 3351, Kansas City, Kansas, 86103.

Once you have drawn the line of progress, you can determine the slope or rate of progress to determine how fast it is going up or down. This can help you predict how long it will take the client to achieve a specific objective. You can compute the slope with the following method.

1. Pick a day and note the rate of the line for that day. For example, if you pick the first day on Figure 4-14c, the point on the line of progress for that day (not the actual data point) is 7.5.

2. Count off 7 days into the future and note the rate of the line of progress at that point. In the example, it would be the eighth day and the rate is 4.5 (see Figure 4-14c).

3. Divide larger number by the smaller—in this case, divide 7.5 by 4.5. The quotient is 1.67.

4. If the line is going down, label the slope ÷ (divide). In this case, the slope is ÷ 1.67. This means that every week, the data are decreasing by a factor of 1.67 (about a 67 percent reduction every 7 days). If the line is going up, label the slope × (times), which indicates that the rate is multiplying (i.e., increasing by a certain rate, such as × 2.0).

After you have computed the slope, you will want to know if it is significantly different from zero (i.e., is the line actually different from a flat line?). What are the chances of finding a slope that is different from a horizontal slope? You can do this by using Fisher's Exact Probability Test (Siegel, 1956). As a "rule of thumb," you can be pretty sure that a slope of less than 1.25 is probably not different from a flat line. Whether a slope greater than 1.25 will be significant depends upon a probability viewpoint on variability—that is, how "scattered" the data points are around the line-of-progress. You can also test the differences between two slopes (e.g., before and after counseling) by using the binomial test (Siegel, 1956). Other methods for analyzing this kind of data, often referred to as time series analysis, are available (see Gottman and Leiblum, 1973).

CONCLUSIONS

Because counseling is primarily concerned with the growth and change of individuals, this chapter has considered methods for the systematic study of an individual. The integration of counseling research and practice has always been desirable, but it has been much more illusion than reality. A major reason for this discrepancy is inherent in our limited view of what constitutes "acceptable" research methodology. By relying on designs that compare one group of subjects to another, the effects of a counseling or training procedure on individual subjects are lost.

Through the use of both qualitative and quantitative methods, counselors can learn more about how the individuals are changing and the factors that influence that change. Intensive case studies can help counselors understand unique cases, disconfirm prevailing theories, and generate "hunches" about cause and effect relationships.

Quantitative methods that involve a series of observations over time can be used to study cause and effect relationships between counseling interventions and individual change. By using different design features such as baseline, multiple baselines, multiple subjects, and time-lagged interventions, counselors can investigate questions of causality, generalization, and replication. The variety of intensive experimental designs allow the counselor/researcher to design an investigation to answer the particular question of interest rather than choose a question to fit a preselected design.

Research, like counseling, is a process. Specific techniques, theories, and methods are useful in both counseling and research but learning to be effective at either requires practice and experimentation. However, both counseling practice and research involve "seeing" and understanding clients more clearly. Consequently, by improving your ability to study individual change, you will also improve your ability to counsel effectively.

REFERENCES

Allport, G. W. *Personality: A psychological interpretation.* New York: Holt, Rinehart and Winston, 1937.

Anton, J. L. Intensive experimental design: A model for the counselor/researcher. *Personnel and Guidance Journal,* in press.

Bandura, A. *Principles of behavior modification.* New York: Holt, Rinehart and Winston, 1969.

Campbell, D. T. and Stanley, J. C. *Experimental and quasi-experimental designs for research.* Chicago: Rand McNally, 1966.

Chassan, J. B. *Research designs in clinical psychology and psychiatry.* New York: Appleton-Century-Crofts, 1967.

Davison, G. C. and Neale, J. M. *Abnormal psychology: An experimental clinical approach.* New York: Wiley, 1974.

Dukes, W. F. N = 1. *Psychological Bulletin,* 1965, *64,* 74–79.

Dustin, R., and George, R. *Action counseling for behavior change.* New York: Intext Educational Publishers, 1973.

Edwards, A. L., and Cronbach, L. J. Experimental design for research in psychotherapy. *Journal of Clinical Psychology,* 1952, *8,* 51–59.

Fisher, R. A. Studies in crop variation. *Journal of Agricultural Science,* Part II, *11,* 1921, 8–35.

Flanders, N. A. *Analyzing teacher behavior.* Reading, Mass: Addison, Wesley, 1970.

Franklin, B. J., and Osborne, H. W. (Eds.) *Research methods: Issues and insights.* Belmont, Calif.: Wadsworth Publishing Co., 1971.

149

Gottman, J. M. Time-series analysis in the behavioral sciences and a methodology for action research. Unpublished doctoral dissertation, University of Wisconsin, 1971.

Gottman, J. M., and Leiblum, S. R. *How to do psychotherapy and how to evaluate it.* New York: Holt, Rinehart and Winston, 1974.

Gottman, J. M., McFall, R. M., and Barnett, J. T. Design and analysis of research using time series. *Psychological Bulletin,* 1969, *72,* 299–306.

Hall, R. V., Cristler, C., Cranston, S., and Tucker, B. Teachers and parents as researchers using multiple baseline designs. *Journal of Applied Behavior Analysis,* 1970, *3,* 247–255.

Hannam, J. W., Thoresen, C. E., and Hubbard, D. R. A behavior study of self-esteem with elementary teachers. In M. J. Mahoney and C. E. Thoresen (Eds.). *Self-Control: Power to the person.* Monterey, Calif.: Brooks/Cole, 1974.

Hersen, M., and Bellack, A. S. A multiple baseline analysis of social skills training in chronic schizophrenics. *Journal of Applied Behavior Analysis,* 1976,*9,* 239–245.

Kazdin, A. E. Self-monitoring and behavior change. In M. J. Mahoney and C. E. Thoresen (Eds.), *Self-control: Power to the person.* Monterey, Calif.: Brooks/Cole, 1974, 218–246.

Kazdin, A. E. Methodological and assessment considerations in evaluating reinforcement programs in applied settings. *Journal of Applied Behavior Analysis,* 1973, *6,* 517–531.

Kazdin, A. E., and Klock, J. The effect of nonverbal teacher approval on student attentive behavior. *Journal of Applied Behavior Analysis,* 1973, *6,* 643–654.

Krumboltz, J. D. Future directions in counseling research. In J. M. Whiteley (Ed.), *Research in counseling.* Columbus, Ohio: Charles E. Merrill Co., 1967.

Krumboltz, J. D. and Potter, B. Behavioral techniques for developing trust, cohesiveness and goal accomplishment. *Educational Technology,* 1973, *13,* 26–30.

Krumboltz, J. D., and Thoresen, C. E. (Eds.), *Counseling methods*. New York: Holt, Rinehart, and Winston, 1976.

Krumboltz, J. D. and Thoresen, C. E. *Behavioral counseling: Cases and techniques*. New York: Holt, Rinehart and Winston, 1969.

Lazarus, A. A., and Davison, G. C. Clinical innovations in research and practice. In A. E. Bergin and S. L. Garfield (Eds.), *Handbook of psychotherapy and behavior change*. New York: Wiley, 1971, 196–216.

Lewin, K. *A dynamic theory of personality—selected papers*. New York: McGraw-Hill, 1935.

Liberman, R. P. Behavioral methods in group and family therapy. *Seminars in Psychiatry*, 1972, *4*, 145–156.

Liberman, R. P. A behavioral approach to group dynamics. *Behavior Therapy*, 1970, *1*, 141.

Lofland, J. *Analyzing social settings: A guide to qualitative observation and analysis*. Belmont, Calif.: Wadsworth Publishing Co., 1971.

Lubin, B. Adjective checklist for measurement of depression. *Archives of General Psychiatry*, 1965, *12*, 57–62.

Medley, D. M. and Mitzel, H. E. Measuring classroom behavior by systematic observation. In N. Gage (Ed.), *Handbook of research on teaching*. Chicago: Rand McNally, 1963.

Miller, E., and Warner, R. W. Single subject research and evaluation. *Personnel and Guidance Journal*, 1975, *54*, 130–133.

Mischel, W. Toward a cognitive social learning reconceptualization of personality. *Psychological Review*, 1973, *80*, 252–283.

Rimm, D. C., and Masters, J. C. *Behavior therapy: Techniques and empirical findings*. New York: Academic Press, 1974.

Risley, T. R., and Hart, B. M. Developing correspondence between the non-verbal and verbal behavior of preschool children. *Journal of Applied Behavior Analysis*, 1968, *1*, 267–281.

Risley, T. R., and Wolf, M. M. Strategies for analyzing behavioral change over time. In J. Nesselroade and N. Reese (Eds.), *Life-span developmental psychology: Methodological issues.* New York: Academic Press, 1972.

Schmidt, J. A. Research techniques for counselors: The multiple baseline. *Personnel and Guidance Journal,* 1974, *53,* 200–206.

Schwarz, M. L., and Hawkins, R. P. Application of delayed conditioning procedures to the behavior problems of an elementary school child. In R. Ulrich, T. Stachnik, and J. Mabry (Eds.), *Control of human behavior, Vol. 2.* Glenview, Ill.: Scott, Foresman and Company, 1970, 271–284.

Sidman, M. *The tactics of scientific research: Evaluating experimental data in psychology.* New York: Basic Books, 1960.

Siegel, S. *Nonparametric methods for the behavioral sciences.* New York: McGraw-Hill, 1956.

Skinner, B. F. The operational analysis of psychological terms. *Psychological Review,* 1945, *48,* 193–207.

Skinner, B. F. *Science and human behavior.* New York: Macmillan, 1953.

Thigpen, G. C., and Cleckley, H. *The three faces of Eve.* Kingsport, Tenn.: Kingsport Press, 1954.

Thoresen, C. E. The intensive design: An intimate approach to counseling research. *The Counseling Psychologist,* in press.

Thoresen, C. E. Intensive designs: An intimate approach to counseling research. Paper presented at American Educational Research Association, New York, 1972.

Thoresen, C. E., and Anton, J. L. Intensive counseling. *Focus on Guidance,* 1973, *6,* 1–11.

Thoresen, C. E., and Anton, J. L. Intensive designs in counseling research. *Journal of Counseling Psychology,* 1974, *21,* 553–559.

Thoresen, C. E., and Mahoney, M. J. *Behavioral self-control.* New York: Holt, Rinehart and Winston, 1974.

White, O. R. *The split-middle: A quickie method of trend analysis.* Eugene, Ore.: Regional Resource Center for Handicapped Children, 1972.

Whiteley, J. M. (Ed.). *Research in counseling.* Columbus, Ohio: Charles E. Merrill Co., 1967.

CHAPTER 5
Participant Observation— Rediscovering a Research Method

Richard M. Balaban*

Participant observation is a valuable research method for attaining an intimate, close-up view of individuals, groups, and settings. Participant observation enables counselors to study a wide range of research and evaluation problems by observing people's actual behaviors and interactions with key persons in important settings.

Although participant observation produced a number of seminal works in the 1930s and 1940s, psychology's premature push for scientific respectability elevated the experiment to center stage and excluded the more qualitative approaches such as participant observation. Only recently have counselors and mental health professionals "discovered" participant observation, a method long found useful by sociologists and anthropologists.

This "new" method for counselors has two interdependent aspects. The "participant" aspect requires the researcher's involvement in the setting to gather data about a particular individual, group, or entire social system; the "observer" aspect of this method requires the researcher to record observations conscientiously. The participant aspect thus relates to the researcher's presence and active involvement as a doer in a setting and the observer aspect to the functions as a researcher (Schwartz and Schwartz, 1955).

*I wish to thank Dr. Murray Levine, State University of New York at Buffalo, for his major contribution to my research experience and understanding of participant observation. Dr. Steven Lynn was most helpful in his detailed criticism of an earlier draft. Lee Goldstein, in particular, as well as Cathy Carey, Mary Dygert, Gordon Gibson, and Andrea Klein lent their support in important areas.

Participant observation may require the researcher to enact various research and evaluation roles and tap numerous data sources (McCall and Simmons, 1969). The most common research role for a participant observer is that of "participant-as-observer" (Gold, 1958; Junker, 1960) who informs the subjects of the research aims. For example, a college counselor investigating the socialization aspects of being a student may spend a good deal of time in the student union, classes, and informal student interviews (Becker, et al., 1961; Merton, et al., 1957). The counselor may thereby learn about longitudinal development and change in student values, attitudes, and social interactions. The participant observer may also be a "complete participant" (Gold, 1958; Junker, 1960), an actual member of a system who conceals the research aims from those being studied. A counselor, for instance, may evaluate a rehabilitation program in a state hospital by enrolling as a "client" to gather direct information about program impact. The counselor may thereby reduce the likelihood of staff altering their behavior or routines (Rosenhan, 1973). As a complete participant one can learn about the effect of the program on one's own functioning and those of the patients and can experience directly the staff's attitudes, skills, and relations with patients. The complete participant role also enables a counselor to study groups that may generally bar outsiders because of their illegal or intimate activities (Riecken, 1956; Riesman and Watson, 1964).

Participant observers generate data from observations, interviews and notes on behaviors, thoughts, and activities in ongoing social settings. The researcher's active involvement in a setting is a key element of data-gathering in participant observation. Such researchers gather data from observations about the behavior of others and themselves. For example, an employment counselor may go through the hiring process to better understand and document employer–applicant interaction. The employment counselor may learn the difficulties clients face in getting jobs. If the participant observation data showed that clients performed poorly during the interviews, the counselor may revise any training or counseling program to include more client preparation for the job interview situation.

Counselors' introspection of their own thoughts and feelings is useful as data in evaluating service-providing settings (Balaban, 1973). For example, a counselor may better assess the quality of service rendered at a community mental health center by posing as a client. The counselor can report how she or he felt about the initial telephone contact, the amount of time waiting for the first appointment, the atmosphere in the center, and the understanding and concern of the community mental health center staff.

The participant observer may also interview respondents about their views and behaviors. The college counselor mentioned previously could ask students about changes in their self-concepts based on their socialization experiences. Finally, the participant observer may also develop working relationships with informants who are experienced and knowledgeable about a particular setting. Thus, a counselor in a prison may cultivate data-gathering relationships with articulate and perceptive guards and inmates in order to learn more about prison life. The guards may describe the demands of their job, their views of the inmates, and their relationships with inmates and other guards. The inmates may discuss their feelings about imprisonment, relationships with other inmates and guards, and their separation from family and friends.

This chapter presents the methodology of participant observation—the research and evaluation processes and limits of the participant observer's entry, involvement, and data-gathering. The applicability of participant observation to counselors' research and evaluation activities in a number of different settings, such as schools, community mental health centers, state hospitals, prisons, and drug treatment programs is demonstrated. Also illustrated is how participant observation can gather valuable data to help counselors better understand and evaluate: (1) client problems in a group and systems context; and (2) the stress and supports experienced by other care–givers and the counselor's relationship to these care-givers.

THE METHODOLOGY OF PARTICIPANT OBSERVATION

The methodology of participant observation entails a number of issues that shape the research and evaluation process, as well as its data. Counselors will find the following participant observer areas relevant to their own research and evaluation activities: (1) entry into the setting; (2) involvement in the setting; (3) method of gathering data; and (4) response to potential limits of the method.

The Participant Observer's Entry into the Setting

The participant observer encounters a number of problems during the entry process. The researcher's data-gathering efforts depend on permission to conduct and continue research, adaptation to people's suspicions, and acceptance for the ongoing research activities.

Participant observers generally require the permission of leaders in the research site to conduct their research and evaluation activities. These "gate-keepers" often determine whether a participant observer will be allowed to accomplish the intended work and, therefore, the participant observer must gain their support.

Even with the leader's sanction, the participant observer's entry may arouse suspicion and anxiety (Dollard, 1937, Wax, 1960). If a counselor is doing research in an institutional setting, the owners or directors must sanction the study. As a result, the staff and clients may suspect that the counselor is an agent of management and will "check up" on them (Blau, 1964). The staff may be especially anxious about the results of the study if the director introduces the researcher as a program evaluator. Just as those evaluated may feel anxious, participant observers also experience a degree of uncertainty and discomfort during the development of new relationships (Powdermaker, 1966).

The researcher may also feel discouraged by the limited amount of data collected in the early stages of the study (Blau, 1964; Wax, 1960). The participant observer's discouragement with the data and relationships with people stem, in part, from often being in a vulnerable position. The participant observer generally enters an ongoing social system of which he/she is not a part only to face suspicion and hostility alone. The researcher must learn to overcome an insecurity that can accompany even a friendly acceptance in the setting (Powdermaker, 1966). Most participant observers are subject to the fear and vulnerability of an untimely termination of their study by leaders in the setting.

Participant observers can overcome people's suspicions and their own discouragement by establishing a solid data-gathering base, communicating competence, and maintaining access to data through leader support and the enactment of an effective research role.

It is natural for researchers to be concerned with explaining their presence to people and dispelling any suspicion. It is generally true that, if participant observers communicate friendliness and good intentions and keep confidences, people will probably accept them. Whyte (1943), as other participant observers, learned that his acceptance:

> . . . depended on the personal relationships I developed far more than upon any explanations that I might give. . . . If I was all right, then my project was all right; if I was no good, then no amount of explanation could convince them that the book was a good idea. (p. 300)

Participant observers further develop relationships and build trust with the significant individuals within the setting by promising and maintaining confidentiality (Bain, 1960; Gullahorn and Strauss, 1960). Preserving confidences marks the participant observer as a trusted individual, alleviates suspicions, and aids in the eventual development of a working rapport.

Maintaining confidentiality helps relieve anxieties about repercussions that may result from the information people share with the participant observer. As researchers, counselors can maintain confidentiality in the published reports by disguising identities, locations, and attributes (Geer, 1964; Lynd and Lynd, 1937).

The participant observer's acceptance and data-gathering may also depend on the continued support of the formal leaders who can help ensure their subordinates' cooperation. For example, if a counselor is evaluating a guidance program in a girls' reformatory, the ongoing assistance of the institution's administrator and the counseling program's director are required for sustained access to sources of data about the girls, counselors, and the program site. Once the participant observer has gained permission for entry into a setting, the assistance of the *informal* leaders of the girls' and counselors' subsystems becomes imperative. Similarly, the participant observer's work in a field study may hinge on having a solid relationship with informal leaders (Whyte, 1943).

Furthermore, the participant observer's research or evaluation role may provide a license to gather data about various aspects of a program or research setting. For example, if a counselor is evaluating a volunteer tutoring program in a prison, interacting with such diverse individuals as the program's director, the volunteers, the prison superintendent, and the inmates and guards will afford a more well-rounded evaluation of the program than could be attained from any single perspective. Legitimate access to the three major subgroups of the program (i.e. the inmates, guards, and volunteers) enhances the counselor's acceptance and data-gathering efforts. Such access to data is particularly valuable in total institutions, such as jails or prisons, which are often not open to researchers or evaluators (Heffernon, 1972).

The Participant Observer's Involvement with the People and the Setting

The researcher's active involvement while observing is an excellent means of capturing data about people's spontaneous interactions without disrupting the social fabric. "It has the value of offering to perception the actual, natural human contact with all the real feelings present and unguarded" (Dollard, 1937, p. 18). Participant observers can learn a great deal by maintaining an active position for recording data, developing working relationships with people, and immersing themselves in the field or program setting (Bruyn, 1966; Liebow, 1967; Wax, 1960).

The participant observer's involvement in a setting during the initial research phases is especially effective for formulating the important questions. The researcher in an unfamiliar setting generally does not know what questions or data are important (Dollard, 1937). The researcher can also gain answers to questions unasked. Such an approach provides data through the participant observer's own experience and also helps attenuate the anxiety aroused by methods that confront people with questions about themselves and their activities.

Investigators who initially pursued interviewing in areas of their central research interests were often disappointed in the results because they found that asking numerous questions tended to exacerbate people's fears (Richardson, 1960). People also became impatient with constant questioning (Bain, 1960). Some researchers stopped asking questions about controversial issues and gained information through their day to day involvement in the setting. They felt that this approach was necessary for obtaining valuable data (Riesman and Watson, 1964). A counselor who is evaluating a milieu therapy program in a physical rehabilitation center may spend time in the setting, learn about the program routines and activities, and experience the environment, program, and people firsthand. The counselor can thereby observe and evaluate the effectiveness of the facility and the program in accommodating the physical handicaps of the clients. Through participant observation, the counselor can also informally record notes on client comments and progress regarding their emotional and psychological adjustment to their handicaps.

Initially, it may be best to ask only the least threatening questions until one achieves adequate rapport. Otherwise, one may unwittingly ask embarrassing or indiscreet questions (Dalton, 1964). Whyte (1943), for example, learned the inadvisability of inquiring too closely about people's activities before a degree of trust and rapport had been established. One of the leaders in the setting cautioned Whyte (1943):

> Go easy on that "who," "why," "when," "where," stuff, Bill. You ask those questions, and people will clam up on you. If people accept you, you can just hang around, and you'll learn the answers in the long run without even having to ask the questions. (p. 303)

Likewise, a counselor who is evaluating a jail program would be wise not to ask the guards questions about physically subduing inmates or inmates questions about contraband in the jail until very solid relationships had been developed over a lengthy period of time.

The participant observer's involvement in a setting can help provide an inside view of a particular culture. For example, Polsky (1962) found that spending time with juvenile delinquents helped him understand ". . . the frame of reference by which they perceive each other and the world" (p. 120). Dollard (1937) describes some of the skills required of a participant observer during involvement in a setting:

> He can use a good ear for the overtones in a social situation; for the little clues and contradictions in the statements and behavior of others; for jokes made at his expense; and for the implicit boundaries which guide his relationships to others, and which oftentimes are not visible until he has transgressed them. People may not tell him directly what he wants to know, perhaps may not know how to, and they will certainly not be able to give him a theory of their culture. What they will do is illustrate it for him, set it out, and in the best case be their true selves before his eyes (Dollard, 1937, pp. 18–19).

These skills require intensive observation and detailed recording of events.

The Participant Observer's Method of Recording

By becoming involved in and recording notes about activities, the participant observer may better understand a setting or program. An effective participant observer learns to balance firsthand involvement in the setting with a second-party detachment. The value of the participant observer rests with an ability to understand how the people being studied think, feel, and behave, while he or she maintains a detached observer stance, which allows for accurately recording and incisively interpreting data (Powdermaker, 1966). Without both participating and observing, the researcher would either not have access to crucial data or be too involved in the setting to accurately conceptualize experiences and observations (Gullahorn and Strauss, 1960; Vidich, 1955).

My own various participant observation experiences in the roles of participant (counselor or teacher), a consultant to human service agencies, and a program evaluator illustrate the mechanics of conducting participant observation and some of the drawbacks of this method. My data consisted of notes on observations, activities, thoughts, feelings, and insights. I sometimes jotted down the participant observation notes during the day, but typically recorded most of them after work. The following entry is from my journal:

> My typings are always expansions upon my notes. Greater detail is filled in and attendant thoughts arise in comparing present with past events. I am trying to understand what it all means and how to get a better grip on the situation through insight and possible action.

The typed report was a much enriched version of the notes of the day, which were usually a cryptic shorthand of occurrences. (See also Dalton, 1964).

Taking notes during the day was valuable because the mood of the class, my feelings, and the events taking place often changed abruptly, as my journal indicates:

> I take notes during the day, which is necessary to capture the vacillating feelings, thoughts and incidents. It gives a better feel for what happens not just day to day but incident to incident; moment to moment. Further, it is not uncommon for me to feel helpless one moment while the next moment brings great events and I am happy and proud of my students.

Typing notes soon after they were recorded is an effective way to obtain a reasonable representation of what occurs. Dollard (1937) provides a rationale for this as he asserts, "New impressions should be painstakingly and immediately recorded in writing because they soon cool off and the sensitive edge of one's reacting mental surface is dulled by repetition" (p. 20). This data-gathering approach allowed for the freshest recall of feelings and events. Otherwise, one does not get a thorough account; many details, emotions and events are lost and more and more inaccuracy occurs.

> Feel much better when I can type up the day's account that very same day—that is, come up with what I can honestly feel to be a complete account of the day's happenings including my own thoughts and feelings. There may be, and often are, thoughts and remembrances which come up on later days which I make note of and try to date as accurately as I can as to when they had occurred. I don't feel badly about this as long as I feel good about having written that somewhat "complete" account.

Such a complete accounting was often difficult to accomplish. Events and feelings arose so rapidly that it was just not possible to record everything.

The Participant Observer's Response to the Limits of the Method

The limits of participant observation entail the researcher's bias or selectivity, taking things for granted due to involvement, inability to understand one's own impact on the situation, conflict between one's participant and observation roles, and great amount of energy and time expended. In response, research relationships have been developed to provide systematic aid to participant observers and minimize the effects of these potential problems. These relationships include: (1) a "knowledgeable other" who is not directly involved in the setting but has an ongoing supervisory relationship with the participant observer and generally has a great deal of experience in settings similar to the research site; (2) highly experienced observers or participants in the research site who can check on the accuracy of the participant observer's recordings; (3) an "adversary" who cross-examines "each specific bit of evidence from which the investigator wishes to draw an inference" (Levine, 1974, p. 674) and develops rebuttals to data gathered to support a proposition.

Participant observers who write about their own activities should be especially alert to problems of bias and selectivity and prevent resultant errors through the use of a knowledgeable other. A knowledgeable other can help the participant observer gather as unbiased a sample of events as possible. As I recorded in my journal, the knowledgeable other "told me to think through what I am *not* recording." This admonition helped me to gather new areas of data I had previously found threatening. When doing participant observation in the role of a teacher, I naturally wanted my writings to reflect positively (though honestly) on my functioning as a teacher. Although I was trying to generate as accurate a series of recordings as possible, I was facing many personally threatening crises in the classroom. I found that, for about the first month, I scarcely documented events that reflected negatively on my teaching performance. I therefore inaccurately underrepresented these occurrences in my journal. The following participant observation note portrays a capsule view of situations that were arduous to endure as a participant (a teacher in this case), let alone record as an observer:

> It took five days to have the guts to face myself and make note of this incident. I let my students return singly to our room from lunch to keep them from causing trouble. I used this method because I have had a hard time keeping them in quiet, orderly lines.
> They still banded together, and made enough noise to disturb another class whose teacher came out to glare at us. I immediately sent the remainder of the kids to our room by another route and ducked up that way myself. When I returned to class, I was furious and really let them have it. I had been exposed. When similar events passed seemingly unnoticed, I didn't get angry at my kids. I am ashamed of myself for taking it out on my class.

This kind of incident was very difficult to record because it did not inspire good feelings toward myself.

The participant observer can use another researcher to take notes independently and compare recordings afterwards as a second means of counteracting bias (Levine, 1974; Whyte, 1951). Riesman and Watson (1964) learned that comparing notes of events helped a researcher "to greater understanding of his own biases and preoccupations and to greater understanding of his own pattern of recall and forgetting . . ." (p. 253). Such assistance affords a fuller sampling of events and interpretations.

The participant observer's discussion of the findings with an outsider can also help overcome the blind spots that may develop due to researcher involvement.

> We can hardly avoid becoming personally involved and thus shut out valuable data. We can help ourselves to some extent by simply being aware of the tendency of taking things for granted. Then it is useful to have someone outside of the situation to whom we regularly describe and explain our observations. The outsider does not take anything for granted, and his questions are a safeguard against growing blind spots. If we write progress reports at fairly frequent intervals, we will find, as we read them over, points at which explanations are weak or at which they are needed and not provided (Whyte, 1951, p. 510).

The knowledgeable other, who is not so involved as the participant observer, can ask questions to lend a detachment to the analysis and a counterbalance to the researcher's immersion in the setting. The knowledgeable other can thereby help the participant observer make explicit that which is taken for granted after becoming involved. One such instance recorded in my journal states:

> I told the knowledgeable other that the hostility displayed by patients in a state hospital could be understood in terms of their favorite attendant leaving the ward. While obvious, I had not thought of this explanation until my discussion with the knowledgeable other.

Thus, supervision of a participant observer's work helps provide a more accurate and insightful account.

The researchers' ability to comprehend their own impact on the situation being recorded is another area of concern in participant observation (Vidich, 1955). For example, learning to conceptualize my own influence on an event was a skill that I developed only through discipline and experience.

> When first observing counselors who were consulting in a state hospital, I noted that they seemed nervous and ill at ease. I later learned that they felt uncomfortable because I was taking notes. They were not used to people following them around and recording their activities. We agreed that I would remain on the scene but that I would record notes only after the events had occurred. After some practice, I improved my memory, was more sensitive to what was occurring, and understood more clearly my own impact on a situation.

This improvement in my use of the method ironically presents a methodological difficulty. I changed as a researcher during my involvement in the setting (Levine, 1974). Therefore, as a research instrument, this participant observer became differentially calibrated at different points throughout the research project (Webb, Campbell, Schwartz, and Sechrest, 1966).

Whyte (1951) also tries to minimize this difficulty when he recommends placing two participant observers in a setting so that "each will have opportunities to observe the other in action and to check on how people are reacting to him. This provides the student with a valuable check on himself" (p. 512). Thus, another observer can provide feedback about the participant observer's effect on the situation.

A noninvolved knowledgeable other can also help the participant observer understand and resolve the potential conflict between participant and observer roles and duties. For example, some researchers have reported feeling guilty about using others for purposes of collecting data. This guilt impeded their responsibilities as participants and precluded them from effectively carrying out their duties as observers (Powdermaker, 1966; Riesman and Watson, 1964).

Another variation of this conflict occurred when one of my research assistants did participant observation in a jail. He became overwhelmed by the needs of the inmates, and the guards persuaded him to help a number of these inmates. Therefore, this research assistant temporarily set aside his research role in order to perform a counselor function. We discussed this matter and I helped him understand how to handle his compassion for the inmates' plight, and continue his data-gathering efforts. He was able to work out this conflict and sustain a research role. Had he not been able to do so, such overinvolvement would have caused my assistant to drop out of the research role.

An "adversary" would be especially conscientious in scrutinizing data collected by this particular research assistant. The adversary would try to determine if the research assistant displayed consistent patterns of error in gathering or interpreting data and would have another observer—what Levine (1974) terms a "reviewer"—make independent observations of the events recorded by this research assistant. The adversary might also require that this research assistant receive ongoing supervision from a clearly neutral member of the research team. If the data gathered by the research assistant was indeed consistently lacking in objectivity, the adversary would reveal this finding in a section of the research report. In addition, the adversary would present any re-interpretations of the assistant's data that had emerged from analyses based on other sources.

The researcher's involvement may also impede the observational and recording process. Such involvement may be so captivating and energy-consuming that, on some occasions, the basic duty of recording events does not receive adequate attention. This problem arose during my involvement as a counselor participant and made it difficult to take notes of some events.

> *I was so engrossed in the case conference that I did not fulfull my duties as a participant observer by taking copious notes. In addition, I was so exhausted afterwards that I did not reconstruct what had occurred.*

A knowledgeable other could encourage this participant observer to return to the task of recording the events of this case conference and stress the importance of doing so.

The amount of time required to record entries is another shortcoming of this method, particularly when many events occur. Sometimes, however, there is insufficient time to record everything (Blau, 1964; Dalton, 1964). For example:

> *While I have been writing up my notes about the counseling program in the jail for over three hours today, I still have not captured all my impressions and observations. Every remembered event triggered another recollection. Although exciting, this process is both time consuming and occasionally frustrating.*

A knowledgeable other's assistance could support this participant observer's efforts in order to help counterbalance the expenditure of time entailed in the research.

COUNSELORS AND PARTICIPANT OBSERVATION

Valuable participant observation data require an effective entry, involvement, data-gathering, and response to the limits of the method. Such data can contribute to: (1) counselors' understanding and evaluation of problems in a group and systems context; and (2) counselors' understanding of and relation to other care-givers. I shall describe how these classes of problems can be studied by the diverse methods employed by participant observers including observations, informal interviews, and recordings of daily experiences or participation. I have sometimes changed the context within which the participant observation data were gathered in order to depict the applicability of participant observation to counselors' research and evaluation activities in a great variety of settings.

Counselors' Understanding and Evaluation of Problems in a Group and Systems Context

A participant observer's observations of group dynamics may help evaluate program effectiveness. School counselors, for instance, often become swamped by referrals of teachers' most disruptive students. Whether these youngsters should be worked with in the classroom or in the counselor's office is a central question. A principal may initiate an in-service program to help teachers develop skills in disciplining such students and in mobilizing group dynamics of these students' peers to help the teacher maintain appropriate behavioral control. Evaluating this program may, in part, entail having a counselor spend time in teachers' classrooms, interacting with small groups of students containing the disruptive youngsters, and recording events involving the effect of teacher and peer impact on disruptive behaviors of the targetted youngsters. The counselor's following observation reveals the powerful influence that a teacher and peers exerted upon such a youngster:

> Robert was upset and tore up his homework assignment. He hides often and runs out of the classroom. When he hid today, the teacher ignored him as did the other kids and he just got back to work. Thus, it was helpful that he did not get attention for his non-constructive behavior.

This incident illustrates that changes in the teacher and peer behaviors were sufficient to control certain dysfunctional behaviors of this youngster. However, when the counselor first began observing, this student was gaining attention for many inappropriate, limit-testing behaviors. By working with the teacher on curbing this youngster's disruptiveness, positive incidents such as the one quoted became more frequent and the teacher was less likely to refer such a youngster to a counselor. This development alleviated the pressures on this aspect of the counselor's direct service load. If counselor observations in other classes revealed similar findings, these data would provide some evidence for concluding that the in-service program enhanced teacher effectiveness in constructively relating to socially disruptive youngsters.

A participant observer's informal interviewing of respondents can also promote better understanding of the relationship between care-givers and clients. In one instance, house parents asked a counselor to study the problems they faced at a youth detention center. One basic question was "Who is in charge here?" The counselor was able to generate informal interview data by talking with people in the setting and learning about the social control techniques used by the house parents and their consequences. In this case, the counselor learned that the house parents had difficulties with certain youths picking on one another and not following staff directives. The following participant observation entry, reported by a house parent to the counselor, provides a view of this house parent's growing mastery over her charges' maladaptive behaviors toward each other after arduous trial and error efforts:

> The detainees relate better than expected when they are put on the line. For example, Gayle often complained to me that the other girls picked on her. I told Gayle that she should behave today and ignore the kids' taunts. Then I told everyone else not to bother Gayle. For the first time, Gayle did not report being hassled.

This incident shows the importance of staff members stating explicitly their expectations. As a result, the counselor's data regarding the presence or absence of this important aspect of social control helped house parents understand the effectiveness of such a technique in handling small groups of similar youngsters. These data would have been strengthened if interviews with the detainees also revealed their need for firm direction from their care-givers.

A counselor can use participant observation in daily professional life to help understand problems that arise in, reflect, and are created by the structure of a social system. For example, a counselor in a community mental health center took notes on observations, interviews, and contacts with the local school's special education teachers, students, and administrators. In this situation, special education classes contain high risk segments of the school population because the students have been unsuccessful in adapting to regular classes. This participant observation attempted to derive a firmer understanding about the special education program and the students' relationship to other students, teachers, and elements of the public school system. The following participant observation account by the counselor reveals how a lack of structure for integrating special education students into a regular class negatively affected the students and the teacher.

> I began to receive a number of similar referrals from the same special education teacher. The students were said to be anxious and regressing in their academic and social functioning. After meeting with these students, I talked with their teacher. I learned that these youngsters were the ones who were functioning up to grade level in different subjects. Therefore, the special education teacher was trying to re-integrate them in the regular classes where those particular subjects were being taught. Because of a lack of structure in the school for meeting with

the regular class teachers, the special education teacher felt "uptight" about burdening them with his students and felt uneasy because of a lack of guidance as to what the best placements would be. The students were not adequately supported in this situation of uncertainty and therefore were feeling upset during this time period.

The absence of an appropriate administrative structure lessened the students' chance for a successful adaptation to a regular class. The lack of communication between special education and regular class teachers prevented discussion and implementation of the best student placements, and the ways students could be supported during the difficult transition period. Participant observation can discover the effect of certain administrative procedures on the students' success or failure in that regular class placement. If the mission of this counselor had been to evaluate aspects of the special education program, these data would have revealed one of the program's shortcomings.

Counselors' Understanding of and Relation to Other Care-givers

The value of participant observation extends beyond helping counselors understand client problems involving group and system dynamics. The process of collecting data about these problems also illuminates the functions and perspectives of the care-givers in the research setting. The counselor's research and evaluation activities require an understanding of these care-givers. Doing participant observation may help the counselor better understand other care-givers by providing data about: (1) The care-giver's situation and job demands; (2) the support that the system gives these care-givers to meet those demands; and (3) how the counselor's own role and skills differ from, and complement, those of the care-givers being studied.

Participant observation enhances a counselor's understanding of the stresses that other care-givers experience in their work. The issue of staff "burn out" in people-serving agencies is a crucial one (Freudenberger, 1974). One such counselor studied staff stress in a group foster home by working on a number of day, night, and weekend shifts. The counselor observed and experienced the difficulties encountered by the staff and interviewed them about their views concerning the emotional demands and rewards of their work. The following account provided the counselor with an appreciation for the constant pressures that staff members were facing:

The staff's behavior is constantly scrutinized by the youngsters who frequently call them liars when a staff "promise" was not fulfilled. This "promise" may

have consisted of a staff member's nod, wave of a hand, or a mumbled "o.k."
while engrossed with someone else. Such close scrutiny and split-second deci-
sions drain the staff's emotional strength.

The counselor learned that these pressures often led to conflicts between the staff and the youngsters. This account gave the counselor a feel for the limitations to be considered if the administrator of the group foster home planned any change efforts. That is, the counselor's awareness of the multitude of demands placed on the staff helped prevent the mistake of recommending any cumbersome change efforts that would require a relatively distraction-free staff for effective implementation. Further, such data would alert the counselor to the potentially unsettling problem of high staff turnover if these stresses were not counterbalanced by the provision of sufficient supports in the system.

Participant observation can help counselors evaluate an agency's ability to provide adequate supervision to support the efforts of its front-line staff. For example, a counselor who was evaluating the supervision of staff at a treatment facility for addicts spent time "hanging out" at the center to learn about the functioning of the outreach workers. Her observations confirmed the following account reported to her by one of the outreach staff about a lack of on-going supervision.

Although my supervisor keeps telling me that he is there to help me out, I do not
feel comfortable asking him for advice. He is the guy judging my work so I do
not want to show him my weaknesses.

Awareness of this situation can help the counselor understand the outreach workers' difficulties in coping with the demands of their work. Such an understanding led the counselor in this situation to recommend that the facility's director supply regular supervision for the outreach staff and be more careful in assessing a worker's ability to contribute to a planned intervention without such continuous assistance.

Participant observation can help the counselor understand the role demands, goals, and methods of other professionals that may be similar or different from those of the counselor. The greater the counselor's knowledge, the more likely he or she will function effectively in both a therapeutic role with clients and in a consultive role with other care-givers. Further, the counselor will be more likely to be accepted by other professionals and thereby in a position to understand and resolve various problems. For instance, counselors and teachers sometimes have differing perspectives of students. A counselor at an institution for the mentally retarded used her own experience in that setting to generate data. These experiences provided information about the varying roles and functions performed by different professions in the same setting. The counselor gathered information through a mixture of observations in the classroom, counseling office, staff meetings, and interviews with staff about their aims, roles, views of problems and interventions, and feelings about cooperative work efforts with other professionals. The following data reveal how the counselor had to re-adjust her view of a situation to conform more functionally to that of a client's teacher.

> Bart was upset because he did not finish his math test. When I have previously worked with children, I tried to help them understand their feelings. In this instance, I would have discussed Bart's disappointment with his exam. However, I realized that a teacher demands more than understanding feelings. A task remains to be completed—the math exam. The child must perform well on a specific exam. It is not enough to help him understand his feelings. Therefore, much more is demanded of a teacher and the students.

A counselor generally focuses more on client feelings, while a teacher's emphasis rests more with client behavior or performance. For counselors to work together effectively with teachers and other care-givers for the client's benefit, they should understand such differences in perspectives and emphases. Doing participant observation can provide information that will help counselors work toward maximizing the utilization and coordination of varying care-giver skills and abilities and minimizing situations of potential conflict.

CONCLUSION

Participant observation enriches counselor understanding of individuals, groups, and social settings. The counselor's proficient entry, involvement, and data-gathering increase the production of cogent insights about activities, thoughts, and feelings, despite the problems inherent in this method of research. The intimate perspective and access to data available through participant observation enables counselors to discover the important dimensions of research problems and programs. Such discoveries aid in the development of hypotheses about key social phenomena. Counselor involvement in a setting allows for conducting longitudinal studies of essential events and changes that occur over time. Therefore, participant observation provides data for understanding and evaluating client problems, care-giver responses, and program impact.

These valuable contributions may well form the foundation for the rightful acceptance of qualitative methods such as participant observation. I believe that this acceptance will lead to increased usage, greater knowledge,

REFERENCES

Bain, R. K. The researcher's role: A case study. In R. N. Adams and J. J. Priess (Eds.), *Human organization research*. Homewood, Ill.: Dorsey Press, 1960.

Balaban, R. M. The contribution of participant observation to the study of process in program evaluation. *The International Journal of Mental Health*, 1973, *2*, 59–70.

Becker, H. S., Geer, B., Hughes, E. C., and Strauss, A. *Boys in white: Student culture in medical school*. Chicago: University of Chicago Press, 1961.

Blau, P. M. The research process in the study of *The dynamics of bureaucracy*. In P. E. Hammond (Ed.), *Sociologists at work*. New York: Basic Books, 1964.

Bruyn, S. *The human perspective in sociology*. Englewood Cliffs, N. J.: Prentice-Hall, 1966.

Dalton, M. Preconceptions and method in *Men who manage*. In P. E. Hammond (Ed.), *Sociologists at work*. New York: Basic Books, 1964.

Dollard, J. *Caste and class in a southern town*. Garden City, N. Y.: Doubleday, 1937.

Freudenberger, H. J. Staff burn-out. *Journal of Social Issues*, 1974, *30*, 159–165.

Geer, B. First days in the field. In P. E. Hammond (Ed.), *Sociologists at work*. New York: Basic Books, 1964.

Gold, R. L. Roles in sociological field observations. *Social Forces*, 1958, *36*, 217–223.

Gullahorn, J. and Strauss, G. The field worker in union research. In R. N.

Adams and J. J. Priess (Eds.), *Human organization research.* Homewood, Ill.: Dorsey Press, 1960.

Heffernon, E. *Making it in prison.* New York: Wiley-Interscience, 1972.

Junker, B. H. *Field work: An introduction to the social sciences.* Chicago: University of Chicago Press, 1960.

Levine, M. Scientific method and the adversary model: Some preliminary thoughts. *American Psychologist,* 1974, *29,* 661–677.

Liebow, E. *Tally's corner: A study of Negro streetcorner men.* Boston: Little, Brown, 1967.

Lynd, R. S. and Lynd, H. M. *Middletown in transition.* New York: Harcourt Brace Jovanovich, 1937.

McCall, G. J., and Simmons, J. L. *Issues in participant observation: A text and reader.* Reading, Mass.: Addison-Wesley, 1969.

Merton, R. K., Reader, G. G., and Kendall, P. L. (Eds.) *The student-physician: Introductory studies in the sociology of medical education.* Cambridge, Mass.: Harvard University Press, 1957.

Polsky, H. W. *Cottage six.* New York: Russell Sage Foundation, 1962.

Powdermaker, H. *Stranger and friend.* New York: Norton, 1966.

Richardson, S. A. A framework for reporting field-relations experiences. In R. N. Adams and J. J. Priess (Eds.), *Human organization research.* Homewood, Ill.: Dorsey Press, 1960.

Riecken, H. W. The unidentified interviewer. *American Journal of Sociology,* 1956, *62,* 210–212.

Riesman, D., and Watson, J. The sociability project: A chronicle of frustration and achievement. In P. E. Hammond (Ed.), *Sociologists at work.* New York: Basic Books, 1964.

Rosenhan, D. L. On being sane in insane places. *Science,* 1973, *179,* 250–258.

Schwartz, M. S., and Schwartz, C. G. Problems in participant observation. *American Journal of Sociology,* 1955, *60,* 343–354.

Vidich, A. J. Participant observation and the collection and interpretation of data. *American Journal of Sociology,* 1955, *60,* 354–360.

Wax, R. H. Twelve years later: An analysis of field experience. In R. N. Adams and J. J. Priess (Eds.), *Human organization research.* Homewood, Ill.: Dorsey Press, 1960.

Webb, E. J., Campbell, D. T., Schwartz, R. D., and Sechrest, L. *Unobtrusive measures: Nonreactive research in the social sciences.* Chicago: Rand Mc-Nally, 1966.

Whyte, W. F. *Street corner society.* Chicago: The University of Chicago Press, 1943.

Whyte, W. F. Observational field-work methods. In M. Jahoda, M. Deutsch, and S. W. Cook (Eds.), *Research methods in social relations,* Vol. II. New York: Dryden Press, 1951.

CHAPTER 6
Evaluating Programs: Models and Strategies

Harman D. Burck

Most counseling, guidance, and human services are rendered more on the basis of faith and good intentions than they are on the basis of whether they are effective in meeting their claims. A broad review of professional journals in the helping professions (clinical, counseling, social work, rehabilitation, etc.) reveals a myriad of research articles that are trivial and irrelevant to field situations. Also, a lack of interrelatedness and unity is evident. This is shocking because few professions or enterprises in our society have enjoyed the financial gravy train for so long, and yet been so immune in accounting for themselves. However, with shrinking resources for society's helping services, and more subpopulations wanting a share of the money (elderly, mid-life clients, etc.), the party is over, and the mandate from the general public, as expressed through legislators and governmental bureaucrats is quite clear: Counselors—account for yourselves!

Previous chapters have dealt with many of the reasons for this state of affairs: inappropriate use of group means to indicate change; inappropriate observation systems; lack of follow-up, lack of commitment to depsychologize human services, and failure to defend our output in operational, measurable terms, and so on. In this chapter we look at several additional reasons. The central theme here is a hard plea for the practitioner to consider seriously different ways to demonstrate accountability, notably by greater use of contemporary and emerging evaluative methods. We don't need more research, we need better and more appropriate evaluations (Burck and Peterson, 1975). In this chapter, we (1) look briefly at some definitions in order to have a greater common base for understanding some of the terminology, (2) forcefully contrast the concepts of evaluation and research so that readers can examine some of the "rigorous scientific" notions with which they were heavily dosed in undergraduate and graduate research courses (as they were being doused with statistics), (3) provide an introduction to some of the more recent and emerging evaluation models, and (4) present three examples of evaluation of human services programs.

TERMINOLOGY

Certain differences in definition between the terms evaluation and research lead to confusion for practicing counselors who are being charged with accountability of their efforts. Here are some definitions; in all cases emphasis has been added.

What is evaluation? It may be defined as

> the systematic process of judging the worth, desirability, effectiveness, or adequacy of something according to definite criteria and purposes. In a broad sense, evaluation can be defined as the process of deciding the value of something or as the science of providing information for decision-making (Sauber, 1973, p. 89).

> including the task of: establishing desired objectives, collecting and organizing information to assess the accomplishment of objectives, judging the adequacy of accomplishments, and making decisions for improving programs (Wysong, 1972, p. 33).

> a judgment of merit, sometimes based solely on measurements such as those provided by test scores but more frequently involving the synthesis of various measurements, critical incidents, subjective impressions, and other kinds of evidence (Ebel, 1965, p. 450).

> the process of delineating, obtaining and providing useful information for judging decision alternatives (Stufflebeam, et al., 1971, p. 40).

Evaluation, then, always consists of at least three parts: (1) process, (2) outcomes, and some (3) judgments of worth or value.

What is research? It is designed to advance knowledge, that is, to depict, correlate, conceptualize, and test.

> These criteria do not include practical considerations—they do not require findings to be relevant to current operating problems, useful to practitioners, or translate into new products (Stufflebeam, et al., 1971, p. 72).

It is

> a science concerned with the study of process or the interdependence of events or phenomena . . . it usually involves the test of some hypothesis concerning the relationship between an independent or "causal" variable and a dependent or 'effect' variable: i.e., the more a, the more b (Suchman, 1967, p. 12).

Research is concerned with furthering the individual disciplines and deals with problems generated and solved within the disciplines themselves. It involves the search for theoretical models that explain and predict phenomena of some definable kind and with the means for measuring and codifying the phenomena.

Research is

aimed at the advancement of scientific knowledge. There is no need for research to be immediately useful or practical, and there can be great concern for making sure that the exact relationship between independent and dependent variables is known (Oetting and Hawkes, 1974, p. 435).

From these definitions we can conclude that the aim of evaluation is to establish worth, effectiveness, and efficiency, whereas the aim of research is to describe relationships of cause–effect between and among variables. There is some overlap, yet there are some variations, at least in degree, that allow us to speak of evaluation and research as separate kinds of activities. Table 6-1 is an attempt to highlight and illustrate some of these differences. No attempt is made to suggest that either evaluation or research is any better than the other, or is to be valued any more than the other. The point is that traditional research models are often insufficient and inappropriate to address the many demands and constraints found in the delivery of human services.

Table 6-1 reveals that research, in comparison to evaluation, tends to be more theory oriented and discipline bound, exerts greater control over the activity, produces more results that may not be immediately applicable, is more sophisticated in complexity and exactness of design, involves less judgment of the researcher, and is more concerned with explanation and prediction of phenomena. Conversely, evaluation is more mission oriented, may be less subject to control, is more concerned with providing information for decision-makers, tends to be less rigorous or sophisticated, and is concerned primarily with explanation of events and their relationship to established goals and objectives. One primary difference between the two activities is that evaluation is done at the site of the intervention (in the field, usually), which allows much less control over all variables.

With evaluation emerging as a distinct set of purposes, methodologies, roles, and outcomes, there appears to be a new discipline being formed, which has been referred to as *evaluation research* by Wortman (1975) and by Suchman (1967) and as *evaluative research* by Nelson (1975). Clearly, the amount of control that the investigator has over the situation (all variables) is one of the important single dimensions that determines how close

TABLE 6-1

CHARACTERISTICS OF EVALUATION AND RESEARCH

DIMENSION	EVALUATION	RESEARCH
	DIFFERENCES	
Purpose	To collect information for decision-making	To provide knowledge that is more generally valid
	To explain	To explain and predict
	Mission-oriented	Theory-oriented
Process	Systems approach models (e.g., CIPP, PERT)	Traditional experimental designs (randomness, hypothesis testing, rigorous controls, sophisticated statistical analyses, operational definition, etc.)
	Treatment intervention usually cannot be reported completely because often not fully controllable or recordable	Treatment intervention can be reported more completely because more controllable and recordable.
	Concerned with relationship between outcomes and established goals	Concerned with relationship between independent and dependent variables
Level of control	Process more general—minimal amount of control	Order of events quite specific—great control
Control subjects	Use of nonequivalent control Ss often used	Use of equivalent control Ss
Setting	In the work or delivery-system situation, *in vivo*	Controlled setting, *in vitro*
Social context	Embedded in a social network	Relatively free from social influence
Personnel	All personnel (intervenors and evaluators) must endorse and cooperate for maximum impact	Cooperation important but not as crucial because of greater control over situation
	Program usually cannot be started over again	Research study can usually be restarted
Instrumentation	Usually constructed for specific program (home-made); high content validity	Standardized measures usually used; reliability and validity already established
Measurement/data	Less precise	More precise
	Use of available data permitted	Decided beforehand (pre-designed and carefully selected)

180

TABLE 6-1 (continued)

CHARACTERISTICS OF EVALUATION AND RESEARCH

| | DIFFERENCES | |
DIMENSION	EVALUATION	RESEARCH
Objectivity	Judgmental—evaluator's values are explicit and usually respected	Less judgmental—researcher's values show more implicitly, if at all
Cost effectiveness/benefit	Specific to program/intervention	More generalizable
	Great concern	Less concern
Use of outcomes	To effect immediate change—to assist decision-makers	Advance scientific knowledge
	Immediately applicable; practical	Theory building and reconceptualization
Outcome	Is a qualified recommendation or set of recommendations	Is a conclusion, for example, accept/reject the null hypothesis

evaluation is to research and vice versa. This is best described by Airasian (1974):

> Because evaluative research is performed in functioning social settings, its conduct most often represents a compromise between the demand for methodological rigor and the reality of the politics and existing role demands of the social setting. While the laboratory model of research methodology, with its emphasis upon causality, control groups, and random sampling, is an optimal model to emulate, in most program evaluations it is difficult to attain the precision and control inherent in laboratory studies. (p. 664)

In any event, a great amount of activity is taking place in moving toward the construction of new kinds of evaluative models (which are more sensitive to the real field setting), and devising more appropriate strategies and techniques.

EVALUATION STRATEGIES

In this section we discuss briefly several currently used evaluative strategies and models. The intent is not to provide the reader with an in-depth and extensive coverage of all models and strategies (there are too many for our space here), but to give some examples of the ones more commonly used, and to provide appropriate references. A word of caution: Because there are no commonly agreed upon criteria for sorting and classifying evaluative approaches into systems, models, strategies, or techniques, and since there is overlap among these categories, the reader may well disagree with our classification. Feel free to rearrange them according to your own criteria. Also, *no one* model is being presented as the ideal one for all uses and occasions, as we shall see later.

Research Design Model

This is one of the more traditional and popular models of evaluation, often used when a decision-maker wants to establish a causal relationship between variables (e.g., attribute change to an intervention). Tuckman (1972) feels that the advantages of this model are that it is logical, allows the research to establish cause and effect relationships (or inferences about them), and provides the conditions for making systematic comparisons. Here are the basic steps:

Step 1.   Identification of the aims and objectives of the program (the dependent variable).

Step 2.   Restatement of the aims and objectives in behavioral terms (an operational definition).

Step 3.   Construction of a content-valid test to measure the behaviorally stated aims and objectives (measurements of the dependent variable).

Step 4.   Identification and selection of a control, comparison, or criterion group against which to contrast the test group (the independent variable).

Step 5.   Data collection and analysis.

It is obvious that this model is derived from the more traditional scientific method, although Tuckman has done an excellent job of attempting to modify it for field settings.

Context-Input-Process-Product Model (CIPP)

This model is used to establish the relationship among inputs, processes, and outputs within a social context, in order to make judgments about worth, effectiveness, and efficiency of a system. Stufflebeam and his colleagues (1971, p. 40) define educational evaluation as the "process of delineating, obtaining, and providing useful information for judging decision alternatives." Hence, basically, the purpose of evaluation is to obtain the right information to pass on to decision-makers. To meet this objective, this group has come up with four types of evaluation: context, input, process, and product.

CONTEXT EVALUATION.   This type serves decision-making in the continued planning of an ongoing program. It is diagnostic in nature and attempts to discover discrepancies between program goals and objectives and the results of the program. Decisions must constantly be made about program goals, target groups and their needs, behavioral objectives, and identifying underlying potential problems. The results of this kind of evaluation are changes and modifications in the program that would result in greater congruence between intended and actual program outcomes. Some examples of this can be seen in the Career Information Service Program later in this chapter. The problem was documented and program goals and objectives were stated. Program evaluation and the mechanics for revision and modification were built in. (The reader is also referred to the Discrepancy Evaluation Model.)

INPUT EVALUATION.   Whereas context evaluation identifies and clarifies the program goals, input evaluation provides information to make the goals attainable. Input evaluation supplies information about the means necessary and available to move toward the program goals. It is an assessment of resources and provides the answers necessary to select and design a project. Feasibility and availability of resources and strategies are decided here. It deals with resources, costs, and benefits, and determines their best use in meeting the program objectives. Examples of this type of evaluation are PERT (Program Evaluation and Review Technique) and the Delphi Technique. In our program example of CCIS described later in this chapter the space, facilities, resources, budget, media, manpower all had to be considered in determining what the CCIS program would look like.

PROCESS EVALUATION.   With a course of action approved (context) and the program operating (input), process evaluation appears on the scene. "Process evaluation has three main objectives—the first is to detect or predict defects in the procedural design during the implementation stage, the second is to provide information for decisions, and the third is to maintain a record of the procedure as it occurs" (Stufflebeam, et al., 1971, p. 229). Of course, if the input-evaluation decisions have been clear, concise, and concrete, the process evaluation task will be that much easier. A good process evaluation will include assessment of interpersonal relationships and the monitoring and managing of communications, resources and logistics, and physical facilities. Formative evaluation is one method used in process evaluation. Again, in our CCIS program, an example of process evaluation might be how well students are performing on the various modules, or how well the student volunteers are doing as a result of a workshop.

PRODUCT EVALUATION. This has been our traditional way of measuring a program; that is, at the end or at the product stage. But, in this sense, attainments are measured during the program, as well as at the end of the intervention. "Whereas context evaluation *determines* the specifications for product evaluation, input evaluation *provides* the specifications for process evaluation. Product evaluation *investigates* the extent to which objectives have been or are being attained; process evaluation the *extent* to which procedures are *operant* as intended" (Stufflebeam, et al., 1971, p. 223). Specifically, product evaluation focuses on the extent to which goals have been achieved. Usually, product evaluation is identical to Summative Evaluation. Some consequences of a product evaluation could be decisions to modify, refund, continue, or terminate a program. In the CCIS program, the product evaluation would speak to the matter of students being able to do the performance objectives as stated.

These four types of evaluations, which are based on the types of decisions that must be made, represent some of the most original and sophisticated thinking, and one wonders why they are not used more than they are.

Medical Approach

More traditional forms of research and evaluation concern themselves with previously set goals and objectives, and measure and interpret data collected in terms of those preset standards. The medical approach to evaluation is concerned with these intended outcomes, but, in addition, is interested in the side effects of the intervention (unintended outcomes) in the lives of the recipients; in the helping relations, we cannot always be sure that our intervention strategy will have impact only in the area we intended. For example, helping clients wrestle with and resolve some choice points in their career development might well have the side effect of higher GPA or better parental relationships. The medical approach is quite concerned about the client's affective reactions to the treatment process, and seeks to explore and explain the ecological context in which the treatment is applied (i.e., the client's social and environmental factors as well as psychological ones). Hence, not only the desirability of the outcome is important, but also process and style must be taken into account (Anderson, Ball, and Murphy, 1975).

Economic Model

These models have been referred to variously as time-effort systems, effort systems, management information systems, management cost systems, management by objectives, and others. This model probably has greater control over the quality and quantity of human services than any other one discussed in this chapter. As Nelson (1975) so forcefully points out:

> . . . accountants record time spent (effort) doing direct services, or in meetings, travel, research, etc. A cost per unit time in each activity becomes feasible and quite easy to calculate. In so doing, accountants have done what psychologists and other mental health workers have failed to do: they have developed a short term, easily communicable, relatively low cost evaluation system. (p. 707)

Although this model can be extended to amount of change divided by dollars invested equals effectiveness, usually it takes a straightforward dollars invested/product (in terms of people seen, patients released, etc.) approach to evaluation, and seldom speaks to the issue of quality of treatment or impact on behavioral change.

Discrepancy Evaluation Model

Provus has been the leading advocate of what is termed the discrepancy evaluation model. According to him (Provus, 1971), "evaluation is primarily a comparison of program performance with expected or designed program, and secondarily, among many other things, a comparison of client performance with expected client outcomes" (p.12). This type of evaluation searches for differences between an ideal and actual state of affairs, or, put another way, it looks for those differences in a program between what was intended and what, in fact, obtained. Great use is made of needs assessments and transactional evaluations. An example of this model is a situation where an evaluator is called in to assess a hotline crisis telephone operation. Discovering that the number of suicides and other mental health problems had not decreased since inauguration of the program, the evaluator might point out to program decision-makers that there is a discrepancy between the intent, specific goals, and objectives of the service and its actual and real impact on the community.

Adversary Model

One of the most unusual and promising, but now impractical, evaluation models to be presented here is the adversary model proposed by Levine (1974) and Kourilsky (1973). They have questioned many of the assumptions regarding the scientific enterprise, and then drawn an analogy between the goals and objectives of scientific methods and the adversary model followed by the legal profession. Levine states

> . . . the scientific enterprise as a whole follows an adversary model, both within the narrower confines of a single experiment and within the social organization of science. By an adversary model, I mean that we are dealing with a situation in which there are claims, and counterclaims, and arguments and counterarguments, each side advanced by an advocate who attempts to make the best possible case for his position. (p. 661)

Levine then goes from the analogy to show how various judicial techniques can be applied to evaluation and research (e.g., rules of evidence, direct and circumstantial, rules of law, etc.). In a very tentative fashion, Levine states: "I do not know how such a system would work, and I am certain that with experience we would find it necessary to develop a variety of 'designs' for collecting appropriate data" (p. 672). Finally, he rests his case, thus: "There is nothing in what I have said to exclude data gathering . . . of a type familiar to us now. Nor am I advocating that we substitute wholly and completely this type of approach for experimentation. I am arguing that we need a classification for types of problems that are best handled by different modes of approach and that the experiment needs to yield the place of honor, or at least to share it, with other forms of research" (p. 674).

This is an untried model. Only one study has been reported to date —that performed by Stake and Gjerde (1971) in which they summarize arguments most favorable to a program for talented youth, and then arguments that are most critical of the program. The reader is the decision-maker and judge.

Formative/Summative Evaluation

The basic difference between these two types of evaluation has to do with the point of emphasis—process or outcomes. Formative evaluation is concerned with program effectiveness, with the *process* of testing materials, describing subgroups, defining the goals, retesting and modifying the pro-

gram. In fact, formative evaluation begins with the task of problem conceptualization and is subsequently concerned with the development and modification of the program as it unfolds.

The summative evaluator begins *after* the treatment has been properly
developed and implemented and is involved with the task of determining
how effective the program is in attaining earlier set objectives. The summative evaluator provides data and feedback for the program developers for
further revision, modifications, or applications.

Essentially, formative evaluation aims to systematically and consistently improve the program, whereas summative evaluation focuses on
determining the overall effectiveness of a program. For a more detailed
explanation of these types of evaluation, see Bloom, et al. (1971) and Scriven (1972).

Transactional Evaluation

This strategy is concerned with the assessment of the adequacy of communication among program participants. Much field evaluation takes place
in professional settings that are inhospitable and even hostile to evaluative
efforts. This resistance is seldom overt, but some well-designed evaluations
have been sabotaged by noncooperation and actual program manipulation.
Transactional evaluation takes the crucial variable of people into consideration and through a series of questionnaires and interviews, confrontations,
and other group dynamic techniques, endeavors to induct innovation and
new programs into a social system. (See Rippy, 1973.)

Categories of Criteria

Suchman (1967) proposes five categories of criteria according to which the
success or failure of a program may be evaluated: effort, performance, adequacy of performance, efficiency, and process. These categories are interrelated; let's look at each of them briefly:

- *Effort* represents the assessing of input or energy, regardless of what
  the output is. This is similar to input in other models because it
  attempts to answer the question "What was done?" Effort provides
  no evaluative answers in itself, but is related to performance and
  particularly efficiency.

- *Performance* measures the results of effort, not just the effort itself.
  There may have been a lot of effort in a particular program but no

payoff in performance. After performance has been measured, this must be compared with the original objective to estimate value.

- *Adequacy of Performance.* "This criterion of success refers to the degree to which effective performance is adequate to the total amount of need" (Suchman, 1967, p. 267). This measure informs the evaluator how effective a certain program has been in terms of total population need. It is a very relative measure and depends on the level at which the program sets its goals.

- *Efficiency* represents the ratio between effort and performance. For example, if we find that a program has worked well (that is, comes close to meeting goals and objectives), we might want to know if there is an alternative way to get the same results. In other words, the same results may be obtained with less money, less trained personnel, or other choices.

- *Process.* In many studies the four previous components are enough to satisfy many evaluators—that is, to determine whether or not a program was successful, and to what degree. But process involves checking on the *why* (the reasons) a program was or was not successful, or, as Suchman states, "Making sense of the evaluative findings is the basic reason for adding a concern with process to the evaluation study. Otherwise one is left with the descriptive results of the evaluation, but without any explanations" (p. 46).

Conclusions About Evaluation Strategies

We have now looked at several of the more popular and commonly used evaluative strategies and models. In summarizing this section, we can see that they are derived from a diversity of theoretical and philosophical bases and vary among many dimensions: from simple to complex, from generally useful to specifically useful, tried to untried. For the person who is just beginning to get interested in evaluative methods, this array must appear to be a hodgepodge of meaningless meandering on the part of evaluators; perhaps this is true. And maybe this state is a healthy one and a stage we must go through. More importantly though, as one looks at the vast array of services being rendered, logically it seems that no one evaluative model or method is *the* one. Selection of a model must depend on the population served, the purpose of the program, and more particularly what it is the program sponsors and decision-makers want to find out. One important theme does seem to pervade the literature in this relatively new multi-disciplined endeavor, and this is that the traditional scientific models used so long in psychology and education and which were borrowed in their entirety from the physical and natural sciences, simply are not relevant and flexible enough to monitor and evaluate the host of human and educational services being rendered in the field.

EXAMPLES OF PROGRAM EVALUATION

Now that we have defined some terms, examined some of the differences between evaluation and research, and glanced briefly at some models, what does all this mean to practitioners who are, so to speak, out there holding the bag; that is, the people on the firing line who are providing the best services they think their clientele needs and for which they have been hired? In their own right, most practitioners are not too interested in the theory behind the Delphi system or PATH analysis. Practitioners need instructions, assistance, and some guidelines to help them find out if what they are doing really makes a difference in the lives of the clientele, and some suggestions on how to communicate this to program sponsors and financial supporters. This is what we attempt to do in this section. Three examples of program evaluation are presented. The first is an actual career information system that has been implemented at a large state university; the other two situations are hypothetical, but similar to programs that are operational in many settings.

We will build our own model eclectically for purposes of this section. Obviously, you will see that, just as in more traditional research, our values manifest themselves in the very nature of this model and in what and how we evaluate. Let's pause now, to make our model explicit. We are not suggesting that this model or any of the foregoing ones is *the* only proper way to be accountable. It is *one* way and you are encouraged to criticize, and build your own for your situation.

We are suggesting the following five basic steps in program evaluation and will use them as the format for the evaluation of the three programs.

PROBLEM DOCUMENTATION. A careful documentation of the problem (e.g., needs assessment) enables the setting of clear and reasonable objectives for which a program may be held accountable. Documentation may be derived from existing records, special surveys, interviews, or other reliable and comprehensive sources, including experiential and empirical data.

STATING GOALS AND PERFORMANCE OBJECTIVES. The principal objective of an evaluation of a service program is to determine whether program activities are effective in reaching program goals. Goal statements describe program outcomes in general behavioral terms that are not directly measurable. Therefore, in order to serve as meaningful guides, goal statements are reduced to measurable performance objectives. Performance objectives are statements that include three elements: (1) a specific behavior, (2) an assessment situation, and (3) a minimum standard of performance. (See Mager, 1962, for a detailed explanation.)

Two categories of goal statements can be used to describe the intended outcomes of a service program: Terminal Program Outcomes and Ultimate Outcomes. Terminal Program Outcomes concern skills mastered, knowledge gained, or attitudes acquired at the time a client leaves the program. On the other hand, Ultimate Outcomes state the impact the program intends to have on clients' attitudes and behavior for a period of time after they leave the program. This latter category concerns the degree to which the intended efforts of the program were internalized into the life styles of clients.

Once goals with performance objectives have been articulated for both Terminal Program Outcomes and Ultimate Outcomes, the nature of the program itself becomes meaningful and concise. This is a crucial step in program planning and evaluation—it describes *what* the program is about, *where* it is going, and how one knows whether the *what* has been attained.

PROGRAM DESIGN. Once a program leader has articulated goals and performance objectives, activities to accomplish these are then planned. Unfortunately, too many service agencies employ a cart-before-the-horse planning strategy in program development by outlining activities before desired outcomes have been stated. Clear program objectives provide an efficient guide for selecting activities either from already successful programs with similar objectives or from the creation of new techniques derived from theory or from clinical hunches.

PROGRAM REVIEW FOR REVISION AND IMPROVEMENT. We have decided to use formative and transactional evaluation (Bloom, Hastings, and Madaus, 1971; and Rippy, 1973) as a review and revision cycle of our program development. You will remember that the former concerns the evaluation of specific activities within a program as they contribute to the attainment of performance objectives; transactional evaluation concerns an assessment of the adequacy of communication among program participants. Examples of formative evaluation studies include the following: the assessment of the impact of a trip to a factory on client attitudes about an occupational field; the determination of whether teachers learned basic principles of affective education from a workshop; an assessment of whether individuals retain information about the hazards of drug abuse after watching a series of films on the topic. Most often, a short home-made test used in a pretest--posttest design (Tuckman, 1972) is adequate to substantiate the effectiveness of a given activity in facilitating the attainment of objectives.

Transactional evaluation concerns assessment of the adequacy of communication among the participants in a program. Often when programs become ineffective, the reason can be traced to a breakdown in communication among the involved individuals. Examples of transactional combinations include counselor–client (did the client carry out a plan of action set forth in the counseling session?), counselor–administrator (did the counselor and the administrator agree on program performance objectives and acceptable activities?), and counselor–teacher (did teachers support the counselor's program by allowing students to be released from class for participation?).

NOTING AND REPORTING PROGRAM OUTCOMES.   It is difficult for anyone to know about the effectiveness of a service program without a system for documenting and reporting the program and its outcomes to other professionals. Too often, service programs carry on new and useful endeavors that are neither evaluated nor reported. Hence, practitioners do not have access to new programs and techniques and administrators receive little feedback information on which to base decisions. All service programs should conduct evaluation activities and disseminate their findings. One fairly effective disseminating process is through national ERIC (Educational Resources Information Center) networks.

This is our eclectic model of evaluation. Let's now go step by step to indicate how we might go about evaluating three service programs. The first program is an operational one, while the other two are hypothetical but typical of numerous operating programs.

Program One—A Career Information Service

In 1973, Robert Reardon, a counseling psychologist at the University Counseling Center, Florida State University, became concerned about the inadequate assistance most undecided and confused students received in that center and from the university generally. Vocational counseling is low in prestige among counselors; as a result students presenting these problems in counseling centers are usually shunted to practicum or intern students by senior staff (for a detailed account of this professional problem see Reardon and Burck, 1975). Reardon decided to do something about this situation, and the result was the establishment of a unit called the Curricular-Career Information Service (CCIS), a voluntary, multimedia based, self-help outreach program. The following actual evaluations were made of this service. (Although CCIS has been evaluated using the CIPP model, and two of the modules have been used in dissertation research, we will use our eclectic model.)

PROBLEM DOCUMENTATION.   First, a comprehensive investigation of all campus units that were supposed to have an impact on the student's academic and career planning was conducted. This included articulation programs, admissions, orientation, registration, advising, and the counseling center. Local surveys of faculty, administrators, and students were conducted. Next, the local situation was compared with national polls and reports on adolescent career-planning problems. These data indicated that between 50 to 60 percent of entering students wanted assistance in career planning, and did not feel that their high schools or colleges were providing sufficient help. A real need was documented.

STATING GOALS AND PERFORMANCE OBJECTIVES.   Specific goals were developed to meet some of the student needs. Although several were listed for each, the following are examples:

Students will be able to:

a.   Describe mistakes and problems in career planning among college students

b.   Use a theoretical model for career decision-making in developing their own career plans

c.   Identify their primary areas of academic and career interest early in their college years

d.   Locate and use information relevant to their most important academic/career alternatives

e.   Identify university and community resources available for assistance in the development of academic/career plans.

Goals and objectives were also developed for the university (e.g., the university will develop resources and materials to support the efforts of faculty, advisors, counselors, and others). For each of the modules, performance objectives and criterion rates were established.

PROGRAM DESIGN.   Having established the need and stated some goals and objectives, a program was designed. CCIS utilized an extensive library of books, pamphlets, and other materials. The most innovative aspect was the development of five modules that were on videotape and involved the viewer in an interactive way. These five modules parallel the five objectives set forth above. Creative art work with brief subtitles made this approach appealing. Also, CCIS utilized 110 audio and 10 video cassette tapes, focusing on descriptive information about college majors and postbaccalaureate vocational alternatives. The procedures and materials used in CCIS were constantly reviewed and modified as feedback about the program was analyzed. In addition, peer-advisors were oriented and trained as paraprofessionals for CCIS and were available to clients.

PROGRAM REVIEW FOR REVISION AND IMPROVEMENT.   Process evaluation included student reactions to the modules (each student was given an evaluation form on every visit). These evaluations were tallied and discussed at weekly staff meetings where *all* personnel were asked to bring notes and logs that they kept about program operations, satisfactions, dissatisfactions, and so on. If new modules had been added, each client/participant was asked to complete a brief evaluation form. In addition, over 15 local and outside experts observed the program operations and provided their evaluations at staff meetings. Also, follow-up questionnaires were mailed to all persons who had used the service. On the basis of this information constant changes and modifications were made in the service. In this case the selection, training, and performance of resident hall assistants as CCIS paraprofessionals was generally unsatisfactory because of disinterest, resentments, lack of skill. One revision was the total removal of one module and specific changes in two others. Another change was that resident hall assistants were no longer used as peer helpers but were replaced by graduate assistants and graduate students in counseling practica.

NOTING AND REPORTING PROGRAM OUTCOMES.   Numerous local reports of evaluation have been made to students, faculty, and administration. Two doctoral dissertations have been completed (see Fisher, Reardon, and Burck, 1976) based on CCIS studies. Annual reports have been made to the sponsors, the Vice President for Student Affairs, and other academic personnel. Attempts have been made to gain national visibility and to report program outcomes (Reardon and Minor, 1975).

Program Two—Affective Education

PROBLEM DOCUMENTATION. After a lengthy faculty meeting recently, many teachers were expressing a desire to learn more about affective educational programs. The principal said he would look into the matter. He called in a consultant in this area, who, in turn, called on an outside evaluator who was to work closely with the county-wide Director of Research and Evaluation. The two evaluators immediately prepared and mailed a questionnaire to all teachers in the county concerning their knowledge and interests in the area of affective education. The results of the survey indicated that 65 percent of the teachers in the elementary schools wished to learn more about affective education and 40 percent indicated a willingness to experiment with this type of approach in their classrooms.

STATING GOALS AND PERFORMANCE OBJECTIVES. The terminal goals were stated by the evaluators: after a two-week workshop, participants ($N=20$) will obtain high levels on ratings of understanding, listening, ability to reflect feelings, and communication skills in one-to-one dialogues. This was understood not to be the total meaning of affective education, but these skills were certainly agreed upon as basic.

The terminal performance objective was listed this way: Given a role-playing situation, a participant will display high levels (3.5 or better on Carkhuff Scales) of understanding, listening, and communications accuracy, to be assessed by peer-participants.

The ultimate goal was that the teachers would be able to provide group experiences with free expression of feelings, and the ultimate performance objective was that 50 percent of the teacher-participants would use group experiences at least three times per week in their classes, three months after the workshop.

PROGRAM DESIGN. A two-week workshop was set. About 15 percent of the eighty hours was devoted to didactic and traditional instructional activities; about 20 percent of the time was given to demonstration/role-playing types of activities supervised by trained observers and believers in affective education; and the remaining 65 percent of the time was spent in small groups on self-exploration and personal growth exercises. The emphasis was on dealing with the affect in interpersonal relationships. In addition, as follow-up and to ensure greater transfer of training, each teacher was observed in the classroom for two (unannounced) hours per week and given feedback about performance.

PROGRAM REVISION AND IMPROVEMENT. Formative evaluation was done by the county Director of Research and Evaluation. At the end of each day during the workshop, he or she conducted small group interviews with participants and consultants to gain information about progress, feeling, and other reactions. Also, the director had each participant complete a questionnaire designed for this study, probing learnings and perceived progress. This information was given to the consultants in order that they might make changes and modify the workshop as appropriate. All written information was kept anonymous by the evaluator. Summative evaluations were secured by an outside evaluator and included consultant ratings of individual teacher progress, as well as peer and self-evaluations of levels of performance. Finally, each week, each participant was observed in the classroom and rated as to levels of affective functioning displayed in interaction with students.

Transactional evaluation involved an assessment of adequacy of group communication, and communication between consultant and participants and between participants. All ratings were done by trained outside observers.

The final step assessed performance objectives; also, an accounting of all monies expended (both for consultants/observers, and teacher time) was completed. Side effects were noted by questionnaires sent to consultants, participants, noninvolved teachers, peers and students in classes taught by participants, and administrators. An attempt was made to ascertain those aspects of the workshop that were most beneficial and those that were not, as well as causal relationship between participation in the program and subsequent behavior.

Program Three: A Drug Abuse Residential Center

In this program we do not attempt to evaluate the center in its entirety, but just one aspect of it, which was a spin-off of a larger annual evaluation. A follow-up survey revealed that 60 percent of the males who were treated for heroin addiction at this drug abuse clinic were unemployed six months after treatment. This fact was reported by many of the addicts as the reason they went back to heroin usage, since employers who learned of their previous addiction either fired them or would not hire them initially. It was a real problem.

Alarmed by this figure, the Director and the Board of Directors decided to implement a vocational education program in cooperation with the Vocational/Technical Center. During the day the clients attended the

Vocational/Technical Center, where special counselors and guidance personnel instituted a program tailored to their needs and interests as well as occupational/vocational training (auto repair, upholstering, barbering, etc.). An evaluator from the local mental health clinic that sponsors this center was secured to evaluate the educational/vocational program. As a *terminal program outcome* he stated the goal: Clients will select a career alternative consistent with interests and abilities as judged by counselors. As a *terminal performance objective*, the evaluator stated that each client selected for this special program would be admitted to a training program for an occupation, or would have secured a full-time job. Ultimately, the goal was that most clients would uphold the responsibilities of full-time employment. The evaluator stated the ultimate performance objective this way: Six months after drug treatment and an appropriate educational training period (depending on choice) 75 percent of the clients would either have been in training leading to a full time occupation or would have held a full-time job (for a period of six months) after termination of their programs.

So, following our model, we see that this *problem was documented* as a side effect of a larger evaluation. The goals and performances were tersely stated, and the educational/vocational program (in addition to the drug treatment program) was designed specifically to take care of the stated problem of unemployment. Weekly meetings were held with all clients to secure feedback on how the program was functioning and several changes were made. Transactional evaluation took place by having twice-weekly meetings of personnel at the drug center, along with counselors and teachers at the vocational/technical center. This kept the air cleared and professional personnel as well as clients had an open forum for discussing what was happening to them and their reactions to it. The results were so good (90 percent met the ultimate performance objective) that the program was written up in brief form and sent to the state coordinating office for drug abuse, which sent it to all other centers in the region.

In retrospect, and as we look over these three program evaluations, we suggest that traditional research methods (control groups, randomness, group mean change, etc.) would have been inappropriate in these applied situations. Although we realize that better evaluative designs might have been offered, a fallback on traditional research methods would not have yielded the information necessary to evaluate these programs.

CONCLUSION

Appropriate and productive evaluation procedures can provide program administrators with information to improve services. Many practitioners view accountability and evaluation from only a punitive standpoint—that is, to determine the imperfections of a program. A more primary purpose of evaluation is to assist in the determination of activities that are effective in reaching program goals and objectives. The information should then be disseminated to the profession at large. Lowering client–counselor ratios, training more counselors, and increasing professional memberships are still important professional matters (Goldman, 1974); yet now is the time for counselors to concern themselves with documenting the quality of services they provide. An appropriate evaluation strategy is one way of getting on with this!

REFERENCES

Airasian, P. W. A book review of Moursand, J. P., *Evaluation: An introduction to research design. Contemporary Psychology,* September, 1974, *19,* 664–665.

Anderson, S. B., Ball, S., Murphy, R. T., and associates. *Encyclopedia of educational evaluation.* San Francisco: Jossey-Bass Publishers, Inc., 1975.

Bloom, B. S., Hastings, J. T., and Madaus, G. F. *Handbook on formative and summative evaluation of student learning.* New York: McGraw-Hill, 1971.

Burck, H. D., and Peterson, G. W. Needed: More evaluation, not research. *Personnel and Guidance Journal,* April 1975, *53* (8), 563–569.

Ebel, R. *Measuring educational achievement.* Englewood Cliffs, N.J.: Prentice-Hall, 1965.

Fisher, T., Reardon, R., and Burck, H. Increasing information seeking behavior. *Journal of Counseling Psychology,* 1976, *23* (3), 234–238.

Goldman, L. It's time for quality. *Personnel and Guidance Journal,* 1974, *52,* (10), 638.

Kourilsky, M. An adversary model for educational evaluation. *UCLA Evaluation Comment,* 1973, *4* (2), 3–6.

Levine, M. Scientific method and the adversary model. *American Psychologist,* September 1974, *29* (9), 661–677.

Mager, R. *Preparing instructional objectives,* Palo Alto, Calif.: Fearon Publishers, 1962.

Messick, S. Evaluative educational programs. In P. B. Mann, *Assessment in* schools, colleges, and society: Report of the conference for education editors and writers. Princeton, N.J.: Educational Testing Service, 1974.

Nelson, R. H. Psychologists in administrative evaluation. *American Psychologist,* June 1975, *30* (7), 707–708.

Oetting, E. R., and Hawkes, F. J. Training professionals for evaluative research. *Personnel and Guidance Journal,* 1974, *52* (6), 435–438.

Provus, M. *Discrepancy evaluation.* Berkeley, Calif.: McCutchan, Inc., 1971.

Reardon, R., and Burck, H. *Facilitating career development: Strategies for counselors.* Springfield, Ill.: Charles C Thomas, 1975.

Reardon, R., and Minor, C. Revitalizing the career information service. *Personnel and Guidance Journal,* 1975, *54* (3), 169–171.

Rippy, R. M. *Studies in transactional evaluation.* Berkeley, Calif.: McCutchan, Inc., 1973.

Sauber, R. *Preventive educational intervention for mental health.* Cambridge, Mass.: Ballinger Publishing Co., 1973.

Scriven, M. The methodology of evaluation. In C. H. Weiss (ed.), *Evaluating action programs: Readings in social action and education.* Boston: Allyn and Bacon, 1972.

Stake, R., and Gjerde, C. An evaluation of *T* City: The twin city institute for talented youth. Urbana, Ill.: Center for Instructional Research and Curriculum Evaluation, University of Illinois, 1971.

Stufflebeam, D. L., Foley, W. J., Gephart, W. J., Guba, E. G., Hammond, R. L., Merriman, H. O., and Provus, M. M. *Educational evaluation and decision-making.* Bloomington, Ind.: Phi Delta Kappan Study Committee on Education, 1971.

Suchman, E. A. *Evaluation research: Principles and practices in public service and social action programs.* New York: Russell Sage Foundation, 1967.

Tuckman, O. W. *Conducting educational research.* New York: Harcourt Brace Jovanovich, 1972.

Wortman, P. M. Evaluation research: A psychological perspective. *American Psychologist,* May 1975, *30* (5), 562–575.

Wysong, H. E. Accountability: Foiled fable or solution? *Impact,* 1972, *2* (3), 32–37.

CHAPTER 7
Longitudinal Research: Studies in a Developmental Framework

Marshall P. Sanborn

In any agency or institution where counseling and guidance activities are aimed at long-range development of individuals or groups, longitudinal study and description of how counselees develop is essential. Schools and colleges, for example, are developmental institutions. School and college counselors need to learn the extent to which students at various age or grade levels show development in personal, social, vocational, and educational areas of concern to the institution. They must be aware of what impact specific guidance and counseling activities have on students.

Research by Garrett and Levine (1962, pp. 430–432) indicates that rehabilitation counseling, like school counseling, must respond to particular needs of individuals as these may be paramount at different stages of development. Rehabilitation agencies are "to achieve maximal function and adjustment of the individual to prepare him (her) physically, mentally, socially and vocationally for the fullest possible life compatible with his (her) abilities and disabilities" (Jaques, 1970, p. 68). Such agencies must learn the extent to which these goals are attained, and the relationship of goal attainment to specific rehabilitation procedures.

Timing of counseling and guidance activities is therefore important and must be predicated on things we are able to learn about developmental stages counselees typically experience. In the broad sense, even psychotherapy is more of a developmental activity than a remedial one. The modern theory of Dabrowski (1972) provides a rich illustration of this, though certainly not the only one. Dabrowski regards phenomena such as guilt as dynamisms—internal forces that propel development. He describes dynamisms as having different meanings and functions at different developmental stages. It may be possible, then, to hypothesize developmental level on the basis of dynamism function, or vice versa. Thus, a practical need for longitudinal study of client development exists in a wide variety of counseling settings. Such study can provide us not only with evidence regarding long-range outcomes of counseling work, but also with implications for how to deal with clients at the time we are working with them.

In this chapter we shall focus on longitudinal study as a practical tool of the practicing counselor. Longitudinal research may often be applied to more "basic" theoretical problems (e.g., Super, 1953; White, 1961; Rothney, Dearborn, and Shuttleworth, 1938), yet our interest here will be on the ways longitudinal research can be put to use within the counseling agency to derive practical implications for agency procedures. We shall try to show how longitudinal study can be built in to routine counseling and guidance activities so as to yield data that will assist us in making immediate decisions about our practice and at the same time furnish the basis for long-range follow-up of counselees.

We shall regard evaluation as the primary goal of longitudinal research in the practical setting; but we shall try to show also how longitudinal data may increase our current understanding of individuals and groups with whom we work, and of environmental forces that affect their lives. It is almost impossible to carry on systematic longitudinal research without discovering that the process generates unexpected knowledge. Data obtained during the course of practical daily applications of guidance procedures, if scrutinized, inevitably lead to new questions, or to the reopening of old ones.

LONGITUDINAL RESEARCH
IN THE PRACTICAL SETTING

The very term "longitudinal research" sometimes frightens people. On looking at the results of a longitudinal study of any magnitude, one can easily get the impression that those who were responsible for its conduct must have had very unusual qualities of ingenuity, patience, and perseverance. Beginning a longitudinal study is somewhat analogous to planting an acorn. One never knows if one will live long enough to see the ultimate product. Yet if we are interested in how long it takes or what conditions are favorable for the acorn to germinate, how to protect the seedling from rabbits, how many inches the sapling grows each year, how nearby foliage affects direction of growth, or when the young tree first provides enough shade to sit in on a hot summer day, we may find sufficient reason to plant the seed and tend it even though we know in advance that the mature tree will shade a later generation.

So it is with longitudinal research in the practical setting. Although counseling and guidance goals are stated in terms that usually imply long-range consequences for counselees, the processes used and the directions taken to work toward those goals are matters of immediate interest. And when the long-range product is examined, it will be in terms of the history of processes, experiences, and events leading up to the culminating point. Data that yielded information of immediate concern in prior years will provide the history.

Thus, it is useful to think of longitudinal study as a *way of systematizing our methods for dealing with immediate questions.* We do not have to wait for many years to begin experiencing the fruits of our labor. At any given point in the process, we are interested in what is happening now. We can trace the development of individuals and groups while we are working with them; and thus we equip ourselves to better understand current progress and needs. We can assess progress of individuals or groups resulting from any given counseling or guidance procedure; and thus derive implications for procedure change and improvement. Finally, we can discover how changing social and economic conditions may alter the needs of counselees, and thereby keep up to date in our focus.

Obtaining data needed for longitudinal study does not necessarily require expensive and time-consuming procedures over and above routine functions of agency staff. Some specialized efforts such as follow-up studies or studies to determine developmental history of counselees before they came to the attention of the agency may eventually be indicated; but the first task, and the prevailing one, is to systematize and document current procedures as much as possible with longitudinal development of individuals in mind.

PRELIMINARY CONSIDERATIONS

As a first step in development of a systematic longitudinal study model, several basic questions about the agency and its clientele must be considered. These questions pertain to agency goals and procedures, and to developmental characteristics of counselees served by the agency. Ordinarily, the primary focus of longitudinal study is on development of counselees in areas of interest to the agency, and on the relationship of agency procedures to counselee development. Processes of data collection and analysis depend on an orderly framework of concepts regarding the agency, its purposes, and its clientele.

What are the counseling and/or guidance objectives of the agency?

The long-range goals of counseling and guidance are usually stated in idealistic and abstract terms. Blocher (1974, p. 7) for example, states that the purpose of developmental counseling is to "maximize human freedom" and that a corollary goal is to "maximize human effectiveness." Miller (1961, p. 10) cites "self-realization" as the goal of guidance. Jourard (1964, p. 60) says that "authenticity" of the individual is the desired outcome, and Thoresen and Mahoney (1974) talk about self-control as the ultimate goal of behavioral counseling. Carl Rogers (1962) has used the term "fully functioning person" to represent the long-range goal of therapy. Such terms as these, or terms at similar levels of abstraction, are often used in counseling goal statements.

These terms represent ideal goals—indeed, lifetime goals of individual development. They denote goals that are so long-range as to be not normally attainable within the limits of counselee contact with a particular counseling agency. School guidance people may subscribe to the concept of "self-realization" as a long-range goal of the guidance program, for example, but self-realization is a process expected to go on long beyond the time when school is a significant daily force in the individual's life. The best the school can do, then, is to try to provide counseling and guidance experiences that further progress of students in the *direction* of self-realization, and with skills, competencies, information, or other tools that it is hoped they will utilize after leaving school. To do this it is necessary to derive an operational definition of the goal and to specify concretely the skills, competencies, attitudes, and understandings to be developed. When these have been specified, agency objectives have been stated.

Similarly, in vocational rehabilitation counseling it may be said that the goals of the agency extend "to restoration of individuality, personality, and human dignity (Pattison, 1957, p. 427)." Yet the agency may realize that the best it can do is to try to provide the counselee with experiences that prepare him or her to return to the mainstream of life where individuality, personality, and dignity will be realized and sustained. The task of the agency, then, is to specify preparatory needs that rehabilitation counselees have and to propose experiences whereby counselees may be assisted to move in the *direction* of the fullest possible re-entry into society and the world of work. In so doing, agency objectives are stated.

In the practical setting, longitudinal study of counselees' development begins at this point. It is the set of objectives that provides focus for study.

Where are counselees in their development at the time we work with them?

This question can be a general one relating to classes or categories of counselees, or it can be an individualized one relating to a particular counselee. It is probably useful in most agencies to ask the questions with both general and individual interest. In the school guidance program we need general data, for example, on children's "typical" levels of development, at various points in their schooling, in areas of concern to school counselors. But when working with any particular child, we must remain aware that his or her development almost certainly will be atypical in some way. Rothney, Dearborn, and Shuttleworth (1938) in the Harvard Growth Studies demonstrated this fact. Those studies were completed with 1400 children; yet after the final profile was drawn, not one individual person fit the profile. The norms did not pertain to a single case.

Nevertheless it is in study of the general question that we may incorporate a theoretical system whereby we order thoughts about human development. In attempting to determine counselee needs and counseling objectives within a developmental framework we need a model to describe developmental events counselees may generally be expected to experience—either as the "natural order of things" or as a function of our efforts to assist their development. We may then assess needs, design activities, and document progress in terms of the model.

The model used may be a simple paradigm whereby we order our thinking about an agency—a specific set of developmental phenomena—or it may be a highly complex theory intended to order thinking about the whole range of possibilities in human development from birth to death. A rehabilitation hospital brochure, for example, describes expected stages of development in the rehabilitation process of persons who have suffered spinal cord injury:

1.   shock, disbelief, denial

2.   anger, guilt

3.   bargaining

4.   depression

5.   acceptance

"The Realities of the Spinal Cord Injury"
Sacred Heart Rehabilitation Hospital,
Milwaukee

It was observed by Davis (1976, p. 11) that these stages resemble those outlined by Kubler-Ross (1969) as typical of the process of adjustment to death or significant loss.

This paradigm is useful for doing direct work with a highly specific group of counselees, and for tracing their development during counseling. In the long run it may be determined that such matters as length of time in each of the above stages, inability to progress, degree of intensity or other variations of particular stages may be explained only by discovering counselees' developmental histories prior to the current problem. When this becomes obvious, then developmental study of counselees on a broader scale is indicated and broader theory will be sought.

Havighurst (1964, pp. 215–236) has advanced a model that may serve as an organizational scheme for counselors in a variety of settings where attempts are made to assist individuals in their vocational development. He describes vocational development as a lifelong process involving six stages:

1.   *Identification with a worker* (Between 5 and 10 years of age). The individual may identify with father, mother, or another significant person. The concept of work becomes an essential part of the "ego-ideal." Appropriate developmental skills include: reading, writing, and calculating; learning physical skills necessary for ordinary games; learning to get along with age mates; learning masculine or feminine social role; developing concepts for everyday living; developing conscience, morality, and values; and achieving personal independence.

2.   *Basic habits of industry* (Between 10 and 15 years of age). The individual learns to organize time and energies to accomplish work. The developmental task of industry is an important achievement.

3.   *Acquisition of identity as a worker* (Between 15 and 25 years of age). Gaining work experience as a basis for occupational

choice, and choosing a vocation are central elements of development. Developmental tasks include: achieving more mature relations with age mates of both sexes; masculine or feminine social role; emotional independence; assurance of economic independence; selecting and preparing for an occupation; acquiring a set of values and an ethical system; preparing for marriage and selecting a mate; starting a family; and getting started in an occupation.

4. *Productive person* (From 25 to 40). The individual strives to master the skills of the occupation and to move up the occupational ladder. Havighurst has not clearly defined developmental tasks associated with this or following stages.

5. *Maintaining a productive society* (Between 40 and 70). The individual sees self as a responsible citizen, accepts civic responsibilities related to the job, and is at the peak of his/her occupational career.

6. *Withdrawing* (Over 70). Contemplating a productive and responsible life. The individual has retired from work and looks back over life with satisfaction, sees that he/she has made a social contribution, and is pleased with it.

Using the Havighurst model as a basis, counselors can organize activities relevant for stages of vocational development expected to occur, and they may trace progress of clients through career development stages and in terms of accomplishment of specific tasks within each stage. They may learn to control and enhance the quality of experience in each stage through ordered activities. And if the work is documented, they may learn to demonstrate how vocational development is furthered by the guidance program.

A more general developmental model is provided by Blocher (1974, pp. 65–87). Stages described in Blocher's model are: organization; exploration; realization; stabilization; and examination. These stages are loosely associated with chronological age, and developmental tasks associated with each stage are described. Blocher's model also may be applied in a wide variety of counseling situations.

Use of a model such as the ones cited above provides order and focus to direct work with counselees as well as longitudinal study of both individuals and groups throughout the period of interest to the agency. Nothing said here, however, should be interpreted as a recommendation that any of the above-cited models be used. Choice of an existing model or development of an agency-specific model is a matter for those who conduct the activities of the agency.

No matter what model or theory is used, procedures developed to answer the question above—both in the general sense and in terms of each individual—are critical. These procedures are essentially counselee appraisal procedures. The quality of everything that follows depends on the quality of the appraisal system developed. As Allport (1937) has put it:

> (The psychologist) will strive to be scientific in the true sense of the term because he will describe his subjects before he takes any action . . . and he will realize that his counsel will only be as good as his data . . . permit. (pp. 95–96)

What counseling and guidance procedures will be utilized to assist counselees' development?

Developmental procedures begin with description of counselees at the time they become users of counseling. Longitudinal study data begins at this point also, and virtually all data needed to pursue adequate longitudinal study can be obtained through implementation and documentation of sound counseling procedures appropriate for the objectives of the agency and the needs of its clients.

John W. M. Rothney, in his most recent book, *Adaptive Counseling in Schools,* has said that large-scale long-term studies may well be left to universities and other agencies that have necessary research resources (Rothney, 1972, p. 158). Yet perhaps no one has done more than Rothney to demonstrate the relationship between actual counseling and guidance procedures and the generation of data needed for longitudinal study. His method of conduct in two pioneer longitudinal studies was to initiate practical counseling and guidance programs in local schools, and then to observe the development of pupils who became engaged in the counseling and guidance program. *Guidance of American Youth* (Rothney and Roens, 1950) describes a pioneer longitudinal study in Arlington, Massachusetts. The book contains a story of how school staff and community members were made aware of the guidance problems of local youth, how a program of counseling and guidance activities was devised and delivered to assist young people with those problems, and what evidence was obtained to show how children developed during and after their experiences in the program.

The study continued for five years through the twelfth grade. A follow-up study was conducted until eighteen months after graduation to determine whether those students receiving counseling experienced better educational and vocational development.

A second book, *Guidance Practices and Results* (Rothney, 1958), contains a report of how counseling and guidance programs of the kind that were, or could be, carried on in local schools were initiated in four school systems where they did not previously exist. All efforts were made to approximate procedures that were feasible in schools. Students who took part were followed up until 10 years after high school.

In each of these research reports it was demonstrated that data needed for longitudinal study of counselees are generated by the counseling procedures employed, and by the counselors and counselees who participate. It was also shown that these data may have both immediate implications for counselor practice and later value for longitudinal study of counselee development.

The basic model described in both reports involves five steps: (1) defining objectives of the counseling program; (2) devising appraisal procedures whereby counselee problems and progress with respect to the objectives may be assessed; (3) implementing a program of activities to further counselee development in the direction of the objectives; (4) documenting activities and their effects on counselees; and (5) follow-up.

If longitudinal data are to be adequately developed, Step 4 is critical. All activities clearly aimed at counselee development must be documented, and effects on counselees must be assessed. This step actually has both immediate and long-range utility. The immediate value is that both counselor and counselee must attempt to record the meaning of a particular procedure at the time it is implemented. The act of recording the procedure may be utilized as a way of assisting the counselee to organize his or her thoughts and reactions to the experience more coherently then if documentation were not required. At the same time, the agency is provided with ongoing appraisal of counselee progress, on the basis of which next steps appropriate for the counselee may be hypothesized. The long-range utility is in the fact that, once documented, both the procedure and the counselee developmental pattern are subject to accurate study at some later time.

What criteria will be used to assess counselee development?

When the data from which longitudinal study grows are developed through counseling and guidance activities, the question of what criteria to use is of

FIGURE 7-1   Documentation of a Vocational Guidance Activity
and Examples of Counselee Reports

UNIVERSITY OF WISCONSIN
Research and Guidance Laboratory

Career Visit

Name _____Bernard W._____ Date ___October 19, 1976___

Name of Professor ___Mr. Jones_____

Office Address ___3321 Sterling_____

Professional Field ___Physics_____

In what specific area of this field are you most interested? ___Nuclear Phys___

Please comment on your impressions of the visit:

No. 1: (Bernard)

"The visit and interview I had with Mr. Jones was interesting and informative as to the Physics field which he represented. Mr. Jones first made a general outline as to the specific classes that a Physics student would be required to take during the four years of undergraduate work. He explained the type of work and education that you would encounter during the four years of study. It gave me an idea as to what to expect if I go into that field of study. What Mr. Jones said was encouraging and answered some of the questions and doubts that I had about a course in Physics. I now have a good idea as to what to expect as far as classes and work are in this line.

"Mr. Jones was open to any questions I would ask and answered them very completely. When I had run out of questions and he didn't have anything more, he took me through the Physics building and provided me with an interesting account as to what was taking place in each department. The tour was very much to my liking and gave me a chance to observe the work being done as well as the equipment used."

No. 2: (Henry, after an interview with a Professor of Law)

"The interview was one of the most informative half-hours I have spent. I learned that the law profession isn't nearly as crowded as I had heard. He explained that the number of law graduates today is about the same as 10 years ago and that they are spread over a wide variety of fields.

"I also learned that an early decision about going into law isn't necessary. I was urged to get a broad, liberal arts education and not to worry about a final decision. English and Social Studies are most important.

"The interview was valuable to me because it helped me to crystallize some ideas I had been developing."

No.3: (Gladys, after an interview with a Social Worker)

"I was favorably impressed by my interview with Mrs. C. I felt that she knew her field very well and gave me some of the answers I sought.

"She had graduated from Miami University in Ohio and told me about its program in Social Work. She felt that there, as almost everywhere, the first step to becoming a Social Worker was the acquiring of a B.A. in sociology, but that to get good jobs and be proficient a master's in Social Work was required.

"She also outlined some of the things she had done, such as working with the Urban League in Chicago and as a case worker. She told me which she liked best and why, and the things I might be expected to do in the various branches of Social Work."

No. 4: (John, after an interview with a Physician)

"The interview itself was interesting yet not that informing. The doctor seemed either pressed for time or not very interested in relating his knowledge of the medical field. I asked questions and he answered them reasonably well with little or no elaboration. I didn't have many questions, so the interview didn't last very long. I enjoyed it yet I don't know that it was that beneficial to me."

No. 5: (Morton, after an interview with a Math Researcher)

"After freezing while walking to Van Vleck Hall, I had to clear 'security' before my professor could be reached. Finally, I entered his office and spent most of the ten minutes discussing college math courses.

"Comment on the discussion—valuable, but the professor was unprepared to meet me".

both immediate and long-range concern. Just as it is necessary to describe the counselee at the outset, it is necessary to trace the counselee's development throughout the course of counseling. Activities and procedures are based, at any given point, on what is known about the counselee. What do we look at to determine counselee progress?

Criteria are to some extent defined by clear statements of agency objectives and by the procedural model employed in the counseling program.

CRITERIA BASED ON SPECIFIC PROCEDURES.   A simple example or two may help illustrate how longitudinal data are extracted from the activity itself, and how the criteria used to trace development are drawn from the objectives served by the activity.

At the Research and Guidance Laboratory, University of Wisconsin (Rothney and Sanborn, 1966), a longitudinal program has been under way for a number of years to develop and demonstrate counseling and guidance activities appropriate for high ability high schoolers. One objective of the Laboratory is to help students learn the things they need to know about career opportunities, and one of the activities carried on to serve this objective is a program of direct interviews with persons who are actually engaged in careers of interest to the students.

Students are asked to state career fields of most interest to them. Then an individual appointment is arranged for each student with a person who is involved in the field of current interest. After some brief training in how to conduct a career interview, the students go to their respective resource person and carry on the interviews, or in some cases they may spend one or more days "shadowing" the person on the job. We are interested in knowing whether this program is helpful to the students in learning some of the things they need to know about careers.

As a simple follow-up activity students are asked to give written reactions to the visits. In different situations these reactions could be written or oral, and the assignment could be highly structured, semistructured, or unstructured, but *reactions should be obtained and recorded from every counselee who participates.* The assignment serves three purposes: (1) it requires the counselee to organize and report his or her thoughts about what was learned; (2) it furnishes longitudinal data; and (3) it provides implications for follow-up activities, program changes, and long-range criteria for determining individual development.

Figure 7-1 contains an illustration of one simple assignment used to document career visits, together with several examples of actual counselee reactions. It can be seen from the examples in this figure that a wide variety of experiences may result from the same procedure. On the basis of a large number of reactions such as the above we may determine that:

1. Counselees and/or resource persons may need some pre-interview preparation regarding the kinds of questions to deal with in a career interview.

2. Some resource persons, even though they say that they are interested, should be deleted from the list of people to whom we refer counselees.

3. In some situations we need to allow time or make advance preparations for such things as security clearance.

4.   In general, the procedure is worth doing, since it promotes for many counselees the kind of knowledge we are interested in.

Thus the reaction assignment serves as a small thought problem for the counselee concerning how he or she profited from the visit, and at the same time it furnishes us with evidence of what happens because we carry on the program. *In later years we may determine if actual career choice is related to the program, since basic data we need to discover this is now recorded.*

The examples given in Figure 7-1 involve only counselee testimony. If more "objective" evidence of the effects of career visits were desired, an instrument could be developed to assess what kinds of facts can be reported by counselees as a result of having participated.

Another example is drawn from the attempts of the Research and Guidance Laboratory counselors to systematize parent contacts. After considerable experience in working with parents, a guide to parent conferences was devised (see Figure 7-2). The guide was developed as an aid to counselors in working with parents to attain the following goals.

- To inform parents about characteristics of their children that they may not be aware of.

- To stimulate action of parents to meet developmental needs their child shows.

- To facilitate communication between the parents, the school, and the student.

- To discover points of view and other parental characteristics that affect the student's development. (Sanborn, Pulvino, and Wunderlin, 1971, p. 2)

Criteria for examining parental involvement in the student's life, then and in the counseling program, are:

- Increased parental understanding of their child.

- Parental action taken in the interest of serving counseling objectives.

- Parental understanding of the counseling program and its objectives as recorded in conference records.

- In the long run, effect of parental participation on the development of the student in areas of concern to the Laboratory.

The left side of the form shown in Figure 7-2 ("Counselor's recommendations") is completed at the time the counselor is working with the counselee. This may be done solely by the counselor, or it may be done jointly with the counselee. When completed, it becomes a basic guide to use when conducting the parent conference.

FIGURE 7-2   Documentation of a Parent–Counselor Conference

PARENT–COUNSELOR FORM

Name of Student ____John_____ Grade _11___

Date of Student Interview _____ Date of Parent Interview:_____

Counselor _____Smith_____

Attended Parent Conference: Mother only ( ) Father only ( ) Both (X) Other( )

If other than parents, explain: _____

The following topics are often covered in parent interviews. Any one may or may not be considered at any session, and others may be added:

1. Work and study habits
2. Choice of subjects
3. School activities
4. Community and church activities
5. Use of leisure time
6. Occupational choice
7. Choice of post-high school education
8. Financing college
9. Reading practices
10. Test interpretation
11. Nature of the Laboratory program
12. Part-time employment

Counselor's recommendations for discussion with parents:

Parent's remarks and reactions:

1. Consider choice of college. This may be determined by occupational choice. If he decided to go into architecture he will probably go out of state. If engineering, will go to U. of Wisc. Inform parents of elements involved in each choice.

1. Was topic discussed? (x)Yes ( )No. Much discussion of this matter. Parents took notes and said they would discuss it fully with John.

2. If John will assemble his work in drawing and architectural drawing, it can be submitted to an expert in this

2. Was topic discussed? (x)Yes ( )No. Specific plans were made for a date on which they would encourage

The right side is completed at the time of the conference. Any topics discussed not originally on the guide are also recorded. Parents' reactions, points of view, and stated intentions regarding any of the topics are recorded briefly immediately following the conference.

By checking back at a later time with parents, their children, or others, it is possible to determine whether any action was taken as a result of the conference. Since the original transaction has been recorded, this follow-up can be done accurately. Research on the effects of parent conferences where

field to get his or her judgment and suggestions.

John to assemble his work. It was then promised that the counselor could help to arrange a time for a conference with an architect. This had been discussed with John and he agreed to do so.

3. John seems to be an excellent selection to be first student in this school to do an independent study project. Would parents support idea? Explain to parents what is involved.

3. Was topic discussed? (x)Yes ( )No. Parents had some doubts about whether John would have time but it was suggested that the independent study would be substituted for, not added to, his regular work. They said they would discuss it with John.

4. In view of father's recent illness is there special need for financial assistance? In any case inform parents of steps necessary to seek scholarship support, and loans if necessary.

4. Was topic discussed? (x)Yes ( )No. They will fill out financial aid forms.

5. Suggest that John consider joining book club. He tends to narrow down his reading to science and may need to explore other areas.

5. Was topic discussed? (x)Yes ( )No. They thought this was a fine idea. Have many books at home but John is very selective in choice. They were concerned that he was narrowing his reading too much and would encourage him to try the book club for at least one semester.

Additional counselor comments: (Note particularly if parents promised to take any action on any area so that a check can be made the following year.)

Parents vitally interested. Seemed to be in agreement on all matters considered but mother is somewhat concerned about John's tendency to get involved in too many activities.

this form was used have led to implications as to how counselors should approach parents on topics where parental action is desired (Camp and Rothney, 1970; Henjum and Rothney, 1969; Jessell and Rothney, 1965).

Later, when we are interested in the more long-range questions related to Laboratory goals for human development, we have a record of parental involvement and can obtain from parents and counselees evidence concerning the impact of parental activities on the experiences and development of the counselee. Furthermore, systematic involvement of the parents in current activities paves the way for securing their cooperation when historical or follow-up data are needed. This gives an advantage to those who must secure 100 percent follow-up returns from a population or from a representative sample of that population some time in the future.

These two examples have shown how objectives, procedures, and criteria are interrelated in the formulation and conduct of longitudinal study. So long as the study can be related to specific goal-oriented experiences and outcomes, then the data are of immediate interest. So long as each activity documented is related to long-term goals, then the data are of long-term interest. Criteria in either case are specific to the activity being documented.

LONG-RANGE USE OF A SPECIFIC PROCEDURE.   Two related studies that were carried on over a seven year period may serve to illustrate the relationship between immediate and long-range use of criteria. The first study (Sanborn and Niemiec, 1971) was an attempt to determine if cumulative records of counselees could be used to gain knowledge about certain values thought to be related to career choice. The investigators classified historical data including the content of personal essays; record of activities, interests, reading, and other pursuits; answers given by the counselees in past years to structured personal data questionnaires; reports of parent conferences; and scholastic records in order to arrive at a ranking of materialistic, social, and personal values for each subject. The matter of immediate interest was whether in counseling the cumulative record data could be used to assist counselees in identifying their own values, even though statements about the values had not been solicited directly in the past. Later it became a matter of interest to know whether the value rankings established previously had remained stable. In the second study, McMahon (1973) followed up the original subjects seven years after high school to discover whether their value priorities had remained the same. He established the fact that although certain patterns of stability existed, there were certain changes that happened more often than would be expected by chance. It appeared from the results of the two studies that counselors could talk with youngsters about their values with some confidence that they would have stability into early adult life, but that certain values (e.g., recognition) may be given less importance in later years than they had while the individual was in school. Thus, the follow-up may enrich our understanding of immediate data.

The criteria used in the first study were matchings of value hierarchies obtained by direct and indirect methods. In other words, the research established that the things subjects said about their values in a direct structured interview, and the things their counselors said, could be verified by study of four-year cumulative records of things they had said and done in the past. That is, it would be possible to assist counselees in value clarification by using existing appraisal data. The criterion for the second study was matching of the original value hierarchies with those obtained by direct structured interviews seven years later. In each case the criteria were specific to a particular counseling activity, and to a particular issue in career development of young people.

CRITERIA REFLECTING GENERAL AGENCY GOALS. Long-range criteria are often related more to global objectives of counseling than to one specific activity. When this is the case, criteria may be more difficult to establish. Ultimately, the selection of such criteria involves operationalizing concepts about broad objectives of counseling. If we take the broadest view, our objectives are as broad as life itself, and this would be reflected in the criteria selected. It is necessary to determine what constitutes desirable general outcomes of counseling and what criteria can be used to assess them. At different times by different researchers a wide variety of criteria have been employed. Travers (1960) grouped these criteria into two general categories:

Subjective, for example:

Personal happiness

Satisfaction with status

Satisfaction with vocational choice

Sense of social adequacy

Satisfaction with counseling received

Objective, for example:

Improved achievement

Personal adjustment

Emotional stability

Occupational choice

Social adjustment

In assessment of any of the above, many types of measures have been used.

There are certain difficulties associated with assessment of any of the long-range criteria thus far utilized. Most subjective criteria, for example, involve securing testimony of clientele but it may be difficult to substantiate this testimony. Misinterpretations, exaggerations, understatements, and deliberate or unintentional deceptions can occur. Furthermore, testimony on such factors as happiness or satisfaction with status may be transitory. A respondent may be happy with his or her status one day, but not the next. Satisfaction with counseling received does not suffice either as evidence of the effectiveness of the process or as evidence of counselee development. Leona Tyler concluded after a survey of research based on client satisfaction that clients like counseling by approximately a three to one margin. She observed that "the same sort of evidence can be obtained for the success of fortune-tellers, phrenologists and faith healers" (1969, p. 218).

Objective criteria have limitations too. In studies of school and college counseling, for example, academic achievement, as reflected by class grades, has often been utilized as a criterion of student development or counseling success; but use of this measure rests on the assumption that getting good grades reflects healthy adjustment or development. This is not necessarily true. Assessment of emotional "adjustment" or comfort involves a similar difficulty. At least one theorist (Dabrowski, 1972) asserts that emotional upset precedes positive development. Furthermore, assessment of "appropriate" vocational plans requires some knowledge or judgment about what is appropriate; emotional and social factors may be culturally or situationally specific, and therefore difficult to judge in terms of appropriateness. Shosteck (1955), for example, concluded that the guidance program in one large city needed improvement because the proportion of high schoolers with professional level vocational aspirations was more than twice as large as the proportion of the existing work force actually engaged in professional level occupations. Only in retrospect could it be discovered that by the time those youngsters could have completed post-high school training for professions, the proportion of persons in the work force who were classified as professionals had more than doubled! What appeared to be inappropriate at the time of Shosteck's study seemed appropriate later.

Conjoint use of both objective and subjective criteria may be employed to correct weaknesses of each. *An additional help is to have data from previous counselee contacts that sheds light on the meaning of current assessments,* whether they be subjective or objective. Longitudinal documentation furnishes these data. Suppose, for example, we are to follow up all counselees who graduated from high school in 1967. Among other things, we are interested in finding out about the relationship of past counseling and guidance activities to their vocational choices and achievements. We ask the following question, among others, on a printed questionnaire:

Check below the response that best reflects your attitude about high school counseling and guidance activities you took part in for the purpose of *choosing an appropriate vocation:*

( )   very helpful

( )   helpful, but not enough

( )   of very little help

( )   did more harm than good

When all the questionnaires are returned, we find that we have responses to this question from Bernard, Henry, Gladys, John, and Morton (see 1967 Career Visit comments included in Figure 7-1). If the senior career visits were the *only* career guidance experiences these persons had while in high school, we might speculate that they would answer the above question differently from one another. Because we have data from the 1967 activity, we may also speculate *why* each person answers as he or she does. If other career guidance and counseling events took place during high school, and if these have been adequately documented, such events can be taken into account in evaluating the meaning of the follow-up responses. Although the question yields only subjective data, we may find it possible to support the data by means of both subjective and objective data from the past. Reasons for expressed satisfaction or dissatisfaction may be hypothesized, and factors related to current viewpoints may be traced.

When do we cease to assume significant influence of counseling?

If we look at broad goal statements made by various leading writers in the field, they seem to bear the implication that if we are to look for counselee development in terms of broad goals, we must do so for some time into the future. Consider the following examples:

The purpose of counseling is to help people to become self-sufficient and effective problem solvers. (J. D. Krumboltz and C. E. Thoresen, 1969, p. 209)

The development of a reasonable independence in a client who takes responsibility for himself, his behavior, his choices and decisions, and his values and goals. (C. H. Patterson, 1962, p. 13)

> We will be working with you, your parents, and your teachers over a period of years to see if we can help you to understand yourself better than you otherwise might, so that when you have to make important decisions you will be better prepared to do so. (J. W. M. Rothney, 1972, p. 54)

> Assist the student to choose and make progress towards educational and vocational objectives which will yield maximum satisfaction . . . and aid the student to set his aspirations in terms of his potentialities. (E. G. Williamson and E. S. Bordin, 1941)

Such words and phrases as "self-sufficient," "effective problem solver," "independence," "takes responsibility," "make important decisions," and "maximum satisfaction" all seem to refer to characteristics that counselees would manifest in some durable way after counseling has terminated. Although perhaps no agency retains its counseling relationship with the typical client long enough to view the "finished product," any serious attempt to describe the impact of counseling on persons must involve some determination of whether directions established during counseling are pursued after counseling. But how long can we realistically expect to secure meaningful data from past clients?

Rothney (1963) illustrated that the intervention of time, with its concomitant cultural change, introduces difficulty in establishing relationship between counseling and later life.

A recent study by Hartz (1973) has shown that a number of client variables of interest to counseling researchers are systematically related to the historical context in which counselees live. He compared ten-year follow-up data obtained from subjects of the Wisconsin Counseling Study, who graduated from high school in 1951, with similar data obtained from a matched group of subjects from the Research and Guidance Laboratory who graduated in 1963. Results revealed systematic differences between the two groups. The 1963 graduates were less often married, married later, had fewer children, had higher levels of education, were less often active in civic affairs, and were more widely dispersed geographically than their 1951 counterparts. On subjective criteria they reported different reasons for choosing their vocations; they were more ambivalent regarding their current status; they were less satisfied with previous education and counseling; and they were less satisfied with their experiences during the first 10 years after high school than were the 1951 subjects.

In a variety of other ways the subjects revealed differences that could be associated with the different historical contexts in which they lived. Although the global criteria of interest to school counselors have probably not changed much during the 20 year span, perhaps beliefs about appropriateness should have changed. What does it mean, for example, if we discover that in current time persons are more often deciding not to marry within ten years after high school graduation; or to marry at a later time? What does it mean if we discover that they are less satisfied with their current status, or have less confidence in their career choices than has been true in the past? What are the implications for counselors? These are the kinds of questions that can be raised by studying progress of counselees over a long period of time.

Perhaps there is no general answer to the question of how many years follow-up should be carried on beyond termination of counseling. Each agency must determine its own answer, based on its own objectives. However, a universal policy should be that when agency goals involve counselee development beyond the time when the counseling is done, study of clientele beyond counseling is indicated. Serious study of follow-up data is almost certain to stimulate new thinking about the appropriateness of agency goals and procedures.

DEVELOPING A LONGITUDINAL RESEARCH PLAN

In describing a model for longitudinal research we will emphasize documentation of counselee development related to or concomitant with specific agency activities. It is probably obvious to the reader by this time that we advocate the process of defining specific objectives (within the limits of long-range goals of the agency), implementing activities designed to meet those objectives, and incorporating into each activity a means for recording what transpired and what was accomplished. This is done activity by activity. In the long run, data on general agency goals will be the result. In the meantime data on current counselee experiences and reactions will accrue.

There are only a few basic principles which, if adhered to, greatly facilitate longitudinal study of counselees. These same principles facilitate current work with counselees, since they have the effect of providing focus for current contacts and stimulating both counselor and counselee thinking regarding the meaning of counseling experiences.

Concentrate on Agency Goals

We have already discussed the advantage of specifying the general counseling goals of interest to the agency. We have discussed also the advantage of using some theory or model whereby developmental phenomena can be classified. Once these have been at least tentatively accomplished, they provide guidelines for the kinds of activities to incorporate and the kinds of data needed for tracing progress.

At the University of Wisconsin Research and Guidance Laboratory, for example, general developmental goals include: (1) assisting counselees to learn about their own abilities, interests, values, and motives, especially as these are relevant to choosing careers and setting life directions; (2) assisting counselees to learn about and take advantage of developmental, educational, and career opportunities open to them; and (3) assisting parents and teachers in providing counselees with appropriate experiences related to the above. All activities generated by the Laboratory are designed to serve one or more of the above objectives. All records kept in counselee cumulative files are obtained during the course of the activities themselves.

As might be expected when working with thousands of young people over a number of years, Laboratory counselors become involved in a wide variety of "problems" or "crises" in the counselees' lives that are brought to the attention of the agency by the counselees and not by means of systematic agency procedures. These matters are not recorded and are not incorporated in gross longitudinal studies, because they are usually not relevant to any of the agency goals. Over a period of years, for example, the staff may become aware of a number of unwanted pregnancies and provide advice and counsel to persons concerned; but no attempt is made to document and classify such matters in terms of agency objectives. Instead, longitudinal records are concentrated on positive development in areas of general interest to the agency.

In an agency where goals are to provide sex education, or to assist women in reaching decisions about whether to become pregnant or what to do about unwanted pregnancy, then some record of unwanted pregnancies, procedures utilized in working with clients, and outcomes would be relevant. On the other hand, there would be no meaningful way in such an agency to classify and utilize data of the type systematically collected at the Research and Guidance Laboratory, even though such information may become available from time to time in individual cases.

This is not to suggest that incidental data be ignored by the agency. Sometimes it may be possible by means of such data to identify common needs or problems of clientele that are not being addressed but are within the scope of the agency. When this happens, new agency goals and activities can be instigated, and some means for incorporating new data into the longitudinal picture can be developed. Until these have been systematized, however, it is suggested that existing agency goals provide the limits for longitudinal data collection.

Document all Relevant Activities

Any activity carried on by the counselor with the counselee, or any activity the counselee becomes engaged in as a part of the total counseling process, should be documented. The only exceptions would be activities not germane to agency goals. Ideally, the documentation process will include some provision for the persons involved in an activity to report their evaluative reactions at the time the activity takes place or immediately afterward. Figures 7-1 and 7-2 contain examples of brief methods for documenting specific activities. In each case the method is designed to record who was involved, what transpired, when, and, from the viewpoint of the recorder, what results were experienced. Once these things have been recorded it is possible to check viewpoints of others involved, if desirable, or to follow up at a later time to attempt to determine effects of the activity.

Documentation procedures need be neither lengthy nor laborious. Most of the time they can be completed by the recipients of counseling rather than by agency staff. The immediate effect is to encourage participants to think about what has happened and what importance, if any, the activity has for them. In the long run it is possible to review accurately the activities of the agency with any given counselee, group of counselees, or with other persons who participate in the counseling process.

Use a Variety of Data Sources and Types

Some of the data necessary in longitudinal study of client development can come only from the counselee. Some may best be obtained from the professional viewpoint of the counselor. Often the best source is a "significant other"—parent, teacher, spouse, or perhaps a clinical resource person. Usually no single source is adequate, and information on a single issue must be obtained from several sources. Data that are all obtained from a single viewpoint—say, the counselor's—on the basis of a single activity, such as the interview, are not likely to appear substantial over time.

It is usually possible to secure both objective and subjective data concerning counselee development, and both types should be sought. If, for example, a counselor has suggested to the parents of a counselee that a certain action should be taken by them, it is one thing to secure their reaction to the suggestion, but quite another to discover what action the parents actually take. It is yet another to try to assess effect of the action on the counselee. It may be desirable to get some testimony from the counselee regarding the effect; but if some learning goal was intended, some way to try to assess what was learned is also needed.

A potential effect of involving all functionaries in the documentation process is that all of them may understand better what the counseling process is intended to accomplish and what kinds of progress are being made. Later, if asked to recall their own roles in a particular activity and to relate the activity to a current situation, they may be better able to provide meaningful information.

Specify Data Sources

Any instrument used to document a counseling activity should be designed to secure exact information regarding who was involved, when the activity took place, where, who is completing the report, and what techniques were used to secure information, as well as any special circumstances of note. Any of these factors may be essential information in understanding the significance of an activity, and any of them may be necessary at some later time if follow-up information is desired.

Provide for Repeated Assessments

In order to derive a developmental picture it is necessary to secure repeated assessments over time, of the phenomena of interest. Whether the problem is to assess school achievement, vocational development, attitudes about the self, interpersonal relationships, self-sufficiency, or future aspirations, activities that yield parallel data over time are needed.

In some instances it may be important to provide for repeated assessment with exactly the same instrument. An inventory such as the Adjective Check List (Gough and Heilbrun, 1965), for example, or the Mooney Problem Check List (Mooney and Gordon, 1950) may be repeated when counselee responses to exactly the same items are desired. In other instances, however, parallel data may be obtained using dissimilar sources. As a simple example, stated vocational plans may be related to later vocational training, to jobs actually engaged in, or to stated future plans. How repeated assessments are to be obtained can best be determined by the agency staff in terms of what information is desired and what is feasible to secure within the limits of agency procedures and goals.

Revise Meaningless Activities

It may seem unnecessary to suggest that meaningless activities be eliminated or revised. Yet one of the results of serious longitudinal study of counselee development is likely to be that meaningless activities come to light. Sometimes these are activities that have long been engaged in and subscribed to by agency staff. It may be discovered, for example, that no relationship can be established between results of a certain vocational interest inventory administered during counseling and actual vocational choices made by counselees at some later time. When this becomes obvious, either the inventory or the way it is used in counseling should be questioned. Or it may be discovered that a certain activity designed to elicit action on the part of counselees or significant others seldom or never can be associated with actions desired. When this is the case, the activity should be changed or eliminated. It may be learned that a certain procedure does not lead us to any understanding of how individual counselees differ from one another. We may, for example, administer a certain mental test to a number of counselees only to discover that there is little or no variability of performance, or we may ask a certain question on a follow-up questionnaire to which virtually all counselees respond alike. If so, then we may eliminate the measure unless there is some compelling reason to identify the few who deviate from the many.

In longitudinal study as well as in counseling, the primary reason for identifying and eliminating meaningless procedures is to economize on time and improve competency. Time is probably the most expensive commodity in counseling, and time probably vies only with competency as the commodity in shortest supply. Both commodities may be enhanced when uselessness is eliminated. In general, there are perhaps three indicators that an activity may be meaningless: (1) no relationship between the activity and developmental phenomena of interest to the agency; (2) no change in behavior of counselees or significant others as a result of the activity; (3) no meaningful variability in the data yielded by the activity. If any one of these indicators is present, then the activity should be questioned.

Secure 100 Percent Response

If data collection procedures are routinely built in to counseling activities carried on by the agency, then longitudinal records can be developed concerning the total population of counselees during the time they are involved in counseling. Ideally, the study of these data would involve the total population. For certain purposes, however, it may be neither feasible nor necessary to work with the total population. Instead, a sample can be identified, with due care taken to ensure that the sample can be defended as representative of the population under study.

A number of sources are available that contain descriptions of sound sampling procedures (e.g., Hillway, 1964, pp. 195–199; Wallen, 1974, pp. 84–110). Here we shall stress only that once a sample has been identified as representative, data from some proportion of that sample is not necessarily representative. It is especially true in follow-up studies that researchers often encounter difficulty securing returns from all members of the group under study. No matter how respondents can be shown to resemble the non-respondents, they differ systematically in that they responded. The meaning of this difference is a matter of pure speculation. Therefore, it is important to secure data from all members of the group.

Experiences at the Research and Guidance Laboratory have led us to believe that if during the course of counseling the counselees have regularly participated in the longitudinal study process, their participation in post-counseling follow-up is easier to secure. Whenever counseling activities are documented, it is probably useful in the long run to discuss with counselees or others who furnish the data how the information is being used at the time and why the data they furnish are important. It is also desirable to inform them that the agency will probably be contacting them in the future to find out their current status and some of their thoughts about the counseling they received. If these things are done at the time the agency is serving the counselees, the likelihood may be improved that at some later time the counselees will recognize the importance of the information they can supply.

Analyze Both Case Data and Gross Data

One of the advantages of systematic collection of longitudinal data is that the information obtained can be analyzed either in terms of groups or case by case. Both kinds of analysis are useful. It may be important, for example, to try to describe typical developmental characteristics of groups served by the agency, or to determine in some general way the effects of a given activity on agency clientele. Useful general differentiations may be discovered regarding a wide variety of classes or categories of counselees —males, females, gifted and talented, emotionally disturbed, parents, adolescents, disabled persons, retired persons, and so on. Yet when the data regarding a single individual are analyzed, it is almost certain that generalizations regarding the group to which that individual belongs will be modified. Gross data analysis is useful for description or understanding of groups, but is of very little use for understanding any particular individual.

Usually when a case is considered in depth it will be discovered that data not supplied through the usual agency activities are necessary to a further understanding of the individual. Methods used in developing an adequate case study are presented by Rothney (1968) together with several examples of case studies of school and college age persons. R. W. White (1961) has provided excellent long-range studies of "normal" persons with complete discussion of case study methods he used and applications of case data to theory. Amble and Bradley (1973) illustrate, among other aspects, the effects of differing viewpoints on the interpretation of case data. Study of these three sources should provide the reader with a keen sense of humility regarding generalizations about people, an understanding of the uses of the case study in counseling, and some knowledge of useful methods for case research and analysis.

CONCLUSION

Longitudinal study of counselee development should be regarded as an essential feature of any agency where counselee development is a goal. Systematic longitudinal study is useful not only for understanding long-range developmental phenomena of interest to the agency, but also for making current decisions about counseling practice. The primary advantage of longitudinal study is that it provides data necessary for both immediate and long-range evaluation. These data can be used to answer questions about populations or specified target groups of agency clientele, or they can be used in systematizing knowledge of individual cases.

Longitudinal study can be implemented in a counseling agency as a routine feature of the counseling activities regularly carried on. The initial task is to develop systematic documentation procedures whereby agency activities with counselees can be recorded as they occur. Documentation should include a record of who was involved, what transpired, when, and what effects of interest to the agency and/or the counselee were experienced. The kinds of activities to be documented, and the kinds of effects to be recorded, are those pertaining to the general counseling goals of the agency.

The process of gathering longitudinal data need not be laborious or time-consuming. Actually, a well-planned documentation procedure may save time or enable agency staff to utilize time more efficiently than it otherwise would. Figure 7-2 illustrates how a method for planning efficient use of parent conference time doubles also as a documentation procedure feeding into the data on activities and consequences for counselee development. Figure 7-1 shows how data may be obtained from the counselee in the form of a brief record of his or her own reactions to a vocational guidance procedure. In each illustration, efficiency may be improved through organization of thinking and planning of the counselor or counselee. An inventive counseling staff may produce a variety of simple procedures such as these that tend to help them organize current work more efficiently, keep counseling activities focused on counseling goals, and at the same time furnish longitudinal data.

It is likely that most counseling activities of an agency can be documented adequately only if the agency staff themselves devise the procedures to be used. The kinds of activities engaged in, the purposes they are intended to serve, and the relationship of each to agency counseling goals must be examined. Criteria for assessing consequences of each activity and for tracing progress of counselees must be established. The process of accomplishing these tasks is almost certain to generate among staff members important questions about how staff time is used and what effects ought to be expected of time use. Thus, even at the outset of a longitudinal study plan, agency staff are encouraged to think systematically about the efficiency of what they do.

Later, when longitudinal data begin to accrue, counselors can start to examine immediate effects of counseling activities. At this time another series of questions is almost certain to arise. Most of these questions will concern whether what agency staff and counselees are spending time on can actually be defended in terms of progress toward counseling goals. On the basis of evidence, revisions in counseling procedure can then be proposed. In this way systematic longitudinal data may provide impetus for more economical use of agency time and resources.

REFERENCES

Allport, G. W. *Personality: A psychological interpretation.* New York: Holt, Rinehart and Winston, 1937.

Amble, B., and Bradley, R. *Pupils as persons.* New York and London: Chandler, 1973.

Blocher, D. H. *Developmental counseling.* New York: Ronald Press, 1974.

Camp, W. L., and Rothney, J. W. M. Parental response to counselors' suggestions. *The School Counselor,* 1970, *17,* 200–202.

Dabrowski, K. *Psychoneurosis is not an illness.* London: Gryf, 1972.

Davis, E. A. Case studies of recent quadraplegics. Unpublished M. S. paper, University of Wisconsin, Madison, 1976.

Garrett, J. E., and Levine, E. S. *Psychological practices with the physically disabled.* New York: Columbia University Press, 1962.

Gough, H., and Heilbrun, A. B., Jr. *The Adjective Check List.* Palo Alto, Calif.: Consulting Psychologists Press, 1965.

Hartz, J. D. A cross-historical comparison of ten year follow-up studies of talented young people. Unpublished Ph. D. Dissertation, University of Wisconsin, Madison, 1973.

Havighurst, R. J. Youth in exploration and man emergent. In H. Borow (ed.), *Man in a world at work,* Boston: Houghton-Mifflin, 1964.

Henjum, R. J., and Rothney, J. W. M. Parental action on counselors' suggestions. *The Vocational Guidance Quarterly,* 1969, *10,* 54–58.

Hillway, T. *Introduction to research.* Boston: Houghton Mifflin, 1964.

231

Jaques, M. E. Rehabilitation counseling: Scope and services. Boston: Houghton Mifflin, 1970.

Jessell, J. C., and Rothney, J. W. M. The effectiveness of parent–counselor conferences. The Personnel and Guidance Journal, 1965, 44, 142–146.

Jourard, S. M. The transparent self. New York: Van Nostrand Reinhold, 1964.

Krumboltz, J. D., and Thoresen, C. E. Behavioral counseling: Cases and techniques. New York: Holt, Rinehart and Winston, 1969.

Kubler-Ross, E. On death and dying. New York: Macmillan, 1969.

McMahon, R. Value development and superior achievers. Unpublished Ph. D. dissertation, University of Wisconsin, Madison, 1973.

Miller, C. H. Foundations of guidance. New York: Harper and Row, 1961.

Mooney, R. L., and Gordon, L. V. Mooney Problem Check List. New York: Psychological Corporation, 1950.

Patterson, C. H. Counseling and guidance in schools. New York: Harper and Row, 1962.

Pattison, H. A. The handicapped and their rehabilitation. Springfield, Ill.: Charles C Thomas, 1957.

Rogers, C. R. Toward becoming a fully functioning person. In A. W. Combs (ed.), Perceiving, behaving, becoming. Washington, D. C.: Yearbook of the Association for Supervision and Curriculum Development, 1962.

Rothney, J. W. M. Adaptive counseling in schools. Englewood Cliffs, N.J.: Prentice-Hall, 1972.

Rothney, J. W. M. Educational, vocational and social performances of counseled and uncounseled youth ten years after high school. Cooperative Research Project No. SAE 9231, U. S. Office of Education, Washington, D. C., 1963.

Rothney, J. W. M. *Guidance practices and results.* New York: Harper and Row, 1958.

Rothney, J. W. M. *Methods of studying the individual child: The psychological case study.* Waltham, Mass.: Ginn-Blaisdell, 1968.

Rothney, J. W. M., Dearborn, W. F., and Shuttleworth, F. K. *Data on the growth of public school children.* Society for Research in Child Development Monographs, Vol. 3, No. 1, Washington, D. C.: National Research Council, 1938.

Rothney, J. W. M., and Roens, B. A. *Guidance of American youth.* Cambridge, Mass.: Harvard University Press, 1950.

Rothney, J. W. M., and Sanborn, M. P. Wisconsin's research-through-service program for superior students. *Personnel and Guidance Journal,* 1966, *44,* 694–699.

Sanborn, M. P., and Niemiec, C. J. Identifying values of superior high school students. *The School Counselor,* 1971, *18,* 237–245.

Sanborn, M. P., Pulvino, C. J., and Wunderlin, R. *Research reports: Superior students in Wisconsin high schools.* University of Wisconsin, Research and Guidance Laboratory, Madison, 1971.

Shosteck, R. How well are we putting across occupational information? *Personnel and Guidance Journal,* 1955, *33,* 265–269.

Super, D. E. A theory of vocational development. *American Psychologist,* 1953, *8,* 185–190.

Thoresen, C. E., and Mahoney, M. J. *Behavioral self control.* New York: Holt, Rinehart and Winston, 1974.

Travers, R. M. W. A critical review of techniques of evaluating counseling. In G. F. Farwell and H. J. Peters (eds.), *Guidance readings for counselors.* Chicago: Rand McNally, 1960.

Tyler, L. E. *The work of the counselor.* New York: Appleton-Century-Crofts, 1969.

Wallen, N. E. *Educational research: A guide to the process.* Belmont, Calif.: Wadsworth, 1974.

White, R. W. *Lives in progress.* New York: Holt, Rinehart and Winston, 1961.

Williamson, E. G., and Bordin, E. S. The evaluation of vocational and educational counseling. *Educational and Psychological Measurement,* 1941, *1,* 5–24.

APPLICATIONS IN FIELD SETTINGS

CHAPTER 8
The School Counselor as Environmental Researcher

Roger F. Aubrey and Francis W. McKenzie

Research, whatever its ultimate form, is basically systematic inquiry. The genesis, focus, and priorities of research by school counselors are determined by the conditions, the actors, and implied scenarios of their school settings. To understand what research efforts ought to be for counselors in school settings, we first need to look at who counselors are, how they emerged in schools, and what ambiguities they face in role and function.

THE "ORIGINS" OF SCHOOL COUNSELORS

Throughout the country's schools are ex-teachers who, refurbished with a few courses, were commissioned at some point in recent time as guidance counselors. Launched as an administrative response to minimize some local pupil problems, these newly created personages found themselves confused as to who they were and what they were expected to accomplish. Over the past few decades they attempted to supply "cures" and "solutions" to a broad spectrum of educational problems.

Often problems in schools were "identified" and adopted with a singular sense of ownership. Targets and foci became "underachievement," "passivity of the learner," "alienation of the learner," "lack of self-adjustment," "poor study habits," and "academic failure."

Part of the collective role problem of counselors has been rooted in their origins. Counseling with dubious "ancestry" in psychotherapy and the world of work came from outside the primary instructional family of traditional subject matter. Coming late on the scene gave counselors little intellectual or academic legitimacy in the eyes of subject-matter teachers. More tolerated than welcomed on the established educational turf, counselors were allowed to deal with the undesirable educational residue left by subject-matter specialists who were indifferent to all save their own academic areas. They were expected to control or otherwise motivate that large percentage of pupils who either could not, or would not, fully function in the existing knowledge-dispensing courses and sequences. In short, they were expected to concentrate their efforts largely with the leftovers that the tradition-legitimated specialists did not, or could not, "motivate" or teach.

Like it or not, how counselors feel about their legitimacy significantly affects the degree of assertiveness they take in the questions they feel they should or do pursue. It determines also the extent of their risk-taking in examining the traditions, folklore, and customs of their schools. Finally, legitimacy plays a major role in the sharpness of focus counselors turn on the psychological imponderables, uncertainties, and anxieties facing their students, colleague teachers, and themselves as well.

"Legitimacy" is an issue of major consequence. The paradox of the "turf and time" poses a distinctive access problem to their pupils. The literature rarely acknowledges that *open access to their pupil clients is relatively denied counselors in the vast majority of American schools, both elementary and secondary.*

Unlike their fellow teachers, few counselors have had their own classrooms, space for teaching, or settings for discussions and group work. Likewise, there is an absence of guidance time blocks in the daily or weekly schedules of schools. Few counselees can get to their counselors without either cutting a class or securing a teacher's permission to be excused from a class lesson.

What guidance becomes, or shall become, is highly influenced by the sufferance and tolerance of colleague teachers. At best, teachers regard guidance as a somewhat mysterious and doubtful presence; a regular annoyance that causes pupils to be periodically drained away from the important stuff of education, namely their classes.

THE NONSTATIC
SCHOOL ENVIRONMENT

School environment is a complex set of variables involving expectancies, belief systems, and surface relationships that are both peer-to-peer and age differentiated. A school actually is a combination of what it once was created to be, what it has emerged into, what different persons wish it to be, what different persons make it to be, and how it is perceived differently by those in charge, those employed by it, and those pupils "in custody," its primary consumers.

Structurally, schools appear to be unmodifiable and unchanging. Actually, they are in the throes of constant change, but not uniformly so. Parts of schools resemble themselves a decade or two previously. Some elements are hardly comparable to six months earlier. A school's variability and predictability of emphasis are more a phenomenon of collective individual behavior than that of policy decisions, administrative fiat, or departmental regulation.

Any presumably desirable improvement in the school's responsiveness to the needs of its students and teachers starts with individual concern. It is then transmitted in ripples and small increments until there is a cluster of concern whose collective voice can get attention. Eventually, this results in sanction to move from unofficial concern to official concern, and from there on to study or investigation.

Today's Student

Collectively, students today are a vastly different aggregation of young people than those who preceded them, even a half-generation ago. They enter school earlier (early education programs, day care and nursery programs); they are also older (mandated special education programs to age 21, junior college and post-high-school technical programs). Such students have a high probability of having moved from several communities or between several schools in their K–12 years.

The probability of growing up in a one-parent family is fast approaching a one-out-of-three likelihood. Today's students include drug users, drug abusers, and pregnant students eligible for abortions or adoption arrangements.

Services and institutional programs of federal and state agencies, clinics, detention centers, as well as specialized schools for the handicapped, the blind, deaf, mentally retarded, and the crippled are being closed or reduced at an unimagined and unanticipated rate.

Students who did not enter school, enter; those who did not stay, stay; and those who can hardly function are now politically positioned to "function." Neither "average," "typical," nor "predictable," today's pupils are everyone's children, with the full spectrum of needs and problems. With vastly broader and unique needs, the schools, however unready, have to gear up rapidly for new demands and new kinds of effectiveness.

THE RESEARCH ROLE
OF THE COUNSELOR

Whether the only pupil personnel worker in a school, or one of several, the counselor is the only generalist. It is therefore inevitable that he or she is the one to whom most constituencies press their concerns or demands. Counselors are obviously almost hopelessly overextended with far fewer fingers than the ever growing holes in the dikes call for. If for no other reason than achieving some semblance of personal and professional effectiveness, counselors must initiate inquiry, obtain data, assess situations and persons, and enter into problem-solving and decision-making arrangements with others. Obviously, goals, objectives, strategies, and programs are necessary. To move to this level of function, counselors need a basic research stance to determine what is functional, what is dysfunctional, what is effective, what is ineffective, and, most especially, what are the priorities for their time and capabilities.

Kehas (1975) has succinctly outlined the counselors' aversions to both research and notions of research. He sees counselors as identifying research with science; science as antithetical to the humanities and hence as dehumanizing. Thus, he observes "research" identified as an incongruity if not a threat to the integrity of human experience.

Kehas, however, reassures counselors that such perceived threats can be diminished if they regard "research to be treated as hypotheses, not givens, especially when dealing with individuals" (p. 46). He further elaborates that (a) schools have not generally encouraged research from within, (b) counselors have not systematically investigated questions about their work, (c) although counselors do raise questions, these questions usually have not become the substance of actual inquiry, and (d) that others, usually outside agencies and graduate institutions who live on research, as a result, have decided on what is to be researched and what are the important questions.

This latter point of Kehas is perhaps the most critical one because it is most central to basic philosophical and operational questions. The issue here is whether counselors intend to remain as passive robots in the institutionalized machinery, or whether they will legitimize and authenticate their questions and those of their students into appropriate frames of inquiry. These frames of inquiry could then lead to more desirable alterations in the structure of the institutions of education, while encouraging the maintenance of the idiosyncratic integrity of all the personalities involved on the educational turf.

The counselor who seeks to play a research role is enmeshed in a vortex of constraints. Dependent on the acceptance of teachers as a potentially valuable colleague, eager to become an effective advocate for students, the counselor usually has not yet been established.

The stronger the counselor's image of advocacy is perceived by others, the greater the possible suspicion that they (teachers, parents, principals, etc.) are the targets. If they come to see the counselor as moving in on grounds and issues not in their own interest, all kinds of countervailing behaviors can be expected from them.

Obtaining Sanction

An astute counselor–researcher who wishes to survive initial relationship booby traps wisely decides to be neither a lone performer nor a "star." Mature examination of local circumstances usually suggests that there exist sufficient concern, frustration, and desire for improvements in all the membership groups of public education to sanction and "authorize" some research efforts. The critically necessary first step is to help build a rationale of self-interest for each group's buying into the process. Common ownership of topics for investigation has the potential of moving through data gathering to a true engagement in common cause in problem solving and problem resolution. In fact, little that will be useful can be accomplished without such a support base. Otherwise, opposition, in some form, is a predictable outcome.

Acceptance of a counselor, particularly a counselor who questions and seeks answers, is highly dependent on the recognition of the usually present quid pro quo, namely the teachers' implied or stated "What can you do for me?" question. If this question is anticipated and woven into broader and more justifiable perspectives of inquiry, partnerships are established and the inquiry has a broader base of authorization and support.

In the setting of formal schooling, the counselor needs to fully recognize the internal resistances to change. Despite new buildings, special facilities, multimedia, special courses and the like, American education has remained relatively unaltered during the lifetimes of all those generations still alive. The illusion of change persists, as do old, repetitive, unassessed practices.

Defining a New Role for Counselors

Counselors, unlike most teachers, are free from commitments to any one or more of the subject matter traditions. Students, in their varied developmental and idiosyncratic characteristics, become the subject matter equivalents for counselors. Counselors are agents provided by the institutions to assist students in managing their own interests, capacities, and destinies. Helping students negotiate their needs within the range of school resources and expectancies is a major expectancy role. Counselors, by now, should have divested themselves of any sense of obligation to "adjust" pupils to school. We would like to believe that counselors have gone well beyond the first timid steps of intervention and helped the institution adjust itself to the varying and highly individualized needs of pupils.

As an advocate for pupils, teachers, and parents, the counselor must have eyes that really see, ears that really hear, and courage to pursue the why of dysfunctional behavior, the why-nots for proposed actions, and the inherent resistance and avoidance in all persons surrounding the educative and mental health tasks of pupils.

Whatever the tracings of avoidances are in the counselors' own past, the demands of the guidance role pressures playing the role of "inquirer," "data-source," "planner," "advisor," and "advocate" all call for a high involvement of intellectual curiosity and conceptual analysis on the part of the counselor. The customary intuitive and emotional affinities of "therapist" are totally insufficient. This is not said to disparage the therapeutic dimension of counseling but rather to emphasize that these other traits and role demands call for a broader acquisition of more cognitive and rational competencies.

As a curious traveler in this educational space called a school, counselors can see what others are blind to, to question the unquestioned, to seek out the unknown and to think the unthinkable. They can start to negotiate new roles and relationships beginning with those things which are not staked out, or are neglected, or are unanticipated by others.

Brokering

One can imagine the implications and consequences following the announcement of the first school in the country to place a moratorium on the usual courses, clock hours, schedules, grade levels, and teaching–learning arrangements in order to open all kinds of alternative options proposed by a counselor-led student, teacher, and parent study. Assume that in its place a variety of teacher–learner resources (tutoring, seminars, consultations, outside visitations, inside invitational visitations, pupil research assignments, etc.) were all made available to students prescriptively, based on assessments of adequacies, inadequacies, needs, and preferences.

Such a school wherein guidance counselors orchestrated the matching of individual student circumstances with periodic rearrangements of teacher resources would signal, perhaps for the first time, a real measure of the potential yields of truly individualized education.

The school counselor as broker, blending needs with resources, adding and subtracting as needed, could truly revolutionize the whole educational system in favor of its two main players: pupils and teachers.

In less ambitious and more modest terms, any such brokering of pupil needs that secures an improved match of instructional resources gives a local school a chance to opt for more desirable individual outcomes, first by direct exchange of pupil data, followed by fully appropriate uses of teacher resources.

The Counselor as a School's Research Catalyst

The counselor is uniquely positioned to become the pivot for data gathering and planning in the school. Counselors are expected to interview others, to have general as well as specific information, to explain, and to interpret both the school and the outer world. The crucial goals are to focus on more significant questions, involve significant persons for the tasks, obtain a sense of the important, and persuade all to be willing to drop old beliefs and practices in face of new information and new implications for subsequent behavior.

Systematic and multidirectional inquiry is the counselor's best protection from the chronic and ever present professional diseases of insulation, isolation, obsolescence, procrastination, misdirected energy, and ineptness. Although not a universal patent medicine in itself, inquiry offers a first stage platform for the treatment of actual and potential ailments and pitfalls of institutional health.

Our concept of the counselor as a catalyst for educational inquiry rests heavily on (1) the unique opportunity to serve multiple constituencies without overidentification with any, (2) the fact that all other players (teachers, students, parents, and administrators) have clearly defined and expected roles from which they cannot move with impunity, (3) the fact that the counselors' early-on handicap is often a distinct asset, namely, that their role potentials are only vaguely perceived by others.

The counselor's initial task is to determine what is going on in the school, how it matches or differs from what is expected to go on (as differently defined by each constituency), and what should go on in terms of appropriate learning sequences and reasonable mental health goals.

At this juncture, we would make the point that imaginative, energetic, curious, and empathic counselors are uniquely positioned to observe, assist, and relate to teachers and pupils.

The Counselor's Research As Self-Study and Accountability

Counselors are in elementary and secondary schools primarily to effect change in the behavior of children and adolescents. As change agents, *counselors may personally bring about development in students* by such activities as individual and group counseling, classroom guidance projects, and curricular work. Counselors may also *influence change indirectly* by consultation work with other significant adults in students' lives such as teachers and parents.

Regardless of the vehicle selected by the counselor in reaching students, there is a need to review periodically the effectiveness of various intervention techniques and their impact on student behavior. The best manner in which this periodic review can be accomplished is by carefully formulating short- and long-range goals and putting them in writing. In turn, these goal statements should be linked to counselor intervention techniques so a causal relationship can be established between means–ends, techniques–goals. Unfortunately, this rarely occurs and counselors frequently find themselves unable to account for the multiple uses of their time and how this influences student development. To achieve such goals, time must be organized, controlled, and mobilized into priority units of work.

Accountability for counselor performance is the responsibility of each school counselor. In effect, this means that each school counselor should be able to delineate time and skill utilization throughout the school year. Further, school counselors must be able to justify the allocation of their time and skills in relation to clearly stated objectives for students. Without explicit goal statements, counselors are continually adrift, their time dissipated and unproductive, and personally faced with multiple expectations and competing demands from numerous publics.

Pragmatically, school counselors require a set of clear and written objectives because of increased pressure for accountability by the taxpaying public and school administrators. Professionally, school counselors need evidence of goal attainment to validate claims that their interventions actually do make a difference in the lives of students. Ideally, and more importantly, school counselors need hard data in order to determine priorities for reaching students in schools.

What Phenomena Should the Counselor Study?

If counselors are to conduct research and studies in schools, it is imperative for them to possess a clear and concise idea of what it is they are to study and investigate. Schools are notorious for swallowing up legions of interested and conscientious researchers. The problem is, there are simply so many fascinating activities and behaviors in schools that one can easily become sidetracked or overinvested in relatively few areas to the neglect of those of real importance.

The crucial question for any school counselor conducting research is how to determine what phenomena should be studied in their particular school setting. Should counselors focus on their immediate daily interventions with students and the effectiveness of their own skills and techniques? Even this simple question is more complex than it appears. In effect, if one is actually to study counselor practices, it is necessary to separate out the counselor's behavior and technique from the actual short- and long-range impact on student behavior. These are really two distinct questions and lines of inquiry. Therefore, this question really requires observation and assessment of both counselor and counselee in addition to a careful analysis of specific methodology.

In considering what phenomenon is most in need of study in a particular school, it is obvious that a great amount of school behavior is not really the domain of counselors. Granted, it might be interesting to know the impact of administrator style on the reward system of teachers and the subsequent effects on mathematics achievement in ninth graders. However, the pursuit of this type of research by school counselors is quite inappropriate and entirely outside the realm of significant guidance and counseling concerns.

RESEARCH AS NEEDS ASSESSMENT AND PROGRAM INVENTORY

Many counselors have found it helpful to conduct periodically a needs assessment in order to determine what school areas are in need of examination. A needs assessment is actually a convenient means for identifying factors underlying guidance and counseling objectives. In this sense, a *needs assessment is a method of gathering and compiling hard and soft data underlying the stated objectives of the guidance and counseling programs of a given school.* A broadly designed needs assessment can also be a means of generating new goals for a guidance and counseling department.

In devising a guidance focused needs assessment, it is desirable to begin with broad and general categories of student needs. In turn, these categories should lend themselves to a breakdown of smaller parts with greater specificity. The counselor's task is to determine which categories or subcategories are most worthy of time, energy, program development, and research. In many instances, this final determination is solely in the hands of the counselor and the ultimate priorities will be largely influenced by local school conditions.

Where Do "Needs" Come From?

At this point, it might be well to ask where do the needs being assessed come from? Do they emanate from the pupil, the school, the community, the family, society? Do counselors have to assess all needs, much less meet them? Are all needs legitimate areas for counselor inquiry and intervention?

The needs of children and adolescents stem from many sources. Counselors, therefore, must carefully examine these sources before deciding the merits and legitimacy of alternative requests. For example, many needs of children and adolescents are predetermined by schools and educators. We are told children have a "need" to read, write, spell, and so on. To this end, schools are erected and filled with audiences of pupils and educators. Children then come to schools and their "need" to achieve is put into action. Unfortunately, adults fail to remember that many children are not motivated to respond to many of the tasks superimposed by adults to "meet their needs." If anything, many of the needs of these children are ignored or frustrated by efforts of the school, and the counselor is then expected to "adjust" these students to unrealistic demands.

Other sources of potential student needs are highlighted in the findings of the behavioral sciences. Social psychologists, and more particularly developmental psychologists, have identified a number of age and/or developmentally related tasks of children and adolescents (Loevinger, 1976; Piaget, 1967). Beginning with Sigmund Freud, and extending through subsequent investigators such as Harry Stack Sullivan, Jean Piaget, Erik Erikson, Robert Havighurst, Lawrence Kohlberg, Jane Loevinger, and others, a number of stage theorists have postulated a series of universal stages of human development. The majority of these psychologists have identified at each stage certain central tasks and skills necessary for successful passage through each stage in preparation for the succeeding stage. They too have therefore identified certain "needs" of students.

The needs of students are also determined by broad social, economic, and political events in our country and in the world (Barker, 1968; Bennis and Slater, 1968; Duncan, Featherman, and Duncan, 1972; Goldenberg, 1971). Currently, for example, the guidance profession has been urged to get on the career education bandwagon. The changing economic picture in this country has made realistic career planning a necessity for young people because of major changes in lifetime career patterns. The same phenomenon of change has resulted in the past ten years in drastic alterations in the chemical dependence (alcohol and drugs) of Americans in general. Whether these are situational needs, innate drives, or reactions to stress and anxiety, they are certainly forces to be reckoned with.

Finally, the profession of guidance and counseling has identified certain "needs" in the students we serve. These include self-actualization, dignity, justice, tolerance, relief and release from pain and suffering, and so on. Counselors are enjoined to meet and fulfill such needs as part of their professional responsibilities to counselees.

The needs of the audiences we serve are therefore an amalgam. They represent both legitimate and occasionally suspect or questionable considerations. However, all must be examined and carefully evaluated before priorities are weighted and ordered. It is at this point that specific counselor interventions are planned and time and energy committed to selected tasks and functions.

Conducting A Needs Assessment

The creation of a needs assessment for a particular school or school district can be arrived at by a variety of means. For example, if an entire school district wished to identify some major categories of student needs, it would be advisable to have a committee go about this task. This needs assessment committee should have a broad representation and include students, parents, teachers, administrators, and guidance personnel. Its focus would be the identification of a small number of critical student needs that spanned the ages and/or grade levels of that school system.

The work of the counselor on such a committee is critical and takes two forms. First, the counselor must endeavor to keep the perspective of the committee members on a broad plane, away from the nitty-gritty. The counselor's role is to elevate discussion and dialogue so that high order needs are the focal point of the committee. In accomplishing the job of avoiding mundane and nonproductive topics, the second role of the counselor emerges—to stimulate the committee by actually presenting examples of need categories.

Although a committee is preferable, a student needs assessment could be conducted by a small group or an individual counselor. If this were to occur, the group and/or counselor could begin determining need categories by soliciting suggestions via questionnaire or interview from students, teachers, and others. Another possible approach would be the construction

FIGURE 8.1   Student Needs Assessment

Column A—NEED CATEGORY	Column B—SUBCATEGORIES	Column C—PROGRAMS TO MEET NEEDS
Current and future economic considerations	Use of leisure time Increase of women in job force Multiple job-shifts	No programs Counselor-led women groups Career education resource center
Life survival skills	Assertiveness Communication ability Decision-making Problem-solving	Course offered to all high school students Interpersonal skills unit offered Use of College Board Deciding Program Part of all-school freshmen orientation
Social-emotional demands on students	Peer group pressure Sex-role differentiation Alcohol and drug taking Sexual experimentation Competition Early independence Making friends	Voluntary groups, individual counseling Counselor-led women groups, nothing for males Outside referral Individual counseling only No programs No programs Friendship groups on informal basis

Difficult transition periods	New teachers and/or school	Extensive group orientation program
	Family moves	No programs
	Puberty	Cross-over teaming with health personnel
	Open versus closed classrooms	No programs
	School departmentalization	No programs
	School graduation	Individual counseling of all seniors
Developmental tasks and/or needs	Stability and predictability	No systematic programs
	Affiliation	
	Security	
	Task accomplishment	
	Competency	
	Recognition	
School demands	Basic skill acquisition	Counselor review of all folders and follow-up
	Use of time	Individual counseling, no programs
	Choice of courses and options	Group and individual conferencing
	Social rules of behavior	No programs
	Increased learner independence	No programs
	Independent use of resources	No programs

in advance of a limited number of categories by the group or counselor. In turn, these predetermined needs could then be sent out to interested parties for comments and suggestions.

It is probably evident that a needs assessment profile is one means of "smoking out" what a given school or department determines as basic student needs and how that school or department proceeds in meeting these needs. Figure 8-1 is a hypothetical example of one such school, and the need categories represent one manner of conceptualizing student needs. In turn, Column B is an attempt to break down the original needs listed in Column A into small units in order to allow for easier program assessment. Finally, Column C determines, vis-à-vis action programs, where an actual school or school system places its priorities. This matching of stated needs with ongoing programs provides the framework whereby counselors can order, reorder, and build program priorities.

In conducting a student needs assessment, it is critical to begin with the actual needs and not the programs developed to meet these needs. Note in Figure 8-1, for example, the need category (under Column A) of *developmental tasks and/or needs*. The corresponding item in Column B breaks this category into subcategories. However, Column C indicates that there are no systematic programs to meet these needs. As a consequence, this program deficiency must be examined. The lack of programs in this area could be the result of a deliberate ordering of priorities and the necessity for limiting certain school programs. On the other hand, this deficiency could be the result of inadequate planning or an oversight on the part of that particular counselor or department.

RESEARCH AS IDENTIFICATION OF PROBLEMS

There is a fallacy, or at least a misconception, in construing research as something that is done after the fact or event. In other words, research need not be viewed as something exclusively devoted to outcomes related to practice. Instead, research can also be used as a vehicle to generate effective and efficient practice. The student needs assessment just presented is one example of creating important guidance and counseling priorities. In that example, the work of the counselor was determined by identifying key social, economic, political, educational, humanistic, and developmental considerations affecting students.

Another manner in which counselors can determine and establish guidance and counseling priorities is by the identification of preexisting problems or needs of students. Although basically remedial in nature, this type of research is extremely important in initially analyzing the composition of a given school or school district. What follows is an example of seeking out student needs rather than allowing the squeaky wheel phenomenon to override reason. Although the example to follow is fictional, the process of need determination could be applied by any counselor to any school or case load of counselees.

The Riverdale School District over the past four years has added one counselor to each of its six elementary schools in a concerted effort to deal with preventive mental health. Initially, this effort was seen as an attempt to identify and help young children before minor difficulties erupted into major academic and emotional problems. A further component of the program included elementary counselors consulting with teachers and assisting them in classrooms with a variety of group activities.

Currently, the elementary counseling program is in serious trouble. In at least two schools the teachers are openly critical of the counselors and their unavailability for referrals and crisis counseling. In yet another school, the parents have become vocal for similar reasons. Strangely, in three schools the teachers and parents are quite supportive of the counselors and have voiced no criticism since the inception of the program.

At a recent meeting of the elementary counselors, Peggy Cook asked the group if they would help her in gathering data to analyze the current problems she and two other counselors were experiencing. Peggy felt that much of the current criticism was based on teacher–parent lack of knowledge regarding the idiosyncratic character of the various elementary schools and their particular needs. In turn, these differences in individual school makeup necessitated varying priorities and use of time and resources. However, without data and information to justify the use of their time, the counselors in these schools were being judged as if conditions in all schools were the same. In short, without some supportive documentation, people could well wonder at differences in style and time usage among the six schools.

The concern of the counselors in identifying critical factors predetermining the use of some of their time and energy stemmed in large part from some basic demographic differences among the six schools. For example, all of the counselors were aware that School E contained over one-third more students than did Schools A, C, and F. This fact alone meant that the counselor in School E would operate somewhat differently than colleagues in smaller buildings. However, size of student body was only one of many key indicators determining counselor priorities.

As the counselors listed and discussed what demographic factors were most critical in their respective schools, a consensus was reached to study nine factors. These factors are listed in Figure 8-2 under the heading *School Indicators*. All counselors then gathered the data in their respective schools concerning each of the nine factors. These data were tabulated by listing total numbers of students falling under each *School Indicator* and the percentage of the total student body this represented. In effect, all counselors drew up a demographic profile for their own schools and then the counselors as a group designed an all-elementary school demographic profile.

Figure 8-2 is one means of depicting some of the crucial factors that press upon counselors as they attempt to allocate their time and resources. It is readily apparent that Schools D and E stand out as institutions with much greater need than Schools A or F. It is also obvious that problems are not merely related to numbers or size of school. A host of factors impinge on any institution and these must be recognized and dealt with before priorities are established.

The representation of a student body by key *School Indicators*, as depicted in this figure, can be done by any counselor for a given school or simply for the total group of students assigned to a counselor. For example, a counselor in a high school of 3000 students with an assigned load of 300 students could do such a demographic profile on just those 300 students. The resultant information may indicate that the counselor has been neglecting one segment of his or her counselees or it may show that a disproportionate amount of counselor time has been spent on the wrong audience. In either case, such research can enlarge the perspective of the counselor and open up new possibilities for time usage and resource allocation.

RESEARCH AS STUDYING THE ENVIRONMENT OF THE SCHOOL

There are at least two major aspects to the research function of the school counselor. The first has been emphasized in previous sections of this chapter. Counselors have a responsibility to examine their own intervention postures and the effect these produce on the lives of students. Put another way, counselors need to periodically study the use of their time and competencies in the school and how this brings about change in students.

A second major aspect of the research function of the counselor pertains to the environment of the school. The counselor in this regard is ascertaining the climate of a particular school and the impact of this atmosphere on the many individuals within that environment. Counselors are interested in this phenomenon because they realize that an environment over a period of time exerts considerable influence on the individuals who

FIGURE 8.2 Demographic Profile of Riverdale School District's Elementary Schools

SCHOOL INDICATOR	SCHOOL A		SCHOOL B		SCHOOL C		SCHOOL D		SCHOOL E		SCHOOL F		DISTRICT TOTALS	
Total Number of Pupils	290		360		320		410		440		300		2120	
Number and percent of minority students	29	10%	72	20%	16	5%	144	35%	220	50%	9	3%	490	23%
Student turnover rate per year by number and percent	41	14%	90	25%	48	15%	189	46%	194	44%	15	5%	577	27%
Number and percent of children from single-parent homes	35	12%	101	28%	45	14%	160	39%	207	47%	39	13%	587	28%
Number and percent of special education pupils	12	4%	18	5%	22	7%	57	14%	97	22%	18	6%	224	11%
Number and percent of pupils receiving aid to dependent children	9	3%	54	15%	32	10%	107	26%	154	35%	12	4%	368	17%
Total number and percent of previous year's referrals to pupil services department	58	20%	97	27%	70	22%	164	40%	220	50%	45	15%	654	31%
Number and percent of pupils achieving below grade level expectation	35	12%	58	16%	45	14%	148	36%	242	55%	30	10%	558	26%
Number and percent of nonEnglish speaking students	2	1%	9	2.5%	7	2%	41	10%	52	12%	0	0%	111	5%

inhabit that environment (Bloom, 1964, Katz and Kahn, 1966; Sarason, 1971). They therefore desire information about this climate in order to make decisions about appropriate interventions to alter or modify that environment.

The study of school climates need not limit counselors by restricting their focus to only "big picture" issues. Obviously, it is equally important for counselors to do research on the practices they engage in each and every day. Even more so, counselors need to study the effects of these practices on the attitudes and behaviors of the individual students they serve. However, before deciding on or hurriedly implementing intervention practices, counselors need to thoroughly examine the audiences they serve to determine what practices are appropriate and relevant.

Determining the pulse and impact of a school on its inhabitants can appear to be an overwhelming task. However, the means for accomplishing this end are limited only by the imagination and resourcefulness of the counselor. Here we focus on some methods of gathering such information beginning with the microcosm of an individual student and ending with the macrocosm of the entire school.

Shadowing

One technique for assessing the impact of the environment of a school on the lives of students is *shadowing*. As the name implies, shadowing is simply a method of closely following the life and experience of someone else. It is a form of participant observation, which is described in chapter 5. Like a good detective, the shadower records the experiences of the person he or she is shadowing. On occasion, the shadower may even vicariously enter this experiencing of events in order to confirm or validate impressions. One example of this type of shadowing follows.

Judy Henderson was concerned about the general atmosphere of Roosevelt Junior High School. As a counselor to 400 seventh and eighth graders, she was increasingly aware of a general feeling of listlessness, apathy, and indifference among students. They seemed bored and tuned out on much of what went on in the school. Nothing seemed to excite or motivate the students, and Judy had noted that even clubs, activities, and athletics all suffered from a lack of participants.

One morning in mid-November, Judy Henderson closed her appointment book for the day and headed for the opening homeroom period in Mr. Scott's class. She sat down next to Sally Becker and asked her if she would mind if she accompanied her for the remainder of the day wherever her schedule took her. Judy also asked Sally's permission to take notes throughout the day and to check these notes with Sally at the end of the school day.

For the remainder of the day, the counselor shadowed Sally Becker. This meant following the girl from class to class, staying with her as she chatted with other students between classes and during lunch, taking part in physical education and other classes, and even accompanying her to the bathroom.

By the conclusion of the day, Judy Henderson was exhausted. She had attempted to keep a running log of the day's activities, but at times this had been impossible. She therefore had to bring her log up to date before sharing the day with Sally. Once this had been done, the two of them began with the morning homeroom period and worked through recorded impressions of the day.

What Judy Henderson discovered in one day of shadowing a student was that her school resembled a highly organized military base. Every minute of the student's day was completely filled with predetermined experiences and inflexible scheduling. Students literally had no time during the school day for either socializing or friendly exchanges with their peers. The demands of the institution regarding rules and regulations were rigid and allowed no input from students. The demands of the teachers on the school and after-school time of students were similarly rigid and unyielding. In short, the school neither asked for nor sought feedback from students on how the institution affected them as human beings.

As a counselor, Judy Henderson had a number of options regarding the data she collected. The information could be presented to the principal with a series of suggestions and recommendations. She could also address a faculty meeting and ask them to deal with this matter. Conceivably, these data could also be the focus of a parent–teacher meeting or the counselor might wish to discuss it with small groups of students.

Shadowing need not be restricted to a single student, such as Sally Becker. A counselor could just as well follow an entire class for a day or possibly some faculty members or the school principal. However, it should be noted that shadowing is impressionistic and limited to the direct observation of the shadower. Let us now consider a more refined manner of gathering data on a larger segment of the school as we increase our focus to an entire classroom.

Assessing Classroom Environment

The classroom environment in any school is the guts of that system. Notwithstanding a recent host of new structural, curricular, and organizational innovations, the lifeblood of any school is still found in individual classrooms. As such, it behooves school counselors to familiarize themselves with instruments and methods that go beyond raw observation and *make intelligible student life in classrooms* (Corrigan, 1969; Fox, Luszki, and Schmuck 1966; Fox, et al., 1975; Jackson, 1968; Lortie, 1975).

What occurs in classrooms is extremely important to school counselors because they have a vested interest in the social-emotional development of students. This aspect of student development should be shared and worked on by teachers as well as mental health specialists. In a similar fashion, counselors are also concerned with the cognitive-academic development of students. However, *what unites counselors and teachers is a mutual concern for the total well-being of each individual.* Much of this concern occurs in the crucible of daily classroom activities, relationships, and happenings.

Assessing classrooms is not a new activity in the field of education. Flanders (1970) almost two decades ago devised a number of sophisticated measures to record the behaviors between and among teachers and students. A number of other educational researchers have also been active in this area over the past thirty years (Amidon and Hough, 1967; Cornell, Lindvall, and Saupe, 1952; Medley and Klein, 1957; Medley and Mitzel, 1955; Walberg, 1969; Withall, 1949). However, the bulk of these endeavors was geared toward increasing teacher efficiency in imparting instruction. They were not designed as tools for mental health specialists in diagnosing potential problems nor as instruments to record change in pupil psychological attitude and behavior over time.

The case that follows is an example of a counselor utilizing a classroom climate instrument for guidance ends. A brief description of this instrument is included so the reader will have some understanding of this particular inventory, its uses, and purposes.

The Brook Elementary School has seen many changes in the past two years. A principal with thirty years of experience (twenty in the Brook School) retired two years ago and a new, inexperienced principal has arrived. Immediately, the new principal set up a one year in-service program centering on open classrooms and team teaching. Although the program was voluntary in nature, over half of the school's 35 teachers signed up for the training sessions and the majority implemented these concepts the following year.

A year ago also saw the arrival of an elementary school counselor. Bert Jones had been an elementary teacher in an adjacent school in the district and, on completing his Master's degree, became the first full-time elementary school counselor in the district. As a counselor, Bert Jones surprised many teachers by spending a great amount of time in classrooms observing children, consulting with teachers, and conducting programs of psychological education.

Some teachers in the Brook School, especially those who did not participate in the year-long seminar, questioned Bert Jones' use of time. They felt the counselor should be available throughout the day to see unruly, disturbed, and underachieving students in his office. When challenged by these teachers, Bert Jones responded by saying that he felt his presence in the classroom had produced many desirable effects on children. The problem was that Bert Jones had a difficult time documenting this statement.

At a state convention, Bert Jones had an opportunity to discuss his problem with several other elementary school counselors. One counselor informed him of a classroom inventory that assessed many of the classroom areas Bert was concerned about. This counselor had used that instrument to identify a number of children with specific learning and emotional problems; the inventory could also be used for pre and posttesting of group and classroom affective education programs as well as for judging the impact of open classrooms on children's behavior. This particular instrument is called the Barclay Classroom Climate Inventory (1976) (BCCI), and it was specially designed to measure social interaction and expectation variables for elementary and junior high school children.

Bert Jones soon discovered that the BCCI contained 42 short scales measuring (1) self-competency skills, (2) vocational awareness, (3) teacher expectations, (4) behavioral reinforcers, and (5) peer judgments. Further, these scales were to be simultaneously completed by self, group, and teacher. The results were tabulated by a computer that would print out a group report for the entire class, an individual report for each child, and summary tables related to the overall characteristics of the children and suspected problem areas.

The BCCI was initially attractive to Bert Jones because it was developed for use in small and large groups and covered a wide range of behavior. For example, the total pattern of responses for each student was analyzed in a computer and then converted into a summary table that indicated suspected problems for each child in such areas as self-concept, group skills, self-control skills, verbal skills, physical skills, vocational development, cognitive development, and attitude toward school. Armed with these data on an entire classroom, Bert Jones could then approach teachers with diagnostic information calling for various intervention strategies. In addition, the BCCI User's Manual contains over fifty suggestions and strategies for individual and group approaches to specific problem areas.

The instrument therefore seemed to Bert Jones a possible answer to many of his concerns. It could be utilized for an evaluation of some of his experimental group counseling and curricular approaches in classrooms. It could also be used as a basis for identifying and/or confirming referrals made by teachers. In some cases, teachers desiring information on the effects of open and traditional classrooms on children's behavior could utilize this instrument for that end. Finally, the data derived from this instrument might also be used by the counselor in consultation work with parents, teachers, and the school administration.

The problems of Bert Jones obviously will not be "solved" by any instrument or assessment device, even though this area has shown promise and expansion (Epstein and McPartland, 1976; Miller, 1973; Miller, Gum, and Bender, 1972). At best, such aids will give him some new data or check points with which to compare older impressions and subjective information. In turn, by revisiting and reexamination of earlier conclusions, some new hypotheses could be generated and tested.

Assessing Total School Climates

Only in recent years has any substantial attempt been made to study the total environment of schools (Bloom, Hastings, and Madaus, 1971; Sarason, 1972; Smith and Keith, 1971; Watson, 1967). Obviously, the magnitude of any effort to study the entire climate of schools is staggering. Schools contain students, teachers, administrators, mental health specialists, supervisors, custodians, bus drivers, cooks, secretaries, aides, graduate students, volunteers. But schools are not only people. What of the physical plant, the manner in which it is organized, rules and regulations, the numerous operational plans and procedures, the manner in which time is structured and utilized? And these are only additional pieces of the pie. What of the school curriculum, the scope and sequence of courses within each discipline? How are the students assigned to these curriculum divisions, and what happens to students moving too slowly or quickly through these curricular experiences? Who determines placement and changes in placement? How are students (and teachers) evaluated, how do changes in curricula occur, and so on?

The climate of schools is made up of many parts and elements. Together they may be greater than the whole. The critical question for the school counselor is always one of selective perspective and emphasis. Just what aspect of schooling is most essential for counselors to consider and what major questions about a given institution are most in need of investigation? Consider the following.

Frank Hays and Mary Webb are two high school counselors in a large suburban school. Recently, the guidance department has come under attack by the local parents' association for being "unresponsive to the students and parents." Specifically, parents have charged that counselors are not available to students or parents when desired and that poor communication exists between counselors and teachers. Also, a dramatic upsurge in alcohol and drug-taking in the community has been placed in the guidance department's lap as a major responsibility.

The counselors in this school, especially Frank Hays and Mary Webb, feel these charges are unwarranted. Nonetheless, they have been given responsibility by the principal and superintendent for answering these complaints. At first, the counselors considered making up a simple questionnaire that students would fill out during homeroom period. However, Frank and Mary felt this device would simply be seen as an in-house way of answering charges and therefore suspect by parents and school administration.

What Frank and Mary wished to do in answering these charges was to take the primary focus of the attack off guidance. Instead, they wanted a study that would concentrate on the entire school and at the same time honor the charges against guidance. They asked the school administration for permission to use a school climate instrument developed by Educational Testing Service and titled Questionnaire for Students, Teachers and Administrators (1973) (QUESTA).

The QUESTA instrument possesses one entire section devoted to an evaluation of school guidance and counseling activities. Like all sections in the instrument, a series of questions addressed to this area is completed simultaneously by all students, teachers, and administrators. When scored, QUESTA breaks out all three groups separately and allows for comparisons between attitudes held by all three groups in regard to specific topics, departments, procedures, and so on. In this manner, a school can gain information about the degree to which the students, faculty, and administrators are satisfied or dissatisfied with various parts of the school and with student development. The instrument also gives data related to the nature and values of the school's subgroups, sources of tension and dissatisfaction, and so on.

For the purposes of Frank Hays and Mary Webb, the QUESTA instrument was ideal. It allowed for a fair evaluation of the guidance department but did not put the spotlight solely on this area alone. Rather, by focusing on the school's understanding of the workings of the total environment, it enlarged the original intent and served a much more constructive end. Finally, the instrument gathered sufficient data to allow the school to improve the total educational environment by suggesting actions based on data and not subjective impressions.

RESEARCH AND THE
DAILY ACTIVITIES
OF COUNSELORS

Little has been said to this point on the day-to-day work of the counselor and research. Instead, the focus has primarily been on the use of research in establishing worthy counseling objectives and the study of school and classroom life. If this seems strange, then perhaps a look at how many counselors spend their time is in order.

In a classic study of school counselors, Armor (1969) found that much of what passes for counselor work could be classified as clerical and semiadministrative functioning. Obviously, the fact that counselors spend inordinate amounts of time in noncounseling work is of interest as well as significant. However, it is hardly an area worthy of research *unless one would undertake research to investigate and possibly change this situation.*

Compounding the problem of counselors frequently using large amounts of their time in noncounseling endeavors is the problem of apathy and indifference. As Kehas (1975) has noted, "Counselors themselves are not systematically investigating questions about their work. . . . the questions and issues on which research is founded have been and are being established by persons other than counselors or other school people" (p. 46–47).

The twin problems of nonconsequential activity and indifference have been instrumental in slowing any major effort among school counselors to do research. Those studies and collections of research on school counselors have by and large been conducted by university personnel (Cramer, Herr, Morris, and Frantz, 1970; Volsky, et al., 1965; Whiteley, 1968). Rarely have counselors contributed to the literature and body of existing knowledge on school counseling.

The recent hue and cry throughout the educational world concerning accountability has undoubtedly raised interest in research among counselors. In fact, many accountability models demand some validation of counselor time usage and performance. Essentially, these models have forced counselors to state in clear and simple terms the overall objectives of their programs. In addition, accountability models have demanded that some criteria be advanced (usually in behavioral terms) to assess student growth over specific time periods.

The spur of accountability could force a new surge of interest in counselor research. However, it could also simply result in a greater amount of traditional data gathering. For example, many counselors and/or school guidance departments do yearly studies on drop-out rates, number of high school graduates continuing education or going on to two and four-year colleges, schoolwide achievement test averages by grade equivalents or percentile rankings, and so on. These studies are then analyzed and distributed with a tacit understanding that guidance and counseling have somehow influenced the factors under study.

Unfortunately, yearly studies of achievement test results, drop-out rates, and the like do not accurately reflect the work of the counselor. Counselors do, of course, have an investment in these areas and certainly do influence student behavior but these types of studies overlap considerably with teacher behavior. In other words, teachers have as great or greater influence on many of these behaviors as do counselors. It is therefore impossible to sort out the impact of a given counselor, vis-à-vis a student's achievement test results, from that of the many teachers working with this student each day.

Accountability models in some cases have suggested other means whereby counselors can study their work with students. For instance, behavioral contracts have become increasingly popular among counselors in work with both individuals and groups. These behavioral contracts lend themselves easily to research and study because they require the clear statement of predetermined goals in behavioral terms. For example, a behavioral contract of a student experiencing academic problems could read, "I will meet with my counselor each Monday and Friday morning at 9:00 a.m. to discuss my work in English and Science. We will go over my tests and assignments during the week and once a month we will also meet with my teachers. I would like to raise both of these grades from a low C to a B by the end of the first semester in January."

The example just cited is a rather simple way of looking at change in student behavior. The use of behavioral contracts does place a clear responsibility on the student for specific outcomes and allows the counselor to validate data by observable phenomena. It has a weakness if the counselor is engaged in long-term work with students or if the intended outcomes are difficult to state in behavioral terms. For example, a counselor engaged in group work who wished to develop decision-making skills in students may feel this is a developmental process extending over many years. As a consequence, the fruits of the counselor's work may not show up in a predetermined period of time. In fact, the results of this work may show up only after the student leaves school and is forced to deal with various career and work choices.

Research conducted by school counselors can take many forms; this chapter has illustrated only the tip of the iceberg. We have suggested that apathy, indifference, haphazard planning, lack of tenacity, inadequate topics, and poor use of time are only a few of the obstacles along the way. However, all of these can be overcome by the counselor desirous of examining both practice and setting to ultimately better the life of students.

CONCLUSION

The emphasis on school environments in this chapter has been a deliberate attempt on the part of the authors to depart from traditional research emphasis on counseling, especially one-to-one counseling. Our desire has been to demonstrate that significant changes in schooling can occur only by research on the total environment of a student, and not simply that created in a counselor's office.

For too long the promise of guidance and counseling has eluded students. Part of this promise can be attained by the school counselor assuming a more active role as a researcher of the conditions underlying the atmosphere of schools. The counselor too is part of this environment and how the counselor chooses questions and seeks data to clarify these hypothesis may, in and of itself, change the conditions in that atmosphere.

REFERENCES

Amidon, E. J., and Hough, J. B. (eds.). *Interaction analysis: Theory, research, and application.* Reading, Mass.: Addison-Wesley, 1967.

Armor, D. J. *The American school counselor.* New York: Russell Sage Foundation, 1969.

Barclay Classroom Climate Inventory. Lexington, Ky.: Educational Skills Development, Inc., 1976.

Barker, R. G. *Ecological psychology.* Stanford, Calif.: Stanford University Press, 1968.

Bennis, W. G., and Slater, P. E. *The temporary society.* New York: Harper and Row, 1968.

Bloom, B. S., Hastings, T., and Madaus, G. *Handbook on formative and summative evaluation of student learning.* New York: McGraw-Hill, 1971.

Bloom, B. S. *Stability and change in human characteristics.* New York: Wiley, 1964.

Cornell, F. G., Lindvall, C. W., and Saupe, I. L. An exploratory measurement of individualities of schools and classrooms. Urbana: Bureau of Educational Research, University of Illinois, 1952.

Corrigan, R. E. *A system approach for education.* Garden Grove, Calif.: R. E. Corrigan Associates, 1969.

Cramer, S., Herr, E., Morris, C., and Frantz, T. *Research and the school counselor.* Boston: Houghton Mifflin, 1970.

Duncan, O., Featherman, D., and Duncan, B. *Socioeconomic background and achievement.* New York: Seminar Press, 1972.

263

Epstein, J. L., and McPartland, J. M. The concept and measurement of the quality of school life. *American Educational Research Journal,* 1976, *13,.* 15–30.

Flanders, N. A. *Analyzing teacher behavior.* Reading, Mass.: Addison Wesley, 1970.

Fox, R., Luszki, M., and Schmuck, R. *Diagnosing classroom learning environments.* Chicago: Science Research Associates, 1966.

Fox, R., Schmuck, R., Egmond, E., Ritvo, M., and Jung, C. *Diagnosing professional climates of schools.* Fairfax, Va.: Learning Resource Corporation, 1975.

Goldenberg, I. I. *Build me a mountain: Youth, poverty and the creation of a new setting.* Cambridge, Mass.: MIT Press, 1971.

Jackson, P. W. *Life in classrooms.* New York: Holt, Rinehart and Winston, 1968.

Katz, D., and Kahn, R. *The social psychology of organizations.* New York: Wiley, 1966.

Kehas, C. D. What research says about counselor role. In H. Peters and R. Aubrey (Eds.), *Guidance: Strategies and techniques.* Denver, Colo.: Love Publishing Company, 1975, 45–61.

Loevinger, J. *Ego development,* San Francisco: Jossey-Bass, 1976.

Lortie, D. C. *School-teacher: A sociological study.* Chicago: University of Chicago Press, 1975.

Medley, D. M., and Klein, A. Measuring classroom behavior with a pupil-reaction inventory. *Elementary School Journal,* 1957, *57,* 315–319.

Medley, D. M., and Mitzel, H. E. Studies of teacher behavior: Refinement of two techniques for assessing teachers' classroom behavior. New York: Board of Higher Education, City of New York, Division of Teacher Education, Office of Research and Evaluation, 1955.

Miller, G. D. (Ed.). Additional studies in elementary school guidance: Psychological education activities evaluated. St. Paul, Minn.: Division of Instruction, Minnesota Department of Education, 1973.

Miller, G. D., Gum, M., and Bender, D. Elementary school guidance: Demonstration and evaluation. St. Paul, Minn.: Division of Instruction, Minnesota Department of Education, 1972.

Piaget, J. Six psychological studies. New York: Random House, 1967.

Questionnaire for Students, Teachers and Administrators. Secondary School Research Program. Princeton, N. J.: Educational Testing Service, 1973.

Sarason, S. B. The culture of the school and the problem of change. Boston: Allyn and Bacon, 1971.

Sarason, S. B. The creation of settings and the future societies. San Francisco: Jossey-Bass, 1972.

Smith, L., and Keith, P. M. Anatomy of educational innovation. New York: Wiley, 1971.

Volsky, T., Magoon, T. M., Norman, W. T., and Hoyt, D. P. The Outcomes of counseling and psychotherapy. Minneapolis: University of Minnesota Press, 1965.

Watson, G. (Ed.). Change in school systems. Washington, D. C.: National Education Association, 1967.

Walberg, H. J. Predicting class learning: An approach to the class as a social system. American Educational Research Journal, 1969, 6, 529–542.

Whiteley, J. M., (Ed.). Research in counseling. Columbus, Ohio: Charles E. Merrill, 1968.

Withall, J. Development of a technique for the measurement of socioemotional climate in classrooms. Journal of Experimental Education, 1949, 17, 347–361.

CHAPTER 9
The Counselor as Researcher in the College Community

Ursula Delworth

Counseling in the college and university community can be an exciting experience and there are several significant functions for counselors on campus. Helping individual students with personal, educational, and career problems; developing and implementing programs to reach large numbers of students; and training/consulting with paraprofessionals and other members of the college community are some of the main services being offered.

Counselors are beginning to view themselves as researchers as well as service providers on campus. They are realizing the importance of evaluating their work as well as learning to see the value in knowing more about their students as a basis for planning services and programs. Colleges often provide unique resources for this study, such as expert consultation, research facilities, and the opportunity for association with faculty and students. By using these resources, counselors can develop skills and understandings that will allow them to know more about what they are and could be doing. The research function can be rewarding and enjoyable for counselors, and it has great potential for enhancing the lives of students.

Studies done in the past few years can tell us a great deal about college students and their interaction with the counseling process. Perhaps more importantly, they also point to many unanswered questions, and to problems with many of the research methods utilized.

RESEARCH ON COUNSELING
AND COLLEGE STUDENTS

Three reviews in recent volumes of the *Annual Review of Psychology* (Layton, Sandeen, and Baker, 1971; Pepinsky and Meara, 1973; Whiteley et al., 1975) provide fairly comprehensive looks at the recent research in college counseling and regarding college students. Only a fraction of the issues can be dealt with here.

Counseling Services

Much of the current discussion and research in the literature deals with three areas: counselor roles and services, counselor training, and counselor interventions. Some pertinent topics in each area are presented in more detail.

COUNSELOR ROLES AND SERVICES.   College counseling centers, in colleges regardless of size, indicate that they offered three main services: (a) counseling for personal problems, 96 percent; (b) counseling for study problems, 92 percent; and (3) counseling for choice of major field, 91 percent (Anderson, 1970). A number of surveys done over a ten year period (Warman, 1960, 1961; Wilcove and Sharp, 1971; Resnick and Gelso, 1971) indicate that college counselors see their most appropriate role as that of counseling students with personal problems. However, students, faculty, and other student services staff indicated priority for academic and educational counseling, although they included personal counseling as an appropriate function.

COUNSELOR TRAINING.   The core facilitative or counselor-offered conditions proposed by Carkhuff (1969) and others have formed the basis for much of the increasingly skill-oriented training offered to counseling students. These conditions include empathy, self-disclosure, and confrontation. Studies by Carkhuff (1969) and Truax and Mitchell (1971), among others, offer considerable evidence supporting the relationship between these conditions and client change. Although more recent research has raised questions concerning the dimensions and, in particular, the validity of rating counselors on the conditions at one period (Gurman, 1973), these conditions have become the basis for a number of training approaches (Carkhuff, 1969; Kagan, et al., 1967; Ivey, 1971; Danish and Hauer, 1973; Brammer, 1973; Egan, 1975).

In addition, research has indicated that nonprofessionals can be trained using these methods (Carkhuff, 1969), and an increasing number of college counselors are now utilizing one or more of these core approaches to train residence hall staff members and other student paraprofessionals in the helping role (Delworth, Sherwood, and Casaburri, 1974).

INTERVENTIONS.   There has been a significant increase in both use of and research on behavioral approaches in college counseling. Such techniques as setting observable behavior goals with clients and using desensitization procedures have been effective for a variety of client problems (Bandura, 1969; Krumboltz and Thoresen, 1969; Suinn, Edie, and Spinelli, 1970; Mehrabian, 1970).

Among other key developments has been an expansion of services beyond remedial, direct services to individuals. A model that incorporates preventive and developmental services to both groups and institutions has been developed by Morrill, Oetting, and Hurst (1974). This model provides a basis for many of the newer outreach programs on campus in which 80 percent of counseling centers are reported to be involved (Morrill and Oetting, 1970). However, limited research on the effectiveness of such interventions has appeared in the literature.

As with research in other areas, research on college counseling suffers from a variety of methodological difficulties. Small numbers in treatment or training groups, lack of controls, and lack of randomization are among the largest problems in the research that has been done. The research also suffers from lack of replication of studies, where the same intervention or training approach would be used with different groups of clients, subjects, or trainees, and with different counselors or trainers. In addition, Carkhuff (1966) states that "we must move further into the environment of the client if we are to account fully for the effects of counseling" (p. 471).

College Students

Researchers in higher education are increasingly studying the college student and the college environment as a basis for determining appropriate interventions on campus. The work of Astin is probably the most ambitious undertaking in this area. This work is a longitudinal study of (a) administrative characteristics, (b) environmental stimulus factors such as peer environment and classroom environment, and (c) the college image (Astin, 1968). Among some of the most important findings in this work thus far for college counselors are the following:

- Students' career choices change to conform more and more to the dominant model choice of their peers as they progress through the undergraduate years (Astin and Panos, 1969).

- Individual student achievement is neither improved nor impaired by the intellectual level of classmates, the level of academic competitiveness, or the financial resources of the institution (Astin and Panos, 1969).

- Marriage and living off campus contribute substantially to students' chances of dropping out of college (Astin, 1975).

Astin and others (Newcomb and Feldman, 1969; Chickering, 1969) have made recommendations to colleges based on their data. Unfortunately, as yet few studies have been done on students and their interactions with the campus environment at specific colleges. Such studies are necessary in order to design appropriate interventions and services for any specific college population.

DIRECTIONS FOR
COLLEGE COUNSELING

College counseling in the 1970s is apparently still highly invested in direct services to individual students who have concerns of a personal, educational, and vocational nature. However, many centers are currently involved in some type of outreach programming, which often focuses on preventive and developmental services and the use of students as paraprofessional counselors. There is an increased emphasis on large-scale longitudinal research that describes college students and their campus, and predicts outcomes of the interaction between student and college environment.

Counselors are increasingly involved in looking at the effectiveness of their work and training and in trying to understand the needs of the often diverse groups of students who enroll in colleges today. Problems, however, remain for counselors as they attempt to understand their students and the impact of counseling in the lives of these students. Among the predominant problems are the following:

Current research on counseling interventions generally has many methodological problems that make it difficult for counselors to trust and use what is being reported.

There has been little research done on the newer outreach efforts undertaken by counseling centers, and often limited knowlege of how to do this work—and gain support for doing it.

There has been limited attention paid to the process and outcome of setting relevant and realistic goals for counseling services.

There has been limited attention to study of students and their interactions with the college environment on individual campuses.

The student development approach articulated by Layton, Sandeen, and Baker (1971) speaks to these issues. They view student development as the product of person–environment interaction, or the "result of the interaction of student characteristics, including expectations of college, and the opportunities, demands, restrictions and sanctions, concerns and indifferences of the college environment and its subcultures" (pp. 533–534). Layton et al. contend that in order to develop programs and methods, counselors need to adopt models of human behavior that take into account not only the qualities of individual students, but of the setting in which students live. Unless counselors can look first at what their college is all about, and what is happening to students in their specific college environment, they run the risk that their interventions—no matter how successful—will have peripheral impact on the lives of students. This idea—inherent in an ecosystem approach—serves as an organizing framework within which questions of appropriate goals and valid, effective services can be asked and answered. Because of the great importance of the ecosystem approach and its promise as a framework for counselors and other student personnel workers, most of the remainder of the chapter focuses on it.

ECOSYSTEMS

The ecosystem model is a research and design process utilizing an ecological approach. The essence of such an approach is the interaction that occurs between persons and their environment, or how an environment affects people, their work, their leisure, and their personal growth. The model was developed at the Western Interstate Commission for Higher Education (1973) and based on much of the current thinking in social ecology and student development.

Traditionally, colleges have responded to students who were not adjusting to their campus environments by easing them out or referring them to a service (often counseling) that would aid them in making an adjustment. Rarely has attention been paid to institutional adjustments in terms of programs, policies, or physical spaces. Even when new services have been offered or existing ones expanded, this is rarely done on the basis of systematic data concerning person–environment fit. Ecosystem theory does not deny that some students should leave college or that some students will need individual assistance while in college. What it does assert is inclusion of an alternative option—the design of environments that ameliorate and prevent unnecessary problems and enhance student retention and growth. In other words, the approach introduces a "quality of life" dimension to viewing the campus. Such design is necessarily based on research regarding students and the college, and the transaction between them, or the person –environment fit.

The ecosystem model's design philosophy, as articulated in the WICHE report *The Ecosystem Model: Designing Campus Environments* (1973) is rooted in eight basic assumptions about persons and environment:

1.   The campus environment consists of all the stimuli that impinge on the students' senses and includes physical, chemical, biological, and social stimuli (policies, relationships, physical spaces, programs).

2.   A transactional relationship exists between college students and their campus environment; that is, the students shape the environment and are shaped by it.

3.   For purposes of environmental design, the shaping properties of the campus environment are emphasized; however, the students are still viewed as active, choice-making agents who may resist, transform, or nullify environmental influences.

4.   Every student possesses capacity for a wide spectrum of possible behaviors. A given campus environment may facilitiate or inhibit any one or more of these behaviors. The campus should be intentionally designed to offer opportunities, incentives, and reinforcements for growth and development.

5.   Students will attempt to cope with any educational environment in which they are placed. If the environment is not compatible with the students, the students may react negatively or fail to develop desirable qualities.

6.   Because of the wide range of individual differences among students, fitting the campus environment to the students requires the creation of a variety of campus subenvironments.

7. Every campus has a design, even if the administration, faculty, and students have not planned it or are not consciously aware of it. A design technology for campus environments, therefore, is useful both for the analysis of existing campus environments and the design of new ones.

8. Successful campus design is dependent on participation of all campus members including students, faculty, staff, administration, and trustees or regents.

The model's process is utilized to identify shaping properties in the campus environment in order to eliminate dysfunctional features and to incorporate features that facilitate student educational and personal growth. For example, a physical space might be altered, or a policy changed. In other instances, a service might be offered to help a specific group of students such as mature women cope with stress in the environment and better utilize educational opportunities.

The model can be applied at a macro-level to study and design environments for the entire campus community. It can be applied at a micro-level to study and design subenvironments for groups within the campus community such as residence hall students, students who are members of ethnic minority groups, or students majoring in biological science. And it can be applied to route individual students to a physical environment, service, or program that has been demonstrated to be meeting student needs. This would be considered an individual design project, and is usually the one most familiar to counselors.

The ecosystems approach consistently takes the values and goals of the institution into consideration, translating these into environments (buildings, curricula, policies, services) that contain mechanisms to reach the stated goals. Student perception and behavior are assessed to provide data on how well the student–environment fit is working, and how well the changes improve this fit.

COUNSELORS AND AN ECOLOGICAL APPROACH

A few counselors and agencies have begun to systematically apply an ecological framework to their work, and many others are utilizing some of the ideas and methods discussed in this approach. In a time of limited resources, decreased support for higher education among the public and in the legislatures, and increased accountability regarding counseling services, it makes sense for counselors to study this approach and devise ways to use it to enhance their impact on students and the college.

Counseling services that have assessed the needs of students and the parent institution, built their system of services based on these needs, communicated the availability of services to students, and evaluated and reported these services are currently reported to be experiencing much better success than those agencies not involved in such activities (Kelly, 1975). Such an approach is basically ecological, and answers three questions vital for every counseling endeavor: (1) What are the goals and objectives of counseling services on this campus? (2) What methods are counseling services using to meet these goals and objectives? and (3) How well are these goals and objectives being met?

Setting Goals and Objectives

A system developed at Colorado State University (Hurst, Moore, Davidshofer, and Delworth, 1976) serves as one example of using an ecological approach in setting goals for a counseling agency. The staff designed a ten-step sequence to set and meet agency goals, yet allow for staff member individuality. The first two steps relate specifically to setting goals and objectives.

Step One: Identify and/or define institutional goals. This step is designed to emphasize the interdependence between the counseling center and the larger institution. Because college goals will differ, and some may not be clearly stated, the Colorado State group adopted the American Council on Education (later reprinted as part of Creager, 1968) conceptualization of the higher education process (Figure 9–1). This conceptualization is general enough to apply to all institutions of higher education and yet specific enough to complement most college goal statements. The conceptualization is helpful in deriving agency goals and objectives that are relevant to institutional goals.

Step Two: Derive agency objectives from institutional goal statements. Morrill and Hurst (1971) proposed a role for a counseling agency that is one example of how an agency may derive its objectives from the broader statement of institutional goals. Their statements are as follows:

1. To provide students with those skills, attitudes, and resources prerequisite to maximum utilization of and success in the learning environment.

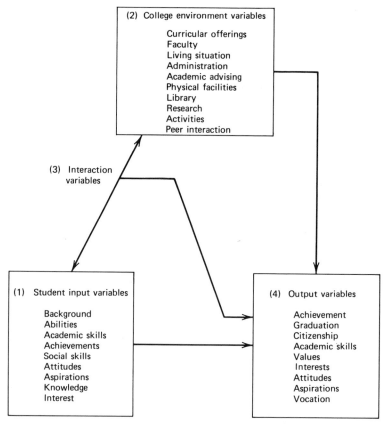

FIGURE 9.1.   Primary Variables in Higher Education

2. To contribute to, modify, and enhance the university environment according to established principles of learning and human development.

3. To acquire information about students, their environment, and their interaction in order to provide a data base for relevant programming to achieve objectives (1) and (2) above.

The first statement is an objective derived from the first group of variables in the ACE conceptualization. The second was derived from the second group of variables, and the last statement relates to the third group of variables and includes both of the other two groups.

Methods for Meeting Goals and Objectives

Once overall goals and objectives have been set and priorities determined, specific services are derived, and the entire system monitored. An important provision of such processes will be negotiation between staff members so that high-priority services, based on assessment of student needs, will be offered, while at the same time staff members will have opportunity to exercise their own skills and interests.

Evaluating How Well Goals and Objectives Are Being Met

Evaluation, or evaluative research, is aimed at collecting data on the effectiveness of programs or services that will help in making decisions. Evaluators are not concerned with proving or disproving a specific theory. Instead, they are concerned with whether a specific program should be continued. Evaluation data on effectiveness serves as the basis on which additional factors (such as program costs and campus support) are looked at in the decision-making process. Without data, counselors risk continuing programs just because they are fun to do and don't cost much!

Program monitoring is a vital part of this process and should be distinguished from evaluation (Oetting, 1976). Monitoring provides data on number of students involved in services, how staff hours are spent, and so on. This is helpful information for both agency staff and higher administrators, but does not tell the agency if a program or service is effective.

COUNSELOR COMPETENCIES IN AN ECOLOGICAL APPROACH

As counselors begin to appreciate the viability of an ecological approach, they come to see that the entire system is built on research, on *knowing* enough about the campus community and its inhabitants—students, faculty, and others—to design environments that will prevent problems and facilitate growth and well-being. Research alone, however, will not automatically lead to desired changes. Counselors also find that they must be able to work with professional colleagues and students in order to gather and disseminate such research. They must be able to demonstrate the effectiveness of new designs, be they programs, policies, or changes in physical space. Little of this necessary knowlege is easily obtainable via the established path of "pure research" or scientific inquiry. Certainly, knowledge of statistics and experimental design is needed (at least by someone in the agency), but much more is required. What is needed most of all are new techniques, better applications of little-used methods, consultation skills, and the willingness to try approaches that have not yet been proven or recorded in the literature.

Obviously, the specific expertise of counselors in delivery of services such as individual counseling and training is still vital. What is added in the ecological approach is that there are new tasks to learn, and that research, in one form or another, is a basic part of these tasks. Further, since doctoral-level counselors and psychologists are usually as inexperienced in some of these approaches as masters-level counselors, graduate students, and undergraduate students, no one group of counseling personnel has all the answers. The ecosystems approach requires new learning for all, and encourages the unique contributions of each type and level of professional expertise.

A process for using an ecosystem approach at the micro-level (agency or department) has been developed at the Western Interstate Commission for Higher Education (Aulepp and Delworth, 1976). The model comprises five stages.

Stage I involves the establishment of a planning team, based on the assumption that successful campus design is dependent on participation of a variety of campus members. Students, faculty and administrators and staff from the target environment (e.g., residence hall system or counseling center) are always included.

Stage II concentrates on determining what aspects of the environment the planning team wants measured in terms of student perceptions.

Stage III is involved in the development of a technique or techniques to measure perceptions and also to assess *why* students hold their perceptions. That is, planners want to know what has happened to students to cause their perceptions. Without such information, there is insufficient data for redesign purposes. For example, we may discover that 90 percent of the students have negative perceptions of the counseling center, but we do not know whether these perceptions are based on attitude or behavior of counselors, the physical setting, insufficient information, or a variety of other factors. Until the planning group has this information, it is in danger of making the wrong redesign in the center.

Stage IV involves administering the assessment techniques and conducting an initial data analysis.

Stage V includes processes for the subsequent redesign of the environment as well as suggested procedures for evaluating the effects of the redesign in terms of reaching agency and institutional goals.

There are a number of competencies that counselors must gain in order to effectively apply an ecosystem model. As a minimum, they must be able to:

- Understand the organization of the campus community and be able to work with a variety of professional colleagues (administrators, faculty, other student services staff).

- Assess the needs, perceptions, and behavior of students, across various groups, and in a variety of environments and thus determine the person–environment fit.

- Work with students as colleagues in planning and implementing research and service designs.

- Do evaluative research on services, programs, and other activities.

- Interpret and communicate research data and recommendations to members of the campus community.

- Develop and implement programs and services in a systematic manner.

Each of these skills is discussed in more detail, with examples from various college campuses.

Working in the Campus Community

Counselors have to know how the institution functions to get its work accomplished, both formally and informally. Written information (such as organizational charts) is helpful, but rarely gives much insight into the informal process. Counselors thus must develop a "network" of knowledgeable faculty, students, administrators, and staff who can give them clues regarding how the system "really" operates; that is, who on campus are the persons of influence.

It is vital that counselors tune into the "climate" or "political realities" on campus. Without such insight, they risk developing programs and services that are based on student need but are unacceptable to campus traditions or values. Once the realities are known, counselors can decide to (1) set aside a controversial or unacceptable program, or (2) devise methods to gain support for the program before it is offered.

There are a number of ways to gather needed information on "climate." One campus group asked a sample of faculty, students, administrators, and staff to rank current and potential services in order of importance. They followed up to determine if low-ranked services were seen as merely low priority or were unacceptable to some group or groups.

When counselors desire to develop a program that is important to students, but negative political realities stand in the way, they would do well to involve influential campus members in the planning and implementation of the program. At one campus, need was demonstrated for increased education and communication in the area of sexuality. In this church-related, private college, however, there were many constraints against moving into this area. Counselors invited key administrators and campus ministers to become part of a planning group. The result was a program that met student needs in a manner the college could support.

Counselors need professional colleagues in the campus community on an ongoing basis for information about the campus, to help assess person–environment fit, to be their "reality testers," and for support. Many times also, such colleagues become involved in the offering and evaluation of counseling services. On one campus a core group of leaders for a marital enrichment workshop is composed of campus ministers. A number of faculty are involved in the counseling service's ethnic relations effort on the same campus.

Determining Person–Environment Fit

Counselors have to be able to determine the congruence between what students need and want in the college environment and what students are getting—the "fit" between student and environment.

Such an assessment might look at the entire campus (macro-level) or a subenvironment (micro-level) such as the counseling service or the residence hall system. The assessment might also examine a specific group of students, such as mature women returning to college, freshmen, or graduate students. Ideally, counselors would probably want to look at the fit between students and counseling services first. The increased skills and credibility gained through this endeavor should make it easier to join with other persons and groups in assessing other environments on campus.

Certainly, in any effort, counselors must be sure to involve at least several appropriate campus members in planning the study. Such input gives a wider perspective, and often results in more credibility on campus.

There is probably no end to the approaches to be used in this assessment. The following are among some currently being utilized on campuses across the country.

Listing current or possible services of a counseling agency and asking students to rate or rank these in (a) importance, (b) availability, and (c) success in meeting student needs.

Listing needs or interests and having these rated or ranked in the same manner as above. In this instance, it is helpful to ask students to indicate *how* or *where* the need or interest is being met.

Interviews with students (either fairly large groups or in-depth interviews of a few students).

Questionnaires that gather student perceptions of various campus environments, or different aspects of one environment.

"Environmental referent" forms (Aulepp and Delworth, 1976) that follow perceptual questionnaires and ask students to give more information on *why* they hold their perceptions and what they think should be done regarding any given situation.

Goal statement inventories, which ask students to rate college or agency goals in terms of "is" and "should be."

Observations of student behavior in various environments at various periods.

Demographic data on students to determine factors in dropping out versus staying in school or other information (Astin, 1975).

Assessment of personality and/or developmental stage that can be compared with demographic data to determine optimum environments for different students.

Interviews with key "sensors" (those with maximum student contact on campus). Such persons will include faculty, but other groups can also be important. On one campus, women who served food in the student union cafeteria were found to have a great deal of valuable information regarding student concerns and needs.

Interviews or questionnaires given to selected groups of students at stated intervals.

Telephone surveys. One large university has set up a telephone survey service with trained students as interviewers. Any agency or organization can request help in designing a survey that is then implemented by the service.

There are many more techniques and methods in current use. Probably the most productive assessments utilize more than one method to gather information, especially if one method chosen is a standardized instrument. Such instruments can be very useful, but they are limited in that they may not ask questions about what campus members sense are the crucial issues on a given campus. They often lack "face validity" with students by using unfamiliar terms or asking about environments that do not exist on a specific campus.

Additionally, more creative methods can be devised. One suggestion (as yet untried) is to equip students with inexpensive cameras and ask them to record "positives" and "negatives" in their experience during a week's time. Interviews could then be held to specify the picture's meaning; for example, an empty dorm room might signify a student's lack of friends and worthwhile activities.

The same methods can be used to assess fit between the environment and persons other than students (e.g., faculty or staff). Some studies compare student perceptions with those of faculty members (Huebner, 1975).

Working with Students as Colleagues

Undergraduate students have an important (though often overlooked) part to play in all aspects of an ecological approach. Certainly they are the primary targets of study and design, but they are also valued colleagues in planning and implementing this work. Students often have a better idea of what approaches (both for research and delivery of services) can work. They usually have more credibility in approaching peers for assessment or in program implementation and evaluation. Perhaps most of all, they ask important questions and they help to keep professionals "on the track" of some of the crucial but difficult issues that counselors and other staff find hard to face.

There has been a rapid rise in student paraprofessionals on campus, and many of these have been used by agencies to deliver services to the student population. In addition, students are currently involved as:

Members of teams planning person–environment assessment and design

Implementers of research projects

Program evaluators

Interpreters of research data

"Change agents" to implement designs based on studies of person–environment fit

Developers of new programs and services, either alone or in conjunction with a counseling or other campus agency; crisis lines and birth control clinics are probably the outstanding examples in this area

Students themselves can gain much by their involvement in such activities. They acquire new skills and added self-confidence. Their participation can increase their sense of belonging and contributing to the campus community. In addition, many are able to "test out" possible vocational plans and acquire letters of recommendation for graduate school or future employment. A number receive money or academic credit for their work.

Counselors who take the time to involve students in their work usually gain added insight into student pressures, concerns, and values. They gain new and innovative ideas on how to approach problems, and also benefit from the help of dedicated, skilled students to implement ideas and plans. In return, counselors should be sure to train, supervise, and consult with students, especially when students are working on tasks that are new to them. In many cases, students and counselors are actually learning a new approach together.

In the new "consumer society" students expect to monitor and improve the quality of their educational experience. Counselors can involve them in doing this—to the benefit of the students, the counselors, and the campus community as a whole.

Evaluative Research

Evaluative research is done on programs and services in order to make decisions regarding whether to continue such programs or how programs may be modified to become more effective. It is not a conservative process in that decisions must be made about programs based on the best data available rather than on absolute "proof" that a program works. If there are alternative explanations of data, the counselor-evaluator and the decisionmakers must weigh these carefully, and decide what alternatives are the most likely. If the best estimate is that a program works, then it might be continued (other factors such as cost being taken into consideration) and further evaluation done.

This approach clearly differs from scientific inquiry, which aims at advancing scientific knowledge. An example might clarify the difference. A marital enrichment workshop is being run for student couples. The evaluation plan calls for measures of attitude toward self and partner, and behavior change in terms of self-report and report by the partner on specific objectives regarding communication, intimacy, and fighting styles. There are enough participants for the group, but not enough for a control group. It is possible to get pre and post scores, but the design is not very good in terms of scientific inquiry. Any changes *could* be due to the program itself, but could also be a result of such factors as a feeling on the part of the participants that they have been designated as a special group, statistical regression, maturation, expectancy, or even the charisma of the group leader. Although some of these possibilities are less likely, others have led to significant research results. Therefore, from the point of view of scientific inquiry (and the view of most journal editors), the study has minimal value. However, if positive results are obtained, the program may be continued, building in a control group (or using the participants as their own control), perhaps running groups with different leaders, and perhaps using a "placeboid" group that would undergo some form of "treatment" but not receive the program itself. If results are negative, evaluators and decision-makers will want to consider, among other things, whether their evaluation plan was really measuring change. If the program is considered very important, then it might be rerun with more careful evaluation.

Evaluative research, although often lacking some of the rigor of scientific inquiry, is equally important because it helps counselors and others make "real life" decisions. It allows counselors to carry on their work in a more responsible, ethical, and productive manner, and it aids counseling agencies in becoming more accountable to the college as a whole.

However, counselors should not assume that evaluation plans are always poor research designs. Evaluators who think about possible crucial alternatives to explain data *ahead of time* may well be able to modify their plans so that these alternatives can be more safely rejected when results are in. It is important, however, to realize that in the "real world" of evaluation it is typically impossible to control for all potential sources of error, at least in any one study. Therefore, evaluation of programs and services becomes an ongoing process, or "way of life" in which successive studies continue to demonstrate program effectiveness through elimination of sources of error. Even studies with severe limitations are often more useful than no data at all—at least as a start!

Interpretation of Research

In the past, counselors have often thought that doing good research —scientific research and evaluative research—was sufficient. What they are coming to realize is that administrators and other members of the campus community many times do not make a clear connection between data and meeting goals and objectives in their own areas. What is needed are ways of interpreting and communicating research findings in a manner so that these decision-makers can hear and act on the findings.

One university planning group chose to issue a series of brief reports on their study of person–environment fit in residence halls, each dealing with a different area of study. They combined this with meetings with key administrators and staff members of concerned agencies. They also had a general overview of the study and its results published in the university newspaper.

A community college planning group presented their questionnaire to department chairpersons and faculty, and asked which items or areas of the assessment were of most importance to that department. A tailor-made report of results (both perceptions and reasons for these) was then developed for each department.

Program Development

All of the previously discussed competencies are important in the development and implementation of effective programs and services. In addition, a definitive *process* for program development is needed. This process should indicate specific methods, techniques, and a sequence for utilizing the competencies and applying any other skills that are important (e.g., review of relevant research on programs similar to the one being planned; group leadership).

Most counselors develop a sense of program planning through experience. The danger here is that they may spend a good deal of time gaining such experience at the expense of good programming. It would help counselors to (1) work with experienced colleagues in developing a program planning process, and/or (2) take an already developed process and adapt it to their specific situation. One example of such a process was developed by Moore and Delworth (1976).

KEY AREAS FOR STUDY

In doing both scientific and evaluative research, counselors will want to address themselves more systematically to some key issues in college counseling. In addition to issues on individual campuses that need the attention of counselors in terms of research, there are a number of issues or areas of study that appear relevant to the college counseling field as a whole. Among these general issues are the following:

The Effectiveness of Paraprofessional Counselors

Students and other paraprofessionals are being utilized more and more as deliverers of counseling services (Layton, Sandeen, and Baker, 1971). Although such helpers have been effective in a wide variety of service areas, counselors cannot assume that paraprofessionals will be as effective as professionals in any given program on a specific campus. Careful studies of professional versus paraprofessional effectiveness are currently few in number, and are generally case studies of one program. Well-designed, multivariate, longitudinal studies are much needed. Studies of comparative effectiveness of various training approaches with paraprofessionals (as with professional counselors) are also needed.

Career Counseling Approaches with Various Groups of Students

There has been a proliferation in recent years of approaches and methods for career counseling with college students. Layton, Sandeen, and Baker (1971) assert that vocational development theorists agree in conceptualizing choice making as "a dynamic and complex process with the growth of the individual of central concern" (p. 543). Research such as that by Faunce (1968) has increased our knowledge of the relation of personal characteristics to career choice. Little attention has been paid to what career choice approaches are most effective with specific groups of students. It may be that students vary considerably in terms of their ability to utilize various approaches. Methods that rely heavily on students' ability to seek out information and resources on their own may be most effective for some. Other students may need and value the support and structure of a group in order to facilitate their career exploration. Counselors should study learning styles and match these with career counseling approaches in order to maximize success for each student.

Effectiveness of Training and/or Consultation in the Campus Community

Counselors have begun to invest a great deal of effort in training and consulting with other staff on campus (e.g., residence hall staff, departmental groups). Generally, evaluation of these activities consists of a report by the trainees or consultees on how they perceive the help given, and sometimes a few examples of how they are using the help. Counselors need to develop clear objectives for such interventions (even for brief interventions) and systematically evaluate how well those objectives were met. Objectives (and subsequent evaluation) would be concerned with such issues as the following:

Skills learned by trainees or consultees.

Specific uses made of the training or consultation by trainees or consultees.

Effectiveness of these uses.

Further service requested by trainees or consultees.

Ability of trainees or consultees to generalize skills to new situations.

Effectiveness of Audio, Visual, and Written Materials

As these methods replace live counseling interventions, evaluation must be done to determine if such materials are as effective, or even more so, than the same service performed by a counselor. Because such materials often are part of a program sequence, it is important to know if they add to or detract from the overall effectiveness of the program. For example, do video or audio career guidance materials facilitate the student's information acquisition and decision-making to the same (or greater) extent than meeting with a counselor? Do written "homework" materials facilitate skill practice in marital groups between sessions?

Programs and Services to Enhance Development

Sprinthall and Erickson (1974), Ivey and Alschuler (1973), and others have stated that counselors must become psychological educators, using their skills and knowledge to promote personal growth through the curriculum. A number of models of cognitive and ego development (Kohlberg, 1969; Loevinger and Wessler, 1970) have relevance for college students. It is now up to counselors to study these models, and develop the mechanisms and programs that will enhance development in students. One promising start in this field is Erickson's (1975) report on a program of deliberate psychological education to enhance growth for women college students. Several colleges are experimenting with enhancing values and personal development through a variety of curriculum offerings, using counselors as planners and consultants.

CONCLUSION

College students continue to be the most highly studied group in the counseling field. Yet much of this research is limited to a particular small population and institution, and does not speak to issues of transforming research data into more effective programs and services. It is essential that counselors focus their efforts toward research models and strategies that will have positive benefits in the lives of students.

An ecological or ecosystems approach represents a solid framework for both research and intervention in the field of college counseling. Such an approach allows research to become a "way of life" for everyone involved in counseling services. It facilitates the setting of counseling goals and objectives based on the mission of the institution and the needs of students, the development and implementation of useful programs and policies, and the demonstration of program effectiveness. In addition, it brings counselors into a collaborative role with administrators, students, faculty, and other members of the campus community. It allows counselors the opportunity to be seen as full partners in the demanding tasks of building "quality of life" on campus and thus enhancing growth both for students and institutions of higher education and increasing the value of counseling work on campus.

REFERENCES

Anderson, W. Service offered by college counseling centers. *Journal of Counseling Psychology,* 1970, *17,* 380–382.

Astin, A. W. A program of research on student development. *Journal of College Student Personnel,* 1968, *9,* 299–307.

Astin, A. W., and Panos, R. J. *Educational and vocational development of college students.* Washington: American Council on Education, 1969.

Astin, A. W. *Preventing students from dropping out.* San Francisco: Jossey-Bass, 1975.

Aulepp, L., and Delworth, U. *Training manual for an ecosystem model.* Boulder, Colo.: WICHE, 1976.

Bandura, A. *Principles of behavior modification.* New York: Holt, Rinehart and Winston, 1969.

Brammer, L. M. *The helping relationship: process and skills.* Englewood Cliffs, N.J.: Prentice-Hall, 1973.

Carkhuff, R. R. *Helping and human relations,* Vols. 1 and 2. New York: Holt, Rinehart and Winston, 1969.

Carkhuff, R. R. Counseling research, theory, and practice—1965. *Journal of Counseling Psychology,* 1966, *13,* 467–480.

Chickering, A. W. *Education and identity.* San Francisco: Jossey-Bass, 1969.

Creager, J. A. Use of research results in matching students and colleges. *Journal of College Student Personnel,* 1968, *9,* 312–319.

Danish, S. J., and Hauer, A. L. *Helping skills: A basic training program.* New York: Behavioral Publications, 1973.

Delworth, U., Sherwood, G., and Casaburri, N. *Student paraprofessionals: A working model for higher education.* ACPA Student Personnel Series No. 17. Washington, D.C.: APGA Press, 1974.

Egan, G. *The skilled helper.* Monterey, Calif.: Brooks/Cole, 1975.

Erickson, V. L. Deliberate psychological education for women. *Counselor Education and Supervision,* 1975, *14* (3), 297–309.

Faunce, P. S. Personality characteristics and vocational interests related to the college persistence of academically gifted women. *Journal of Counseling Psychology,* 1968, *15,* 31–40.

Gurman, A. S. Instability of therapeutic conditions in psychotherapy. *Journal of Counseling Psychology,* 1973, *20,* 16–24.

Huebner, L. A. *An ecological assessment: Person–environment fit.* Unpublished doctoral dissertation. Colorado State University, 1975.

Hurst, J. C., Moore, M., Davidshofer, C. O., and Delworth, U. Agency directionality and staff individuality. *The Personnel and Guidance Journal,* 1976, *54,* (6), 312–317.

Ivey, A. E. *Microcounseling: Innovations in interviewing training.* Springfield, Ill.: Charles C Thomas, 1971.

Ivey, A. E., and Alschuler, A. S. An introduction to the field. *The Personnel and Guidance Journal,* 1973, *51,* (9), 591–597.

Kagan, N., Krathwohl, D. R., Goldberg, A. D., Campbell, R. J., Schauble, P. G., Greenberg, B. S., Danish, S. J., Resnikoff, A., Bowes, J., and Bondy, S. B. *Studies in human interaction: Interpersonal process recall simulated by videotape.* East Lansing: Michigan State University, Educational Publication Services, 1967.

Kelly, B. C. What's in at U.S. counseling centers: An inside view by an outside observer. *Dialogue,* June, 1975, 1–3.

Kohlberg, L. Stage and sequence: The cognitive-developmental approach to socialization. In D. Goslin (Ed.). *Handbook of socialization theory and research,* New York: Rand McNally, 1969, 347–480.

Krumboltz, J. D., and Thoresen, C. E. *Behavioral counseling cases and techniques.* New York: Holt, Rinehart and Winston, 1969.

Layton, W. L., Sandeen, C. A., and Baker, R. D. Student development and counseling. In P. H. Mussen and M. R. Rosenzweig (Eds.). *Annual Review of Psychology,* Vol. 22. Palo Alto, Calif.: Annual Reviews Inc., 1971, 533–564.

Loevinger, J., and Wessler, R. *Measuring ego development,* Vols. 1 and 2. San Francisco: Jossey-Bass, 1970.

Mehrabian, A. *Tactics of social influence.* Englewood Cliffs, N.J.: Prentice-Hall, 1970.

Moore, M., and Delworth, U. *Training manual for student service program development.* Boulder, Colo.: WICHE, 1976.

Morrill, W. H., and Oetting, E. R. Outreach programs in college counseling: A survey of practices. *Journal of College Student Personnel,* 1970, *7,* 226–234.

Morrill, W. H., and Hurst, J. C. A preventive and developmental role for the college counselor. *Counseling Psychologist,* 1971, *2,* 90–95.

Morrill, W. H., Oetting, E. R., and Hurst, J. C. Dimensions of counselor functioning. *The Personnel and Guidance Journal,* 1974, *52,* (6), 355–359.

Newcomb, T. M., and Feldman, K. A. *The impact of college on students,* Vols. 1 and 2. San Francisco, Calif.: Jossey-Bass, 1969.

Oetting, E. R. Evaluative research and orthodox science. *The Personnel and Guidance Journal,* 1976, *55,* 11–15.

Pepinsky, H. B., and Meara, N. M. Student development and counseling. In P. H. Mussen and M. R. Rosenzweig (Eds.), *Annual Review of Psychology,* Vol. 24. Palo Alto, Calif.: Annual Reviews Inc., 1973, 117–150.

Resnick, H., and Gelso, C. Differential perceptions of counseling role: A reexamination. *Journal of Counseling Psychology,* 1971, *18,* 549–553.

Sprinthall, N., and Erickson, V. L. Learning psychology by doing psychology: Guidance through the curriculum. *The Personnel and Guidance*

Journal, 1974, *52,* (6), 396–405.

Suinn, R., Edie, C., and Spinelli, P. Accelerated massed desensitization: Innovation in short-term treatment. *Behavior Therapy,* 1970, *1,* 303–311.

Truax, C. B., and Mitchell, K. M. Research on certain therapist interpersonal skills in relation to process and outcome. In A. E. Bergin and S. Garfield (Eds.), *Handbook of psychotherapy and behavior change.* New York: Wiley, 1971, 299–344.

Warman, R. E. Differential perceptions of counseling role. *Journal of Counseling Psychology,* 1960, *7,* 269–274.

Warman, R. E. The counseling role of college and university counseling centers. *Journal of Counseling Psychology,* 1961, *8,* 231–238.

Western Interstate Commission for Higher Education. *The ecosystem model: Designing campus environments.* Boulder, Colo.: WICHE, 1973.

Whiteley, J. M., Burkhart, M. Q., Herman-Harway, M., and Whiteley, R. Counseling and student development. In M. R. Rosenzweig and L. W. Porter (Eds.), *Annual Review of Psychology,* Vol. 26. Palo Alto, Calif.: Annual Reviews Inc., 1975, 337–366.

Wilcove, G., and Sharp, W. H. Differential perceptions of a college counseling center. *Journal of Counseling Psychology,* 1971, *18,* 60–63.

CHAPTER 10
Rehabilitation Counseling and Rehabilitation Research

Dwight R. Kauppi

The range of research relevant to the rehabilitation counselor is broad, just as the domain of the rehabilitation counselor is broad. Many forces have shaped the roles of rehabilitation counselors and the kinds of research that have been done that aid them in their work. This chapter delineates the domain of rehabilitation counseling and examines several of the major research streams, with implications for the practitioner. Suggestions are offered both for using and doing research.

THE DOMAIN OF REHABILITATION COUNSELING

Rehabilitation counseling is not always clearly distinguished from other practices of counseling or guidance. If asked to tell what's different about rehabilitation, the typical rehabilitation counselor will mention the work with "deviant" clients, the focus on client assets rather than liabilities, the emphasis on practical, life-functioning goals, and the use of a multidisciplinary team to achieve holistic service to the client. When it is pointed out that these elements are not exclusive to rehabilitation (nor indeed are they present in every instance of rehabilitation), the typical rehabilitation counselor will nonetheless insist that rehabilitation counseling is meaningfully different from other kinds of counseling.

Rehabilitation counselors may be wrong in many specific instances when they insist that they are different. Still, rehabilitation counselors in general share many characteristics and these have many implications for the research that is relevant to the task. For one thing, the rehabilitation counselor's clients are all "deviants," persons who are in some significant characteristics well beyond the middle 50 percent of the population. This deviance may or may not be readily apparent, but is acknowledged by all clients in the act of accepting the services of a rehabilitation counselor. Just about all of a rehabilitation counselor's clients have objective problems. This is in contrast to many other counseling caseloads, where the clientele may be healthy, financially secure, well entrenched and accepted in the mainstream, with many skills and advantages, but who feel a need that brings them in for counseling. As a result, rehabilitation counselors must work with both intrapsychic and external problems. The intrapsychic reactions of a client are important, although the typical rehabilitation counselor may spend relatively little time trying to modify them directly. Intrapsychic problems often include the client's view of self as a damaged person, and ambivalence about trading an easy dependence for the rigors of trying. Other problems often present include: unemployment, pain, poverty, disfigurement, familial rejection, social ostracism, the possibility of future disability or death, and all the other personal, medical, and social difficulties people can face.

In addition to working with clients, rehabilitation counselors work with many other persons and institutions. They must relate to a family that is sometimes helpful, sometimes overprotective, occasionally rejecting. They deal with problems of the labor market, the economy, the insurance and workmen's compensation laws, and the social services industry. They must cope with a sometimes hostile community. They must deal with the politics of agencies, local, county, state and federal government, and a variety of professions.

The methods available to rehabilitation counselors are similarly varied. They use, of course, the traditional individual and group counseling techniques employed by counselors in most settings. For many rehabilitation counselors, though, the "50 minute hour" in the office has been replaced by individual and informal sessions in a variety of locales: at the client's home or place of employment, at a work evaluation station, in a rehabilitation center, or hospital—wherever the client is. The rehabilitation counselor typically has access to various other professionals and paraprofessionals, with all their expertise and techniques. The use of so many workers is necessitated by the different problems affecting many life areas presented by most rehabilitation clients. In order to integrate the work of all the specialists in a "holistic" manner, a team is necessary.

The focus of rehabilitation is on the strengths and assets of the client, rather than on pathology and weakness. There is a subtle but significant difference between saying "this person can't walk, except with crutches" and saying "this person can walk, with crutches." The intent of rehabilitation workers is not making the client "well" or "curing" the condition, but rather achieving the highest level of functioning possible. As a result, the rehabilitation counselor's interest in the evaluation of clients is in measures of strength.

So the answer to the question "What is special about rehabilitation counseling?" seems to require several parts. Rehabilitation counselors generally focus on the assets of their clients, work as part of a team concerned with the client's total functioning, toward practical goals of independence and self support, and use a variety of techniques to help clients with many internal and external problems. Certainly some counselors who do not call themselves rehabilitation counselors would claim the same distinctions, at least some of the time, and some rehabilitation counselors would not always fit this description. Still, the description is generally more true of rehabilitation counselors than not, and can serve to guide a consideration of the research that is significant to rehabilitation counselors.

RESEARCH RELEVANT
TO REHABILITATION
COUNSELORS

In an effort to give a flavor of the research literature without attempting a comprehensive review, this chapter describes research relevant to the rehabilitation counselor in four categories: research on specific disabilities, rehabilitation counseling service delivery, rehabilitation constructs, and research utilization. This listing is not exhaustive nor are the categories mutually exclusive. Purposely omitted are the kinds of research that are of interest to counselors in general, such as research on counseling and vocational psychology. Some of that research is accomplished under the support of rehabilitation funding, and gets reported in rehabilitation journals, but it is not considered here. Also omitted is the vast amount of primarily medical research.

Specific Disability Research

A very large body of the research of interest to rehabilitation counselors has been done on the rehabilitation of persons with specific disabilities. Research reported is generally on some special characteristic of the group (such as the handicapping effect of the disability, or the particular personality or social problems presumably shared by persons with that disability), or on some special techniques of rehabilitation useful with persons with that disability. This research is undertaken for a variety of scientific, practical, and political reasons. Some disabilities present severe social problems, either because they are widespread (such as mental retardation), or because they present very serious handicaps (such as quadriplegia). Public concern may lead to legislation that provides support for research on particular disabilities. Perhaps as important as any factor, the presence of centers and organizations devoted to particular disabilities stimulates and supports such research by political action, financial support, and access to data.

Rehabilitation counselors may find their practices greatly influenced by some of the studies done with particular disabilities. For example, the disability of mental retardation formerly was thought to preclude work and vocational rehabilitation. Even though mentally retarded persons were eligible for vocational rehabilitation services, they were not accepted in large numbers. At the same time, studies were done and reported showing that many mentally retarded persons could work. One of the best known was the study by Baller (1936), which reported on a group of adults who had been classified earlier as mentally deficient. This same group was followed up later by Charles (1953), and even later by Baller, Charles, and Miller (1967). The results, like those of many other such follow-ups, show that many mentally retarded persons are gainfully employed. They may not, as a group, be earning as much as a comparison nonretarded group, but there are many individuals who are self-supporting and in other ways indistinguishable from the population at large. Their appearance may be a mask covering actual incompetence (Edgerton, 1968), but they certainly are, as a disability group, suitable for vocational rehabilitation.

Mental retardation also offers many examples of research on special rehabilitation techniques. Often the programs demonstrated have to do with early identification and special education, special workshops, special techniques for behavioral management, and jobs that are uniquely suitable for the mentally retarded. These studies are likely to be reports of what has been done or observed in the field, leaving the usual questions that result when there are no real control groups or precise criteria. Still, most rehabilitation counselors might find such research to be very interesting, and a source of ideas for useful techniques.

The research on other specific disabilities is surprisingly similar. There are reports that discuss the unique aspects of the disability; such research shows that, despite popular opinion, people with the disability can be rehabilitated. And there are reports of special techniques, and special problems in working with that disability, usually including the notion that early identification and intervention are important, that specialists in the disability can do the best job, and that the attitudes of the counselor and the client are important.

A variety of physical and psychiatric disabilities have been the subjects of such research. Also treated as disability groups have been older disabled workers (Muthard and Morris, 1961), welfare recipients (Hamilton and Muthard, 1973), and offenders.

Research on Rehabilitation Counseling Service Delivery

A large volume and a wide variety of studies can be included in the general category of "service delivery." There are studies to test one or another new (or old) method of getting rehabilitation services to clients. There are studies to establish the technology for assessing various aspects of service delivery. Some studies look at the work behavior, attitudes, and environments of counselors and other rehabilitation workers. There are studies of the sociology of rehabilitation. Of special interest to the counselor are studies of counselor effectiveness and function.

One kind of research effort of great importance to the counselor is the search for better criteria of successful rehabilitation than the old-fashioned, simple "closed-employed." One example of such a measure grew out of the Woods County project (Reagles, Wright, and Butler, 1972). They combined 20 vocational and extravocational items into a scale that would yield a single score, but would reflect more of a client's rehabilitation status than simple employability. In addition, they hoped to use the scale as an index of rehabilitation progress, through the use of change scores.

The desire for a single score that would reflect more than just vocational success may be futile. Bolton (1974) used a factor analysis of measures of client vocational and personal adjustment, to determine if there was enough similarity among the measures to justify lumping them together. He concluded that the vocational dimension was independent of the psychological dimensions, which suggests that they should be treated as separate criteria. Even concern only with vocational aspects may call for a more complex index. The Minnesota DVR (1972) has developed a Case Difficulty Index. This index supplements closure rate as a measure of counselor performance, by adding two more dimensions to the measurement: counselor time and effort, and a measure of the average difficulty of such clients. Thus, a counselor who works with a severely disabled caseload will not be penalized for a lower closure rate. Despite all the efforts to find a new criterion, however, the one most used is still the number of cases closed because employed.

Generally, questions about what rehabilitation counselors do or what rehabilitation counselors are like are asked directly, by getting a sample of counselors and asking them in one way or another. In an emerging profession, the results of such research can be important in providing practitioners with models, and with a sense of where they belong. The following studies are examples of interesting methodology or careful procedures. In an application of the critical incidents technique, Jaques (1959) asked each of the counselors in her sample to give examples of incidents in which they considered their efforts to be especially effective or ineffective. The incidents were then analyzed. Among other results, Jaques concluded that within her sample of state agency counselors in several midwestern states, trained counselors were more likely than untrained counselors to see their counseling function as important.

Another major study of what rehabilitation counselors do and think was reported by Muthard and Salomone (1969). They used a carefully devised sampling plan to solicit respondents from around the country, so that their final group included subjects proportionately representative of the population as to employment setting, training level, experience, and geographic distribution. In 15 large cities, a total of 378 rehabilitation counselors completed a number of questionnaires in two half day sessions. Questionnaires included a rehabilitation counselor Task Inventory devised for the study, plus other special and standardized questionnaires to index job satisfaction, attitudes toward the profession, vocational needs and preferences, and a variety of other variables. The data pool was analyzed using factor analytic techniques, which the authors then examined for applications to counselor preparation and role assignment. They suggest, for example, that the way task importance, desirability, and satisfaction responses clustered indicates that separate work roles might be established for coordinating and for counseling so that counselors with different backgrounds and talents could be used differentially. They saw evidence for role strain in the unrealistic role expectations displayed by many of the rehabilitation workers' colleagues. Dozens of other hypotheses were tested and conclusions drawn on the basis of this large, carefully devised and collected data pool.

A series of studies of rehabilitation counselors has been carried out by sociologists Marvin B. Sussman and Marie R. Haug, and their colleagues and associates at Case Western Reserve University. Most of their studies have been reported as working papers (Sussman, Haug, and Trela, 1966; Sussman and Haug, 1970), but a concise report of some of their research on rehabilitation counselor careers appeared in the *Journal of Rehabilitation* (Sussman, Haug, Hagan, Kitson, and Williams, 1975). Using questionnaire survey techniques with sometimes phenomenal response rates (324 out of the 326 rehabilitation counselors graduating in 1965 responded to their mailed questionnaire), Sussman and Haug have taken a sociologist's look at where rehabilitation counseling students come from and where they go, separately, as compared to other rehabilitation workers, and in the context of the New Careers movement. Their work has been both praised (Research Awards Committee of ARCA, 1971), and criticized (ARCA Research Committee, 1973; Haug and Sussman, 1973). The most controversial part of their project has been the study of where rehabilitation counselors come from, and what happens to them when they complete their training. In their study of rehabilitation counselors who graduated in 1965, Sussman and Haug found that one-third had left the field of rehabilitation counseling within one year after graduation. Although there were many possible explanations, such an attrition rate could have serious implications for those responsible for funding and administering rehabilitation counselor training programs. Their finding was criticized because of the restrictive definition of rehabilitation counseling used to determine who had left the field, and the lack of any comparison with other professions. These criticisms were answered in their 1972 follow-up of the 1965 graduates (Sussman, Haug, et al., 1975), which found that the combined proportion of "employed out of rehabilitation" and "not employed" was 10 percent for rehabilitation counselors, an attrition rate that was lower than all but 3 of the 13 disciplines studied. They found also that, compared to students from other disciplines, rehabilitation counselors came from lower social class backgrounds, made their occupational selection later in life, were third highest in income, had the highest percentage claiming personal disability (23 percent), and were third highest in proportion of blacks.

There are many studies demonstrating or testing some aspect or method of delivering rehabilitation counseling. Most of them are demonstration project reports, rather than true experimental studies utilizing no-treatment controls. Rehabilitation counseling shares with other service delivery systems in the difficulty and expense of doing such experiments. Like the studies mentioned above, research on service delivery can be useful in providing information on how rehabilitation counselors are used, what they think, and what developmental history they follow.

Research on Rehabilitation Constructs

Many studies in rehabilitation could be best categorized as research on rehabilitation constructs such as attitudes toward disability, acceptance of disability, and motivation for rehabilitation. There are many such constructs used to describe the factors that influence the behavior of clients, families, employers, rehabilitation workers, and society at large. Of course, research includes many constructs of interest to *all* counselors, such as empathy or self-concept, as well as the ones discussed here as more or less unique to rehabilitation.

The attitudes of people in general and clients in particular toward disability and disabled persons have long been considered crucial to various aspects of the rehabilitation process. A much used tool in research on these attitudes has been the Attitude Toward Disabled Persons (ATDP) scale (Yuker, Block, and Younng, 1966). The ATDP asks the subject to agree or disagree with statements about the adjustment problems of physically disabled persons. In general, the scale is scored so that the more a subject sees physically disabled people as not different from other people, the more the score will be in the "accepting" direction. Many studies have been done to norm and validate the scale, and to establish the correlates of the thus measured attitudes.

As with any deviant group, it is presumed that societal attitudes toward the disabled motivate much of the prejudicial behavior displayed toward them, so that learning more about such attitudes can help conquer barriers to employment and produce other benefits. Research with the ATDP has not always revealed such a powerful attitude as being specific to the disabled, but rather suggests that it may be a part of a larger ethnocentric attitude (Chesler, 1965). Another possibility is that such attitudes are multidimensional, with various social and personal components that may be present to varying degrees in different subjects in relation to different disabilities (Siller, 1976).

Issues regarding the nature of attitudes toward the disabled are studied because if such attitudes do indeed influence so much significant behavior, then the change and control of these attitudes becomes very important. Usually, studies of how to change attitudes are experiments that either provide subjects with contact with disabled persons or give information about disability using ATDP score changes as the measure of attitude change (Evans, 1976).

The "acceptance of disability" by a disabled person has long been considered as a significant determiner of that person's behavior in the rehabilitation process. Sometimes the construct is used in the other direction, as when a client's adjustment is said to reflect "denial" of the disability. The construct generally is used to indicate where a client is in a process of adjustment, which is thought to involve the shifting of values and meanings away from a physical and disability centeredness to a broader perception (Wright, 1960). Despite its apparent importance, the construct has not been much researched. It is most usually used clinically, often as an after-the-fact explanation for observed client behavior. For example, a client who does not participate in rehabilitation treatment will be said to be resisting because of denial of the disability. When measurement of the construct is required, the ATDP is often used, on the presumption that disabled persons who have positive attitudes toward disabled persons in general also have positive attitudes toward themselves and therefore accept their disability.

A scale to measure Acceptance of Disability (AD) was constructed by Linkowski (1969, 1971). He followed the suggestion of Dembo, Leviton, and Wright (1956) that the process of adjustment to disability involved value shifts in four areas: enlargement of scope of values, subordination of physique, containment of disability effects, and transformation from comparative values to asset values. He wrote items to exemplify each area, resulting in a 50 item self-report questionnaire using a Likert scale. Evaluation of the resulting scale proved it to be adequately reliable. It showed a significant and substantial relationship with the ATDP. The separation of acceptance into four parts was not supported because the items based on each part were highly intercorrelated, and a factor analysis revealed only one sizeable factor.

Both attitudes toward the disabled and acceptance of disability are important constructs in rehabilitation. They are used along with many other constructs to explain a variety of behaviors on the part of the disabled, families, counselors, employers, and the general public. Like other constructs in counseling and psychology, it has been easier to create constructs than to find evidence for their operation. Much hard work remains before the constructs used so much in talking about rehabilitation counseling are adequately measured and verified.

Research on Research Utilization

An important and growing component relevant to rehabilitation counselors is the work on research utilization. In a book devoted to research for the counselor, it seems appropriate to look closely at the ways in which the use of research by rehabilitation counselors has been tested.

With a strong emphasis on the support of research by the federal Vocational Rehabilitation Administration, research reports have accumulated at an increasing rate. By 1962, federal grants for support of research and demonstration totalled $37 million for 540 special projects (Lofquist, 1963). By 1970, the number of research and demonstration grants had grown to almost 1700, and their report-producing capabilities had been joined by the

19 Research and Training Centers and nine Regional Rehabilitation Research Institutes (Levine, 1970). When Muthard (1974a) compiled a bibliography of reports and articles relevant to vocational rehabilitation, the listing included over 6000 articles.

In the beginning not much attention was paid to the growth of report literature. Some of the visitors to Washington, D.C., would bring back stories of the size of the room required to hold final reports from all the projects. Rehabilitation workers who read project reports complained about their length and turbidity. Occasionally, counselors would be amazed to discover that a rehabilitation research project they had never heard of but which sounded very interesting was being conducted at a university only a few miles away.

Such observations and complaints plus the emphasis in rehabilitation on practical matters led to concern for developing ways of applying this research. In 1966, the Director of the Vocational Rehabilitation Administration appointed a research utilization task force (Usdane, 1968). The Joint Liaison Committee (1967) of the Council of State Administrators of Vocational Rehabilitation and The Rehabilitation Counselor Educators held a conference on the communication, dissemination, and utilization of rehabilitation research information. At about the same time, a research utilization branch was formed within the division of Research and Demonstration Grants. A variety of programs were begun to find ways to get research information to the front line worker in a manner that would make it useful.

Extensive listings of research resources have come from the Regional Rehabilitation Research Institute at the University of Florida. Their publications include listings of experts in rehabilitation (Muthard and Crocker, 1971), information centers (Muthard, Rogers, and Crocker, 1971), and reports and publications of Research and Demonstration projects and other relevant HEW grantees (Bailey and Muthard, 1968; Dumas and Muthard, 1970; Crocker, Muthard, Reinhardt, and Wells, 1973: Muthard, 1974a). Efforts to get the research into a useful form have included a project to write easy-to-read summaries of research projects (Muthard, 1974b), and the use of audiovisual briefs (Engstrom, 1975). Efforts to get practitioners to use results have included the establishment of research utilization specialists in some state agencies (Hamilton and Muthard, 1975), visiting consultants (Butler, 1975), planned learning experiences (Kunce and Hartley, 1975), and other methods developed by the Research Utilization Laboratories (Soloff, Goldston, Pollack, and White, 1975; Robinault and Weisinger, 1975).

It follows that a field committed to research will look for research to demonstrate the effectiveness of various utilization projects. An interesting study testing a basic assumption behind the need for research utilization efforts was reported by Bolton and Soloff (1973). They examined the extent to which an employability scale developed at the Chicago Jewish Vocational Service was utilized, through searching the literature for references, putting advertisements in journals, and mailing questionnaires to persons who had requested information about the scale. Although no extraordinary distribution efforts had been made beyond publishing the scale, announcing its availability, and publishing research reports, 48 practitioner and research applications of the scale were found. This led the authors to conclude "we suggest that without change agents, more research results get put to use than utilization theorists now believe" (pp. 77–78). Although there can be no doubt that much useful research goes unused, the wall between research and practice must have some openings.

What are the channels through which information passes? Muthard and Crocker (1975) collected data on the sources of information used by 37 state-level supervisors in 11 state vocational rehabilitation agencies. The journal most read by their respondents was the *Journal of Rehabilitation*. Their professional reading habits varied, with 20 percent having 75 or more volumes, and 16 percent fewer than ten volumes in their professional libraries. When they needed professional information, most of them used personal contacts, either with their own colleagues, or people with experience in other agencies. Professional literature was not seen as very useful, for reasons that included the belief that their own problems are unique, the need for fast action, and the difficulties of locating, reading, and understanding research. The finding that personal sources are more valued than literature strengthens the position of Salomone (1970) and others in recommending research utilization conferences.

The specific research utilization tools growing out of the research utilization projects have been evaluated in a variety of ways. One of the published listings of projects was evaluated by Crocker and Muthard (1972). They sent questionnaires to a sample drawn from 2000 recipients of the "Index to Rehabilitation Research and Demonstration Projects 1955–1970" (Dumas and Muthard, 1970). Responses were received from 63 percent (235) of their sample. Of the persons responding, 27 percent had never used the index for anything, while 73 percent had used it at least once, most often as a referral source or to get information regarding a client problem. Almost half (46.9 percent) had tried to get at least one copy of a project report. The evaluation of the index was highly positive, which fit the authors' informal experiences. Most users of the index were researchers and administrators.

Evaluations of the Rehabilitation Utilization Specialist Programs are reported by Hamilton and Muthard (1975) and Glaser and Backer (1975). The former report sees the programs as successful in that they survived, gained acceptance, and brought about agency changes. Glaser and Backer report a more complete evaluation done through field visits, questionnaires, and document analysis. Their criteria were various evidences of impact, set in a conceptual or clinical approach to evaluation. They concluded that since the projects survived, were visible, had won endorsement, had affected system operation, and had produced other evidence of impact on the agencies, they were a valued new resource for some of the agencies.

Butler (1975) reports an evaluation of the visiting consultant method of research utilization. A sample of 18 consultation visits was analyzed in depth, through either a visit to the agency or a telephone interview. The consultation was seen as helping satisfactorily, with the usefulness and satisfaction depending at least in part on the institutional characteristics of the agency, and on the user's perception of the consultant.

Research utilization efforts in rehabilitation counseling have gone far in developing a variety of methods for getting research results into the hands of the counselor. More important, there has been a concerted effort to test the effectiveness of various dissemination and utilization methods and models. Although much remains to be done, the field of rehabilitation counseling has done a great deal to bring about a better understanding of how counselors can be helped to use research.

EVALUATING
REHABILITATION RESEARCH

As a general conclusion of this survey of rehabilitation research, we can say that there are many studies that do have specific application, some generalizations that are of limited help to the practicing counselor, and a few principles that can be counted on. The practicing counselor probably does learn more of value from supervision and colleagues than from reading rehabilitation research reports. This rather pessimistic view of the impact of rehabilitation research is consistent with the results of an evaluation of policy-related rehabilitation research recently conducted by a group of economists at Rutgers University (Berkowitz, Englander, Rubin, and Worrall, 1975, 1976). They examined abstracts of rehabilitation projects done between 1955 and 1973 to locate those in which an attempt was made to relate various services to a change in client status. They located 477 reports, and collected information about each project's methodology. Each report was then rated on a 10 point scale on the adequacy of its scientific methodology, and its policy utility. Overall 44 percent of the projects were rated "poor" methodologically, with only 17 percent rated highly. The usefulness of the projects in setting policy was only slightly better, with 32 percent rated low and 26 percent highly. They suggest that the usefulness of a project is closely related to the adequacy of its methodology, and rehabilitation research is not very good, methodologically.

However, before seriously suggesting that because of its imperfections rehabilitation research should be eliminated or ignored, a broader perspective is necessary. As Miller (1976) and Noble (1976) suggest in their responses to the Berkowitz et al. (1976) study, the methodology of rehabilitation research is no worse than the methodology of research on intervention in other areas. Although it is important to know the ideal in conducting evaluations, practical alternatives must also be kept in mind. Like old age, rehabilitation research looks better when the alternatives are considered.

RESEARCH DONE
BY THE COUNSELOR

Should rehabilitation counselors do research? Can the already overburdened counselor be expected to find time to think of problems, devise methods, collect data, and reach conclusions? As it is so often, the answer to such questions is "yes and no." If by research we mean the sort of activity that leads to publications in the professional journals, then the answer is probably "no." Most counselors cannot afford the time it would take to learn to use the tools of research and begin producing publishable articles. But if by research we refer to the kinds of things counselors might do to learn more about their own practice, their own clients, their own office, their own situation, then the answer is "yes," rehabilitation counselors can and should do research.

Actually, the "no" may be a bit premature. Almost any issue of a rehabilitation professional journal includes at least one author whose title is "rehabilitation counselor," so some practitioners are doing research. A substantial proportion of the respondents to a survey of the publication preferences of the readers of the Rehabilitation Counseling Bulletin expressed a desire to see more practitioner written articles (Kauppi, 1975), so there is an interest in reading such research. Practitioners who feel that the research being done is not relevant may do well to bring about relevance through their own research. A cooperative effort between researchers and practitioners might be the most fruitful way of conducting and reporting research, as recommended by Berkowitz, et al. (1976). The professional researcher can furnish the tools while the professional counselor can furnish the realism and applicability.

Research might not seem so far removed from rehabilitation counselors if they did more of it, and thus realized that research is not something done by strangers at a university, but is performed every day by ordinary people. Most rehabilitation counselors already do some things approaching local research. Whenever anyone makes systematic observations in order to answer questions he or she is doing research, and it isn't only Ph.D's in laboratories who can and should do it. The typical rehabilitation office or center is full of questions and the data to answer them. If rehabilitation counselors can train themselves to look for data rather than speculating about answers, they can find many interesting and valuable research projects.

The local research projects done by the rehabilitation counselor will probably not be the same as those conducted by full time researchers. The practitioner will be wise to avoid studies that would involve instruments that require computer scoring or extensive statistical analysis. Similarly, studies that depend for their value on generalization to large populations, or that utilize complex inferential statistics may be beyond the practitioner's ability. But even after such projects have been eliminated, many studies remain to be done by the practicing counselor. Such local studies can include looking at tools, resources, procedures and practices, caseloads, and the characteristics of people and groups in the community.

Specific Local Studies

Most of the tools used in vocational rehabilitation do not have local validation. For some, national studies have been done and it is presumed that the results apply to local situations. In other cases, research was done at the place the tool orginated and is applied elsewhere on that basis. Too often, tools are used with no data whatsoever as to whether they are actually useful to the counselor. Local research can supply some useful and interesting data.

For example, most work evaluation units use a variety of job samples, tests, and tasks to evaluate the vocational potential and ability of their clients. Counselors who use the units generally get impressions of the relative usefulness and validity of each of the tasks. Sometimes counselors feel that certain tests are very useful in evaluating potential for certain kinds of jobs, and ignore client performance on other tests. The effective use of a work evaluation unit can be improved with answers to a variety of researchable questions including:

Which tasks are seen as most useful by the work evaluators? rehabilitation counselors? clients? potential employers?

Are the tests administered in a standardized manner?

Would a change in instructions make a substantial change in client performance? Does it make a difference in client performance if the test is completed alone or in a group of clients? At the beginning of the client's stay, or later?

Is there a relationship between client performance and age? sex? education? disability? Any other demographic or experience variable?

If you gave clients the same test a few days after they took it the first time, would they get the same score? If you gave them the test 3 or 4 times in a row, would their scores go down or up?

The answers to these questions are often already sitting in the agency's data files, waiting to be put together. In other instances, all counselors need to do is get the cooperation of their colleagues in keeping a few notes, making a few observations, or answering a few questions. Answering questions such as the above can increase the usefulness of work evaluation test results.

An example of such a simple study took place at a large rehabilitation center a few years ago (Kauppi, 1963). The center's work evaluation unit was using a simple repetitive assembly-disassembly task ("washer–nut–bolt") as a means of assessing basic finger dexterity. Results on this test were generally interpreted as reflecting clients' ability to use their hands, with high scorers showing some potential for assembly or similar work, while low scorers were thought to be either unmotivated or unable to use their hands well. Norms were based on local clients, since no other norms were available. In order to collect some data on how nonclients might perform, the entire staff of the center was asked to do washer-nut-bolt. All but one person did, so that data on the performance of about 35 persons was available. The results were amazing and changed the interpretation of washer–nut–bolt results considerably. There was no overlap between the scores of clients and staff. The highest scoring client had not done as well as the lowest scoring staff person! This might not be surprising if all the clients had disabilities that might impair their dexterity, or if the staff were all from a group of highly able individuals. But both groups were highly heterogeneous, with the majority of clients not physically disabled, while several of the staff were. Clearly, some factor other than finger dexterity greatly influenced scores on the washer–nut–bolt, a fact that would not have been discovered if the little local research project had not been done.

The "shop talk" of colleagues can be a fruitful source of local research questions regarding resources. Local resources often get reputations for certain kinds of performance; when such reputations are based on unverified hunches rather than data, an opportunity is raised for local research. For example, some trade schools get a reputation for building their enrollments by guaranteeing placement to all graduates, accepting anyone who applies, and withholding final graduation from all clients they cannot place. Such a reputation could be investigated by examining the files of the local state vocational rehabilitation office to answer the following questions.

> How many clients have been referred to the school? How many have been turned down? How many have graduated? How many have jobs for which their training was relevant? How long were the nongraduates retained as students?

Similarly, some rehabilitation facilities have the reputation for "creaming," that is, accepting or working only with easy-to-place clients. Some facilities get a reputation for being especially effective with particular client groups. These kinds of reputations could lead to studies that asked questions in a way similar to those asked about the school.

Local studies of resources can be done only where the rehabilitation counselor has access to appropriate data, such as a state vocational rehabilitation office. There is a danger, too, that the data might be used unfairly, or that the resources being so studied might object. Such studies must be conducted carefully, but it should be the case that systematically collected data are less dangerous than uninformed speculation.

Counselors who work in small offices, or who have only their own case files to examine, will be limited in the kinds of local resource studies they do. It may still be valuable for them to collect such data as a basis for their own opinions, but ordinarily one caseload is not enough to form conclusions about the utility of a resource.

Another fruitful area of local research is the practices and procedures of an office or other work unit. Here too, coffee break conversations can provide questions to ask. Practically every new operating procedure that is instituted stirs up a variety of opinions concerning its effect. Too often, these opinions don't get beyond the talk stage, and the new procedure becomes an old procedure with no check on whether it did what it was supposed to. A research minded counselor might find it very interesting to convert some of the opinions into a form that allows the collection of some data, so that the procedure can be evaluated. For example:

Does a new method of getting general medical examinations result in reports that are longer, more detailed, or more useful by some judgment? Do they come more quickly?

Does a new system of referring clients for vocational testing result in more counselors using the service? Are more tests given? Are the counselors satisfied? Do they still use testing at the same rate six months later?

Does a new system of maintaining case recording on clients result in more up-to-date notes? longer recording? more detailed records? Are the counselors satisfied? Do they still perform the same six months later?

Does a new procedure of in-service training actually lead to more counselor time spent in training? Is the time equally distributed, or are some counselors doing it all? Are counselors more satisfied with it? Do they know more after the training?

The unit of interest can be the individual counselor. Professionals who wish to learn something about their own methods might think of many kinds of data that would be useful. Some agencies with access to computers already give counselors feedback on a variety of caseload information, such as the number of cases in each status, the length of time spent in each status, and so on. Counselors who do not have access to computers can collect their own information, to answer questions about their own caseloads, such as:

How many clients are interviewed each week? Are some clients seen more often than others? What kinds of clients are seen more often? less often? About how long is the average interview? What is the topic of long interviews? short interviews?

How many different rehabilitation plans are developed? How many different vocational goals? How often is the job at closure related to the original vocational goal? Is there any evidence of stereotyping of rehabilitation plans? Vocational goals?

Does making regular stops at a referring agency increase the number of referrals? Does a personal letter to the physician speed the medical report? Does a detailed letter requesting information needed from a specialist result in a more comprehensive report?

What activity takes up most of the time? How much time is spent in what might be called counseling? clerical work? placement?

Caseload characteristics and their changes are also a fruitful source of local research data. The task is made much easier when the data are collected routinely and processed by a computer, but even a lone counselor with a hand calculator can collect the data to answer some questions. Keeping case summary data on a file card or sheet makes it easy to sit down once a month or so and sort the cases into various categories. This allows the counselor to keep track of such caseload questions as:

What are the basic characteristics of the caseload, in terms of age? sex? marital status? ethnic background? education? number of dependents? disability type? source of referral? age at disablement?

Have these basic characteristics changed appreciably? Have any changes followed a change in the regulations, office procedures, and practices of the counselor? Is any disability or other group of clients increasing or decreasing in proportion?

A final area of local research pertains to the characteristics of the community. The community studied could be as small as the staff of a local office, or as large as a major city or state. Coffee break conversations again are a source of questions that interesting data can be collected to answer. The technique used will often be a survey questionnaire, but the ingenious researcher will find many other sources of data, including some already available. Some time spent learning sampling techniques could save much effort. Data can be collected to answer such questions as:

Do the employers in the town know anything about affirmative action legislation? Is their knowledge related to the size of their company, or any similar factor? Of the employers who know, how many are acting? What are they doing?

How many vocational rehabilitation agencies in this community use paraprofessionals? What do they use them for? How do they hire them? Are they satisfied with their performance?

How many self help groups are there for the disabled in this community? Are they mainly single-disability groups, or do they admit anyone who is interested? What needs do they see as most important for the community? How do they function?

Many might object to calling such local studies "research," and they may be right. We have not, it is true, said anything about the hypothetico-deductive system, the statistics of inference, parameters, or Graeco-Latin squares. What rehabilitation counselors discover doing local studies will not change the course of the profession, and they will not create much in the way of universal knowledge. But if examining data is better than specula-tion, and if rehabilitation counselors in doing local studies gain knowledge about their own practice and learn something about research, then these studies are worth doing, whatever they're called.

Doing the Study

Obviously, no universal procedure for doing local studies could be given. A few suggestions are in order, however, since most research reference books offer considerably more advice than the beginning local researcher is able to use.

1. It is a good idea to specify the questions in advance, and to spend some time refining them. It may be easiest to start with a coffee break statement, such as "mentally retarded clients seem a lot easier to place on jobs since the local ad campaign." Before any data can be collected, that statement needs to be refined. First of all, who is meant by the reference "mentally retarded"? Just those people who have "mental retardation" as a primary disability in the state VR caseload? What is meant by "easier"? That there are more clients placed? That more job openings are available? That there is less apparent resistance by employers? That clients are more willing to work? What is the comparison group? What about "jobs"? Does this include sheltered work? On-the-job training? Jobs outside of those tradition-ally reserved for mentally retarded? When is "since the local ad campaign"? Does the question imply that the ad campaign was effective in increasing employer acceptance?

After such refinement, the question may be more on the order of "the number of clients with M. R. as the primary disability on the local VR office caseload who have been closed as rehabilitated in competitive work in the local community is larger for the period July 1 to December 31 than it was for the same group during the same period the previous year." If the ques-tion is still one of interest, then the next step can be taken.

2. If the question is carefully specified, then the data to be collected will be easily described. In the example cited, closure rates are the basic data, and the specific counts to be made are readily determined. At this stage the counselor–researcher may discover that although the data needed are

clear enough, they are not available. If this happens, and no substitutes can be found, then it is probably necessary to start over with another question.

3. The next step is to collect the data. In general, it is best if the data collection can be built into a routine system, or if the counselor–researcher can do the collecting. If something can go wrong, it will, and what may seem like the simplest instructions will get impossibly garbled. Data requiring subjective judgment is acceptable, if it can be shown that other equally trained judges would make more or less the same judgments. Avoid complicated questionnaires and indirect paper-and-pencil measures of constructs hardly anyone understands. When in doubt, collect the data that are simplest and most directly related to your question. To avoid a kind of contamination, with some studies the data should be collected and stored without being examined until the end of the project.

4. The "simplest is best" method is recommended for examining and analyzing the data as well. The first step is to look at the data; if they look significant, they probably are. Such a procedure would make many statisticians and researchers wince, but with local studies the small differences that may achieve statistical significance with the right manipulation probably don't have practical significance to the local counselor–researcher. Of course some statistical analysis may be unavoidable or even desirable, in the form of means, standard deviations, and maybe even some correlations. And on occasion a statistical test of significance may be used. But it is rare that the counselor–researcher who has done a careful job with the basics will find occasion to use complex statistics.

5. The last step is to write up the study, and distribute copies to people who might be interested. This write-up serves several purposes. It is a form of discipline and gives closure to a process that might instead just peter out. It provides a reinforcement for the counselor–researcher and those who cooperated. It stimulates systematic thinking about the subject. And if the results of the study are significant, then a write-up makes it more likely to be used. Publication in a national journal is always a possibility even for local research, if it is well done and the results are interesting.

6. Finally, a good last step is to plan the first step of the next study, taking into account the mistakes that were made this time around.

CONCLUSION

Research is as important for the rehabilitation counselor as it is for all counselors. The rehabilitation counselor has an interest in all the research of counseling, plus the research pertaining to rehabilitation and the counselor's role in that process. Research relevant to rehabilitation counseling is extensive, but difficult to find and apply. Despite that difficulty, the rehabilitation counselor cannot totally delegate the responsibility of reading that research and applying it to practice. To ignore research dooms the counselor to committing and perpetuating the mistakes of others, using modern versions of bloodletting because someone recommended it.

Counselors can do research on local problems and issues of interest to themselves and their colleagues. The value of such research lies not so much in how well it mimics large-scale science as in how well it answers questions of local interest and how well it confers understanding of research.

Rehabilitation counselors are by training and experience a combination of idealist and pragmatist. They seek the best for their clients, with a focus on the functional. Such an approach fits well with research, which seeks truth through a focus on data.

REFERENCES

ARCA Research Committee, A critique of Sussman and Haug's working paper No. 7, *Rehabilitation Counseling Bulletin*, 1973, *16*, 218–225.

Bailey, J. P., Jr., and Muthard, J. E. (Eds.). *Reports and articles resulting from research and demonstration projects: A bibliography: 1968.* Gainesville: Regional Rehabilitation Research Institute, University of Florida, 1968.

Baller, U. R. A study of the present social status of a group of adults who, when they were in elementary schools, were classified as mentally deficient. *Genetic Psychology Monographs*, 1936, *18*, 165–244.

Baller, U. R., Charles, D. C., and Miller, E. L. Midlife attainment of the mentally retarded: A longitudinal study. *Genetic Psychology Monographs*, 1967, *75*, 235–329.

Berkowitz, M., Englander, V., Rubin, J., and Worrall, J. D. *An evaluation of policy-related rehabilitation research.* New York: Praeger, 1975.

Berkowitz, M., Englander, V., Rubin, J., and Worrall, J. D. A summary of "An evaluation of policy-related rehabilitation research" *Rehabilitation Counseling Bulletin*, 1976, *20*, 39–45.

Bolton, B., and Soloff, A. To what extent is research utilized? A ten year follow up study. *Rehabilitation Research and Practice Review*, 1973, *4*, 75–79.

Bolton, B. A factor analysis of personal adjustment and vocational measures of client change. *Rehabilitation Counseling Bulletin*, 1974, *18*, 99–104.

Butler, A. J. Visiting consultant program for research utilization. *Rehabilitation Counseling Bulletin*, 1975, *19*, 405–415.

Charles, D. C. Ability and accomplishment of persons earlier judged mentally deficient. *Genetic Psychology Monographs,* 1953, *47,* 3–71.

Charles, D. C. Longitudinal follow-up studies of community adjustment. In DiMichael, S. G. (Ed.), *New vocational pathways for the mentally retarded.* Washington, D. C.: The American Personnel and Guidance Association, 1966.

Chesler, M. A. Ethnocentrism and attitudes toward the physically disabled. *Journal of Personality and Social Psychology,* 1965, *2,* 877–882.

Crocker, L. M., and Muthard, J. E. Evaluating the usefulness of an informational tool for rehabilitation workers. *Rehabilitation Research and Practice Review,* 1972, *3,* 1–6.

Crocker, L. M., Muthard, J. E., Reinhardt, E. W., and Wells, S. A. *An index to rehabilitation and social service projects: Volume II: 1955–1973.* Gainesville: University of Florida, 1973.

Dembo, J., Leviton, L., and Wright, B. A. Adjustment to misfortune—A problem of social-psychological rehabilitation. *Artificial Limbs,* 1956, *3,* 4–62.

Dumas, N. S., and Muthard, J. E. *Index to rehabilitation research and demonstration projects 1955–1970.* Gainesville: University of Florida, 1970.

Edgerton, R. B. Anthropology and mental retardation: A plea for the comparative study of incompetence. In Prehm, H. J., Hammerlynck, L. A., and Crosson, J. E. (Eds.), *Behavioral research in mental retardation.* Eugene, Ore.: Rehabilitation Research and Training Center in Mental Retardation, 1968.

Engstrom, G. A. Research and research utilization—a many-faceted approach. *Rehabilitation Counseling Bulletin,* 1975, *19,* 357–364.

Evans, J. H. Changing attitudes toward disabled persons: An experimental study. *Rehabilitation Counseling Bulletin,* 1976, *19,* 572–579.

Glaser, E. M., and Backer, T. E. Evaluating the research utilization specialist. *Rehabilitation Counseling Bulletin,* 1975, *19,* 387–395.

Hamilton, L. S., and Muthard, J. E. *Reducing economic dependency among welfare recipients*. Gainesville: Regional Rehabilitation Research Institute, University of Florida, 1973.

Hamilton, L. S., and Muthard, J. E. Research utilization specialists in vocational rehabilitation: Five years of experience. *Rehabilitation Counseling Bulletin*, 1975, *19*, 377–386.

Haug, M. R., and Sussman, M. B., Rehabilitation counseling in perspective: A reply to the critics. *Rehabilitation Counseling Bulletin*, 1973, *16*, 226–238.

Jaques, M. E. *Critical counseling behavior in rehabilitation settings*. Iowa City: College of Education, University of Iowa, 1959.

Joint Liaison Committee. *Communication, dissemination, and utilization of rehabilitation research information*. Studies in rehabilitation counselor training, No. 5. Washington, D. C.: Vocational Rehabilitation Administration, 1967.

Kauppi, D. R. *Washer–nut–bolt, sex, client status, and staff*. Unpublished report, The Minneapolis Rehabilitation Center, 1963.

Kauppi, D. R. Publication preferences and needs of ARCA members: 1975 survey. *Rehabilitation Counseling Bulletin*, 1975, *19*, 323–329.

Kunce, J. T., and Hartley, L. B. Planned interpersonal informational exchanges: The RULE project. *Rehabilitation Counseling Bulletin*, 1975, *19*, 443–446.

Levine, A. S. Introduction in Dumas, N. L., and Muthard, J. E. *Index to rehabilitation research and demonstration projects 1955–1970*. Gainesville: University of Florida, 1970.

Linkowski, D. C. A study of the relationship between acceptance of disability and response to rehabilitation. Unpublished doctoral dissertation, State University of New York at Buffalo, 1969.

Linkowski, D. C. A scale to measure acceptance of disability. *Rehabilitation Counseling Bulletin*, 1971, *14*, 236–244.

Lofquist, L. (Ed.). *Psychological research and rehabilitation*. Washington, D.C.: American Psychological Association, 1963.

Miller, L. Reviewed by Leonard A. Miller. *Rehabilitation Counseling Bulletin*, 1976, *20*, 46–49.

Minnesota DVR. *The Difficulty Index—An expanded measure of counselor performance*. Research monograph No. 1. St. Paul: Minnesota DVR, 1972.

Muthard, J. E. *Vocational rehabilitation index: 1974*. Gainesville: University of Florida, 1974a.

Muthard, J. E. Preface in Regional Rehabilitation Research Institute, *Research in action*. Gainesville: University of Florida, 1974b.

Muthard, J. E., and Crocker, L. M. *Directory of rehabilitation consultants, 1971*. Gainesville: University of Florida, Regional Rehabilitation Research Institute, 1971.

Muthard, J. E., and Crocker, L. M. Rehabilitation state supervisors as knowledge users. *Rehabilitation Counseling Bulletin*, 1975, *19*, 433–442.

Muthard, J. E., and Morris, W. W. (Eds.) *Counseling the older disabled worker* (proceedings of two conferences). Iowa City: College of Education and Institute of Gerontology, State University of Iowa and Office of Vocational Rehabilitation, 1961.

Muthard, J. E., Rogers, K. B., and Crocker, L. M. (Eds.). *Guide to information centers for workers in the social services: 1971*. Gainesville: University of Florida, 1971.

Muthard, J. E., and Salomone, P. R. The roles and functions of the rehabilitation counselor. *Rehabilitation Counseling Bulletin*, 1969, *13*, 81–168.

Noble, J. H., Jr. Reviewed by John H. Noble, Jr. *Rehabilitation Counseling Bulletin*, 1976, *20*, 52–54.

Reagles, K. W., Wright, G. N., and Butler, A. J. Toward a new criterion of vocational rehabilitation success. *Rehabilitation Counseling Bulletin*, 1972, *15*, 233–241.

Research Awards Committee of ARCA. *Abstracts of research in rehabilitation.* Fayetteville: Arkansas Rehabilitation Research and Training Center, University of Arkansas, 1971.

Robinault, I. P., and Weisinger, M. A brief history of the ICD research utilization laboratory. *Rehabilitation Counseling Bulletin,* 1975, *19,* 426–432.

Salomone, P. R. The research implementation process: some reflections and suggestions. *Rehabilitation Counseling Bulletin,* 1970, *13,* 349–354.

Siller, J. Attitudes toward disability. In Rusalem, H. and Malikin, D. (Eds.), *Contemporary vocational rehabilitation.* New York: New York University Press, 1976.

Soloff, A., Goldston, L. J., Pollack, R. A., and White, B. Running a research utilization laboratory. *Rehabilitation Counseling Bulletin,* 1975, *19,* 416–424.

Sussman, M. B., Haug, M. R., and Trela, J. E. *Profile of the 1965 student rehabilitation counselor,* working paper No. 3. Cleveland, Ohio: Case Western Reserve University, August, 1966.

Sussman, M. B., and Haug, M. R. *From student to practitioner: Professionalization and deprofessionalization in rehabilitation counseling,* working paper No. 7. Cleveland, Ohio: Case Western Reserve University, March, 1970.

Sussman, M. B., Haug, M. R., Hagan, F. E., Kitson, G. C., and Williams, G. K. Rehabilitation counseling in transition—some findings. *Journal of Rehabilitation,* 1975, *41,* 27–33, 40.

Usdane, W. M. Introduction in Bailey, J. P. Jr., and Muthard, J. E. (Eds.). *Reports and articles resulting from research and demonstration projects: A bibliography: 1968.* Gainesville: Regional Rehabilitation Research Institute, University of Florida, 1968.

Wright, B. A. *Physical disability: A psychological approach.* New York: Harper and Row, 1960.

Yuker, H. E., Block, J. R., and Campbell, W. J. *A scale to measure attitudes toward disabled persons*. Albertson, N. Y.: Human Resources Center, 1960.

Yuker, H. E., Block, J. R., and Younng, J. R. *The measurement of attitudes toward disabled persons*. Albertson, N. Y.: Human Resources Center, 1966.

CHAPTER 11
Research in Employment and Vocational Counseling Agencies

Wayne P. Anderson

Employment and vocational counseling agencies are living research laboratories waiting for someone to make use of the special opportunities they present for studying the world of work. Their potential, however, remains largely untapped. An examination of the research reports in the vocational journals shows that most vocational research has been done in academic settings and few studies have been done with the clients of agencies (Holcomb and Anderson, 1977). College sophomores do not have the same vocational choice problems as employment service applicants, and counseling methods effective with highly motivated college students may not be so effective when used with a ghetto client in a work incentive program. Counselors working in these agency settings are in a position to find the answers to important questions that are of concern to their clients.

In employment and vocational counseling agencies, data on applicants and the world of work are available or can be collected somewhat easily. From these data descriptive reports or reports based on simple research methods can be prepared that will be useful not only to the staff in that agency but to staff in other agencies with similar clients.

This chapter is not intended so much for the full-time or academic researcher as for the counselor or other worker in an agency where employment or vocational counseling is done. Because of direct contact with the daily problems of clients and applicants, the counselor can often ask and answer meaningful questions that the professional researcher does not encounter. This chapter is designed to point out the issues that must be considered in doing research and to suggest some relevant topics as examples of what the reader might investigate in his or her own agency.

A researcher who is primarily a counselor will need to be attuned to practical questions, and the answers arrived at should make one more understanding of and helpful to clients. Questions may be about client characteristics, methods of counseling, effects of training programs, and so on—"What is the effect of age on an applicant's continuing in a training program?" "What is the most frequent reason new employees quit a job?" "What ability level is needed to complete LPN training?" The answers to questions of this nature will help in planning with clients and assure that resources will be used in the most economical fashion.

In this chapter, frequent illustrations are used from articles on employment and vocational counseling. The articles quoted are intended not only to show how a particular researcher went about answering a question, but also to serve as an introduction to the kinds of problems that people working in employment and vocational counseling agencies are presently concerned with.

Not all of the studies cited in this chapter will meet the criteria for good, generalizable research outlined by Harmon earlier in this book. There may have been too small a sampling of subjects, the expertise of the counselor may be in question, or some other factor may make the data such that the results are of no more than local interest. Although some of the studies chosen for this chapter may therefore be inappropriate for publication in a national journal, they were selected to demonstrate studies that can be carried out in an agency to provide useful information for dealing with local problems. Often the results of these studies can be published in a newsletter, in agency reports, or shared at the various meetings that agency people attend.

My experience has been that statistics is frequently the factor keeping counselors from doing more research. Perhaps counselors tend to be more comfortable with human relations than with numerical ones; however, many studies require the use of only simple statistical procedures. For example, descriptive data often require no more than averages or percentages. When comparing relationships between two factors, such as a score on a test and supervisory ratings, a rank-order correlation may be all that is necessary; in most other cases a product-moment correlation will be sufficient. If there is a question whether the difference between two groups or between test scores is significant, a t-test is often adequate. If the terms t-test and product-moment correlation sound esoteric, be assured that almost any counselor with a bit of guidance, can learn to do these statistics quickly with the aid of a pocket calculator. One can leave the high powered statistics to someone else, or, like me, consult someone who knows how to program problems for the computer and let it do the hard work.

We shall discuss (1) the general problems involved in designing a study, (2) methods of collection of information or facts for analysis, (3) methods of judging the effectiveness of a program or counseling method, (4) some human differences that influence work behavior, and, finally, (5) some important areas for further research.

APPROACHING RESEARCH: DESIGNING THE STUDY

For our purposes two major classifications of research exist: descriptive research and experimental research. Descriptive research often makes use of information already existing and which can be examined with a minimum of effort to discover characteristics of a group or relationships between groups. Experimental research involves those situations where a counselor can control, change, or influence specific events or procedures to discover the effects of such factors as a new counseling technique on the outcome of counseling.

Descriptive Research

In descriptive research a counselor can make a straightforward report or statement of something that exists without having to compare it with something else. A purely descriptive study in a community agency was done by Sollinger (1970) on clients' expectations of what they could receive in the way of services from that agency. In this case, Sollinger used the closed files of his agency as his source of data. He took 300 clients who had registered in one year and categorized and counted their reasons for coming. His major conclusion was that the agency's clients saw it as a place to be tested and to get specific help and advice. They did not recognize the agency as a place to get counseling. The implication of this study was that clients may actually want or at least expect a more limited service than an agency is able and willing to provide.

A basic descriptive study like the above is often a good way to start answering such questions as: "What do clients want from our service?" "Where do our clients come from?" "What is the educational background of our clients?" Data of this nature already exist in most agencies' files.

At other times it may be valuable to compare local data with national or state data, or present with past data to establish trends. Lauver, Gastellum, and Sheehey (1975) examined the illustrations used in the *Occupational Outlook Handbook* to see the sex, age, and ethnic origins of the persons pictured. They then compared these percentages with the percentage of each group in the actual work population. This allowed them to make an estimate of the amount of bias that exists in the occupational material, which is presumably an influence on young people's attitudes toward vocations.

In the two studies cited above the authors were able to make use of data already in existence. There are times, however, when the data do not exist, and the next step is to set up some method of acquiring them.

One method for getting descriptive data is the survey. This usually involves developing a questionnaire or structured interview to find out what attitudes or conditions exist. These tools might be used with counselors, companies, ex-clients, or others. For example, Harkness (1971) was concerned about the hiring practices of government agencies and industrial firms as they related to various types of handicapped people. He was interested in establishing the reasons these agencies and firms give for not hiring the handicapped, and how realistic those reasons might be. Harkness surveyed 280 agencies and firms who had interviewed job candidates at the Northern Illinois University Placement Bureau during the 1969–1970 academic year, asking about their hiring practices regarding people with diabetes, epilepsy, hearing loss, and visual deficiencies.

A more elaborate form of descriptive study makes use of correlations. Correlational studies are most often done of problems where the experimenter cannot or does not want to control what happens and yet wants to know the relationship between two events or factors. The most used correlations in employment agencies would be those that exist between tests (e.g., Wonderlic Personnel Test, General Aptitude Test Battery) and a person's actual performance on a job or learning task. Super and Crites in their book *Appraising Vocational Fitness* (1962) give hundreds of these correlations. Knowing that an interest inventory score or an aptitude test score correlates with some future event, such as adjustment to a job, allows a counselor to be of increased help to a client. If one score or set of scores is known along with the correlation with some measure of job success or satisfaction, this will give some idea of what to expect of the person's later performance. Klein and Trione (1970) compared the scores of individuals who had taken the General Aptitude Test Battery (GATB) with their performance on the High School Equivalency Test (GED). They wanted help in deciding which persons were ready to pass a high school equivalent examination without further study, and who were likely to profit from further study. From this they developed an expectancy table that the counselor could use to help educationally deficient clients decide what they ought to do about taking the high school equivalency test.

Putnam and Hansen (1972), using more sophisticated forms of correlational methods, studied the relationship between self-concept and vocational maturity in young women. On the Tennessee Self-Concept Scale, people with high scores see themselves as having value and worth, and people with low scores see themselves as undesirable, and often feel anxious, depressed, and unhappy. Scores from this test were correlated with the Crites Vocational Maturity Inventory. Their results indicated that a woman's self-concept was useful in predicting her vocational maturity. The authors do point out, however, that most of the variance on a vocational maturity scale is associated with factors other than levels of self-esteem. This points up the fact that many factors influence vocational maturity, and other studies could be done exploring what these factors might be.

Experimental Designs

We are often in a position to control some aspect of the environment, such as the type of training given to an individual or the way in which facts are presented in a class. This allows us to systematically manipulate the influences or factors we wish to study. Usually there are two groups: a control group, for whom things are done on a routine or usual basis, and an experimental group, who are subjected to special conditions. This allows us to test ways of improving our counseling techniques or training methods. The most frequent statistic used in these studies is a t-test or some elaborate form of t-test such as analysis of variance.

When one is working with training techniques, these studies can often be done with a minimum of additional time committed. That is, this research can be done with programs that are scheduled to run anyway.

For example, Keil and Barbee (1973) used 16 persons in an experimental group and 12 persons in a control group to investigate the influence of job interview training on the interview skills of the job applicants. All of the persons being studied took part in a pre-training interview to establish how they usually behaved in an employment interview. For the experimental group, this was followed by training on specific skills that personnel staff have indicated are important in impressing an employment interviewer favorably. A follow-up interview situation with both the experimental and control groups showed that a significant improvement had occurred in the experimental group in their ability to impress an interviewer favorably.

In the Keil and Barbee study, conditions were organized to study the effect of training versus no training. The study was short term and its effects were the result of a few hours of training given to 16 people.

In some situations we may intervene in a program already existing and modify one factor for some groups. This gives us a larger sample to study and an opportunity to apply our methods over a longer period. Jepsen (1972) investigated a new method of providing occupational knowledge for ninth grade classes. Four schools that were already teaching occupational information classes were chosen for the study. Two were assigned the experimental condition, which was the presentation of an occupation on a 20-minute videotape followed by study and discussion. The two schools that served as controls used a more traditional method of reading about the same occupations in nationally produced materials and then discussing them. The effectiveness of the methods was measured by pre and posttests on the accuracy of the students' images about the occupations studied. It was found that the use of videotape presentations helped students gain a more accurate picture of what happens in an occupation.

Combinations of methods may also be used under controlled conditions. Petty (1974) considered the effect of various combinations of oral and written instructions on the understanding of disadvantaged trainees learning industrial skills. By presenting oral and written information in four combinations, he concluded that one must be quite cautious in the use of written instructions with disadvantaged clients. One of his findings is that the best way to give relatively easy job-related information is to deliver it orally.

Sometimes it is necessary to control the information given to subjects so that they are not aware of what is being studied. These deception experiments are not often necessary, but at times they are the best way to get information. Rosen and Jerdee (1974) studied the influence that the sex of a worker has on the personnel decisions made about that worker. The subjects were 95 bank supervisors who were asked to react to a series of items in memorandum and letter form related to a variety of situations in the organization. Among the items were some covering personnel problems that had been written in two or more versions, so as to change the sex of one or more of the characters. That is, some of the managers were making decisions about a worker who was described as a man; other managers were making decisions about the same situation, but the worker involved was described as a woman. Their findings support the statement that there is discrimination against women in decisions related to promotion, development, and supervision.

Up to this point we have been discussing experiments where two or more groups are compared after some form of intervention. It is also possible to use subjects as their own controls, by comparing their scores on pre and postmeasures. We are most likely to do this when we have some control over a situation and can manipulate some factors but may not be able to manipulate others. In some situations we are not able to set up a control group because of the difficulty of refusing service to some applicants.

Occasionally, the researcher is in a position to observe some variable over a period of years in a longitudinal study. Kapes and Strickler (1975) studied changes in work values between the ninth and twelfth grades as related to the kind of curriculum that the students were involved in. The Occupational Values Inventory was used to study the work values. Kapes and Strickler found that five of the seven work values did change over a three-year period, and that at least some of this change appeared to be related to what the student was studying. They also observed that the value placed on salary made the greatest increase and that value intensity changed so that strong values grew stronger and weak values grew weaker.

TOOLS FOR RESEARCH:
THE COLLECTION OF DATA

As should now be clear, facts and data can be gathered in a number of ways. The most frequent ways of gathering data in an agency setting are: (1) the use of files, (2) interviews, (3) scales and questionnaires, and (4) tests. Although these methods may be used separately, they are often used in combination, either with each other or with some of the criteria discussed in the next section.

Files

In most agencies, much information is stored in files, only waiting for someone to ask the right question for them to divulge their answers. Biographical information on application forms or intake sheets can serve as a source of items to relate to counseling outcome, placement history, and so on. Often, a scoring system based on these data can lead to more accurate predictions than tests or scales. At the present time, a number of groups have made attacks on the use of tests in employment situations because it is felt that tests are not fair to all groups and lead us to refuse persons positions in which they might have done well. It may, however, be just as damaging to both a company and an individual to place a worker in a position where failure is likely. This problem of appropriate selection procedures has increased the need to find alternative ways to help people determine the best fit between their talents and employment.

The results of counseling can also be studied using file information. Nagle (1973) studied the number of counselor contacts with disadvantaged applicants and compared that information with later success on the job. The data for his study were collected from the records of 333 disadvantaged applicants in the Columbia office of the Missouri State Employment Service. He used client status as a criterion; that is, whether the client was active, inactive, in training, or employed. His results indicated that there might well be a "magic" number of counseling contacts, between three and five, beyond which clients were not likely to be significantly helped. He concludes that in dealing with disadvantaged clients, any case carried beyond seven contacts should be given careful scrutiny. Similar studies could be done in almost any agency to provide norms about that particular agency's clients, or even to study how specific methods used by different counselors may have affected their clients' later experiences.

Predictive studies could easily be done using the files by going back and checking out what the difference was between those clients who were helped by the services rendered and those who were not.

Interviews

Although files already contain data from interviews, there are situations where special questions must either be included in the regular interviews as a way of collecting information on specific aspects of client behavior, or a special interview must be developed for getting the information needed. In terms of special questions, for example, if a counselor was interested in studying the effect of early role models (e.g., parents) on later vocational aspirations, he or she would include questions covering this in the regular employment interview or counseling session.

On the other hand, one may wish to conduct interviews to collect specific data for a study. An example of this use of the interview would be a follow-up interview of persons who had had counseling to find out what happened to them since and what was their evaluation of how counseling influenced their behavior. Reich (1973) studied the relationship between vocational specialization in school and eventual occupational placement, by doing interviews with former students two to two and a half years after they had left school. He was able to contact 60 percent of the sample to do interviews with them about their occupational and educational experiences since leaving school. He found that 52 percent of these ex-students were employed in fields relating to their high school training. The author went one step further, however, and found that, if placement in clerical and sales are excluded, only 18 percent of the respondents were employed in jobs related to their earlier course work. This additional step provides information that makes one question the value of high school training for later vocational placement. On the other hand, it leaves open for research the questions: How can we make training more relevant? What kind of counseling would have resulted in better placement? Does it make any difference to people if their high school training does not relate to later occupational placement?

Questionnaires and Scales

It may be difficult to make a complete discrimination between questionnaires, scales, and tests; however, for our purposes questionnaires are those devices that deal mostly with attitudes, preferences, values, and indications of satisfaction, but do not have much formal statistical foundation. Scales are questionnaires where the items have been scored or ranked so that a subject taking the scale can be placed on a continuum. Some sample items from different points on a scale are: "I can never find out how I stand with my boss," "On the whole, the company treats us about as well as we deserve," "I am made to feel that I am really a part of this organization." In terms of the numbers of questionnaires and scales available in the area of occupations and vocations, one has almost an embarrassment of riches to choose from in doing research. Two sources of scales are especially valuable. The best source, for the purposes of those working in agencies, is *Measures of Occupational Attitudes and Occupational Characteristics* (Robinson, Athanasiou, and Head, 1969) available from the Institute for Social Research of the University of Michigan at Ann Arbor. This handbook not only provides reviews of some of the important literature, but in addition presents 72 scales that can be used in employment and occupational studies. These scales are evaluated in terms of the language that they use, their relevancy, and reliability, validity, and other statistical concepts. Among other classifications are: general job satisfaction scales, scales for job satisfaction for particular occupations, occupational value scales, work-relevant attitudes, and vocational interest measures.

For a study of other variables, such as self-esteem, dogmatism, values, attitudes toward people, there is *Measures of Social Psychological Attitudes* (Robinson and Shaver, 1973) from the same Institute for Social Research.

If the necessary scale or questionnaire for the research purposes selected does not exist (see the list in Appendix A), counselors will need to develop their own. As an example of a study of this kind, Bingham and House (1973) were interested in the accuracy with which counselors viewed women and work. They developed a 25-item scale of factual information on the subject and mailed it to secondary school counselors in New Jersey. This questionnaire included such items as "On the average, women spend about 25 years in the labor force" (true), "Approximately 40 percent of American women who hold college degrees never marry" (false). Counselors were found to have accurate information on only 12 of the 25 items, and women counselors were found to have more accurate information than men counselors on every item tested.

An interesting use of the Neuroticism Scale Questionnaire was made by Schneider and Stevens (1971) in a study on the personality characteristics associated with job-seeking patterns. The particular scale used measures of assertiveness and passivity. Their initial exploration found that patterns of job-seeking behavior were related to the personality dimension of submissiveness–dominance. In their sample they found that assertiveness and independence were associated with positive job-seeking behavior, and that passivity and dependence were associated with a low readiness for job placement.

In studying such topics as vocational maturity, vocational interests, and vocational values, job scales and questionnaires are particularly appropriate.

Tests

It is difficult to say where the classification of scales ends and that of tests begins; for our purposes, tests contain items that have right and wrong answers, and have definite norms for comparative purposes. The most frequently used tests in employment settings are likely to be some form of aptitude test (including intelligence tests). Interest inventories fall between scales and tests but in most works are treated like tests. The researcher would do well to have a set of Buros' Mental Measurements Yearbooks (available from the Gryphon Press, Highland Park, N. J.) to help in choosing tests. Most agencies already have a collection of tests available for use and in some places also have an ongoing test research program, such as the United States Employment Service has with the General Aptitude Test Battery (GATB).

A unanimous Supreme Court decision in 1971 (Duke Power case) ruled that a relationship must be established between test scores and job performance if the score is to be used in hiring. One should employ similar standards if a test is to be used for counseling purposes as an aid in decision-making. We need to verify any test's value for use with the particular clients with whom we work.

Some studies examine the test itself, but most frequently the test is used as a measure of some underlying characteristic of the client. An example of a simple but meaningful study of the test itself was done by Kapes and Sievert (1973) on the use of plastic pegboards as opposed to wood pegboards on the GATB aptitude manual dexterity (M). A ninth grade class of 1050 boys and girls was used. Students who were tested using the wooden boards performed significantly better (an average of 11 converted score points higher) than did students tested on the plastic board.

Johnson and St. John's (1970) study is an example of how to use a test as a measure of a basic characteristic to make predictions about later behavior. They felt that many of the tests available to counselors are inappropriate for students planning to enter employment in technical, business, or subprofessional occupations. They wanted to find a test to help students choose among various two-year terminal programs. They found the Minnesota Vocational Interest Inventory (MVII) to be an effective instrument for differentiating the interests of students in these programs. An additional finding was that the student's choice of career appears to be more closely related to what he likes than to what the individual believes to be important or valuable.

Another use of tests is as pre and postmeasures to determine if some change occurs as the result of counseling or training. This use is included in the following section on criteria.

CRITERIA

If we are to evaluate the effectiveness of a counseling technique or the adequacy of a vocational interest scale, we must have some standard against which to measure success. The standard used is called the criterion and it is some measurement or judgment against which available data can be compared. Such questions as : "How good is an innovative training program?" "How effective is a particular agency?" will be answered only if we can come up with some measure of "goodness" and "effectiveness." Often, establishing criteria is a matter of counting or compiling numbers of placements or training dropouts, job ratings, or test score changes.

The number of placements made by an agency may be by itself a weak criterion, because some clients will quit or be fired shortly after beginning; therefore, some measure of job continuity would be better. For example, how many applicants remain at a job for three months or more? Varga (1974) used such a definition of placement in his paper on counselor characteristics and client results. The client was considered placed if successfully employed for at least 90 days or if after 90 days still in a training or educational program. Using this criterion for placement, the author found that older counselors and counselors who had placement experience closed significantly more cases than other counselors. It was also found that counselors who had frequent contacts with their client and who saw their goal to be client-employment placed the highest number of cases.

Levison and Easterling (1974), in a study to predict the work-release performance of federal prison inmates, used as a criterion of successful work-release remaining on the job without removal for at least three months. They used correlational techniques to determine how well 29 variables such as age, first arrest, and longest prior sentence could predict work-release performance.

The time-on-the-job criteria are rather straightforward, but may not always be the most meaningful. Actual ability to do a job may be a more important criterion to apply to some cases. If the job is a simple one, with a definite outcome such as number of machines put together, there is little difficulty in making a judgment. On the other hand, for many jobs the job adjustment rating will have to be made by a supervisor. Although this brings in the problem of supervisor bias, it is often the best method we have of rating job performance. Anderson and Cox (1972) used supervisors' ratings on the Work Adjustment Rating Form (WARF) of a group of Neighborhood Youth Corps trainees in order to compare the relationship of intelligence test scores to actual job performance. It was found that a commonly used group intelligence test predicted for whites but not for blacks, in spite of the fact that there was no difference in the average scores of blacks and whites on the Work Adjustment Rating Form.

One set of ratings, those by instructors in a training setting, was used by Trimmer (1974) to predict the criterion, which was another set of ratings, those made by supervisors in an employment setting. Among other findings, the author discovered that ratings based on trainee performance did not predict very accurately the eventual employment performance as judged by a supervisor on the job.

In the previous section we discussed the use of tests. Tests may also be used as a criterion of change. The most usual method is to give the test before and after some experimental condition, and evaluate the changes based on increase or decrease in test score. This assumes that a test has been selected that accurately measures what the counselor is trying to change. Again, Buros and his *Mental Measurements Yearbooks* are the best source of information on tests.

In an example of the use of tests as a criterion, Gordon, Arvey, Daffron, and Umberger (1974) studied racial differences in the impact of mathematics training at a Manpower Development Program. The California Achievement Test (Junior High School level) was administered at successive six-week intervals over a six-month period. It was found that white students profited more from the instruction than black students; this implied that racial differences in mathematical competence may be increased by training rather than reduced.

INDIVIDUAL DIFFERENCES
AND WORK BEHAVIOR

When we speak of tests, scales, and so forth, we are speaking of techniques to measure ways in which one individual differs from another. There are some major factors that must be considered when we study vocational or work behavior because they influence differences in performance on many of the measures we use. The difficulty of generalizing results from one applicant or client group to another is compounded if the groups differ in age, sex, social class, race, or if they have mental or physical handicaps. In addition, there are minor factors that produce variations in some training and work situations. Discovering what these factors are could be one of the goals of your personal research program. We briefly discuss the major factors and then indicate several of the minor factors. For additional information on the influence of individual differences, see Tyler (1965).

Differences in age may influence vocational values, vocational maturity, willingness to learn new material, and the ability to perform on various kinds of tests. We would expect, for example, that tests requiring the individual to work fast would give lower scores to older individuals. In one study involving age, Bjorkquist and Finch (1970) used 44 graduates of two Manpower Development Training Programs to study personal characteristics that influence the client's willingness to move. The results suggested that the age at which a person starts a training program will influence whether or not the applicant will move to accept employment on completion of training. The main implication we are concerned with here is that results from a group at one age may not predict as well for a group that is markedly older or younger.

Many studies are now being done on women, some to prove that there are significant differences between performance of men and women, others to prove that no such performance differences exist. It does seem to have been established, however, that separate norms on certain measures, such as the GATB, are needed. When differences are found, much argument exists as to whether these are basic differences that depend on the biology of the two sexes or are simply the result of cultural experience and training.

Shepard and Hess (1975) investigated the different attitudes women and men have toward whether or not an occupation is male or female. Analysis of reactions showed that both sexes were willing to let women into prestige occupations, but that females were more willing than males to have household and child-caring tasks performed by both sexes.

A third major influence is social class or socioeconomic status (SES). It would seem that there are times when Americans would like to deny social class differences, yet we consistently find that people from different social classes behave differently and have different expectations (Tyler, 1965). Kunce (1970) looked at the relationship of welfare status and SES to employment outcomes following prevocational programs for mentally retarded young adults. About three-quarters of the clients who were neither on welfare nor from the lower SES were successful. About half of the clients who were either on welfare or from the lower SES were rehabilitated, and only about one-quarter of the clients who were both on welfare and from the lower SES were successful. Kunce suggests the need to develop improved strategies for working with highly dependent clients on vocational problems.

Some of the social class influences needing further study in relation to work and employment are attitudes toward society, attitudes toward delay of gratification, family patterns, and language differences.

Race factors have been studied in a number of ways, and it is now clear that race affects test performance, particularly on aptitude and intelligence tests. There is research to show that it also affects performance on personality tests, and there are additional findings that perhaps counselor–client interactions are influenced by race.

In the case of handicaps, we have already pointed out that they influence the attitudes of many employers. Further work needs to be done on the influence of handicaps on test performance, the development of tests that do a better job of appraisal with handicapped people, and the problems of self-esteem and motivation of handicapped persons.

Some of the factors that can also work to influence behavior may seem minor but may actually be reflections of deeper mechanisms. Farley (1975) found that how a woman chooses to style her name is related to the extent that she will express interest in continuing her education. The woman who chooses an independent name style, such as Mrs. Mary Jones, is more likely to express interest in further training.

The background of the client is also a consideration. Eltzroth (1973) compared the responses to vocational counseling of 20 women who had been prostitutes and 20 women who had been household domestics. She found that prostitutes had no expectations from the program, and domestic workers had unrealistic expectations. Only four of the prostitutes completed training and entered conventional employment. Of the former domestic workers, all were successful.

TOPICS AND AREAS OF CONCERN

The vocational/occupational literature has certain topics that are at present popular research areas. This means not only that they are important topics, but also that the researcher has the advantage of a body of literature to draw on for ideas, tools, and techniques. On the other hand, the counselor should not hesitate to do research on topics not mentioned here since he or she is the only one who really knows what will be most useful in a particular setting. The following section indicates some of the present areas receiving attention and some of the questions that might be appropriately asked.

Work Values

What aspects of work are valuable to a person and do these aspects relate to how the individual handles the choices at occupational decision-points? These values differ from interests in the way they are used for research purposes. When we speak of values, we speak of characteristics that may be attached to a number of occupations, such as job security, prestige, salary, responsibility. These usually refer to the kind of psychological reward or satisfactions the individual wants to get from work. Work values might be examined with items with which the subject is asked to agree or disagree. Examples are: (1) People have a right to expect their work to be fun. (2) It is more important for a job to offer opportunity than security. (3) To me, work is nothing more than a way to make a living.

Values could be investigated in terms of the topics that have already been discussed—such as "What are some of the individual differences on work values, that is, do blacks differ from whites, women from men, older workers from younger?" "What is the influence of work values on the decisions that one makes?" "In counseling, do work values influence counseling outcome?" "Do work values influence placement outcome?" One can take almost any one of the topics discussed in the previous sections and use them to study values. The same will be true for most of the other topics we will introduce here.

Vocational Identity

How one's parents reacted to work (family role models) has been cited by many authors as an important element in the development of a person's work behavior. We already know that work role models provided by members of the family are not only a source of identification for a person, but help the individual formulate his or her own feelings about the world of work. It would seem to be important to explore some of the effects that lower socioeconomic role models have on the development of work habits and behavior.

Expectations of Work

The above topics lead to the consideration of the problem of what clients' expectations are of work; that is, what is a definition of good work for a person, and just what does the individual want to get out of it. Some work is already being done in this area, and one study at least has shown that it is important to make a distinction between individuals' aspirations and their expectations. Thomas (1976) studied 118 low socioeconomic status black and white male high school students and found that students were able, given the opportunity, to distinguish between their aspirations and expectations. When the choices were broken down into those two categories, lower SES blacks were not significantly more unrealistic than whites in their occupational expectations.

Job Satisfaction

More follow-up must be done with the clients once they have actually been placed to find out what needs are being met by the job. This would include such questions as: Do you feel at ease in the presence of people under whom you work? Do you feel you are being paid a fair salary for the work you do? Does your present job tire you too much physically? Again, knowing who is satisfied with what kind of job would help counselors make better plans with clients, particularly if working toward long-term job placement.

Vocational Maturity

Research in this area is based on the theory that a person's vocational choice is something that develops over time through a series of decision points. It is this series of choices that then determines the eventual pattern the individual's career will take. Westbrook and Cunningham (1970) point out two uses for vocational maturity measures: first, to assess clients' readiness to make various educational/vocational decisions; second, to identify at an early point the clients with low vocational maturity, thus allowing the counselor to provide special guidance.

Techniques of Counseling

Are the counseling methods developed on highly motivated, intelligent clients really applicable to most agency clients? On this topic we need to do more research on client reactions to counseling methods. This should give us an opportunity to discover some of the factors that result in attitude changes in clients, particularly those relating to disadvantaged and hard-to-place clients.

Changing of Attitudes

More studies are needed on techniques of changing clients' attitudes toward self and toward work. Tiffany, Cowan, and Tiffany (1970) show that we can reinforce appropriate attitudes that carry over into work behavior or decision-making. Other work (Rosenthal and Jacobson, 1968) opens the possibility that we might most effectively influence clients' attitudes by influencing the attitudes of those supervisors and teachers who have primary contact with them.

Cognitive Style

Finally, we may wish to investigate the ways in which clients interpret or view what they see. What are their expectations of people and events? Do they approach situations with ready-made prejudices to which they make reality conform (e.g., seeing occupational success as being the result of influence)?

We also need to look at response style. Is the person impulsive or reflective? Does the client feel that what happens to him or her is internally or externally controlled? Work by Tiffany, Cowan, and Tiffany (1970) suggests that this is important in a client's search for work and how he or she responds to being unemployed.

CONCLUSION

For counselors in an employment or vocational counseling agency, there is not much published research to help with decisions. Counselors in many other settings such as colleges and rehabilitation centers have a better research base from which to deal with their clients. At this time, we are not sure of the ways in which employment or vocational agency clients may differ from clients in other settings. As a result, although answers to their questions have been developed in other settings, these findings do not apply when vocational counselors attempt to use them in their own agencies.

This means that for employment and vocational counselors to have information applicable to their clients, they will need to do some research on their own. Rather than having the study grow out of theory, as happens in many published research papers, most of their research designs will grow out of a more immediate need for answers and the results will be applicable to the specific setting in which they are working.

Although we have been using published research for examples in this chapter, we do this because many of these designs will be useful to anyone working in an agency setting. This is not meant to imply that we will do research only if the results are so broad that they can be generalized and as such published. In fact, it is this very factor that argues for doing local research. Published material, by its very nature, needs to apply to a wide population. Local research can dwell on problems that may be very specifically applicable to a limited group of people or may shed light on a problem of interest because of some specific local conditions. All of this, of course, suggests that some of the most important information to be used with clients will be information generated in one's own specific setting.

REFERENCES

Anastasi, A. *Differential psychology* (3rd ed.). New York: Macmillan, 1958.

Anderson, W., and Cox, W. Intelligence and work adjustment in an NYC population. *Journal of Employment Counseling,* 1972, *9,* 126–129.

Bingham, W. C., and House, E. W. Counselors view women and work: Accuracy of information. *Vocational Guidance Quarterly,* 1973, *21,* 262–268.

Bjorkquist, D. C., and Finch, C. R. The relationship of personal characteristics of MDTA graduates to geographic mobility. *Journal of Employment Counseling,* 1970, *7,* 121–125.

Eltzroth, M. Vocational counseling for ghetto women with prostitution and domestic service backgrounds. *Vocational Guidance Quarterly,* 1973, *22,* 32–38.

Farley, J. Married women's name styles and interest in continuing education. *Journal of Employment Counseling,* 1975, *12,* 91–95.

Gordon, M. E., Arvey, R. D., Daffron, W. C. Jr., and Umberger, D. L. Racial differences in the impact of mathematics training at a manpower development program. *Journal of Applied Psychology,* 1974, *59,* 253–258.

Harkness, C. A. Nondebilitating diseases and industrial hiring practices. *Vocational Guidance Quarterly,* 1971, *20,* 52–53.

Holcomb, W., and Anderson, W. Vocational guidance research: A five-year overview. *Journal of Vocational Behavior,* 1977, *10,* 341–346.

Jepsen, D. A. The impact of videotaped occupational field trips on occupational knowledge. *Vocational Guidance Quarterly,* 1972, *21,* 54–62.

Johnson, R. W., and St. John, D. E. Use of MVII in educational planning with community college "career" students. *Vocational Guidance Quarterly*, 1970, *19*, 90–96.

Kapes, J. T., and Sievert, N. W. Measuring manual dexterity with the GATB: Wooden versus plastic pegboards. *Journal of Employment Counseling*, 1973, *10*, 71–77.

Kapes, J. T., and Strickler, R. E. A longitudinal study of change in work values between ninth and twelfth grades as related to high school curriculum. *Journal of Vocational Behavior*, 1975, *6*, 81–93.

Keil, E. C., and Barbee, J. R. Behavior modification and training the disadvantaged job interviewee. *Vocational Guidance Quarterly*, 1973, *22*, 50–56.

Klein, F., and Trione, V. Use of the GATB "G" score for predicting achievement on the GED. *Journal of Employment Counseling*, 1970, *7*, 93–97.

Kunce, J. T. The challenge of welfare dependency to rehabilitation. *Journal of Employment Counseling*, 1970, *7*, 151–155.

Lauver, P. J., Gastellum, R. M., and Sheehey, M. Bias in OOH illustrations? *Vocational Guidance Quarterly*, 1975, *23*, 335–340.

Levison, R. L., and Easterling, R. E. Predicting work release performance for federal inmates. *Journal of Employment Counseling*, 1974, *11*, 78–84.

Nagle, G. S. Number of contacts with disadvantaged applicants as an indicator of success. *Journal of Employment Counseling*, 1973, *10*, 203–207.

Petty, M. M. Relative effectiveness of four combinations of oral and written presentations of job related information to disadvantaged trainees. *Journal of Applied Psychology*, 1974, *59*, 105–106.

Putnam, B. A., and Hansen, J. C. Relationship of self-concept and feminine role concept to vocational maturity in young women. *Journal of Counseling Psychology*, 1972, *19*, 436–440.

Reich, C. M. Vocational specialization and occupational placement: A follow-up study. *Vocational Guidance Quarterly*, 1973, *21*, 281–287.

Robinson, J. P., Athanasiou, R., and Head, K. B. *Measures of occupational attitudes and occupational characteristics.* Ann Arbor: Institute for Social Research, The University of Michigan, 1969.

Robinson, J. P., and Shaver, P. R. *Measures of social psychological attitudes.* Ann Arbor: Institute for Social Research, The University of Michigan, 1973.

Rosen, B., and Jerdee, T. H. Influence of sex role stereotypes on personnel decisions. *Journal of Applied Psychology,* 1974, *59,* 9–14.

Rosenthal, R., and Jacobson, L. F. Teacher expectations for the disadvantaged. *Scientific American,* 1968, *218* (4), 19–23.

Schneider, L. R., and Stevens, N. D. Personality characteristics associated with job-seeking behavior patterns. *Vocational Guidance Quarterly,* 1971, *19,* 194–200.

Shepard, W. O., and Hess, D. T. Attitudes in four age groups toward sex role division in adult occupations and activities. *Journal of Vocational Behavior,* 1975, *6,* 27–39.

Sollinger, I. Client expectations and the community agency. *Vocational Guidance Quarterly,* 1970, *19,* 16–21.

Super, D. E., and Crites, J. O. *Appraising vocational fitness* (rev. ed.). New York: Harper & Row, 1962.

Thomas, M. J. Realism and socioeconomic status (SES) of occupational plans of low SES black and white male adolescents. *Journal of Counseling Psychology,* 1976, *23,* 46–49.

Tiffany, D., Cowan, J., and Tiffany, P. *The unemployed: A social-psychological portrait.* Englewood Cliffs, N. J.: Prentice-Hall, 1970.

Trimmer, H. W., Jr. Predictive validity of instructor ratings in a skill training setting. *Journal of Employment Counseling,* 1974, *11,* 89–95.

Tyler, L. E. *The psychology of human differences* (3rd ed.). New York: Appleton-Century-Crofts, 1965.

Varga, L. Counseling outcomes: Counselor characteristics and client results. *Journal of Employment Counseling*, 1974, *11*, 2–9.

Westbrook, B. W., and Cunningham, J. W. The development and application of vocational maturity measures. *Vocational Guidance Quarterly*, 1970, *18*, 171–175.

CHAPTER 12
Intervention and Evaluation: Two Sides of the Same Community Coin

Steven J. Danish and Kevin R. Conter

Working in the community—such as in correctional settings, youth service agencies, and in consultation and education programs of community mental health centers—is a recent development for counselors. In many ways counselors are in foreign territory when they work in these settings; the roles they are often required to play make their task even more unfamiliar and perhaps more difficult. The professional community counselor is increasingly less involved in direct service activities (where the counselor counsels directly) and more concerned with providing indirect services such as program planning, implementation and evaluation, consultation, training, supervision of other workers, and administration. The delivery of these indirect services in community settings will be the responsibility of the community counselor of the future (Danish, 1974, 1977; Lewis and Lewis, 1977).

Although it is beyond the scope of this chapter to detail the developments and rationale that precipitated this change in focus, a brief discussion seems appropriate. The delivery of human services is rapidly becoming decentralized. For example, college and university counseling services are emphasizing outreach programs (Warnath, 1973); services are being delivered through a variety of other agencies as the number of individuals in state hospitals decreases (Bloom, 1973); and the criminal justice system is developing more alternatives to incarceration (Brodsky, 1972). In addition to the traditional delivery of human services geared to remedial efforts, services designed for prevention and enhancement are now increasing (Cowen, 1973; Danish, 1977).

Despite the growing number of counselors being produced in our graduate programs, there is little demand for them in community settings—even though the need for service is acute. Unfortunately, as counselors obtain higher degrees they become too expensive for community agencies to hire as direct service providers. The need for less expensive personnel to deliver services has led to the stepped up use of human service personnel. These personnel may have no degree, an A.A. degree, or a B.A. degree but certainly cannot be considered counselors under APA or APGA criteria. In addition to the augmented use of less educated personnel to deliver services, new types of services have been developed to meet the needs within the community. The development of support groups (cf. Caplan, 1976) and teaching-oriented counseling services (Gordon, 1970; Guerney, 1977) are examples of these new services.

Opportunities for indirect service roles are available for counselors, but most counselors are still primarily trained to provide one-to-one counseling services. Skills such as program planning, implementation, and evaluation are not part of the specific training offered to most counselors, despite the fact these topics may be covered in graduate programs. Nor are counselors given training in understanding the unique needs of the community and its social service system. All too often it is assumed that the counseling enterprise will transfer from setting to setting unaltered. Therefore, counselors are often unprepared to function effectively as the indirect service providers in community setting.

For example, across several contexts including correctional settings where guards or volunteers may be used as counselors, Big Brother/Big Sister programs, Foster Grandparent programs, and a variety of crisis center hot-line and walk-in centers, counselors may have the primary responsibility for training and for administering and evaluating the programs. Unfortunately, many counselors are poorly prepared for such roles. They are not familiar enough with the community's needs to know what services are really required and are usually untrained in needs assessment techniques. Further, they may not have sufficient skills to design training programs, implement these programs, or evaluate the program's effectiveness once the needs have been determined.

Community counselors must expand their view of what constitutes appropriate activities within the community, and direct service will be a minimal part of these expanded responsibilities. This chapter provides a framework for conceptualizing evaluation within the community and presents a model of community intervention and evaluation. The first step is to distinguish evaluation research from experimental research methods within community settings.

RESEARCH VERSUS
EVALUATION IN
THE COMMUNITY

As noted in Chapter 1, much of the counseling research has been less than valuable for community settings. A major reason for its failure to be applicable is the emphasis on experimental research methods that impose laboratory research designs on the naturalistic setting in an attempt to achieve maximum quantifiability and experimental control. Its basic purpose is to uncover causal relationships between variables. Although applying proven laboratory research procedures to look for such causal relationships may be appropriate in some research, moving into the community with these methods presents problems not found in an evaluation research model.

Evaluation research differs from experimental research both in terms of purpose and procedure. As already mentioned, the general purpose of experimental research is to generate knowledge concerning the causal relationships between variables. On the other hand, the purpose of evaluation research is to describe each step of the intervention and to assess *both* the impact of each intervention step and the total intervention program. The value of a step-by-step assessment is that the counselor can change any step within the intervention process that is not fulfilling its prescribed goal. This process recognizes that the final result of an intervention is the summed impact of each step of the intervention and the interaction between these steps. Evaluation, then, is a dynamic process in which the counselor monitors each step of the intervention. Evaluation becomes a part of the intervention program development, not a process applied after its development.

The shortcomings of experimental research methods become apparent when they are applied to programmatic interventions. The trend is to label the intervention program the independent variable and the behavior of the target group the dependent variable and hope that the intended changes in the target group's behavior do occur and then attribute these changes to the program. For example, Mannino and Shore (1975) reviewed the effects of 35 consultation outcome studies conducted between 1958 and 1972. The basic question was "Does consultation work?" Although the authors conclude that in 69 percent of the studies reviewed positive changes were demonstrated on the consultee, client, or system level, or some combination of these, the community counselor is left knowing little about what the process of consultation is and its value, and having grave doubts about the validity of the findings. In this case consultation has been labeled the independent variable. Any change in the target group's behavior is attributed to the consultation. No effort was made to detail what the process of consultation was and why it was effective or ineffective. Consultation is not a unidimensional process and even defining it as education-oriented, psychiatric, or group-centered does not help the counselor know how to implement it or what parts are effective and therefore necessary to include. The counselor is at a loss as to whether instituting a reported successful program would be useful for a particular situation. Even if consultation is found to be useful, the counselor still may have little knowledge about how to operationalize the program concretely, what danger signals to look for, or what the critical components of the program are. Faced with this kind of situation, it is little wonder that research in the community is generally considered an imposed, additional task that is time consuming, frustrating, and perhaps only minimally informative.

The distinction between evaluation and experimental research is similar to the delineation between formative and summative evaluation made by Scriven (1967). As he conceptualized the difference, formative evaluation focuses on short-range (proximal) goals, which may be conceptualized as the series of actions utilized in achieving more long-range (distal) goals. The result is that programs are evaluated to determine what works. Continuous monitoring is carried on, and modification, alterations, or reinforcement of the program are introduced when necessary. Outcome studies (summative evaluation), to determine whether distal goals have been achieved, are only conducted following extensive formative evaluations.

A MODEL OF COMMUNITY INTERVENTION AND EVALUATION

During the first sections of this chapter, an alternative role for the counselor has been identified and distinctions have been drawn between experimental research methods and evaluation methods as they apply to the community. Intervention and research in the community often require a significant investment of time and effort both for the counselor involved and the community participants. What follows is an outline for the counselor to use at the beginning of an intervention-evaluation project within the community. It is important to note that while this model presents a sequence of activities, it should not be viewed as rigid or fixed. The activities have been divided into three major stages—planning and identification, implementation, and dissemination—as well as into a series of smaller procedural steps. An effective counselor may need to adapt the order of these activities to meet a particular situation or to accommodate individual styles.

Planning and Identification Stage

The first step in any community intervention-evaluation program requires making contact with the community. Entrance may be gained by serving as or being asked to be a consultant, by volunteering one's services, or by seeking to alter an already established relationship within a community to meet a perceived community need. Using consultation as an example, although the skills, knowledge, and attitudes necessary for effective consultation have been described elsewhere (Caplan, 1964, 1970), a brief discussion of some of the preentry issues a consultant may face seems fruitful. Cherniss (1976) defines several issues that he considers unavoidable and that must be examined before any planning begins. They are: (a) Should one do consultation in this situation? (b) Whose interests is the consultation serving? and (c) What is the primary focus of the consultation? To answer these questions fully a needs assessment, which is discussed below, may be necessary. The issue of entry into the community is discussed here to sensitize the reader to the fact that wanting to work or conduct research in a community will not in itself suffice as a reason for community consultation. Ethical and value questions as well as cost–benefit analyses issues abound.

Following entrance into the community and the clarification that the counselor's needs and interests are consistent with those of the community, *a community needs assessment should be conducted.* Needs assessments involve the development of instruments and a technology to determine the needs of a particular community. By a community we are referring to the large number of formal and informal organizations and agencies that exist, including the school system, human service agencies, business and professional groups, youth organizations, religious organizations, neighborhood groups, and the like. In addition to actual citizen participation in the determination of needs (Bell and Warheit, 1975; Weiss, 1975), epidemiologic assessments (Roen, 1971; Schwab, Warheit, and Fennell, 1975) or census and social statistical data (Stewart and Poaster, 1975; Windle, Rosen, Goldsmith, and Shambaugh, 1975) can be used. When the information is gathered, decisions can be made about what needs exist, what community services the community is aware of, and what services the members of the community feel they need and what investment in time, energy, and funds they are willing to expend on these services. The examination of the services available in conjunction with the determination of the needs for services provide an estimate of community needs.

For example, if a counselor was concerned about the extent of human services being offered to the aged, a needs assessment could be conducted.

By examining census and social statistical data, the counselor could determine the percentage of the population who qualify as elderly. The counselor could then survey existing human service agencies to assess the type and extent of geriatric services offered. Matching this information with an epidemiological survey delineating the medical, psychological, and human service needs of the elderly, the counselor would then be able to determine what additional services could be incorporated into the community, what existing services could be altered to meet unmet needs, or what services could be eliminated to avoid unnecessary duplication and expenditures.

As part of a needs assessment of the community the *counselor may institute evaluation efforts to determine whether the agencies are delivering the services they are committed to.* The counselor must be aware of why the evaluation is being conducted. Evaluation may be thought of ideally as the means to determine if a program or agency is meeting its objectives and should be continued, expanded, altered, or changed. However, as Weiss (1972) notes, there are other reasons for an agency to undertake an evaluation: (a) the decision-makers may be trying to postpone a decision by undertaking a time-consuming evaluation; (b) administrators or decision-makers may be ducking the responsibility of decision-making by seeking an "objective evaluation" and thus avoiding taking sides between opposing factions; (c) the evaluation may be an effort to establish good public relations and support by producing a favorable, though superficial, evaluation; and (d) evaluations may be undertaken simply to fulfill grant requirements, in which case evaluations may be of low priority relative to problems of staffing, budget, and community relations. A decision by an agency to conduct a feasibility study to determine whether a "Half Way House" for drug abusers should be opened within a community could be an example of the "other reasons" Weiss notes for doing an evaluation. The feasibility study could serve as means of postponing a decision, seeking an "objective evaluation," and establishing good public relations with the groups involved.

Counselors should also examine their own personal and professional needs and be certain that the evaluation undertaken is for the "client's" purpose. This will help avoid situations in which a counselor does an evaluation of an agency's service delivery capabilities to pave the way for the counselor's own wishes to deliver a certain service.

The counselor needs to examine the results and impact on the community of the assessment evaluation. If the assessment has indicated that sufficient services exist but the public is unaware of them, the counselor may wish to help design and evaluate a public relations program to acquaint the public with the services. The human service system has not been adept at using the media for public relations purposes. Newspaper accounts and television advertisements for "mental health" tend to be sterile and formal, increasing people's reluctance to use the services. If the media can be used so effectively to sell products, people, and ideas, why can't human services be sold?

If the services are inadequate but the existing agencies do not recognize the inadequacies, the counselor may want to help the citizen–consumer advocate for increased programs. One way to advocate for improved services is to organize the affected group and lobby for the needed services (Alinsky, 1971). Another method might be to contact already existing advocacy groups to gain their assistance. For example, the Massachusetts Advocacy Center (1971; Suffer the Children, 1972) has helped pregnant teenagers and parents of mentally retarded children gain the services they need and are entitled to by law. Advocacy as an intervention has been generally overlooked by counselors. Nonetheless, the process of advocacy training and evaluation is certainly within the domain of the counselor's role.

If it is determined by the assessment and agreed by both the existing services and the community that an additional service (intervention program) is appropriate, the counselor may then wish to focus on the development and evaluation of a new program. Thus, the results of assessment will affect the nature of the intervention proposed and the manner in which it is implemented.

Implementation Stage

If it is concluded that an intervention program is desirable, *the first step is to formulate the intervention goals*. Two sets of goals are necessary. There are long-range (distal) goals and short-range (proximal) goals. The former relate to the goals the community has identified; the latter are subgoals or process goals designed to implement the long-range or distal goals. If at all possible, the counselor should become involved in identifying the long-range community goals. Without the counselor's input the goals may be in such a form that they are unattainable, unmeasurable, or both.

The counselor should assist the community to identify the goals, insofar as possible, in behavioral terms (Mager, 1962). This goal description should also present, as clearly as possible, the status of the community's progress toward achieving the goal and the importance of the goal from the perspective of the community. When the goal has been identified and described, the counselor can then determine who and what groups need to be intervened with, and what skills, knowledge, and attitudes these groups need in order to achieve the distal goal. These individual skills, knowledges, and attitudes needed then become the proximal goals.

For example, the authors and a colleague (Danish, Conter and Ginsberg, 1976) were recently involved in developing a proposal to train police in crisis identification. This proposal was based on a community's decision to develop a Victim-Witness Advocate Program (V-WA). This program is designed to provide effective on-site police management of crises and to allow a smooth transition of a victim or witness of a crime over to the V-WA program's professional staff of counselors. The development of this program was in keeping with the overall objective of increasing the public's confidence in the criminal justice system. To attain this overall objective, the following goals were identified by the community:

1. To determine and classify the number and types of program-related needs of all victims and witnesses that come to the attention of the V-WA Program.

2. To provide the services necessary to address the needs of 100 percent of the victims and witnesses that desire assistance from the V-WA Program, to the degree that:
    a. The V-WA Program or another referral agency has sufficient resources to meet the needs.
    b. The V-WA Program is the appropriate agency in the county to provide or refer the service.

3. To increase the ability of 80 duly commissioned officers to identify victims and witnesses in need of crisis assistance.

4. To increase the number of referrals by law enforcement officers of crisis victims and witnesses to crisis intervention resources.

5. To increase the number of referrals by law enforcement officers of victims and witnesses in need of social services to social service resources.

6. To involve at least 100 volunteers in providing victim-witness assistance in the project.

7. To increase the apparent willingness of the public to report crime in the county by 10 percent within a three-year period.

8. To increase the willingness of the public to assist in the prosecution function by 20 percent within three years by providing testimony, evidence, or information.

In order to meet these goals, especially the third and fourth goals, law enforcement officers must be capable of diagnosing the problems and subsequently referring the victims and witnesses to the appropriate advocate program specialist. If the officers are unable to detect a victim-witness problem and are unaware of how to use the V-WA Program, then the program will be unsuccessful in attaining most of the interrelated goals. Therefore, the purpose of the training program was to sensitize police officers to the various problems that victims and witnesses encounter resulting from crime, to inform the officers on how to correctly diagnose a victim or witness problem, and to educate the police on how the V-WA Program works.

The authors were involved in developing subgoals or proximal goals to help this particular department to achieve the third and fourth distal goals. The following process goals were developed.

a. To identify the causes of crises

b. To identify citizens who are in crisis

c. To identify the officers' reactions to crises and the effect crises have on their behavior

d. To develop a repertoire of behaviors for crisis situations

e. To recognize the consequences of their various responses on the behavior of citizens in crisis

f. To assess the needs of citizens in crisis and be able to determine what kinds of intervention strategies are necessary to facilitate referral

g. To identify referral services in the proposed area

h. To develop an understanding of cultural and ethnic minorities

Following the delineation of the distal and proximal goals, the next task is to clarify three aspects of each proximal goal. First, *it is necessary to ascertain that each proximal goal relates to one or more of the distal goals and whether the proximal goals need to be attained in any specific sequence.* This is essentially an indication of internal consistency, demonstrating that the proximal goals are related to the distal goals. For example, if one of the proximal goals was to have trainees learn how to diffuse marital crises, it would be an inappropriate proximal goal given the identified distal goals. Clearly, however, this goal is appropriate in other situations. Second, *it must be determined whether each proximal goal is measurable and attainable within certain time and money constraints.* For instance, in the example above, although the agency might agree that all the proximal goals listed are important, if they felt that these goals would need to be achieved within the maximum of 30 hours of training and $5000 in expenses, this might affect the nature of the training developed. Third, *one must clarify whether goal attainment involves the learning of a skill or the acquisition of a knowledge or a change in attitude or all of the above.* For example, in the proximal goals listed above, goals b, c, and d require skill learning; a, e, and g involve acquiring new knowledge; and h involves acquiring new attitudes. Goal f involves both learning new skills and knowledge.

After the determination of distal and proximal goals *the underlying principles of these goals should be specified.* This process, called the rationale, includes: why the proximal goal is important, how it contributes to the eventual attainment of the distal goal, and whether proximal goals need to be attained in some specific order and why. Essentially two rationales are developed; one is theoretical, includes the points just mentioned, and is for the program designer and the community, while the second is presented to the trainee and acts as a motivational force to ensure optimal participation. This second rationale, in addition to containing information about the relationship of the proximal and distal goals as described above, would also contain information about the process of learning the skills, knowledge, and/or attitudes necessary for proximal goal attainment.

Following the development of the rationales, a *level of attainment related to both the proximal and distal goals is specified.* The specification of this level enables the community, the participant, and the counselor to know when a functional level has been achieved. The specification identifies a *minimal level* on which participants can build more proficient attainment.

For instance, in a program to teach communication skills to Cub Scout leaders (Conter, 1977), one of the distal goals was that den leaders display a set of interpersonal skills that would facilitate pro-social behavior among the den participants. The accompanying proximal goals were: identifying and reflecting the boys' feelings; recognizing their own feelings and expressing them in a nonjudgmental way; reinforcing appropriate behavior; specifying the acceptable limits for the boys' behavior; and clearly structuring the environment, both physically and verbally, so that the appropriate behavior was facilitated. An example of level of attainment for *one* of the proximal goals—identifying and reflecting the boys' feelings—was: being able to listen to a series of audio-taped statements made by boys and correctly identifying their expressed feelings, and using these feelings in a brief statement demonstrating the leader's recognition of the feelings and their source.

When a level of attainment is specified, *the procedures used to assist the participants to attain each proximal goal can be determined.* The procedures followed can be designed to facilitate evaluation as an ongoing component. For example, a format based on general instructional principles (Gage, 1963; Gagne, 1970) can be followed. The format includes: (a) identification of explicit behavioral objectives; (b) practice or application of skills to be learned; (c) self learning by group discussions; (d) rationale for learning (understanding of importance of certain skills); (e) sequential presentation (learning concept A before concept B); (f) active trainee participation; (g) the use of modeling; and (h) the use of immediate feedback concerning the appropriateness of trainee responses.

This format seems especially appropriate for teaching skills. Having knowledge about the skills is not enough. Effective learning involves acquiring a conceptual understanding of the components of the skill (knowledge); viewing others demonstrate the various aspects of the skill (modeling); and an opportunity to use the skill (practice) (Danish and D'Augelli, 1976).

In using such a model, one's evaluation time could be consumed evaluating the relative effectiveness and efficiency of various learning procedures for attaining proximal goals. One could, for instance, assess whether each component of the proximal goal is necessary, how the component contributes to the proximal goal, which components are most important and which can be left out, what is the most effective way to present each component, and so forth. Essentially, these are "efficiency" questions because in the long run they effect the cost–benefit analysis of the intervention. However, these cost–benefit questions are secondary. The major questions are: does the learning of the proximal goals relate to learning the distal goal, and if the distal goal is learned, is the community "better off" as a result? If both major questions can be answered affirmatively, then the next question is "Can we more efficiently achieve these goals?"

Earlier it was noted that the counselor needs to be involved in identifying the distal goals so they are attainable and measurable. If not, it may be impossible to *determine whether the implementation of a goal has been achieved.* As one moves toward distal goals, the measurement often becomes more general, less sophisticated, and more difficult. Tests and other obtrusive measurements become less useful, and unobtrusive measures become more predominant. For example, in the crisis identification proposal described above, one distal goal related to the number of referrals of victims and witnesses to social service agencies. Using unobtrusive measures, comparison could be made of police and social service agency records three months prior to beginning a program for training officers in crisis identification and referral, immediately following the conclusion of training, and again at a later period to account for a delayed training effect. To interview or test citizen-victims and witnesses during their crises would be of limited value and might be unethical and obtrusive.

Dissemination Stage

The general procedure for reporting results of a research project is to write the results in the form of an article for journal publication. Unfortunately, reports of evaluations of community interventions tend to be written as final reports for the funding agency. Either way, such a procedure directs the flow of information to a professional audience. Although this is an established procedure, evaluators of community intervention must ask for whom this evaluation has been conducted and who is to benefit from the information. Limiting reports of the community intervention to professional audiences negates the real purpose of the intervention—community change. Because community agencies sponsoring the program may also require and benefit from the report, the counselor should make an effort to write the report in language that is understandable, clearly spells out the meaning of the results, and offers guidelines for decisions that might follow from such a report. In other words, the community as a whole should be viewed as the ultimate consumer and as such has a right to demand that reports be written in language understandable and useful to them.

It is insufficient for the counselor to present the information and then view the task as being completed. The counselor must facilitate the use of the information by others for constructive change. This means that the report is not just written in language understood by the organization but that the implications of how the information should be used need to be delineated. The counselor has to consider how the results of the evaluation affect the needs the community identified. The evaluation, then, becomes an intervention in itself and as such the community must be prepared to use the information. Because the community may resist change, the counselor might outline steps toward implementing the changes implied by the information.

The steps would be small, objective, measurable ones, specifying change in terms of behaviors and delineating how the community would know when the changes have been achieved.

If the evaluation is to be an essential part of the community's growth and development, it must be disseminated in a manner that will have maximum impact. Regardless of how well done an evaluation is or its "objective" results, if it does not promote change in its intended program, system, or community, then the evaluation must be regarded as a failure.

For instance, if as a result of a needs assessment with the aged it was determined that there were increasing numbers of complaints from the elderly regarding their transportation difficulties, the following intervention–evaluation–dissemination process might occur. The elderly are usually quite dependent on public transportation yet taxis are often too expensive and buses require a continuous state of mental and physical alertness that some elderly may not be able to maintain. A counselor might have developed an intervention with the bus company like reserving special sections for the elderly near the drivers, having the driver call out street names, and reducing the bus rates for the elderly during nonpeak hours. A comparison of baseline versus post-intervention data should demonstrate a significant increase in the number of riders and rider satisfaction and a decrease in the number of elderly riders exiting on the wrong street.

Although dissemination to professional audiences is important, in order to increase the usefulness and potential impact of the intervention and its results a more active process is necessary. The counselor must "sell" the findings to the community. A cost analysis of the program might be conducted to determine if the increased number of riders and the improved image the bus company gains as a result of the program negates the potential increased operating costs so that the bus company can continue the program. The counselor may need to help the bus company develop a public relations campaign to sell the program and its new image.

CONCLUSION

To follow through on an intervention-evaluation program as we have described the counselor will have to solicit help from people outside the human service and mental health establishments. The counselor must have a real working knowledge of the community and its nonhuman service resources. It is inappropriate for a counselor to use a community to conduct an intervention and evaluation study. One needs to ask "Is this evaluation on, for, or with the community?" Unless the counselor has a commitment to the welfare of the community and intends to follow through on the program to ensure its usefulness, serious questions must be raised about the counselor's purpose. Presentation of results and findings to professional audiences does not fulfill that commitment. Dissemination, then, is an active process and becomes the implementation of the first stage of the model—the planning and identification process.

REFERENCES

Alinsky, S. *Rules for radicals: A pragmatic primer for realistic radicals*. New York: Random House, 1971.

Bell, R. A., and Warheit, G. J. Use of the community survey to estimate mental health needs. Paper presented at the meeting of the American Psychological Association, Chicago, 1975.

Bloom, B. L. *Community mental health: A historical and critical analysis*. Morristown, N. J.: General Learning Press, 1973.

Brodsky, S. L. *Psychologists in the criminal justice system*. University, Ala.: American Association of Correctional Psychologists, 1972.

Caplan, G. *Principles of preventive psychiatry*. New York: Basic Books, 1964.

Caplan, G. *Theories of mental health consultation*. New York: Basic Books, 1970.

Caplan, G. *Support systems and mutual help*. New York: Grune and Stratton, 1976.

Cherniss, C. Preentry issues in consultation. *American Journal of Community Psychology*, 1976, *4*, 13–23.

Conter, K. Interpersonal skill training programs for Cub Scout leaders. Unpublished masters thesis, The Pennsylvania State University, 1977.

Cowen, E. L. Social and community interventions. In P. H. Mussen and M. R. Rosenzweig (Eds.), *Annual review of psychology*, Vol. 24. Palo Alto, Calif.: Annual Reviews Inc., 1973, pp. 423–472.

Danish, S. J. Counseling psychology and the Vail Conference: An invited comment on training settings and patterns. *The Counseling Psychologist,* 1974, *4,* 68.

Danish, S. J. Human development and human services: A marriage proposal. In I. Iscoe, B. L. Bloom, and C. D. Spielberger, *Community psychology in transition.* New York: Haworth Press, 1977.

Danish, S. J., Conter, K. R., and Ginsberg, M. Crisis identification seminar proposal. Unpublished manuscript. The Pennsylvania State University, 1976.

Danish, S. J., and D'Augelli, A. R. Rationale and implementation of a training program for paraprofessionals. *Professional Psychology,* 1976, *7,* 38–46.

Gage, N. L. (Ed.). *Handbook of research on teaching.* Chicago: Rand McNally, 1963.

Gagne, R. *The conditions of learning.* New York: Holt, Rinehart and Winston, 1970.

Gordon, T. *Parent effectiveness training.* New York: Peter H. Wyden, Inc., 1970.

Guerney, B. G., Jr. *Relationship enhancement: Skill-training programs for therapy, problem prevention, and enrichment.* San Francisco: Jossey-Bass, 1977.

Lewis, J., and Lewis, M. *The community counselor.* New York: Wiley, 1977.

Mager, R. F. *Preparing instructional objectives.* Belmont, Calif.: Fearon, 1962.

Mannino, F. V., and Shore, M. F. The effects of consultation: A review of empirical studies. *American Journal of Community Psychology,* 1975, *3,* 1–22.

Massachusetts Advocacy Center. *The way we go to school: The exclusion of children in Boston.* Boston: Beacon Press, 1971.

Roen, S. R. Evaluative research and community mental health. In A. E. Bergin and S. L. Garfield (Eds.), *Handbook of psychotherapy and behavior change: An empirical analysis.* New York: Wiley, 1971, pp. 776–811.

Schwab, J. J., Warheit, G. J., and Fennell, B. An epidemiologic assessment of needs and utilization of services. *Evaluation,* 1975, *2,* 65–67.

Scriven, M. The methodology of evaluation. In *AERA Monograph Series on Curriculum Evaluation.* Chicago: Rand McNally, 1967.

Stewart, R., and Poaster, L. Methods of assessing mental and physical health needs from social statistics. *Evaluation,* 1975, *2,* 67–70.

Suffer the children: The politics of mental health in Massachusetts. The Massachusetts Advocacy Center, 1972.

Warnath, C. F. (Ed.). *New dimensions for college counselors.* San Francisco: Jossey-Bass, 1973.

Weiss, A. T. The consumer model of assessing community mental health needs. *Evaluation,* 1975, *2,* 71–73.

Weiss, C. H. *Evaluation research: Methods of assessing program effectiveness.* Englewood Cliffs, N. J.: Prentice-Hall, 1972.

Windle, C., Rosen, B. M., Goldsmith, H. F., and Shambaugh, J. P. A demographic system for comparative assessment of needs for mental health services. *Evaluation,* 1975, *2,* 73–76.

LEGAL AND ETHICAL ASPECTS

CHAPTER 13
Legal and
Ethical Concerns
in Research

Donald N. Bersoff

*Experience should teach us to be most on our guard to protect liberty when
the Government's purposes are beneficent. . . . The greatest dangers to
liberty lurk in insidious encroachment by men of zeal, well-meaning but
without understanding.*

*—Justice Brandeis dissenting in
Olmstead v. United States (1928)*

Just over a decade ago Reubhausen and Brim (1965) stated that, "It requires
no Cassandra to predict lawsuits by parents, and a spate of restrictive legislation, if those who administer . . . tests in schools—even for the most legitimate of scientific purposes—do not show a sensitive appreciation for both
individual and group claims to a private personality" (p. 1194). If there is
any error to that assertion, it is merely that the authors underestimated the
breadth of concern that has emerged with regard to privacy in all institutional facilities and governmental agencies, not only in educational settings.
In all other respects, there is no doubt as to the accuracy of the prediction.

This chapter explores precisely how courts and legislative bodies have
influenced the conduct of research in colleges, schools, mental hospitals,
prisons, and other institutions where counselors work. To help guide the
discussion, the chapter begins with the presentation of a factual situation
that resulted in a lawsuit against a school system planning to administer

personality tests as part of a drug prevention research and treatment program. The setting of that litigation, known as *Merriken v. Cressman* (1973), provides an instructive framework for understanding the legal bases on which courts decide challenges to experimentation with human subjects. The chapter shows how, in the context of a specific situation, the courts employ the legal doctrines explored in the *Merriken* case and then moves from the courts to the statute books. The federal government has recently become intensely involved in monitoring biomedical and behavioral research, and a variety of governmental agencies and commissions has begun to promulgate regulations and guidelines that now, or soon will, control a vast amount of research. The last part of the chapter deals with the broader and perhaps unsolvable conflict between the researcher's right to know and the individual's right to privacy. To bring together the principles developed in the first five sections, we offer an analytic framework to aid counseling researchers design studies that meet legal and ethical demands and to help counselors evaluate whether they wish to participate in the research of others. Finally, there is a brief personal note in the nature of a plea for greater cooperation between the experimenter and those the experimenter studies.

It may be helpful to highlight the issues raised throughout the chapter at the start. Prime among them are:

1.   In what ways does research invade the private lives of those we study?

2.   In the light of this potential invasion, how must we accommodate our procedures so that we meet both ethical demands and legal requirements?

3.   In particular, what are the kinds of information that our potential subjects should be given so that they may make an informed choice as to their participation?

4.   How do we attain the consent of those who may have a limited capacity to consent—children, the retarded, the severely disturbed—and those whose very situation may preclude free choice—the institutionalized and the imprisoned—while respecting the dignity, humanness, and right to self-determination of these potential research subjects?

5.   When may the risks of injury be so great that the researcher should feel obliged to forego the research even though there may

be some potential benefits to either participants or society as a whole?

It should be stated that the reader will find no cases described in which counselors are defendants; in fact, very few cases involving researchers are to be found at all. With the exception of Merriken v. Cressman (1973), in those few instances where courts have become concerned, the dispute involved biomedical rather than behavioral research or touched on matters alleged to implicate national security. Most research that counselors engage in can be appropriately characterized as having therapeutic intent. Counselors are interested in data-gathering to benefit the participant as well as improve future services. Scientists whose basic aim is research are less likely, as a primary goal, to be interested in the therapeutic benefits to participants and thus become more vulnerable to legal claims by subjects. Furthermore, counselors rarely intend to deceive their clients as part of a research design, unlike some social psychologists who depend on deception to study particular phenomena.

This is not to say that counselors who engage in research should be sanguine about possible legal involvement. The invasion of privacy may occur in significant and subtle ways, from the gathering of data to its dissemination. And, from an ethical perspective, putative participants may be treated as objects when left unserved for the sake of populating a control group. This chapter is, thus, designed to sensitize the counselor planning research to the ethical and legal problems inherent in such an endeavor, whether it involves naturalistic observation, needs assessment, descriptive research using data gleaned from agency files, program evaluation, the study of the effectiveness of several methods of therapeutic intervention, or others of the myriad of possible research strategies described in this book.

A GOVERNMENT AGENCY PLANS A STUDY

In 1970, a survey ordered by the Commissioner of Montgomery County, Pennsylvania, and conducted by a company called Scientific Resources revealed that many children in the county were heavily involved with drugs. (I have depended on an article by Diane Rosen in the January 1974 issue of Civil Liberties for many of the facts presented here but not found in the official written opinion of the court that decided the case.) Most of the children who used drugs, the study claimed, possessed some common characteristics. For example, 80 percent of the identified drug abusers indicated that they felt estranged from their families. On the basis of such data

Scientific Resources proposed to the Montgomery County Drug Commission that they sponsor a drug prevention research and treatment program that was later to be labeled CPI, for the Critical Period of Intervention. All three of the county school districts agreed to participate in the program.

There were two phases to the study: identification and remediation. In the first phase, questionnaires were to be given to eighth grade students and their teachers so that certain students, deemed potential drug abusers, could become part of the remediation program. The teachers were asked to identify pupils who most and least fit eight descriptions of anti-social behavior, for example, "This pupil makes unusual or inappropriate responses during normal school activity." The student form was to be somewhat lengthier. First, students would be asked to assess their own behavior, for example, to state which of the following statements was most like themselves: (1) Someone who will probably be a success in life; (2) One who gets upset when faced with a difficult school problem; (3) Someone who has lots of self-confidence; (4) A student who has more problems than other students. In the next part of the questionnaire they would be asked questions about their relationships with their parents and the behavior of their parents, for example, to indicate whether one or both parents "tell me how much they love me" or "make me feel unloved" or "seem to regret that I am growing up and spending more time away from home." Finally, the students would select from their classmates those who fit certain descriptive statements similar in kind to the ones given the teachers.

The second phase of the study was intervention. When the CPI staff had analyzed all the results, they would compile a list of children who would have significant potential for becoming drug abusers. This list would then be given to the school superintendent who would organize a joint effort among guidance counselors, teachers, school psychologists, and others to provide group therapeutic experiences. One of these experences was called the Guided Group Interaction, a program to which the identified students would be involuntarily assigned. One of its stated purposes was to use the peer group as "a leveller or equalizer insuring that its members do not stray too far from its ranks."

When the program was first developed the school system did not intend to obtain the affirmative consent of the parents for their children to participate. The researchers did plan to send a letter home to each parent as follows:

Dear Parent:

This letter is to inform you that, this fall, we are initiating a Drug Program called "Critical Period of Intervention" (CPI). The aim of this program is to identify children who may be susceptible to drug abuse and to intervene with concrete measures to help these children. Diagnostic testing will be part of this program and will provide data enabling the prevention program to be specific and positive.

. . . We ask your support and cooperation in this program and assure you of the confidentiality of these studies. If you wish to examine or receive further information regarding the program, please feel free to contact the principal in your school. If you do not wish to participate in this program, please notify your principal of this decision. We will assume your cooperation unless otherwise notified by you. . . .

Also, as originally proposed, the study contained no provision for student consent.

Sylvia Merriken, the mother of one of the intended participants in the study, who happened to be a therapist in a drug and alcoholic rehabilitation center, complained to the principal of the school where her son was enrolled and to the school board. The American Civil Liberties Union (ACLU) then announced it would represent Mrs. Merriken in an attempt to permanently enjoin the school from carrying out its plans. The ACLU began by filing a complaint in the appropriate federal district court claiming that the program would violate the constitutional rights of both Mrs. Merriken and her son. It quickly obtained a temporary injunction prohibiting the county from implementing its proposal until the litigation was completed. At that point, two of the three schools in Montgomery County decided to discontinue their participation but the Norristown system, which Mrs. Merriken's son attended, persisted, although it honored the temporary injunction.

When the suit began in earnest the school system offered to change the format of their letter so that affirmative written parental consent to participate would be required. In another attempt at compromise, the school modified the test so that students who did not want to be included could return an uncompleted protocol. But the proposal contained no provision for student consent and no data were to be provided whereby students could make an informed choice about participating.

LEGAL UNDERPINNINGS

Although Mrs. Merriken's lawsuit named school officials as defendants, the legal issues raised by the litigation have relevance to all public institutional settings in which research might be conducted. Schools, after all, are governmental agencies like Veterans Administration hospitals, public colleges, and vocational rehabilitation offices. They are also like mental hospitals and prisons where a great deal of power is delegated to authorities who make decisions of significant import concerning the lives and well-being of others. It is in these settings that counselors are to be found and in which much of their research is planned. Furthermore, like much of the research that counselors undertake, the CPI study was planned in good faith to benefit the participants. What increases the instructive value of a school-based example is that the researcher must consider both the legal rights of those who by law have limited capacity to consent—children—as well as the rights of the participants' primary caregivers—their parents or guardians.

In the context of this chapter, Mrs. Merriken's complaint helps illuminate three important legal principles. First, will courts intervene in institutional affairs or will they respect the discretion of the institution and its professional employees? If they do intervene, on what legal bases would they decide to do so? Second, the ACLU was alleging that the planned research was violating certain constitutional rights of the Merrikens; what reading of the Constitution could they rely on to block a program the school claimed was a matter of important public interest? And, third, were there any other nonconstitutional breaches of a legal duty by the school system? To better understand the specific manifestations of these problems as presented in Merriken, it will be helpful to first spend some time exploring the answers to the questions raised in more general terms.

Judicial Scrutiny of Institutional Behavior

Increasingly, courts have carefully reviewed the behavior of officials who direct, supervise, and work in public agencies. There was a time, however, when institutional behavior went virtually unexamined. For example, courts—pleading lack of expertise—were wary of interfering in the discretion of school administrators to control and educate their students. As late as 1968 the Supreme Court was reaffirming that understanding:

> Judicial intervention in the operation of the public school system of the Nation raises problems requiring care and restraint. . . . By and large, public education in our Nation is committed to the control of state and local authorities. Courts do not and cannot intervene in the resolution of conflicts which arise in the daily operation of school systems and which do not directly and sharply implicate basic constitutional values (Epperson v. Arkansas, 1968, p. 104).

But, it also warned that the "vigilant protection of constitutional freedoms is nowhere more vital than in the community of American schools" (Epperson v. Arkansas, 1968, p. 104).

In the 1970s, it is not at all unusual for the courts to oversee the operation of a wide variety of agencies. In some instances, psychiatric facilities, state schools for the retarded, and prisons have virtually been operated by judicial decree. Private businesses have been ordered to eliminate discrimination on the basis of race, sex, or handicap in their employment practices. And, in a decision that should evoke at least a modicum of anxiety among public officials (including counselors hired by public agencies), the Supreme Court ruled in 1975 that such officials were not absolutely immune from liability for money damages when, under certain circumstances, they violate the constitutional rights of those for whom they are responsible (see *Wood v. Strickland*, 1975).

The Right of Privacy

Is privacy one of those constitutional rights that will be vigilantly protected by the courts? Given recent decisions by the Supreme Court it is very difficult to tell precisely to what extent an individual's claim to a privacy right will be protected, but there is little doubt that such a right, whatever its parameters, is now embedded in the Constitution.

Although privacy, as a constitutionally protected right, has been recognized only in the last dozen years, there were some early intimations that there was legal justification for claiming its protection. In 1891, the Supreme Court declared that "no right is more sacred, or is more carefully guarded by the common law, than the right of every individual to the possession and control of his own person, free from all restraint or interference by others, unless by clear and unquestionable authority of law" *(Union Pacific Ry. Co. v. Botsford,* 1891, p. 251). And, in an impassioned dissent to a decision holding any wiretapping legal (since overruled), Justice Brandeis asserted that the framers of the Constitution had conferred to the private citizen, as against the Government, the right to be let alone that he called "the most comprehensive of rights and the right most valued by civilized men." To protect that right, he continued, "every unjustifiable intrusion by the Government upon the privacy of the individual, whatever the means employed, must be deemed a violation of the Fourth Amendment" *(Olmstead v. United States,* 1928, Brandeis, J., dissenting, p. 480). But, neither *Botsford* nor *Olmstead* explicitly recognized that the right to privacy as such was protected by the Constitution.

In 1965, however, the Supreme Court in *Griswold v. Connecticut* held unconstitutional a state statute prohibiting the distribution of information concerning contraceptives on the ground that the statute violated a married couple's right of privacy. The Court soon made clear that the right was not limited to husbands and wives. In *Eisenstadt v. Baird* (1972) the Supreme

Court stated: "If the right of privacy means anything, it is the right of the individual, married or single, to be free from unwarranted governmental intrusion into matters so fundamentally affecting a person as the decision whether to bear or beget a child" (p. 453).

And so, privacy became a constitutional right. But what did that mean? In *Griswold*, Justice Douglas, who wrote the majority opinion, while finding the right of privacy in the "penumbras" of a variety of constitutional amendments, never offered a definition of privacy. That may have been the judicious tack to take since there has yet to be published a universally accepted description of the concept. There have been several thoughtful attempts to define privacy (Beaney, 1966; Bloustein, 1964; Margulis, 1974; Parker, 1974; Reubhausen and Brim, 1965; Shils, 1966; Westin, 1967), and two somewhat overlapping aspects have been identified as constituting the right. One is the right not to suffer governmental prohibition or penalties as the result of engaging in private activity; the other is to be free from governmental gathering, storage, and dissemination of private information (see Dorsen, Bender, and Neuborne, 1976). However, it is probably true that "the right of privacy is largely a subjective, incorporeal right, difficult to identify and incapable of measurement" (Reubhausen and Brim, 1965, p. 1186). But, whatever else it might mean, there is agreement that at least one component of privacy is the right to determine when and in what manner personal information will be communicated to others.

> The essence of privacy is . . . the freedom of the individual to pick and choose for himself the time and circumstances under which, and most importantly, the extent to which, his attitudes, beliefs, behavior and opinions are to be shared with or withheld from others. The right of privacy is, therefore, a positive claim to a status of personal dignity–a claim for freedom . . . of a very special kind (Reubhausen and Brim, 1965, pp. 1189–1190).

Alternatively,

> The decisive element . . . that defines [a breach of privacy] . . . is the acquisition or transmission of information without the voluntary consent or initiative of those whose actions and words generate the information (Shils, 1966, pp. 282–283).

The judiciary—true behaviorists—never attempted to define privacy but were content to indicate what activities comprised its scope. In *Roe v. Wade* (1973), the case establishing a woman's right to abortion, the Supreme Court acknowledged that the guarantee of personal privacy extended to conduct related to marriage, procreation, contraception, family relationships, childrearing, and education. It is not yet clear whether, or to what extent, the constitutional right of privacy extends to other areas.

But even in the areas just mentioned, the privacy rights guaranteed by the Constitution are granted to adults. A great deal of research that counselors do, however, involves children and so it is pertinent to ask if children have similar rights. Do they also have some legally protectable interest, independent of parents, to a right of privacy? In *Tinker v. Des Moines School Dist.* (1969) the Supreme Court intimated that at least some rights were evenly distributed among children and adults: "First Amendment rights are available to teachers and students. It can hardly be argued that either students or teachers shed their constitutional rights to freedom of speech or expression at the schoolhouse gate" (p. 506). However, the Court has also made it clear that children do not share equally in all provisions of the Constitution. In *In re Gault* (1967), children in juvenile court proceedings were afforded some, but not the entire range of, due process protections granted adult criminals. In *Ginsburg v. New York* (1968) it said that it was rational for the state legislature to prohibit the sale of sexually related material to minors even though it would not be allowed to do so with regard to the sale of the same material to adults. In *Baker v. Owen* (1975), a famous "school spanking" case, the federal district court of North Carolina readily admitted that it was questionable at best whether the law would condone any degree of corporal punishment of adults at the same time it was sustaining the right of the school to use a desk drawer divider on the buttocks of children to maintain discipline.

The Supreme Court's most recent discussion of abortion indicates that in some facets of personal life, certain children will be considered to possess privacy rights even when their expression might conflict with parental wishes. In July 1976 the Court declared unconstitutional a state statute requiring parental consent before a pregnant minor could obtain an abortion. In so doing it said, "Constitutional rights do not mature and come into being magically only when one attains the state-defined age of majority. Minors, as well as adults, are protected by the Constitution and possess constitutional rights" (*Planned Parenthood of Cent. Mo. v. Danforth,* 1976, p. 74). But, it must be remembered that although the Court extended to children the privacy rights previously granted to adults in the earlier abortion cases, matters of procreation have received special treatment by the Court and there is no reason to believe that the independent right of privacy will be honored in other domains where children's interests might be at stake.

The Informed Consent Doctrine

The third avenue in this lengthy, but we hope helpful, detour, the informed consent doctrine, is closely intertwined with the right of privacy. The doctrine emerged as a rule of law in the context of physician–patient malpractice suits. The first clear expression of the concept was delineated over 70 years ago:

> [U]nder a free government, at least, the free citizen's first and greatest right, which underlies all others—the right to the inviolability of his person, in other words, his right to himself—is the subject of universal acquiescence, and this right necessarily forbids a physician or surgeon . . . to violate without permission the bodily integrity of his patient by a major or capital operation . . . without his consent or knowledge (Pratt v. Davis, 1905, p. 166).

By the 1960s the contours of the legal duty of physicians to disclose significant aspects of proposed medical procedures to their patients had been fairly well established. Generally, it is now held that physicians violate their obligations to patients and subject themselves to liability for malpractice if they fail to reveal potential dangers and other important facts concerning suggested treatment or withhold information concerning available forms of treatment. (For some legal perspectives on informed consent see Bersoff, 1976a; Goldstein, 1975; Note, 1974; Plante, 1968; Waltz and Scheuneman, 1969; for a general and most helpful source see Katz, 1972.) The underlying legal and philosophical premise of the informed consent doctrine is the notion of "thoroughgoing self-determination" (Natanson v. Kline, 1960, pp. 406; 1104). As a result, the patient is entitled to all the facts necessary to make an informed, intelligent choice before consenting to medical intervention.

Typically, the duty to disclose is not absolute. It is tempered by what may be called the materiality rule. Physicians need not disclose risks that are likely to be known to the average patient or are in fact known to the particular patient involved due to past experience. Rather, the extent of disclosure is determined by the materiality of the risk. As defined in a leading case, "Materiality may be said to be the significance a reasonable person, in what the physician knows or should know is his patient's position, would attach to the disclosed risk or risks in deciding whether to submit or not to submit to surgery or treatment" (Wilkinson v. Vesey, 1972, p. 689). Thus, at trial the jury must decide whether the physician disclosed enough information for the reasonable patient to make an intelligent decision to accept or reject the proposed treatment. If the prudent juror would have foregone the treatment if apprised of an undisclosed fact or risk, then that fact or risk would be material. Some of the information falling within the materiality rule and thus necessitating disclosure are: (1) inherent and potential hazards of the proposed treatment; (2) alternatives to that treatment; (3) the likely result if the patient chooses to remain untreated. In brief, "To establish consent to a risk, it must be shown both that the patient was aware of the risk and that he assented to encounter it" (Waltz and Scheuneman, 1969, p. 643).

There was no reason for the informed consent doctrine to be limited to physician–patient relationships. In many ways the insensitivity of behavioral and medical researchers to the interests of those they studied matched that of the healers and by the mid-1950s it was clear that scientists were not to be immune from legal constraints. In 1954 a group of professors from law and the social sciences recorded and studied the deliberations of juries with "bugging devices." The researchers obtained the approval of the judges and the lawyers involved, but neither the jurors nor the litigants were aware that microphones had been concealed in the jury room. In 1963 three medical researchers injected "live cancer cells" into 22 chronically ill patients at a New York hospital with the approval of the institution's director of medicine but without the fully informed consent of those injected. (For a lengthy history and description of these cases see Katz, 1972.) In 1972 the American public was finally told that for 40 years, under the leadership, direction, and guidance of the United States Public Health Service there had been a continuing study of the effect of untreated syphilis in approximately 400 black males in Alabama. There was no evidence that consent for participation had ever been obtained.

Of overriding influence as far as behavioral research is concerned, was Stanley Milgram's study of obedience (Milgram, 1963). Central to the startling results achieved was the deception, by the experimenter, of the subjects involved. To briefly recount the design, subjects were told that they would be taking part in a learning experiment. Each subject was assigned to a group of four people, three of whom, unknown to the subject, were Milgram's assistants. One of the assistants was the "learner" in the pseudo-experiment. The subject was to play the role of "teacher" whose function it was to instruct the learner by administering an electric shock when the learner made an error in the memory task. The naive subject was put at a control panel that regulated the shock from mild to extremely intense and painful. The teacher was told to deliver the painful stimulus whenever the learner erred. In reality, no electricity was hooked up to the panel and no learning took place. The subject was deceived concerning the purpose of the experiment. Learners deliberately made mistakes and pretended to feel pain so that the real investigators could determine to what levels subjects would raise the amount of electricity. When subjects hesitated they were urged to continue. Sixty-two percent of over 1000 subjects obeyed the experimenter's commands fully, raising the intensity level of the painful stimulus to the highest point possible. The experiment achieved notoriety not only because of the results obtained but because of the reactions of the deceived subjects. They expressed shame, revulsion, anxiety, and extreme tension during and after the experiment.

The ethics of conducting the research in the first place was soon debated in the psychological literature (Baumrind, 1964; Milgram, 1964) and eventually led to a reconsideration of the American Psychological Association (APA) Code of Ethics regarding research. That examination stimulated the drafting of a lengthy and separate reformulation of ethical principles concerning research with human beings (APA, 1973). In turn, these principles led to a vigorous discussion in print regarding the efficacy of the newly established Code (Baumrind, 1971; Berscheid, Baron, Dermer, and Libman, 1973; Gergan, 1973; Kelman, 1972; Kerlinger, 1972; Menges, 1973; Resnick and Schwartz, 1973; Waterman, 1974). Whatever the debatable points, the APA—the major organization representing behavioral scientists—had at least established minimal ethical guidelines for the design and implementation of research. Soon it would be the turn of the courts and the government to do the same.

MERRIKEN v. CRESSMAN REVISITED: THE COURT DECIDES

Despite the concern regarding the ethics of conducting research with humans, Mrs. Merriken's suit against the Norristown school system and its superintendent seems to be the only reported case in which the issue of privacy and psychological data gathering is dealt with squarely. Although it was decided in a federal district court and does not have the far-reaching effect of an appellate or Supreme Court opinion, because it appears to be the only case of its kind it has received remarkably wide coverage in the legal literature (Moskowitz, 1975; Note, 1974; Recent Cases, 1974; Recent Developments, 1973–74; see also Bersoff, 1975).

Of the many constitutional challenges Mrs. Merriken made, the court entertained only one of them seriously—the right of privacy. The court found that the highly personal nature of the research instrument disrupted family associations and interfered with the right of the mother to rear her child. It said, "There is probably no more private a relationship, excepting marriage, which the Constitution safeguards than that between parent and child. This Court can look upon any invasion of that relationship as a direct violation of one's Constitutional right to privacy" (p. 918). And although there was no precedent to the effect in the Supreme Court, the district court declared that privacy was entitled to as much constitutional protection as free speech. But who possessed this right—the student, the parents, or both? The court seemed ready to answer that question when it declared that "the fact that students are juveniles does not in any way invalidate their right to assert their Constitutional right to privacy" (p. 918). However, the court had not yet reached the essential question of whether the lack of consent by children to the invasion of their privacy would be sufficient to invalidate the research. Apparently reluctant to provide a definite answer it found a means to avoid doing so:

> In the case at Bar, the children are never given the opportunity to consent to invasion of their privacy; only the opportunity to refuse to consent by returning a blank questionnaire. Whether this procedure is Constitutional is questionable, but the Court does not have to face that issue because the facts presented show that the parents could not have been properly informed about the CPI Program and as a result could not have given informed consent for their children to take the CPI TEST. (p. 919)

In essence, the court evaded two important issues; whether the failure to secure the child's consent was independently sufficient to constitutionally discredit the research and second, whether parents as guardians can waive their children's constitutional rights by consenting for them. Rather, the court concentrated on Mrs. Merriken's own right of privacy and found that she was unable to give genuinely informed consent to the invasion of her personal life because the parental permission letter was so inadequate. The court deridingly compared the letter to a Book-of-the-Month Club solicitation in which parents' silence would be construed as acquiescence. The letter was also criticized as a selling device in which parents were convinced to allow children to participate. It was not, as it properly should be, an objective document telling parents of the potentially negative features and dangerous aspects of the program. The court then proceeded to lecture school officials and teach them an important legal lesson:

> The parents are not aware of the consequences [of participating] and there is no substitute for candor and honesty in fact, particularly by the school board who, as the ultimate decision maker as far as the education of our children is concerned, should give our citizenry a more forthright approach. The attempt to make the letter requesting consent similar to a promotional inducement to buy,

lacks the necessary substance to give a parent the opportunity to give knowing, intelligent, and aware consent. (p. 920)

The last phrase in the quotation above is an important one and deserves some more attention. People may waive their constitutional rights. They may confess to crimes even though they have the right to remain silent. They may represent themselves in a criminal trial even though they have the right to an attorney. But waivers of such strongly guarded constitutional protections are permissible only if people first know they possess the privilege against self-incrimination or the effective assistance of counsel at critical stages of a criminal prosecution. It has been immutable constitutional doctrine for the past four decades that waivers of constitutional rights must be voluntary, knowing, intelligent, and done with sufficient awareness of the relevant circumstances and likely consequences. It was in this respect that the request for permission was legally invalid. Mrs. Merriken had the right to waive her right of privacy by consenting to the research and intervention program. But because the request was little more than huckstering, it lacked the necessary substance to afford her the opportunity to meaningfully consent to the exploration of her personal life.

There were more infirmities to the program than those apparent in the information-gathering phase. There were also deficiencies, if not misrepresentation, in its dissemination aspect. Recall that the promotional letter promised confidentiality. But the program itself contemplated the development of a "massive data bank" (to use its own terms) and dissemination of data relating to specific, identifiable students to school superintendents, principals, guidance counselors, coaches, social workers, PTA members, and to those on the school board. And, even if the school system had been more circumspect and had constructed means by which the research data were less widely distributed (or not distributed at all), no promise of confidentiality can supersede a subpoena compelling the disclosure of the material to law enforcement officials. Thus, as the court warned, "[T]here is no assurance that should an enterprising district attorney convene a special grand jury to investigate the drug problem in Montgomery County, the records of the CPI Program would remain inviolate from subpoenas and that he could not determine the identity of children who have been labeled by the CPI Program as potential drug abusers" (p. 916). Parents were not at all informed of this possibility.

Compounding the problem was that the identification instruments did not possess enough psychometric soundness to overcome the hazards that may have flowed from their use. Not only could there have been considerable harm done to children correctly identified (e.g., the self-fulfilling prophecy, scapegoating by peers, loyalty conflicts between parents and children if the latter wanted to participate and were thus forced to reveal personal family information to do so), but equally vulnerable, if not more so, were those children incorrectly identified. The latter possibility greatly concerned the court and in a statement that should terrify those who inappropriately rely on tests to diagnose and classify children, it said, "When a program talks about labeling someone as a particular type and such a label could remain with him for the remainder of his life, the margin of error must be almost nil" (p. 920).

But was there no justification at all for the school system's attempt to identify and treat potential drug abusers? Certainly one could mount a persuasive argument that a program designed to learn about and prevent drug abuse serves an important social end. Courts, when faced with the problem of the infringement of individuals' important or fundamental constitutional rights, often consider the competing interests claimed by the public at large. For example, there is a heavy presumption against prior censorship of the newspapers. But most of the Supreme Court agreed that if the Pentagon Papers had been published in wartime and had revealed current troop movements, freedom of the press and the doctrine forbidding prior restraint of the news would have been submerged in the national interest. Thus, courts will balance the interests of the individual against the interests of the state or society. In *Merriken,* the court acknowledged that if the program had demonstrated adequate public need and had restricted itself to a minimal invasion of privacy, it might have passed constitutional muster. But, after studying all of the evidence, the court struck the balance in favor of the individual:

> [T] *he reasons for this are that the test itself and the surrounding results of that test are not sufficiently presented to both the child and the parents, as well as the Court, as to its authenticity and credibility in fighting the drug problem in this country. There is too much of a chance that the wrong people for the wrong reasons will be singled out and counselled in the wrong manner. (p. 921)*

As a summary, it may be helpful to catalogue a number of the serious infirmities inherent in the CPI Program so that future researchers may avoid its pitfalls.

1. The instrument was not technically sound. It did not possess sufficient psychometric trustworthiness to justify its use in such a sensitive area of research.

2.   Those acting as participant-therapists (primarily school counselors) were considered undertrained for the tasks expected of them. Although the counselor who participates in the research of others may not be as culpable (in a moral, ethical, or legal sense) as the experimenter, it would seem appropriate for counselors to determine for themselves if the research they are requested to participate in is designed to protect the rights of subjects, data gatherers, and experimenters.

3.   The researchers failed to secure the affirmative, written, informed consent of the primary caretaker of the intended subjects, the children, who under traditional law are legally unable to consent themselves.

4.   The researchers gave inadequate consideration to the developing rights of the subjects, who may have had a sufficient protectable interest under the Constitution to require their personal consent.

5.   Absolute assurances of confidentiality were naive and misplaced, thus making consent given under such false promises invalid.

6.   There was the possible dissemination of personal and potentially damaging information to law enforcement officials and a wide spectrum of school personnel. The problem was compounded by planned use of data banks from which the information would be easily retrievable.

Finally, I would like to raise a problem not discussed by the court. Although the planned program involved instruments and interventions that had little proven validity, it was never made clear that the study proposed to the school and later sponsored by it was experimental. The school advertised it as a service rather than what it was—an attempt to identify and remediate serious problems through untested or unvalidated means. In the law, labels alone carry little weight. What the counselor may consider practice the court may consider research. It is the nature of the instruments and their psychometric integrity that determine the safeguards courts will demand before they condone research that invades privacy or provides no demonstrable benefit to the participants. Much of what counselors and other mental health professionals do, even though time-honored, is truly experimental. Counselors will be hard pressed to name those personality, vocational, and ability tests that are so valid that the "margin of error [is] almost nil." The same is true for intervention techniques. Counselors may need increasingly to think of their clients as participants in research and surround them with the protections that such persons deserve.

THE STATUTORY RESPONSE: THE FEDERAL GOVERNMENT SPEAKS

Courts develop rules of conduct in piecemeal fashion and only when litigants present legally cognizable issues. But rule-making bodies such as legislatures and government agencies need not wait for people like Mrs. Merriken to sue errant researchers. When law-makers determine that certain problems need a broader reach than courts can provide, when problems begin to affect a great many people, or for other good reasons, they begin to enact statutes and regulations that have comprehensive effect. This process has begun in human research. The year 1974 may be viewed as the watershed in that respect, offering further evidence that Reubhausen and Brim's (1965) prediction that began this chapter is assuredly true.

In mid 1974 the U.S. Department of Health, Education and Welfare (DHEW) published regulations regarding the protection of human subjects. These regulations govern the activities of those organizations who receive research funds or are accountable to DHEW. First published in the Federal Register (39 Federal Register 18917, May 30, 1974) and now codified as Federal regulations (45 CFR 46), the rules explicitly declare the Department's policy that "no activity involving human subjects to be supported by DHEW grants or contracts shall be undertaken unless a committee of the organization has reviewed and approved such activity and the organization has submitted to DHEW a certification of such review and approval . . ." (45 CFR 46.102(a)). These institutional review boards are to make four major determinations.

1. Whether the risks to the subject are outweighed by both the benefit to the individual and the importance of the knowledge to be gained so as to warrant a decision to allow the subject to accept these risks.

2. Whether the rights and welfare of these persons—called "subjects at risk"—will be adequately protected.

3. Whether legally effective informed consent can be obtained by appropriate and adequate methods.

4.   Whether the design calls for periodic review of the research.

Two definitions made part of the regulations are pertinent here. One is the meaning of "subject at risk." The term includes:

> [A]ny individual who may be exposed to the possibility of injury including physical, psychological, or social injury, as a consequence of participation as a subject in any research, development or related activity which departs from the application of those established and accepted methods necessary to meet his needs, or which increases the ordinary risks of daily life (45 CFR 46.103(b)).

The other definition is the Department's attempt to conceptualize informed consent. Broadly defined, it is conceived as the "knowing consent of an individual or his legally authorized representative so situated as to be able to exercise free power of choice without undue inducement or any element of force, fraud, deceit, duress, or other form of constraint or coercion" (45 CFR 46.103(c)). More specifically, the elements comprising consent include:

- Fair explanation of the procedures to be followed, and their purposes, including identification of any procedures that are experimental.

- Description of any attendant discomforts and risks reasonably to be expected.

- Description of any benefits reasonably to be expected.

- Disclosure of any appropriate alternative procedures that might be advantageous to the subject.

- An offer to answer any inquiries concerning the procedure.

- An instruction that the person is free to withdraw consent and to discontinue participating in the project or activity without prejudice to the subject.

Finally, the regulations prohibit the dissemination of personally identifiable information obtained through research without consent of the subjects or their legally authorized representative (45 CFR 46.119(b)).

Soon after DHEW published these regulations, Congress passed the National Research Act (Pub. L. 93-348, 88 Stat. 342), Title II of which is called "Protection of Human Subjects of Biomedical and Behavioral Research." Its primary purpose was to establish a National Commission whose major task is to identify basic ethical principles that underlie the conduct of human research. The Commission, now in operation, is composed of persons from medicine, law, ethics, theology, the physical and social sciences, philosophy, humanities, government, health administration, and public affairs. At least five of its members must be actively engaged in biomedical or behavioral research with human beings.

In developing ethical principles, the Commission is charged with considering ways in which it can be determined if human subjects are needed for planned research, constructing guidelines for the selection of human subjects, and arriving at a definition of informed consent. Another significant aspect of its work is to identify the requirements of informed consent for those persons whose capacity for giving consent is either absent or limited. In this category fall prisoners, institutionalized mental patients, and children. To accomplish this task the Commission is to consider the adequacy of information given to such persons about the research, the risks, discomforts, and anticipated benefits from the research, as well as the competence and freedom of such people to make a choice for or against their involvement.

The concern for "limited capacity" populations was apparently stimulated by a recent decision that held that involuntarily detained mental patients could not give informed and adequate consent to experimental psychosurgery (Kaimowitz v. Dep't of Mental Health (1973)). (The reach of this holding to prisoners is unclear because the patient in this case had been committed to a state hospital under a criminal sexual psychopath law without a trial of his criminal charges for murder and rape.) The invalidity of consent was predicated on the inherently coercive atmosphere of an institutional setting where release may depend on cooperation with those suggesting surgery as an alternative to indefinite confinement. The court assumed that the absence of meaningful choice on the part of one who has little bargaining power could vitiate any consent given by one in that position.

The Commission in its recommendations to the Secretary of DHEW (1976) has rejected the rationale of the Kaimowitz court. It agreed that institutionalization may lessen the ability of prisoners and mental patients to make uncoerced choices, but asserted that the diminished capacity to consent should not absolutely exclude involuntarily confined persons from the opportunity to benefit from new therapies if those interventions are their best or only hope for recovery from disabling disorders.

The Commission focused on the nature of the institution in which research might be conducted. Although prisons and hospitals may have potential for limiting the capacity of their residents to make "free" choices, the Commission believed it was possible to specify the necessary conditions under which research in closed institutions might continue to be supported by the federal government. With regard to prisons, for example (the Commission as of this writing has not yet completed drafting its guidelines for those committed to psychiatric facilities), it recommended that research concerning the possible causes, effects, and processes of incarceration and studies of prisons themselves could be supported provided that they presented no more than minimal risk or inconvenience to the subjects, that the research was performed by competent persons, and that the proposed study was approved by the Institutional Review Boards required by DHEW. With the same proviso, the Commission also agreed that research on innovative and accepted practices that had the intent and reasonable probability of improving the well-being of the individual prisoner might be conducted. Any other research—primarily that which would not have the goal of benefiting the individual prisoner—could only be conducted if the planned research filled an important social and scientific need, if the reasons for involving prisoners (in contrast to "free living" subjects) was compelling, and if there was a high degree of voluntariness on the part of prospective participants and openness on the part of the institution. Criteria of openness would include adequate living conditions, opportunity to effectively redress grievances, separation of research participation from parole considerations, and willingness of the prison to bear public scrutiny.

Thus, the Commission focused on standards of conduct for institutional authorities rather than on the capacity of the potential subject. As an alternative to forbidding all research in closed settings, it recommended research participation by inmates where there is evidence that a relatively free choice is probable. The consequence is at once to respect the autonomy of the individual as well as to stimulate positive change in living conditions in previously coercive institutions. The recommendations are, of course, not perfect. They may be considered paternalistic and protectionistic insofar as the prisoner is only allowed a choice when the institution meets the requirements of openness and voluntariness or when the research has substantial promise of benefit to the subject.

The situation regarding consent becomes even more complex when the potential subjects are children or those involuntarily committed to mental institutions. Unlike prisoners, these populations are not always presumed competent to make decisions. Substitute or proxy consent by a parent or legally appointed representative has been the traditional solution but there are those—including some members of the Commission, its staff, and its consultants—who feel that the use of third persons to consent for others is a basic denial of human dignity. It is this fundamental question of whether, or under what conditions, selected others may consent or refuse to consent to participation in research with which the National Commission for the Protection of Human Subjects is now grappling.

The Commission does not have the power to make regulations. It is merely advisory and in the two years of its originally scheduled existence (now three by virtue of an extension granted by Congress in October 1976) it will be limited to recommending ethical principles and guidelines to the Secretary of Health, Education, and Welfare. Finally, the guidelines, as they are developed and adopted, will pertain only to research sponsored or supported by DHEW. No doubt, however, any accepted measures will have significant influence on the conduct of research generally since the Commission is also making recommendations to Congress. To date, the Commission has developed guidelines for the protection of fetuses, pregnant women, and products of human in vitro fertilization. The guidelines have since been adopted as as regulations, with the force of law, by DHEW. See 40 Federal Register 33526 (August 8, 1975). Guidelines concerning prisoners have also been published as proposed rules (see 42 Federal Register, 3076, January 14, 1977) but have not yet been adopted as enforceable regulations. Also awaiting approval by the Secretary of DHEW are completed guidelines with regard to psychosurgery and children.

This thicket of regulations, guidelines, codes, and statutes is no doubt confusing. At the very least they may provide a ready reference for those who contemplate federal funding for their research. For counselors and others seeking governmental assistance, it is imperative that they know what rules they will have to abide by to secure and maintain such funding. The regulations are generally useful in designing any research and may have a secondary benefit. If challenged, research designs that rely on federal regulations will probably be accorded significant weight by the courts. Lastly, the plethora of rules illustrates the progression from ethical standards, binding on only those researchers who belong to professional organizations but with little legal significance, to judicial decisions, binding on only the litigants involved, to statutes and regulations, binding on all those contemplated by the laws. Already, 90 percent of human medical research is sponsored by the federal government and for many who plan, conduct, or participate in research, ethical constraints are now legal mandates.

BALANCING THE INTERESTS: THE HARD CASES

The legitimate question may be raised as to whether all this judicial intervention and legislative interference is indeed necessary. The jury bugging case, the Alabama syphilis study, and the cancer research at the hospital in New York are, perhaps, merely isolated anomalies. It can be charged that by using *Merriken v. Cressman* (1973) as an illustrative example, I have unfairly biased the case against research in institutions. The thoughtlessness of the researchers and officials who agreed to employ the CPI Program made *Merriken* an easy case to decide. The appealing nature of the plaintiff's charges allowed the court to iterate some easily applaudable statements concerning privacy and the rights of human subjects. But I should emphasize that the defendant-school system lost, not because it sought to engage in personality research and intervention per se, but because the research design was flawed, the chance of error great, and the public need poorly demonstrated. Given all that, the decision was inevitable.

But what of other instances where planned research does not suffer from such fatal infirmities? Does planning research well end the responsibility of the investigator? The burden of scholarly opinion seems to say no, for there are other considerations beyond the experimental design. Inherent in all research, but especially in the behavioral sciences, is the conflict between the interests of the researcher and those of the subject, a conflict perhaps best summarized in the following observation:

> The respect for privacy rests on the appreciation of human dignity, with its high evaluation of individual self-determination, free from the bounds of prejudice, passion, and superstition. In this, respect for human dignity and individuality shares an historical comradeship with the freedom of scientific inquiry, which is equally precious to modern liberalism. The tension between these values, so essential to each other in so many profoundly important ways, is one of the antimonies of modern liberalism. The ethical problems with which we are dealing . . . arise from the confrontation of autonomy and privacy by a free intellectual curiosity, enriched by a modern awareness of the depth and complexity of the forces that work in us implemented by the devices of a passionate effort to transform this awareness into scientific knowledge (Shils, 1959, pp. 120–121).

Similar note of this tension was made by psychologist Ross Stagner (1967) before a Senate subcommittee concerned with government research:

> Social scientists . . . have a genuine obligation to devise protections for the right of privacy, and to avoid mere psychic voyeurism. At the same time they have a compelling obligation to accumulate data—and meaningful generalizations —about the powerful impulses of loyalty, hostility, fear, and ambition which shape human history. . . .

There is an obvious conflict between the need of society to know and the right of the individual to dignity and privacy. (pp. 757–758)

The conflict between the needs and benefits of research and the integrity of the individual are nowhere more apparent than in the APA's Ethical Principles in the Conduct of Research with Human Participants (1973). Principle 3 of these standards state, "Ethical practice *requires* the investigator to inform the participant of *all* features of the research that reasonably might be expected to influence willingness to participate, and to explain *all* other aspects of the research about which the participant inquires (APA 1973, p. 29, emphasis mine). But, without a pause, it then cautions that "Failure to make full disclosure gives added emphasis to the investigator's responsibility to protect the welfare and dignity of the research participant" (p. 29). Principle 4 exhibits the same ambivalence: "Openness and honesty are *essential* characteristics of the relationship between investigator and research participant. When the methodological requirements of a study necessitate concealment or deception, the investigator is required to ensure the participant's understanding of the reasons for this action" (p. 29, emphasis mine).

The APA Principles undoubtedly reflect an attempt to mediate between the values of science and the values of the individual. Such a compromise may be anathema to those who do not feel that human freedoms should be diluted (I will present that point of view a bit later on), but powerful arguments can be launched against the invocation of what has been called "ethical imperialism" (Gergan, 1973, p. 910). An appeal to absolute abstract moral principles may halt important research too abruptly without first investigating whether informed consent and freedom from deception have any real meaning for research participants and in what ways they affect the accumulation of valid data. If research subjects remain unaffected by the withholding of "all features of the research that reasonably might be expected to influence willingness to participate," if they find experimental deceptions rather intriguing, if they do not care about the rationale of the research, and if their attitudes about life and themselves remain untouched regardless of whether ethical constraints are realized in an experiment, then establishing such principles poses unnecessary hardships for the scientist (Gergan, 1973) as well as obstructing, and perhaps permanently denying, the gathering of potentially important data that may genuinely serve to alter beneficially the environment, the individual behavior of people, and the participants themselves.

In the behavioral sciences, participation in research does not occur through a unidimensional class of experiments. Data may be gathered, for example, by methods such as the following, discussed in other chapters of this book:

Convert or unobstrusive observation or recording of public behavior.

Covert or participant observation in private situations.

Disguised field experimentation in public situations.

Adding research manipulations to existing nonresearch operations (e.g., studying the effectiveness of different styles of counselor-client interaction with counselors who are naturally different).

Obtaining information from third parties (APA, 1973, pp. 30-35).

Thus, the argument continues, differing ethical safeguards may be needed for each kind of research setting. The easiest case is made for dispensing with informed consent in the covert observation of public behavior:

> *Involvement of individuals in this sort of research is minimal and not to be compared with that of research participants in the usual sense. The experience of the "participants" is not affected by the research, and there is no direct or negative effects on them. The case approaches that of historical research (in which the public acts of persons are studied without their consent being thought necessary) or that of research with unobstrusive measures . . . (APA, 1973, p. 31).*

Covert observation does not necessarily consist of violation of privacy and thus the subject may not need to be informed:

> *If a researcher bugs hotel rooms . . . to observe and record sexual behavior this is a clear violation of privacy. But when a researcher observes members of a group interacting even without the knowledge of those observed, there is no invasion of privacy . . . Most research situations in which psychologists observe people are not private because there is ordinarily no communication or behavior of a personal and private nature (Kerlinger, 1972, p. 894).*

Can deception be similarly rationalized? Informed consent concerns the researcher's obligation to provide information but deception involves the researcher's deliberate act of providing misinformation. Unlike the medical scientist who uses deception primarily to assure cooperation of the subject who might otherwise be frightened away, those who study human behavior use deception as an integral part of the experimental procedure:

Without deception, it would be impossible . . . to obtain the kind of information that many psychological experiments are designed to produce. . . . For those who value these lines of research because they represent contributions to knowledge—perhaps even to the betterment of the human condition—it is difficult, therefore, to take the absolutist position that behavioral scientists must refrain from using deception in their experiments under any and all conditions (Kelman, 1972, p. 996).

Deception methodology . . . often serves to facilitate the manipulation of independent variables that otherwise would not be amenable to rigorous investigation and to minimize the extent to which "demand characteristics" are operative in experimental settings (Berscheid et al., 1973, p. 913).

Those who oppose rigorous adherence to the principles of informed consent in all research claim that a legitimate concern about surveillance and deception by political, police and intelligence agencies has been diffused inappropriately into the research context:

Research observation has the basis purpose of obtaining measures of variables. . . . Police and intelligence agencies observe people to obtain information on the past, present, and possible future misbehavior as defined by law or by the agencies. They practice clandestine surveillance. . . . These two forms of observation are utterly different in their intent and purpose (Kerlinger, 1972, p. 894).

One of the consequences of openness and honesty is that research data may be significantly altered. Resnick and Schwartz (1973) studied the effects of fully informed participation. Two groups were exposed to a simple verbal conditioning task performed many times in laboratories with uniform results. One group, labeled "nonethical," was exposed to the task under the usual research procedures (i.e., they were not told the purpose of the experiment). The second group of subjects, labeled "ethical," was exposed to the task after being told explicitly of the purpose, procedure, and hypothesis of the study (i.e., to reinforce the use of certain personal pronouns through verbal conditioning). The results showed significant positive conditioning by the nonethical group. The 14 subjects in this group increased the use of "I-We" pronouns (the ones systematically reinforced by the experimenters) from a mean of 7.00 before conditioning to a mean of 14.43. The ethical group started at the same level (mean = 7.21), but they *decreased* their use of "I-We" pronouns in equivalent trials to 5.07.

Resnick and Schwartz (1973) found that major unanticipated problems were encountered in conducting their experiment that related directly to the conditions under which the groups were studied. Few people volunteered for the ethical group and those that did missed more than half their appointments. In contrast, none of the nonethical group were ever late. Because of the lack of cooperation of those in the ethical group it took five weeks to complete the experiment; those in the nonethical group were run in a week. From all this the authors concluded the following:

> It is possible that people lose their interest in participating in psychological research when it is disclosed fully to them what the research is all about. This may suggest that people enjoy an element of risk and nondisclosure and become bored rapidly with the prospect of participating in something about which they already have knowledge. . . . [Another] possibility is that people may become very suspicious when the experimenter is so totally disclosing and stay away altogether (p. 137).

Epstein, Suedfeld, and Silverstein (1973) found that 80 percent of 300 college students surveyed expected that they would not be told the purpose of the experiment. They considered nondisclosure a generally appropriate feature of research participation. Only 6.7 percent considered deception inappropriate to the research setting and thought that the experimenter was obligated to be honest. The only strong demand the students made was that the researcher provide clear instructions. There is also some evidence to suggest that the need for information is correlated with the nature of the experiment. If the study is perceived to be nonstressful, desire to participate is relatively unaffected by the amount and nature of information provided by the researcher. But if the study appears stressful (such as that by Milgram), participation rates are substantially affected by the information provided (Berscheid et al., 1973).

Thus, the argument concludes, there need not be the ethical imperatives in the behavioral sciences that can be insisted on rightfully in medical research and treatment. Not only have present procedures not been demonstrated as harmful to human subjects but there is evidence that informed consent and honesty may be detrimental to the attainment of important knowledge regarding human behavior. Field experiments, under rigorous adherence to the informed consent doctrine, would be impossible and the vast majority of research dealing with negative affect states would be seriously curtailed (Gergan, 1973; see also Reubhausen and Brim, 1965).

This long string of arguments that stresses the primacy of knowledge acquisition has not gone unmet. Clearly in opposition is the belief that researchers should forego experimentation involving deception and unconsented invasion of privacy. Undoubtedly, Diana Baumrind has been one of the most articulate and persuasive advocates of this view. "There are times," she says, "when the objectives and commitments of the investigator directly conflict with the well-being of the subject, and the code of ethics should contain provisions that at such times unequivocally protect the subject from the investigator" (Baumrind, 1971, p. 887). Children, she feels, deserve special attention. Their right not to be harmed or alienated "must supersede the rights of the investigator to know and to report" (Baumrind, 1971, p. 887). Once society permits some subjects to be deceived or uninformed because it endorses investigators' claims to the overweaning significance and reasonableness of their scientific objectives, then the dilution of individual freedoms begins (Shils, 1966).

Just as alarming is the possibility of alienation as more and more subjects are treated dishonestly. Baumrind (1971) believes that people are less affected by the pain and stress of some experiments than by the loss of trust in themselves and the investigator: "The more serious harmful consequence [of deceit] may be that the subject is taught that he cannot trust those who by social contract are designated trustworthy and whom he needs to trust in order not to feel alienated" (p. 889). Thus, not only will continual deception and involuntary participation jeopardize community support for research (e.g., Nettler, 1959; Sheets, Radlinski, Kohne, and Brunner, 1974) but it can invalidate data as more and more "subjects" become suspicious of all researchers and begin to distrust even honest communications. Eventually, cynical citizens determined not to be made fools of may refuse to help genuine victims, misperceiving real-life events as elaborate field experiments.

> Take a hypothetical example . . . a study in which the experimenter's accomplice feigns a heart attack in a public place. . . . An observer notes the amount and type of help that people offer him. . . . The fact that such events may occur naturally does not, of course, justify staging them for research purposes. In the long run, the proliferation of such experiments would add to the already considerable degree of deceit and irrationality that pervades modern life. Increasing public awareness that such experiments are taking place would add not only to the "pollution" of the research environment . . . but also to the ambiguity of real-life situations that call for helping behavior (Kelman, 1972, p. 999).

Perhaps the fundamental concern of those who would subordinate the researcher's right to investigate to the individual's right to privacy is the dehumanizing effect of secrecy and deception.

> To manipulate men, to propel them toward goals which you—the social reformer—see, but they may not, is to deny their human essence, to treat them

as objects . . . to degrade them. That is why to lie to men, or to deceive them . . . is, in effect, to treat them as sub-human, to behave as if their ends are less ultimate and sacred than my own (Berlin, 1969, p. 137; see also Jourard, 1966).

Researchers tend to regard experimental situations as isolated from the rest of existence so that the usual standards of interpersonal ethics need not apply (Kelman, 1967) and so do things to subjects they would never do in other interpersonal relationships. But, by forgetting that the researcher-participant relationship is also a "*real* interhuman relationship" and judging the experimenter's conduct purely in the context of scientific contribution, "deception—which is normally unacceptable—can indeed be seen as a positive good" (Kelman, 1967, p.5). Ultimately, "where society's sanctioned procedures exhibit a disdain for the value of human personality, that ideal is not likely to flourish" (Kadish, 1957, p. 347).

In sum, then, the fully informed involvement of human participants makes four significant contributions.

> [It] serves society's desire to respect each individual's autonomy and his right to make choices concerning his own life. Second, providing a subject with information about an experiment and encouraging him to be an active partner in the process may also increase the rationality of the experimentation process.
>
> Third, securing informed consent protects the experimentation process by encouraging the investigator to question the value of the proposed project and the adequacy of the measures he has taken to protect subjects, by reducing civil and criminal liability for nonnegligent injury to subjects, and by diminishing adverse public reaction to an experiment. Finally, informed consent may serve the function of increasing society's awareness about human research (Katz, 1972, pp. 523–524.

AN ANALYTIC FRAMEWORK FOR PLANNING RESEARCH

As a way of providing some cohesion to the material presented so far, it may be helpful in this final section to discuss some principal considerations that counselors can refer to in the planning and design of their own research. In developing this framework, I have drawn, in part, from the work of Anastasi (1976), Kelman (1972), and most especially Westin (1966), although I have little doubt that none of them would agree totally with what follows. I, of course, take full responsibility for what is contained therein. I also acknowledge that I will seem overcautious and forbidding in a textbook designed to promote, not inhibit, research. As indicated early in this chapter, much of the concern about research has involved nontherapeutic experimentation involving drugs or medical procedures. Counselors have created little, if any concern. And—with the possible exception of behavior modification research, designs predicated on deception, or the use of psychological tests —social science research has escaped scrutiny. However, in an effort at completeness and to alert counselors to possible problems not entirely irrelevant even to the most benign research, I believe the following material will be useful.

Seriousness of the Need to Conduct Research

Studies may be characterized as therapeutic and nontherapeutic although the distinction is not always clear and consistent. Therapeutic studies are those likely to produce direct benefit to the participant. Subjects in such studies may be classified as intended beneficiaries. Nontherapeutic studies are often, but not always, designed to contribute knowledge about the class of persons of which the subject is a member. Here, where only the class, but not the particular person, may profit, subjects in nontherapeutic research may be classified as incidental beneficiaries. Other types of nontherapeutic research are those studies in which the particular class of subject chosen is irrelevant but is selected only because it is conveniently available.

In evaluating the need to conduct research, the counselor should consider two dimensions—the potential value to society and the potential value to the individual subject. The greater the risks to subjects in comparison to the contribution to society and the more the design includes subjects who will go untreated, the stronger should the experimenter inhibit pursuing the research at all. A great deal of research not only is an intrusion into personal privacy but "also quite useless and unnecessary from any serious standpoint. . . . Much of it is frivolous self-indulgence of the professional of intrusion" (Shils, 1966, p. 306). On the other hand, much of what the counselor might study would serve to preclude unwarranted invasions of privacy. Well-planned needs assessments and carefully designed program evaluation might prevent wasteful gathering of personal data or provide immediate information that ill-conceived interventions should be stopped.

One could construct a hypothetical continuum along which three major reference points might be placed. Near the end where the least compelling reason for doing research would be located are those studies that harm the individual and that promise only vaguely to benefit some amorphous societal interest. In the middle, perhaps somewhat toward the end favoring research, are those studies that enhance institutional decision-making, have no presently demonstrable benefits for the subjects themselves but may aid others like them in the future and possess no more than minimal risk and inconvenience for the incidental beneficiaries. Most compelling are those studies directly aiding the participant.

Availability of Alternative Methods to Meet the Need

When governments curtail individual liberties to achieve a state goal, courts will often declare the method used to achieve that goal unconstitutional. They will impose on the state the duty to devise a less drastic means for accomplishing its purposes. For example, the state would not be permitted to exclude children from public school simply to save money. Instead, the court would order the school board to seek a less drastic alternative such as raising to taxes or increasing class size.

The same principle can be applied to research. Even if the research aim is laudatory, the experimenter should consider the availability of instruments and methods that will not coerce, deceive, leave treatable subjects untreated, or invade privacy. For example, if research on children is contemplated, there should be evidence that the planned study cannot be conducted on adults, that the knowledge to be gained can only be obtained if children participate, and that the information desired cannot be gleaned from natural, nonresearch settings. With prisoners or other institutionalized persons, similar considerations are relevant.

Counselors in closed settings such as prisons and hospitals who engage in research should be sensitive to the possibility that they might be using subjects in those institutions because the population is stable and controllable and not because results may directly benefit the participants. Given the nature of most counselor-conducted research, this is unlikely, but it is still helpful to be aware that considerations of equity demand that the risks of research, including the invasion of privacy, be distributed among the total population, not only those who are accessible and acquiescent.

More likely, it is possible that some research specifically designed to help some participants may leave others untreated. For example, consider a study in which a vocational counselor seeks to discover whether rehearsals of job interviews better prepare potential employees than those without such training. In pursuit of this knowledge, the counselor systematically rehearses an experimental group chosen at random and leaves untrained a control group. It is very likely that the rehearsed group will be more successful in receiving job offers. But what of the untrained group? By virtue of inclusion in a research protocol—notwithstanding its intention to benefit some of the participants—the untreated control subjects receive significantly fewer job offers, a consequence of major economic and psychological importance in their lives. Alternatively, given the scarcity of counselors, it is quite possible that access to their services might be predicated on agreement to become part of an experiment. Even with full disclosure of risks and benefits, such participation may be seen as coerced and inherently unethical. It is in these situations that counselors might wish to pursue other than a research context to study certain questions.

Soundness of the Research Instruments

Counselors and other practitioners should use only those instruments useful in making appropriate decisions about persons and that possess demonstrable psychometric integrity. Many assessment devices fail to meet these criteria (Bersoff, 1973). Projective testing, for example, continues despite the fact that the assumptions on which these tests are based have been challenged and found to possess little substance (Murstein, 1965). A major concern in *Merriken,* it may be recalled, was that one of the end products of the research program was the classification of children as potential drug abusers. The court criticized the assessment tool that would select those particular children, not only because of its personal nature, but because its validity was unproved.

Obviously, different considerations apply when the purpose of the study itself is to establish the reliability and validity of a new instrument. Here, participants deserve a variety of absolute protections. No decisions of any kind concerning the subjects should be made on the basis of test results. None of the information gleaned from the instrument should be disseminated. All test results should be destroyed or protected from subpoena (see Astin and Boruch, 1970; Holtzman, 1971, for descriptions of such procedures). No personally identifiable information should be attached to the test results if there is some compelling reason for their maintenance.

Recognition of the Right to Consent to the Invasion of Private Worlds

If society, including its scientific community, believes in individual humanness, in the principle of self-determination, and in the right of people to be secure not only in their homes but in their thoughts, then it becomes necessary to develop means to obtain, to the fullest extent possible, the consent of those asked to become participants in research. There are, no doubt, practical barriers to genuine informed consent (see generally, Katz, 1972, pp. 609–674), the problems of which are magnified when the principle is applied to those with limited capacity to consent. Nevertheless, researchers should feel duty-bound to strive toward that ideal by more complete disclosure.

Greater adherence to the informed consent doctrine need not mean the end of research, including those studies that depend on covert observation or deception. The use of some modicum of ingenuity might satisfy the needs of both researcher and participant. For example, a pool of possible subjects could be told sometime in advance that they may be deceived or their behavior secretly monitored, though they would not be told when or how. They could then be given the chance not to participate. If Resnick and Schwartz (1973) are correct, subjects may fully agree to such conditions because of the possibility of risk or excitement. There may be a more persuasive reason for obtaining consent before one engaged in covert observation. Some states make it a criminal offense to overhear conversations with a listening device unless all the participants to the conversation are specifically informed. Oregon's law to that effect makes failure to inform punishable by a fine of up to $3000, imprisonment for not more than three years or both (Ore. Rev. Stat. §§ 30.780, 165.540(6) (1973)). A similar statute exists in Maryland. Reubhausen and Brim (1965) point out that such statutes accord no exemption for behavioral research.

The unanswered question in *Merriken v. Cressman* (1973) was from whom should consent be obtained. There is no problem, of course, if the subject is a competent adult. In that instance, it is the individual participant who must consent. Thus, in research conducted in colleges, in agencies designed to rehabilitate the physically handicapped, or in the context of vocational or employment counseling, it is imperative for the participant to consent. But what if the intended subject is a child or is retarded or institutionalized in a psychiatric facility? For children one can invoke two principles as a partial answer. One is the assumption that parents are at least equally capable as institutional staff in deciding what is best for their children (Goldman, 1972). The other is the legal doctrine supporting the primacy of parents to care for their children and to be ultimately responsible for their eduction. Thus, under either one or both of the above, it is essential that parents consent to any proposed research.

However, as Reubhausen and Brim(1965) inquire, "In the case of children . . . while the legal principles may be clear . . . should not a child, even before the age of full legal responsibility, be accorded the dignity of a private personality?" (p.1200). Many writers, I among them (Bersoff, 1976–1977, 1976b; Holt, 1974; Wald, 1974) have suggested that children's rights become more specifically tailored to developmental levels rather than tied to arbitrary age limits. Unless there is a significant risk of irreversible damage or clear and convincing empirical evidence that at particular ages children have not sufficiently developed skills to exercise discretion, neither parents nor the state should have the right to make unilateral decisions that meaningfully affect children. On a purely methodological base, coerced participation leads to uninterpretable, invalid data.

For those institutionalized because of retardation or psychiatric intervention, proxy consent should be avoided to the maximum extent possible. In a paper written for the National Commission for the Protection of Human Subjects, Joseph Goldstein, a professor of law at Yale University, argues strongly that the only one who should consent to research is the potential participant.

> The burden in law for incompetence should be very high. No evidence other than a showing that the patient is comatose should ordinarily be accepted as proof of incompetence. . . . Respect for human dignity should not lessen according to an individual's mental health. But practice does undercut that respect by making provision for "substituted consent" by a legal representative who may be forced upon them without their "informed consent." To accept such proxy consents is to authorize invasions of person and personality without regard to the wishes of the research subject—that is to deny them freedom to choose without saying so (Goldstein, 1976, P. 26).

Thus, primary concern for the autonomy and integrity of the individual may dictate that decisions regarding participation in research be honored regardless of institutionalization or adjudication of incompetency. Possibly, when there is a readily identifiable, direct, and substantial benefit to the health, functioning, development, or well-being of the individual and the individual cannot consent, then a person nominated by the potential subject to act on his or her behalf may consent in the subject's stead. In the event that no such person is or can be nominated, then perhaps a legally appointed representative may consent with the provision that the person designated has been determined most likely to act as the individual might have acted if able to.

Capacity for Limitation and Control of Data

The storage and dissemination of research data is as much of a legal and ethical concern as its gathering (for a general discussion of the problem see Lister, Baker, and Milhous, 1975). The problem is compounded by the development of government data banks. "The maintenance and use . . . of information for purposes other than that originally agreed to, and the threat of confidentiality inherent in its continued maintenance, strongly suggest that the proper course of [those] possessing such data is either to obtain the consent of the individual involved to its continued preservation, or to destroy the data. . . ." (Reubhausen and Brim, 1965, p. 1206).

At this point, there is relatively little protection for the researcher or subject. First, there is no such recognized entity as a researcher-client privilege. In many states now, clients of psychologists in private practice have been accorded the statutory right to privileged communication (i.e., the right of the client to prevent licensed psychologists from testifying in court about communications revealed within the context of a professional relationship), but there is no counterpart for scholars. The case for such a privilege has been made persuasively (Nejelski and Lerman, 1971) but has been rejected by the courts, at least in the context of a criminal investigation (the major case is *United States v. Doe* (1972); for refusing to reveal research sources to a grand jury, Professor Samuel Popkin of Harvard spent eight days in prison for contempt). In addition, researchers cannot guarantee complete confidentiality of data in light of the ability of law enforcement personnel to compel the production of records by subpoena.

In an attempt to provide some protection for human subjects, one group (Carroll and Knerr, 1976) has suggested that all social science organizations adopt the following statement as part of the scholar's ethical obligation to protect confidential sources and data:

> [The scholar] has both an ethical and a professional duty to not divulge either the identity of confidential sources of information and/or confidential data developed in the course of research, whether to governmental or nongovernmental officials or bodies, even though in the present state of American law he or she runs the risk of suffering a penalty. Since the protection of confidentiality is often essential in social science research, and since its continued growth is in the public interest, scholars have an obligation to change or uphold the law so that confidentiality of sources may be safeguarded. (pp. 14–15)

Obviously, the surest way to protect confidentiality is to gather data that is either not personally identifiable or allows for anonymous responses. However, some research requires that data be maintained and identified, as when a counselor studies the long-term efficacy of an experimental counseling technique. In that instance coding may help but there is still the danger that the code may be broken and the information retrieved. Although most researchers find the idea of data destruction abhorrent, destruction of personally identifiable information is another possible safeguard. Some innovative scientists have suggested the use of storage in foreign facilities (Astin and Boruch, 1970) out of the reach of domestic government agencies. At a minimum, as part of the informed consent process, children and their parents should be told of any conceivable limits to the promise of confidentiality. Naive promises of a guarantee of secrecy are misrepresentations of reality.

A FINAL NOTE

This chapter has detailed the consequences when behavioral scientists and practitioners act with insensitivity toward those they study. Invocation of "science" as a talisman to protect those who harm others is no longer possible. Because of those who sought to benefit humankind to the detriment, deception, and denigration of human beings, there is now a vast network of external control monitoring the experimentation process. The absolute prohibition, in most instances, of the use of certain research instruments or designs would be intolerable in a free society, yet freedom also requires that those who are asked to reveal their personal selves be treated with respect for their individual integrity.

When genuine societal interests permit the invasion of privacy without consent, there should be broad sharing of the responsibility for doing so. Potential research participants should be invited to engage with the researcher—become "joint adventurers" to use Paul Ramsey's (1970) phrase—in a dialogue concerning those aspects of the research that might invade privacy, either in its gathering or in its dissemination. I am convinced, with Freund (1969), that comprehensive involvement in the decisionmaking process will not only improve the design of studies but will have the more important effect of acknowledging the equality, mutual interests, and individuality of all participants.

TABLE OF CASES CITED

Baker v. Owen, 395 F. Supp. 294 (M.D. N.C. 1975) *aff'd mem.* 423 U.S. 907 (1975).

Eisenstadt v. Baird, 405 U.S. 438 (1972).

Epperson v. Arkansas, 393 U.S. 97 (1968).

In re Gault, 387 U.S. 1 (1967).

Ginsburg v. New York, 390 U.S. 629 (1968).

Griswold v. Connecticut, 381 U.S. 479 (1965).

Kaimowitz v. Dep't. of Health, No. 73-19434-AW (Cir. Ct. Wayne Co., Mich. July 10, 1973), reported in part at 2 Prison L. Rep. 433 (1973).

Merriken v. Cressman, 364 F. Supp. 913 (E.D. Pa. 1973).

Natanson v. Kline, 186 Kan. 393, 350 P.2d 1093 (1960).

Olmstead v. United States, 277 U.S. 438 (1928).

Planned Parenthood of Cent. Mo. v. Danforth, 428 U.S. 52 (1976).

Pratt v. Davis, 118 Ill. App. 161 (1905).

Roe v. Wade, 410 U.S. 113 (1973).

Tinker v. Des Moines School Dist., 393 U.S. 503 (1969).

Union Pacific Ry. Co. v. Botsford 141 U.S. 250 (1891).

United States v. Doe, 460 F.2d 328 (1st Cir. 1972) *cert. denied*, 411 U.S. 909 (1973).

Wilkinson v. Vesey, 110 R.I. 606, 295 A.2d 676 (1972).

Wood v. Strickland, 420 U.S. 308 (1975).

REFERENCES*

American Psychological Association. *Ethical principles in the conduct of research with human participants.* Washington, D.C.: Author, 1973.

American Psychological Association. Ethical standards of psychologists. *American Psychologist,* 1963, *18,* 56-60.

Anastasi, A. *Psychological testing.* (4th ed.) New York: Macmillan, 1976.

Astin, A.W. and Boruch, R.E. A "link" system for assuring confidentiality of research data in longitudinal studies. *American Council on Education Research Reports,* 1970, *5* (3).

Baumrind, D. Principles of ethical conduct in the treatment of subjects. *American Psychologist,* 1971, *26,* 887-896.

Baumrind, D. Some thoughts on ethics of research—after reading Milgram's "Behavioral Study of Obedience." *American Psychologist,* 1964, *19,* 421-423.

Beaney, W.M. The right to privacy and American law. *Law & Contemporary Problems,* 1966, *31,* 253-271.

Berlin, I. *Four essays on liberty.* Oxford: Claredon Press, 1969.

Berscheid, E., Baron, R.D., Dermer, M., and Libman, S. Anticipating informed consent: An empirical approach. *American Psychologist,* 1973, *28,* 913-925.

Bersoff, D.N. Representation for children in custody proceedings: All that glitters is not *Gault. Journal of Family Law,* 1976-1977, *15,* 27-49.

Bersoff, D.N. Therapists as protectors and policemen: New roles as a result of *Tarasoff? Professional Psychology,* 1976a, *7,* 267-273.

Bersoff, D.N. Child advocacy: The next step. *Education Quarterly*, 1976b (Spring) *7*, 10-17.

Bersoff, D.N. Professional ethics and legal responsibilities: On the horns of a dilemma. *Journal of School Psychology*, 1975, *13*, 359-376.

Bersoff, D.N. Silk purses into sow's ears: The decline of psychological testing and a suggestion for its redemption. *American Psychologist*, 1973, *28*, 892-899.

Bloustein, E.J. Privacy as an aspect of human dignity. *New York Univ. Law Review*, 1964, *39*, 962-1007.

Carroll, J.D. and Knerr, C. Law and the regulation of social science research: Confidentiality as a case study. Symposium on Ethics and Social Science, Univ. of Minn., April 9-10, 1976 (mimeo).

Dorsen, N., Bender, P., and Neuborne, B. *Emerson, Haber, & Dorsen's Political and civil rights in the United States* (Vol 1). Boston: Little, Brown, 1976.

Epstein, Y.M., Suedfeld, P., and Silverstein, S.J. The experimental contract: Subjects' expectations of and reactions to some behaviors of experimenters. *American Psychologist*, 1973, *28*, 212-221.

Freund, P. Legal frameworks for human experimentation. *Daedalus*, 1969, *98*, 314-324.

Gergan, K.J. The codification of research ethics: Views of a doubting Thomas. *American Psychologist*, 1973, *28*, 907-912.

Goldman, L. Psychological secrecy and openness in the public schools. *Professional Psychology*, 1972, *3*, 370-374.

Goldstein, J. On the right of the "institutionalized mentally infirm" to consent to or refuse to participate as subjects in biomedical and behavioral research. Paper prepared for the National Commission for the Protection of Human Subjects of Biomedical and Behavioral Research, 1976 (mimeo).

Goldstein, J. For Harold Laswell: Some reflections on human dignity, entrapment, informed consent, and the plea bargain. *Yale Law Journal,* 1975, *84,* 683-703.

Holt, J. *Escape from childhood.* New York: Putnam, 1974.

Holtzman, W.H. The changing world of mental measurement and its social significance. *American Psychologist,* 1971, *26,* 546-553.

Jourard, S.M. Some psychological aspects of privacy. *Law & Contemporary Problems,* 1966, *31,* 307-325.

Kadish, S. Methodology and criteria in due process adjudication—a survey and criticism. *Yale Law Journal,* 1957, *66,* 319-363.

Katz, J. *Experimentation with human beings.* New York: Russell Sage Foundation, 1972.

Kelman, H.C. The rights of the subject in social research: An analysis in terms of relative power and legitimacy. *American Psychologist,* 1972, *27,* 989-1016.

Kelman, H.C. Human use of human subjects: The problem of deception in social psychological experiments. *Psychological Bulletin,* 1967, *67,* 1-11.

Kerlinger, F. Draft report of the APA Committee on Ethical Standards in Psychological Research: A critical reaction. *American Psychologist,* 1972, *27,* 894-896.

Lister, M., Baker, A., and Milhous, R.L. Record keeping, access, and confidentiality. In N. Hobbs (Ed.), *Issues in the classification of children.* San Francisco: Jossey-Bass, 1975.

Margulis, S.T. Privacy as a behavioral phenomenon: Coming of age. In S.T. Margulis (Ed.), *Privacy.* Washington, D.C.: Environmental Design Research Association, 1974.

Menges, R.J. Openness and honesty versus coercion and deception in psychological research. *American Psychologist,* 1973, *28,* 1030-1034.

Milgram, S. Issues in the study of obedience: A reply to Baumrind. *American Psychologist,* 1964, *19,* 848-852.

Milgram, S. Behavioral study of obedience. *Journal of Abnormal and Social Psychology,* 1963, *67,* 371-378.

Moskowitz, J.S. Parental rights and state education. *Washington Law Review,* 1975, *50,* 623-651.

Murstein, B.I. Assumptions, adaptation level, and projective techniques. In B.I. Murstein (Ed.), *Handbook of projective techniques.* New York: Basic Books, 1965.

National Commission for the Protection of Human Subjects of Biomedical and Behavioral Research. Report on the use of psychosurgery. November 13, 1976 (mimeo).

Nejelski, P., and Lerman, L.M. A researcher-subject testimonial privilege: What to do before the subpoena arrives. *Wisconsin Law Review,* 1971, 1085-1111.

Nettler, G. Test burning in Texas. *American Psychologist,* 1959, *14,* 682-683.

Note. Constitutional law—right of privacy—school program designed to identify and provide corrective therapy for potential drug abusers held unconstitutional. *Fordham Urban Law Journal,* 1974, *2,* 599-610.

Note. Informed consent and the dying patient. *Yale Law Journal,* 1974, *83,* 1632-1664.

Parker, R.B. A definition of privacy. *Rutgers Law Review,* 1974, *27,* 275-296.

Plante, M.L. An analysis of "informed consent." *Fordham Law Review,* 1968, *36,* 639-672.

Ramsey, P. *The patient as person: Explorations in medical ethics.* New Haven: Yale University Press, 1970.

Recent Cases. Constitutional law—right of privacy—personality test used by school to identify potential drug abusers without informed consent of parents violates students' and parents' right of privacy. *Vanderbilt Law Review,* 1974, *27,* 372-381.

Recent Developments. Education—school-instituted program to identify potential drug abusers—right to privacy. *Journal of Family Law,* 1973-74, *13,* 636-638.

Resnick, J.H. and Schwartz, T. Ethical standards as an independent variable in psychological research. *American Psychologist,* 1973, *28,* 134-139.

Reubhausen, D.M. and Brim, O.G. Privacy and behavioral research. *Columbia Law Review,* 1965, *65,* 1184-1215.

Sheets, R., Radlinski, A., Kohne, J., and Brunner, G.A. Deceived respondents: Once bitten, twice shy. *The Public Opinion Quarterly,* 1974, *38,* 261-263.

Shils E. Social inquiry and the autonomy of the individual. In D. Lerner (Ed.), *The human meaning of the social sciences.* New York: Meridian Books, 1959.

Shils, E. Privacy: Its constitution and vicissitudes. *Law & Contemporary Problems,* 1966, *31,* 281-306.

Stagner, R. Problems concerning federal support of social science research. Hearings on S. 836 before the Subcommittee on Government Research of the Senate Committee on Government Operations, 90th Congress, 1st Session, 757-760 (1967).

Wald, P. Making sense out of the rights of youth. *Human Rights,* 1974, *4,* 13-29.

Waltz, J.R. and Scheuneman, T.W. Informed consent to therapy. *Northwestern Law Review,* 1969, *64,* 628-650.

Waterman, S. The civil liberties of the participants in psychological research. *American Psychologist,* 1974, *29,* 470-471.

Westin, A.F. *Privacy and freedom.* New York: Atheneum, 1967.

Westin, A.F. Science, privacy, and freedom: Issues and proposals for the 1970's (Part II). *Columbia Law Review,* 1966, *66,* 1205-1253.

*Statutes and regulations ,are cited in the text only.

CONCLUSION

CHAPTER 14
Epilog

Leo Goldman

This book obviously does not contain all there is to say about research in the counseling field. We have selectively emphasized those methods that appear to us to be of greatest value to the largest number of applied workers in the field—practicing counselors and other helpers. Further, we have for the most part emphasized those applications of research methods that reflect the cutting edges of our field in several settings. Essentially we look at research pragmatically: it should make some contribution to the people and organizations that counselors serve.

This is in no way to imply a value judgment about the comparative merits of so-called basic research and applied research. But we are saying that the research done in the counseling field up to now has neglected the less formal and less quantitative methods. We are also saying that research will not contribute all that it can in this field if practitioners themselves do not participate actively in the identification of topics to be studied and in the planning and conduct of research.

The necessary changes will not be easy to accomplish. Psychology has been struggling for decades with the notion of the scientist-practitioner. Although there are indeed a small number of psychologists who are active as both scientists and practitioners, they are a tiny minority of all psychologists. I think that a major reason for the failure of this model is the unrealistic expectation that people who are practitioners at heart will do truly "scientific" research, which usually means using advanced and complex designs and statistics and building research on well-developed theoretical foundations. This is too much to ask of all but a tiny percentage of practitioners; indeed it is a great deal to expect of most research specialists.

Our vision of the effective practitioner is a person who is constantly alert to the needs of the people and institutions being served and constantly evaluating the usefulness of current programs and activities. Such a practitioner is already a researcher in our conception of research. The methods delineated in this book are in some ways no more than systematic organizations of methods available to effective counselors to study needs and evaluate activities. It is our belief that every counselor, in whatever specialty and whatever setting, should find in this book at least a few methods of research that would be useful in that specialty and setting. There remains the practical problem of reaching the point where practitioners *do* use these methods.

Realistically, there are many reasons why counselors (and indeed applied practitioners in almost all fields) have *not* done research of any kind. At least briefly we should address ourselves to suggestions for changing that situation.

COUNSELORS AS RESEARCHERS: MAKING IT HAPPEN

To attain that brave new world where numbers of counselors do research, a number of changes must occur.

Training of Counselors

In many ways the easiest kind of change to introduce is in preservice counselor training. Instructors of courses in research methods, and advisors on theses, projects, and dissertations should be able to extend their horizons to include the methods featured in this book. They may well face opposition from their "hard science" colleagues and even from former students who believe that, since they did it the hard way, there is no reason why today's students should be admitted to the profession without the rituals that include traditional research. As a minimum, we in the counseling field, along with other applied behavioral science workers, have to reach the point of believing that "soft" research—non-quantitative, action-oriented, seeking to shed light on practical matters more than on theoretical issues—is as worthy of recognition and reward as the traditional research approaches that seek mostly to make theoretical contributions.

The doctoral dissertation plays a key role in this effort to broaden conceptions of research. Those with doctorates occupy influential positions as counselor educators, directors and supervisors of counseling programs, editors and board members of journals, and officers and committee members of professional associations. It is therefore vital that doctoral advisors and committees recognize that in the human behavioral fields the qualitative and even subjective methods of research are not only acceptable but even desirable methods of scientific progress, as well as major contributors to the solution of practical problems faced by practitioners. For both reasons doctoral students should be encouraged to select from a broad variety of both quantitative and qualitative research methods.

Journals and other Publications

One very important way to increase the recognition and "respectability" of these less quantitative methods of research is to have them accepted by professional journals as worthy of publication. Of course, this pertains only to those studies that have some degree of generalizability. There is not much reason to publish reports that sought only to answer local questions, except perhaps in some instances as exemplary models for others who wish to study similar questions in their own locality.

To accomplish such a change in publication practices will require a major policy decision on the part of most journals. For many of the journals it will be necessary to add to their editorial boards or panels of reviewers people who understand and accept the nonquantitative methods of research. For all journals it will be necessary that the persons designated as editors have a broad conception of what is publishable research.

Convention Programs and Workshops

Similarly, those responsible for planning convention programs are in a key position to define what are the acceptable types of research. This means not only accepting program proposals that utilize the kinds of research we have stressed in this book, but also planning sessions of a workshop or symposium nature that will help people understand these methods and learn how to use them.

It will also be valuable for associations, and other who sponsor workshops apart from conventions, to offer workshops that provide specific training in using these methods of research.

Research Awards

A number of professional associations seek to encourage good research by giving awards for the best published research they can find. Certainly the criteria for such awards should not be such as to exclude the less quantitative studies. This will require revision of some of the rating forms used for this purpose that presently do exclude qualitative types of research by asking only questions (about sampling, statistics, etc.) that are applicable to the traditional methods.

In some instances it might be necessary to have two or more categories of research for which awards are given. In a way this would be less than ideal, because of the likelihood that there will be implicit or explicit distinctions between first-class and second-class types of research. But this would still be better than restricting such awards only to the traditional studies that contain all the stereotyped sections on "hypotheses," "methods," "results," and so on, but that are often devoid of any real significance for the field.

It would also be most desirable to grant awards to exemplary local studies, many of which are not necessarily appropriate for publication. Here the purpose would be to recognize the contributions made locally rather than to any more widespread generalization of the findings.

In the Field

If counselors on the job are to do research of any kind, it is vital that their employers regard research as not only an acceptable but even a desirable use of counselor time. Perhaps it will be easier to do this than has been the case in the past if studies can be shown to offer very specific help to the agency or institution in the conduct of its affairs. And that is more likely to be the case if the action-oriented kinds of methods are used rather than those that stress precision of measurement and use of esoteric statistical techniques.

There still remains the problem of time and of convincing supervisors, directors, and board members that their total enterprise will in the long run benefit if counselors take a few hours a week from services and use that time to study the people and communities they serve and their own work. It may be necessary for counselors to start the ball rolling by doing a study on their own time first, to demonstrate its value. But it will no doubt require continuing effort for counselors to receive both the time and the necessary support to do research as part of their jobs.

The Place of the Research Specialist

Finally, it will be extremely important that we find ways to bridge the gap between researchers and counselors. Certainly there will always be a major place for specialists in research, no matter how much research is done by

counselors. The research specialists will be needed as consultants to practitioners who are doing research, and they will be needed for the planning
and conduct of large-scale studies that go beyond a single institution or are
simply so large in scope that they cannot be done by any save full-time
researchers. And, of course, there are the more technical kinds of research
that are beyond the knowledge, skill, and interest of practitioners, but that
will benefit from the counselor's input, as described by Harmon in Chapter
2.

One way to bridge the gap is for agencies and institutions that employ
counselors to establish working relationships with research specialists who
are interested in applied problems and needs. Ideally this is done on a
regular consultant basis, so that the researcher meets regularly with counseling staff to help stimulate research and help them plan studies. If this is done,
we will very likely have much better evaluations of experimental projects
than we have seen in the past. One reason for the inadequacies of the past is
that the research specialist, when involved at all, is brought in after the
program has been planned and funded and even after it is under way.
Another reason, at least in some instances, is that the researcher is not
sufficiently attuned to practical concerns and is interested in more theoretical models of research. Under those circumstances it is almost inevitable
that there will be frustration for all and regrets about the limitations of the
evaluation outcomes. When a practice-oriented researcher teams up with
research-oriented counselors early in the process of developing programs,
we can expect much more effectiveness and satisfaction for both.

Still another place for the research specialist—and another opportunity
to bridge gaps—is in programs and activities aimed principally at research
dissemination. Fortunately, at the time we go to press, there is considerable
support for research dissemination activities, in the form of federal grants
and specific projects in some of the counseling specialty areas. Too often,
researchers have ended their efforts with the results section of the report and
often have to be pressed to engage in any discussion of the implications of
their results for practice. On the other side, practitioners find it difficult to dig
into published research because the sections on related theories, methods,
and results are so far from their interest and understanding.

Systematic programs for research dissemination will demand better
communication between research specialist and practitioner than has been
the case in the past. It will also require imaginative use of audio-visual
techniques and of workshops and other formats that maximize communication and collaboration. There will no doubt be many frustrations, as practitioners discover how limited can be the immediate applications of most
studies, and as researchers learn how limited is the practitioner's interest in

APPENDIX A
BOOKS ON
MEASURES AND SCALES

Bonjean, C.M., Hill, R.J., and McLemore, S.D. *Sociological measurement: An inventory of scales and indices.* San Francisco: Chandler, 1967.

Chun, K., Cobb, S., and French, J. R. P. *Measures for psychological assessment.* Ann Arbor: Institute for Social Research, The University of Michigan, 1975.

Dailey, C. A. *Assessment of lives.* San Francisco: Jossey-Bass, 1971.

Goldman, B. A. and Saunders, J. L. *Directory of unpublished experimental mental measures.* New York: Behavioral Publications, 1974.

Hoepfner, R., Stern, C., and Nummedal, S. G. (Eds.). *CSE-ECRC preschool/kindergarten test evaluations.* Los Angeles: UCLA Graduate School of Education, 1971.

Hoepfner, R., Strickland, G., Stangel, G., Jansen, P., and Patalino, M. *CSE elementary school test evaluations.* Los Angeles: UCLA Graduate School of Education, 1970.

Horst, P. *Personality: Measures of dimensions.* San Francisco: Jossey-Bass, 1968.

Johnson, O. G., and Bommarito, J. W. *Tests and measurements in child development: A handbook.* San Francisco: Jossey-Bass, 1971.

Lake, D.G., Miles, M.B., and Earle, R.B. *Measuring human behavior.* New York: Teachers College Press, 1973.

Loevinger, J., and Wessler, R. *Measuring ego development, Volumes 1 and 2.* San Francisco: Jossey-Bass, 1970.

Robinson, J. P., Athanasiou, R., and Head, K. B. *Measures of occupational attitudes and occupational characteristics.* Ann Arbor: Institute for Social Research, The University of Michigan, 1969.

Robinson, J. P., Rusk, J. G., and Head, K. B. *Measures of political attitudes.* Ann Arbor: Institute for Social Research, The University of Michigan, 1968.

Robinson, J. P., and Shaver, P. R. *Measures of social psychological attitudes*. Ann Arbor: Institute for Social Research, The University of Michigan, 1969.

Shaw, M. E., and Wright, J.M. *Scales for the measurement of attitudes*. New York: McGraw-Hill, 1967.

Simon, A., and Boyer, E. G. *Mirrors for behavior III: An anthology of observational instruments*. Wyncote, Pa.: Communications Materials Center, 1974.

Strauss, M. A., *Family measurement techniques*. Minneapolis: University of Minnesota Press, 1969.

Walker, D.K. *Socioemotional measures for preschool and kindergarten children*. San Francisco: Jossey-Bass, 1973.

Webb, E. J., Campbell, D. T., Schwartz, R. D., and Sechrest, L. *Unobstrusive measures: Nonreactive research in the social sciences*. Chicago: Rand McNally, 1966.

APPENDIX B
SEARCH AND
LOCATER SERVICES

EDUCATION RESOURCES
INFORMATION CENTER (ERIC)

The ERIC network was established by the National Institute of Education (NIE), of the U.S. Department of Health, Education, and Welfare. NIE currently supports sixteen clearinghouses, each one responsible for collecting, selecting, abstracting, and indexing both published and unpublished materials of theoretical, research, and applied interest in its designated content area. In addition to feeding these selected materials into the national ERIC network for dissemination via one of the methods listed below, each clearinghouse also provides direct user services, such as newsletters, magazines, syntheses of the literature on selected topics, and others. Each clearinghouse also will do computerized searches on special topics for users on request.

Each clearinghouse welcomes receipt of two copies of any speeches, papers, or other document that might be appropriate for inclusion in the system. For that purpose, or for special requests not covered by the national ERIC publication and dissemination system, one should address the specific ERIC clearinghouse.

ERIC Clearinghouse on Career Education
The Ohio State University
Center for Vocational Education, 1960 Kenny Road
Columbus, Ohio 43210

ERIC Clearinghouse on Counseling and Personnel Services
University of Michigan
School of Education Building, Room 2108
East University and South University Streets
Ann Arbor, Michigan 48104

ERIC Clearinghouse on Early Childhood Education
University of Illinois
College of Education
805 W. Pennsylvania Avenue
Urbana, Illinois 61801

ERIC Clearinghouse on Educational Management
University of Oregon
Eugene, Oregon 97403

ERIC Clearinghouse on Handicapped and Gifted Children
The Council for Exceptional Children
1920 Association Drive
Reston, Virginia 22091

ERIC Clearinghouse on Higher Education
The George Washington University
One Dupont Circle, NW, Suite 630
Washington, D.C. 20036

ERIC Clearinghouse on Information Resources
Syracuse University
School of Education
Area Instructional Technology
Syracuse, New York 13210

ERIC Clearinghouse for Junior Colleges
University of California
Powell Library, Room 96
405 Hilgard Avenue
Los Angeles, California 90024

ERIC Clearinghouse on Languages and Linguistics
Center for Applied Linguistics
1611 North Kent Street
Arlington, Virginia 22209

ERIC Clearinghouse for Reading and Communication Skills
National Council of Teachers of English
1111 Kenyon Road
Urbana, Illinois 61801

ERIC Clearinghouse on Rural Education and Small Schools
New Mexico State University
Box 3AP
Las Cruces, New Mexico 88003

ERIC Clearinghouse on Science, Mathematics, and Environmental Education
The Ohio State University
1200 Chambers Road, Third Floor
Columbus, Ohio 43212

ERIC Clearinghouse for Social Studies/Social Science Education
Social Science Education Consortium, Inc.
855 Broadway
Boulder, Colorado 80302

ERIC Clearinghouse on Teacher Education
American Association of Colleges for Teacher Education
One Dupont Circle, NW, Suite 616
Washington, D.C. 20036

ERIC Clearinghouse on Tests, Measurement, and Evaluation
Educational Testing Service
Princeton, New Jersey 08540

ERIC Clearinghouse on Urban Education
Columbia University
Teachers College, Box 40
525 W. 120th Street
New York, New York 10027

The ERIC national dissemination system includes the following. Libraries often can be of help in locating these materials and services:

Current Index to Journals in Education, 1969–
CIJE is a monthly publication that indexes and annotates articles appearing in journals in or related to education and all its components. There are also semiannual and annual indexes. Available in many libraries or from Macmillan Information Division, Order Department, Front and Brown Streets, Riverside, N.J. 08075.

Resources in Education,1966/67–
RIE is a parallel publication that covers all forms of material other than journals, including technical and research reports, conference papers, speeches, program descriptions, and similar material. Most of these materials are unpublished and therefore almost impossible to locate without the use of the ERIC system. This too is indexed on a semiannual and annual basis. Available in many libraries or from the Government Printing Office, Washington, D.C. 20402.

ERIC Document Collections
The complete text of all the documents abstracted in *Resources in Education* and not restricted by copyright is available on microfiche or hard copy reproductions from the ERIC Document Reproduction Service, Post Office Box 190, Arlington, Va. 22210. Many libraries throughout the country maintain a complete and continuing collection of the Document Collection on microfiche.

PSYCHOLOGICAL ABSTRACTS INFORMATION SERVICE

This is a group of services available from PsycINFO, the American Psychological Association, 1200 Seventeenth Street NW, Washington, D.C. 20036. The base is the *Psychological Abstracts*, a monthly journal published by APA and containing nonevaluative summaries of the psychological literature as found in journals and books from all parts of the world. There also are semiannual and three-year cumulative indexes.

In addition to the *Psychological Abstracts* and its indexes, which are available in many libraries, APA offers the following locater services:

Psychological Abstracts Direct Access Terminal (PADAT)
An organization leases a computer terminal that then provides direct access to the data base from the organization's own facilities.

Psychological Abstracts Tape Edition Lease or License (PATELL)
The user obtains the magnetic tapes of PsycINFO records on either an annual lease or license basis. This is intended for information analysts and dissemination centers that intend to serve either their own members (lease) or others (license).

Psychological Abstracts Search and Retrieval (PASAR)
This is the service most likely to be used by individuals. The user fills out a form that specifies the topic to be searched and mails it to APA. A printout of relevant abstracts from the *Psychological Abstracts* is mailed to the user at a cost based on the amount of computer time required to perform the search.

COMMERCIAL ON-LINE RETRIEVAL SYSTEMS

Lockheed's DIALOG and System Development Corporation's ORBIT offer services similar to those provided by PASAR, but for many data bases combined. At the end of 1976, DIALOG was providing access to 45, ORBIT to 20 data bases. DIALOG, for example, may search, in response to a single query, ERIC, *Psychological Abstracts*, *Sociological Abstracts*, NTIS (National Technical Information Service reports covering a wide range of disciplines from over 240 U.S. government agencies—more than 500,000 citations), and *Dissertation Abstracts* (again more than 500,000 references to doctoral dissertations since 1861). Search results are in the form of a bibliography, often with accompanying abstracts.

Search costs are based on computer time used and on the number and format of references located; $35 to $50 might be considered average charges. Searches are available at hundreds of sites throughout the U.S and Canada, in Sweden, Mexico, the United Kingdom, and Australia. The number is growing rapidly.

At many institutions costs are subsidized, often through affiliation with an information resource center.

NATIONAL REFERRAL CENTER FOR SCIENCE AND TECHNOLOGY

This is a service arm of the Library of Congress (address its Science and Technology Division, 10 First Street SE, Washington, D.C. 20540). It provides a free referral service by mail or phone in the physical, biological, social, or engineering sciences. The center directs inquiries not to literature but to live sources—names and addresses of organizations or individuals that are known to provide the kind of information one is seeking. The Center also publishes selections from their data base of names and addresses; a 700-page compilation on the Social Sciences was published in 1973 (GPO Catalog no. LC 1.31: D62/2-973) and is available at a price of $6.90 from the Government Printing Office, Washington, D.C. 20402

SMITHSONIAN SCIENCE INFORMATION EXCHANGE

SSIE provides several specialized services, including both custom searches and publication of noncustom research information packages on topics of high current interest (examples of the latter drawn from the Therapy, Rehabilitation and Counseling area within the Behavioral Science division are "Vocational Counseling" and "Rehabilitation of adult and juvenile offenders"). The data bank consists of brief descriptions of research projects as received from over 1300 funding agencies at the time of funding. For custom searches the user may specify the subject, names of investigators, funding organizations, or geographic areas to be sought in the computer search. Because of the nature of this program, it is especially useful for information about research in progress, and for information about which funding organizations are supporting research in designated areas.

INFORMATION RESOURCE CENTERS

Exemplified by RISE in Pennsylvania and SMERC in California but located throughout the country, these are nonprofit, usually government sponsored organizations that, among many other services to educators, prepare full information packages containing actual full text copies of documents and journal articles found through computer searching, a bibliography, a list of resource persons, and so on. Costs vary. An original RISE search in 1976 was $300, a package duplicating a search already on file was $25, and a bibliography alone was $2.50.

"Information Brokers," for profit organizations offering similar services are also available and are the latest development in this fast growing area.

INDEXES AND ABSTRACTS

In addition to the computerized and other special locater services listed above, there are of course the published indexes and abstracts such as the *Education Index, Psychological Abstracts, College Student Personnel Abstracts,* and *Sociological Abstracts.* A university librarian specializing in reference service is usually the best source of help in locating and using these sources.

Name Index

423

Subject Index